Theory of Modelling
and Simulation

Theory of Modelling and Simulation

BERNARD P. ZEIGLER

Professor
Logic of Computers Group
Department of Computer and Communication Sciences
The University of Michigan, Ann Arbor

and

Department of Applied Mathematics
The Weizmann Institute of Science
Rehovot, Israel

ROBERT E. KRIEGER PUBLISHING COMPANY
MALABAR, FLORIDA
1984

Original Edition   1976
Reprint Edition   1984

Printed and Published by
ROBERT E. KRIEGER PUBLISHING COMPANY, INC.
KRIEGER DRIVE
MALABAR, FL 32950

Printed in the United States of America

Library of Congress Cataloging in Publication Data

Zeigler, Bernard P., 1940-
    Theory of modelling and simulation.

    Reprint. Originally published: New York: Wiley, 1976.
    Includes index.
    1. Computer simulation.   2. System theory.   I. Title.
QA76.9.C65Z44   1984   001.4'34   84-19443
ISBN 0-89874-808-9

To my Parents,

Maurice and Sylvia Zeigler

Preface

A THEORY OF MODELLING AND SIMULATION—WHY?

The field of modelling and simulation is as diverse as the concerns of man. Every discipline has developed, or is developing, its own models and its own approach and tools for studying these models. Why then is an overall theory of modelling and simulation necessary?

Why should a college senior or first-year graduate student majoring in biology, aeronautical engineering, or business management be introduced to the general theory of modelling and simulation—yet another discipline not specific to his own? The answer relies on the same reasoning that determined that the student should have acquired at least some grounding in mathematics. Nobody questions the role of arithmetic in the sciences, engineering, and management. Arithmetic is all pervasive, yet it is a mathematical discipline having its own axioms and logical structure. Its content is not specific to any other disciplines but is directly applicable to them all. Thus students of biology and engineering are not taught how to add differently—the different training comes in *what* to add, *when* to do it, and *why*.

The practice of modelling and simulation too is all pervasive. However it has its own concepts of model description, simplification, validation, simulation, and exploration, which are not specific to any particular discipline. These statements would be agreed to by all. Not everyone, however, would say that the concepts named can be isolated and abstracted in a generally useful form.

In response, this book attempts to provide a framework in which the concepts can be sketched in their clear abstract forms; embodying the concepts in concrete modelling situations further serves to illuminate them.

Of what use is such a framework for the specializing student, or the one who later will specialize? It can fulfill the following purposes:

1. Introduce the student to the full range of concepts and tools available in the field, rather than just those currently employed in his discipline.
2. Provide a perspective on the modelling activity of his own discipline, permitting the creative employment of insights and approaches stemming from other disciplines.
3. Provide an understanding of why we model and simulate, what can be achieved, and what cannot be achieved.
4. Provide a universal language for communicating the structure and behavior of models to others, regardless of whether they are conversant with the interpretive frameworks of their respective disciplines.

We have been talking about the theory of modelling and simulation relative to the noncomputer sciences. However, the book is also addressed to those who are interested in general and mathematical systems theory or in the more specialized computer and information sciences. Indeed, the framework developed here reflects several related influences:

- General systems theory, with its belief in an underlying and exploitable unity in all systems, diverse though they may seem.
- Mathematical systems theory, with its attempts to formalize the concepts of system structure and behavior.
- Automata theory, with its formal, logical, and algebraic analysis of the behavior and interrelations of computer-related models.

In this context this book marshals the available approaches and formalisms in order to deal with the particular issues raised by modelling and simulation. Thus the theory presented should introduce the student of systems and computer science to the many open problems in the area needing conceptual and/or mathematical development, as well as furnish a basis for attacking them.

For the veteran practitioner of modelling and simulation, the book I will fill an important gap in the literature between the material that is very abstract and that which is very applied. The reader who has had little formal mathematics may find the going rough. Still, my hope is that he will be led to more clearly perceive the issues faced daily in his modelling efforts.

THE BOOK PLAN

Achieving meaningful communication with two audiences—one that is oriented toward computer science and one that is not—presents a challenge. In response to this challenge the book is divided into three parts. Part 1 introduces the basic framework and underlying concepts in an informal and intuitive way. Part 2 is a formal presentation of the systems theory concepts necessary for a thorough understanding of Part 3, which sets forth the basic formal framework and discusses a number of issues and problems in modelling and simulation with the help of the framework.

Part 1 is designed to be sufficiently self-contained to serve as a basis for introducing both computer and noncomputer science majors to modelling and simulation. Chapters 1 and 2 deal with model description and basic systems concepts. With the conceptual basis so developed, we briefly consider the basic elements of discourse—real system, experimental frame, base model, lumped model, and the computer—and the concepts of simplification, validation, and simulation, which involve relations among the basic elements. Then, by discussing several commonly employed simplification procedures, we raise the question, Under what circumstances can such gross simplifications result in valid models?

Chapters 3 through 7 deal with the dynamics of simulation, that is, with the generation of the temporal behavior of a model. The concept of state and the formal description of models are developed in parallel with the description of how the computer carries out the simulation process.

The last chapter of Part 1 (Chapter 8) returns to the subject of modelling. From our formal basis, we discuss an example of discrete event modelling and introduce the concept of homomorphism as a criterion for valid simplification.

Parts 2 and 3, which are oriented toward students majoring in the computer and systems sciences, provide a basis for a second course in modelling and simulation in which the emphasis is on the application of formal systems concepts to problems in the area.

Part 2 consists of two chapters. Chapter 9 develops a hierarchy of system specifications ranging from the lowest behavioral level to the highest structural level. Chapter 10 develops a parallel hierarchy of preservation relations that interrelate specifications. These morphisms (preservation relations) form a hierarchy in that higher level morphisms imply lower level ones, but not conversely.

Part 3 opens with an axiomization of the basic framework, using the systems concepts developed earlier. A number of problems common to many domains are isolated and formulated within the framework. These problems include model simplification, approximation, validation and pre-diction, structural inference, program verification, and model integration. Subsequent chapters deal with these problems in some depth.

HOW TO TEACH AND READ THIS BOOK

A number of suggestions are offered to the instructor of an introductory course based on Part 1.

The written development is linear and logical. This is necessary for orderly exposition, but it promotes the separation of concepts that should be developed in parallel. Thus the instructor is encouraged to develop alternative lines of development that cut across the chapter demarcations. For example, while introducing the informal description of models (Chapter 1) in lectures, the instructor may assign the Game of Life simulation (Chapter 4) as the first programming exercise. As the students work on designing their programs, the instructor can introduce the concepts of state and transition function in the Game of Life context.

The teaching of simulation languages should be interspersed with conceptual development and keyed to programming exercises. (For students with moderate programming background, two or three languages such as GASP, CSMP, or GPSS can be taught in a one-semester course.) This keeps the students busy applying the principles presented in class. Several excellent books are available for introducing these languages.

Although the material of Parts 2 and 3 is developed at a relatively abstract level, the problems discussed are fundamental and can be pointed out in concrete modelling situations. A similar observation holds for the advanced treatment of stochastic simulation models developed in a number of recent books.

One way of simulating a real modelling and simulation situation is "quasi simulation"—the construction of a base and a lumped model and the testing of the latter against the former. (An example of such a simulation appears in Appendix A.) Students may be asked, singly or in groups, to undertake a quasisimulation in an area of interest. To illustrate the general concepts and problems discussed in class, the students may be given a list of questions to be answered about their simulations in a term paper. A sample question format is presented in Appendix B.

The presentation consists of three kinds of text—*exposition, exercises,* and *problems*. The expository sections present the main thread of the development and often omit minor but sometimes essential supporting arguments. The exercises intended to fill in the gaps usually require a good familiarity with previous material, but only one or two steps in logical deduction beyond that. Problems, on the other hand, range from straight forward application of expository concepts to guided tours of material relevant to the expository text but not developed in it.

Exercises accompany the expository sections they supplement. This is ideal for readers who like to plod through the text, making sure that they fully understand the exposition thus far before proceeding. Those who prefer to grasp the broad sweep of things before filling in the details may skip the exercises on first reading, returning to consider them in subsequent study. The placement of the exercises facilitates this approach.

BERNARD P. ZEIGLER

Ann Arbor, Michigan
August 1975

PREFACE TO REPRINT EDITION

The decade since the first appearance of ''Theory of Modelling and Simulation'' has seen explosive growth in computer science. Computer-based modelling and simulation has likewise experienced a maturation toward a more principled, better quality-controlled discipline. As methodolgy comes increasingly to the fore in simulation practice, the need for a well-grounded conceptual framework becomes more evident.

The present book has not been surplanted as the primary respository of such a framework. In particular, it serves as background for the author's more specialized follow-on work ''Multifacetted Modelling and Discrete Event Simulation'' (Academic Press, London, 1984).

My appreciation is expressed to Krieger Publishing Co. for making this reprint edition available.

Acknowledgments

A new development in science rarely just happens; it arises from a fortuitous coincidence of time, place, and personalities. The ideas underlying this book find their root in the intellectual soil of the Program in Communication Sciences at the University of Michigan, where I received my graduate education, in the mid-1960s. Transcending the formally transmitted facts and ideas was an attitude—a respect for the clarity of logic and mathematics; also an equal respect for the diversity and complexity of nature. But most strongly emphasized was, the importance of the parallel and synergistic development of the mathematical and the natural sciences. Certain tenets of mathematical and empirical modelling were natural partners of this attitude. Although they had not yet received the extensive elaboration attempted here, they were necessary to the current formulation, and as related to it as an embryo to a fully developed person.

The development of these seminal ideas was greatly nourished by my association, first as student and later as colleague, with the members of the Department of Computer and Communication Sciences (which the program later became) and its associated Logic of Computers Research Group,† particularly with A. W. Burks, J. H. Holland, J. F. Meyer, S. Kaplan, R. A. Laing, and R. Weinberg.

Many others, including G. Klir, M. A. Arbib, and B. C. Patten, contributed to the growth of my ideas, stimulating the development of a line of

† During my tenure, the Logic of Computers Group received most of its research support from the National Science Foundation, whose sponsorship of the research that preceded the writing of this book is gratefully acknowledged.

thought by providing a forum in which to present a paper or by asking the right question at the right time.

Crucial, too, has been my association with the many graduate students it is my good fortune to have had. I must thank R. Reynolds, in particular, for his extensive suggestions for improving the clarity of the manuscript. The work of other students, equally helpful, is referenced throughout the book.

I am grateful to H. Hodgson, M. Barto, and S. Motyl who so accurately transformed my unsightly original into a completed manuscript.

My parents transmitted to me our people's ancient reverence of learning, which inspired my efforts. My wife and children nurtured these efforts with forebearance and goodwill. To them, my special thanks.

B. P. Z

Contents

PART 3

11   Framework for Modelling and Simulation   293

12   Valid Model Construction and Simplification   306

APPENDICES

*Theory of Modelling
and Simulation*

Part One

Chapter One

The Enterprise
of Modelling and
Its Communication

We set the stage in this chapter by providing an overview of the modelling and simulation enterprise: its objectives, its entities, and its processes. Subsequent consideration of the importance of communication to participants within this enterprise leads us to the primary focus of the chapter: the informal description of models and their categorization.

1.1 MODELLING AND SIMULATION: AN OVERVIEW

The phrase "modelling and simulation" designates the complex of activities associated with constructing models of real world systems and simulating them on a computer.

From this definition, it is evident that we are concerned with three major elements—real system, model, computer (actually, we elaborate these to a total of five in Chapter 2). When we engage in modelling and simulation, we are concerned not only with the elements themselves but also with establishing certain relationships among them. In particular, *modelling* deals primarily with the relationships between real systems and models; *simulation* refers primarily to the relationships between computers and models.

Thus our subject matter is characterized essentially by three elements and two relations—the modelling relation and the simulation relation, as represented in Figure 1.

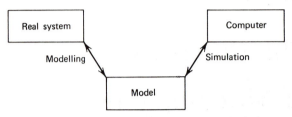

Figure 1   The basic elements and relations of the modelling and simulation enterprise.

By a *real system* we mean some part of the real world, which is of interest. The system may be natural or artificial, in existence presently or planned for the future. A natural scientist, for example, may be interested in such existing real systems as the developmental processes of flowers or the social organization of a bee colony. An engineer may be interested in designing artificial systems planned for the future—for example, a new generation of computers or a new metropolitan transportation system.

As a general rule, we can say that a real system is (or will become) *a source of behavioral data*, consisting in primary form of plots of X against T, where X can be any variable of interest such as the temperature in a room, the number of petals on a flower, or the U.S. Gross National Product, and T is time, measured in convenient units such as seconds, days, or years. An example of such a plot appears in Figure 2.

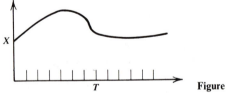

Figure 2   A plot of X against T.

A *model* is basically a set of instructions for generating behavioral data of the form of Figure 2.

Models are often expressed in certain common ways—by differential equations, in automata theoretic notation, or in the discrete event formalism we introduce later. Although it may not be immediately obvious, all these forms of model description provide instructions to "someone or something" for generating data.

That "someone or something" may be the modeller himself if he attempts, for example, to solve a differential equation he has set up. More commonly nowadays, it may be a digital computer that carries out the model instructions suitably encoded as a program. For us then, a *computer* (man or machine) is a computational process capable of generating behavioral data when supplied with suitably encoded model instructions.

Although the model itself does not generate data, we may speak of *model-generated data* or *model behavior*, since it is the model that provides the key instructions to the computer for generating this behavior. We distinguish "model behavior" from the model *structure*, which refers to the particular form the model instructions take. Essentially, behavior is what the model **does**, and structure is **what makes it do** what it does.

Having looked briefly at the three elements, let us consider the two relationships. The *modelling relation* concerns the *validity* of the model, that is, how well the model represents the real system. In the first instance, validity is measured by the extent of agreement between real system data and model-generated data, as portrayed symbolically in the equation:

$$\text{real system data} \overset{?}{=} \text{model-generated data}$$

There are degrees of strength for this validity. The model is *replicatively valid* if it matches data already acquired from the real system. Stronger than this is the condition in which the model is *predictively valid*, that is, when it can match data *before* data are acquired from the real system (or at least "seen" by the model). A third, stronger level of validity concerns the relation between the structure of the model and the internal workings of the real system. A model is *structurally valid* if it not only reproduces the observed real system behavior, but truly reflects the way in which the real system operates to produce this behavior.

The *simulation relation* concerns the faithfulness with which the computer carries out the instructions intended by the model. The faithfulness with which a program realizes a model is often referred to as the *correctness* of the program. We are concerned here with the accuracy of the data produced by the computer. Does the computer faithfully generate the actual model behavior, or does it generate misleading outputs, artifacts of the computer implementation rather than characteristics of the model itself?

Why do we engage in modelling and simulation in the first place? We may have one or more of the following *goals* in mind. We may wish simply to *understand* how a real system works, like a scientist studying nature. In this case we use models to embody *hypotheses* about the underlying and inaccessible structure of reality.

If we are more pragmatically inclined, we may wish to carry out a *parameter study* of a real system, perhaps with a view to *optimizing* certain aspects of its operation. For example, a computer engineer might be interested initially in the effect of various means of scheduling computer jobs on the rate at which these jobs are processed by the computer facility. With this information, he might be in a better position to find a combination that results in a high rate of processing. In this case, we use the model as a *stand-in* or *surrogate* for the real system. There several reasons for substituting a model for a real system. Experimenting with the real system may be *costly* and *time consuming*, or *even impossible* in some situations. Moral considerations, for example, prevent tampering with parameters of the human brain, but one who experiments with a model of the brain is under no such constraints. In addition, computer simulation experiments are completely *repeatable* and *nondestructive*. A rhesus monkey is never the same once its reticular activating system has been removed, but a model can be arbitrarily restarted as if nothing had happened. Finally, the data acquired from computer simulation are often *easier to interpret and to reduce* to statistical and graphical summaries, especially considering the facilities provided by many simulation languages for this purpose.

In the same vein, surrogate simulation models are now beginning to see service in education. For example, medical students can learn the art of drug prescription by interacting with a computer-coded model rather than a real patient. The advantages here in terms of avoiding mistakes in treatment are obvious.

Note that in both the science-oriented and applications-oriented cases we are vitally concerned with *achieving valid models*. In the applications-oriented case, we are interested in replicative validity or in predictive validity. A model of a real patient would have to mimic the human response to all standard drug schedules, but not necessarily to those not yet dreamed up by physicians. But a model of a not-yet-built transportation system should reliably predict what will happen when the system becomes operative. In the scientific case, we are aiming toward structurally valid models, which reveal the workings of nature. (If you are asking yourself whether structural validity is necessary to achieve predictive and replicative validity, you now have the motivation for sticking with the book until the later chapters, where some answers are given.)

To achieve valid models we must of course know how to go about *constructing* models. This involves being able to *describe* models in some kind of expressive language. Since our initial models are usually too complicated, we will have to know how to *simplify* models by retaining only what is relevant to our inquiry. We will have to understand what makes models complex as measured by the resources required by the computer to carry out the model instructions. *Validating* a model requires comparing its behavior with that of the real system. This presupposes that we have *verified* the correctness of the program realization of the model, since we do not want to confuse faults of the program with faults in the model. Thus we must understand the simulation process: its *mechanics*, such as how random variables are realized or how differential equations are integrated; as well as its *strategics*, such as the various approaches taken in sequencing events and activities.

Exercise. Indicate whether each of the following topics relates primarily to one or more of the three elements (real system, model, computer) or the two relations (modelling, simulation):

source of data	model description
behavior	model construction
structure	model simplification
replicative validity	model validation
predictive validity	program verification
structural validity	simulation mechanics
correctness	simulation strategics
goals of modeller	

1.2   COMMUNICATION ASPECTS OF MODELLING AND SIMULATION

One of the most important aspects of modelling, and one of the least appreciated, is communication.

The construction and testing phases of modelling activity provide constant excitement (how will the next run turn out?), generating on their own a motivation for application, diligence, and resourcefulness.

On the other hand, once the modelling challenge has been successfully overcome and the modeller's own curiosity satisfied, he may find it difficult to become enthusiastic about the task of clarifying for himself and communicating to others what he has accomplished. Nevertheless, if these aspects of his activity are not effectively transmitted, the great energy released by the project will most likely go to waste. In other words, what posterity will remember is not the intellectual and emotional gratification accrued to the modeller (though this is what he may remember). The long-term contribution of any modelling effort lies in the benefits it affords, either by direct use or by guidance for further development, to science and industry.

Effective communication, in this context, involves the following aspects:

1. Informal (English or other natural language) description of the model and the assumptions that went into directing its construction.

2. Formal (mathematical or other exact, unambiguous) description of the model structure.
3. Presentation of the program with which the simulation was carried out.
4. Presentation of the simulation experiments performed, and their results and analysis.
5. Conclusions about the range of application of the model, its validity, and its running cost.
6. Relating of the present model to other (past and future) models.

To be more concrete, suppose you are developing a model and intend to use the foregoing list as the format for a report on the completed project. This report may be sent to two classes of people interested in your work: (1) potential users of the simulation program or variations of it—we shall call them the *users*; and (2) people who may not use the program or model directly but may make other uses of it in relation to their own research and development—call them the *colleagues*.

Users include modellers who may run the model as a "subroutine" within their own program, and managers and other decision makers who may use the model predictions to guide decision machinery.

Colleagues include modellers who may be working in alternate or parallel directions within the field, as well as others with a more general interest in the area.

You, the modeller, are included in the users and colleagues. This is a fact worth remembering when you return to the report for information after some time away from the project.

How does our format help communicate to users and colleagues?

The *informal description* of a model plays a fundamental role, both in the developmental and public presentation phases of the effort.

By the developmental phase, I mean the period of activity in which the modeller conceives, programs, debugs, and tests his model. This may involve an extended period of "cut and try" alteration. Your progress in this phase will be facilitated to the extent that you can maintain a clear overall image (or gestalt) of the model which pieces all the parts together coherently. Writing out an informal description of the model, presenting the essentials but not the details, helps one to maintain a clear gestalt of the model as it develops. In the public presentation phase, the *informal description* should help both users and colleagues to grasp the basic outlines of the model and to visualize it within the framework of their prior conceptions about how things work. I am assuming that everyone carries within his head a "world model" and that each one can understand a new model best if he can fit it relatively easily into the joints and supports of his world model structure.

If I am not mistaken, people's world models do not consist of strings of algebraic-looking equations or FORTRAN computer code but are expressed internally much like the English-language way people communicate with one another in normal conversation, scientific or otherwise. Thus an informal description of the model is the most natural and effective way of establishing contact with the reader's intuition and of interfacing your model with his world model. By the way, the report should enable your model to have a lasting effect on the reader's world model—either to add nicely to its prior structure or to jar it into a more adequate one, when the two models conflict.

Relating explicitly your model to other models (aspect 6) will facilitate interfacing it with the reader's world model. Also, along with *conclusions* (aspect 5), it will help the user to decide whether the simulation program is appropriate to his own particular application, and the colleague to assess the implications of the model and its behavior for his own modelling efforts.

Having achieved a general acquaintance with the model structure, both users and colleagues (to varying degrees and on different occasions) may want to get a more detailed and precise view. The *formal model description* (aspect 2) and the *presentation of the simulation program* (aspect 3) should serve this end by supplying a two-layered explication. The first layer is that of the *model* divorced from its program realization. The second is that of the *program* (the instruction sequence by which the model state change operations are actually carried out). The colleague will be primarily interested in the model description, but he may want to consult the program listing for purposes of clarification and cross checking. The user who may have to transport the program from your machine to his, debug it, and/or modify it, will require in addition, a well-annotated, well-documented program description.

Nowadays, programming language designers are emphasizing *readability* (the ability of a language to be understood, somewhat like an essay) and *annotatability* (the facility with which program instructions and segments can be isolated, explained, and commented on). If these features are used to maximum advantage, much of the detail appropriate to the program can be explained directly in the program listing. The formal description can then concentrate on model structure essentials. (Of course, sometimes it may not be so easy to decide what is essential model structure and what is non-essential implementation; we discuss this further in Chapter 16.)

In conclusion, the communication aspects are important in influencing the use and impact a simulation study may enjoy. In this book we lay a foundation for the understanding of each of these aspects. The next section treats the most fundamental communications aspect, that of generating an informal model description.

1.3   INFORMAL DESCRIPTION OF MODELS

In this chapter we advocate that the proper way to informally present a model is to describe its (1) components, (2) descriptive variables, and (3) component interactions.

Generally speaking, the *components* are the parts from which the model is constructed; the *descriptive variables* serve as tools to describe the conditions of the components at points in time (included also are "parameters" that specify the constant model characteristics), and the *component interactions* are the rules by which components exert influence on each other, altering their conditions and so determining the evolution of the model's behavior over time. These concepts are graphically illustrated in Figure 3, which the reader should impress on his memory.

We must assert at the outset that no a priori rules can be given for the choice of components, descriptive variables, or component interactions—their selection is part of the art of modelling. This is as it should be, for each model structure must ultimately be appropriate to the real system being modelled; if we provided rules for the selection of the model elements, we would be setting forth a theory of reality, which is a vastly more ambitious project than is even a theory of modelling. This is not to say that *later* choices cannot be made more insightfully than *earlier* choices (in fact, as the modeller accumulates experience with a particular real system, his facility in this respect should be expected to improve) or that *some* choices cannot be derived from *other* choices (in fact, this is one of our fundamental tenets). However, we cannot expect to prescribe the choice of elements, or even the best way to describe this choice. We simply furnish some representative examples in the hope that the concepts of component, descriptive variable, and component interaction will become workably clear and that the flavor of their description will be imparted. At the section's end we suggest a general format as a guideline for model description.

Please note that the following examples are intended to be illustrative only; they are not touted as potentially valid models of real systems.

1.3.1   Examples

Example 1.   Round Robin Service.   A particular computer time sharing system consists of a computer and five users seated at terminals connected to the computer as in Figure 4.

The computer serves each user in turn moving clockwise (this is called round robin service). When his turn arrives, the user transmits data to the central processing unit (CPU) and awaits a response. When he receives it, he begins to prepare the data for his next turn.

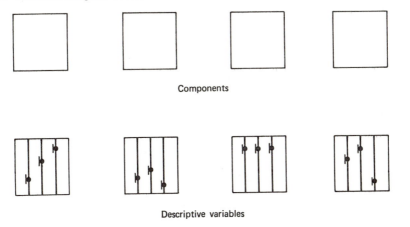

Components

Descriptive variables

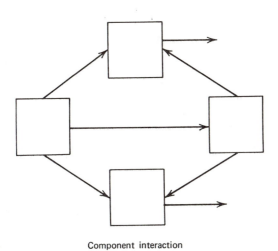

Component interaction

Figure 3 The elements of model description.

Our interest in the model is to study how fast a user completes his program development.

Description

Components

CPU, USER1, USER2, ..., USER5 (the computer is called CPU and each of the users is identified by a number).

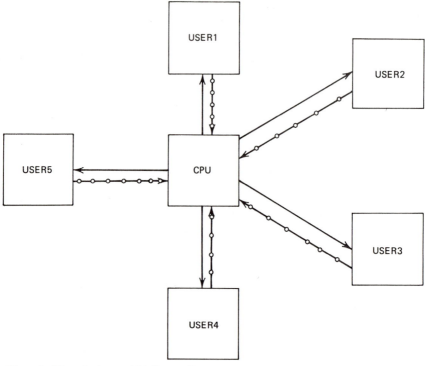

Figure 4   Time sharing model influence diagram.

Descriptive Variables

CPU

WHO · NOW—with range $\{1, 2, \ldots, 5\}$; WHO · NOW $= i$ indicates that USERi is to be serviced by the CPU.

USERi $(i = 1, 2, \ldots, 5)$

COMPLETION · STATE—with range $[0, 1]$ (the real numbers lying between zero and one); COMPLETION · STATE $= s$ indicates that a USER has progressed a fraction s of the way toward completing his program (zero means just starting, $\frac{1}{2}$ means halfway, one means finished, etc.).

PARAMETER

a_i—with range $[0, 1]$; the rate at which completion is attained by USERi.

Component Interaction

1.   The CPU serves each USER in turn at a fixed rate—thus WHO · NOW runs through the cycle 1, 2, 3, 4, 5, 1, 2, ...

2.   When USERi gets his turn (i.e., when WHO $\cdot$ NOW takes the value i), he completes a fraction a_i of the work left to be done [i.e., if his COMPLETION $\cdot$ STATE is s, it becomes $s + a_i(1 - s)$].

Assumptions

1.   The service time given to a USER is assumed to be fixed, thus not dependent on the USER's program. Thus the dotted arrows indicating influence of a USER on the CPU are absent in our model (Figure 4), although they might well be present in a more refined model.
2.   USERi's progress is hypothesized to proceed at an exponential rate determined by his individual parameter a_i.

Example 2.   Dynamics of Government–People Relations.   Consider modelling a country consisting of a government and a people. The government is run by a PARTY in power, either LIBERAL or CONSERVATIVE, and which determines an internal POLICY that may be PERMISSIVE or COERCIVE. The people reacting to governmental actions may be found at any time to be in a state of CIVIL $\cdot$ STRIFE, which is either LOW or HIGH.

Many postulates can be made concerning how the people react to governmental policy changes and how, in turn, the government determines its policy in response to the people's behavior. When such a set of postulates is not self-contradictory or incomplete it determincs, a particular government–people interaction. One set is given in the following as illustration.

Description

Components
GOVERNMENT, PEOPLE

Descriptive Variables
GOVERNMENT
    PARTY—with range {CONSERVATIVE, LIBERAL} indicates the political (idealogical) tendency of the GOVERNMENT.
    POLICY—with range {PERMISSIVE, COERCIVE} indicates the type of policy the GOVERNMENT is following.
PEOPLE
    CIVIL $\cdot$ STRIFE—with range {LOW, HIGH} indicates the general state of unrest in the country among the PEOPLE.

Component Interaction
P1.   A COERCIVE governmental policy is invariably followed in the next year by a HIGH degree of CIVIL $\cdot$ STRIFE.

P2.   Conversely, a PERMISSIVE government is always able to bring about
      and/or maintain a LOW level of civilian unrest in a year's time.

P3.   A PARTY remains in power as long as CIVIL · STRIFE is LOW,
      being replaced within a year's time if unrest becomes HIGH.

P4.   Once in power, a CONSERVATIVE government never changes its
      POLICY; nor does it change the POLICY of its immediate predecessor
      when it first assumes power.

P5.   A LIBERAL government will react to HIGH CIVIL · STRIFE by
      passing PERMISSIVE legislation, but within a year after quiet has
      returned it will invariably become COERCIVE in attitude.

The influence diagram is given in Figure 5.

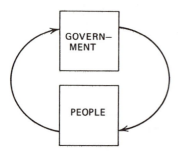

Figure 5   Government–People influence diagram.

Exercise.   What are some of the assumptions made in the model? Provide some
alternative postulates.

Example 3. World System.   The world model of Forrester (see Chapter 5)
has spawned much modelling of the interaction of industry, population, the
environment, and other variables. Here we present a very simplified model
in this class.

Description

Components

POPULATION, POLLUTION, INDUSTRY

Descriptive Variables

POPULATION

POPULATION · DENSITY—with range the positive real numbers;
POPULATION · DENSITY $= x$ indicates that there are currently x
people per square meter of the earth's habitable surface.

POLLUTION

> POLLUTION · LEVEL—with range the positive real numbers; POLLUTION · LEVEL = y indicates that the current POLLUTION · LEVEL of the environment is y units on some unspecified scale.

INDUSTRY

> INDUSTRIAL · CAPITALIZATION—with range the positive real numbers: INDUSTRIAL · CAPITALIZATION = z indicates that the total world industrial assets are currently valued at z dollars.

Component Interaction

1. The rate of growth of POPULATION · DENSITY increases linearly with increasing POPULATION · DENSITY and INDUSTRIAL · CAPITALIZATION; it decreases linearly with increasing POLLUTION · LEVEL.
2. The rate of growth of POPULATION · LEVEL increases linearly with increasing POPULATION · DENSITY and INDUSTRIAL · CAPITALIZATION.
3. The rate of growth of INDUSTRIAL · CAPITALIZATION increases linearly with increasing INDUSTRIAL · CAPITALIZATION and decreases linearly with increasing POLLUTION · LEVEL.

The influence diagram appears in Figure 6.

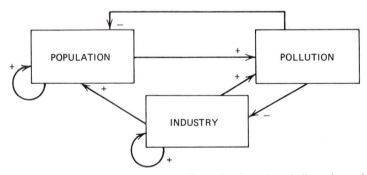

Figure 6 World model influence diagram: plus and minus signs indicate increasing or decreasing direction of influence, respectively.

Example 4. Student Model. In designing a system for computer-aided instruction (CAI), a model of a student was constructed to test the operation of the system. The model included as parameters such constructs as initial knowledge, organizational ability, memory retention, and problem-solving capability whose settings characterized the various student makeups. Here we present a much simplified illustrative version.

The student model was designed to take the place of a real student undertaking a CAI session (Figure 7). The model initially receives a document number from the CAI system and decides whether the levels of the concepts relevant to this document are sufficiently high; in the affirmative case, the model reports that it has "understood" the document (i.e., it outputs UNDERSTOOD); if not it outputs NOT · UNDERSTOOD. Depending on this response, the CAI system selects another document number for presentation, the model considers the next document, and so on.

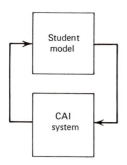

Figure 7   CAI system—student model interaction.

The documents and concepts mentioned are constituents of the particular CAI course being taught to the student and their numbers and interrelation also appear as parametric inputs to the model.

Description

Components

INPUT · REGISTER—displays the number of the document directly being presented to the model.

CONCEPT · 1, CONCEPT · 2, ..., CONCEPT · N_{CON}—the concepts characterizing the CAI course currently being "taught" to the model; there are N_{CON} of them.

OUTPUT · REGISTER—displays the response of the model.

Descriptive Variables

INPUT · REGISTER

DOCUMENTS—with range $\{1, 2, ..., N_{DOC}\}$; DOCUMENT $= x$ indicates that the xth document is currently being presented to the model.

CONCEPT · i ($i = 1, 2, .., N_{CON}$)

STRENGTH—with range $[0, 1]$; STRENGTH $= q$ indicates that CONCEPT · i has been learned to a fraction q of full comprehension.

OUTPUT · REGISTER

Y—with range {UNDERSTOOD, NOT · UNDERSTOOD} with the obvious interpretation.

PARAMETERS

Characterizing the student

Δ_U—with range the positive reals; reinforcement increment when DOCUMENT · UNDERSTOOD.

Δ_N—with range the positive reals; reinforcement increment when DOCUMENT NOT · UNDERSTOOD.

Δ_F—with range the positive reals; forgetting increment when concept unused.

Characterizing the course

N_{DOC}—with range the positive integers; the number of DOCUMENTS.

N_{CON}—with range the positive integers; the number of CONCEPTS.

For each DOCUMENT x

x-RELEVANT · CONCEPTS—with range the subsets of {1, 2, . . . , N_{CON}}; the CONCEPTS that are relevant to the understanding of DOCUMENT x.

DIFFICULTY(x)—with range the positive reals; the level difficulty of DOCUMENT x.

Component Interaction

When a DOCUMENT x is input to the model, the following procedure is carried out:

1. The x-RELEVANT · CONCEPTS are scanned, and based on a comparison of their total STRENGTH and the difficulty level, DIFFICULTY(x) of the DOCUMENT, a decision UNDERSTOOD or NOT · UNDERSTOOD, is outputted.

2. For each x-RELEVANT · CONCEPT · i: if DOCUMENT x was UNDERSTOOD, CONCEPT · i's STRENGTH is incremented by an amount Δ_U (to represent a reinforcement); if DOCUMENT x was NOT · UNDERSTOOD, CONCEPT · i's STRENGTH is incremented by an amount Δ_N (to represent some learning from use, even if the use was not totally successful); thus usually $\Delta_U > \Delta_N$.

    For each non-x-RELEVANT · CONCEPT · j: the STRENGTH of CONCEPT · j is decremented by amount Δ_F (to represent the tendency to forget a concept when it is not used).

Assumptions

1. Since the model has components representing concepts but not documents, it is being assumed in effect that the real student does not maintain

representations of documents as such but immediately decodes them into the relevant concepts, of which he does maintain a memory.

2. Course concepts are unrelated or "orthogonal" to each other; thus the condition of one is not directly correlated to that of another. (Concepts do interact indirectly, however, by way of interaction rules 1 and 2.)

3. Concept comprehension increases when a concept participates with other relevant concepts in the dissection of a document. This increase is greater when the document contents are understood than when they are not.

4. Unused concepts are forgotten.

5. A student reports that he "understands" the contents of the document when and only when the concepts relevant to it are comprehended at a sufficiently high level.

Example 5. Passenger Transportation. A very active field in simulation has to do with "discrete event" models of bus, airline, and other transportation systems. We present a simple model here of a hypothetical bus shuttling between two stations. Passengers may board the bus at either station and remain on the bus for as many stops as they wish, because presently no check is made of passengers' tickets once they are on the bus. The bus company, interested in whether it should invest in personnel or equipment for this purpose, has initiated the model development.

Description

Components

INPUT · GATE · 1
INPUT · GATE · 2
STATION · 1
STATION · 2
BUS

Descriptive Variables

INPUT · GATE · i ($i = 1, 2$)

· ARRIVING · i—with range the nonnegative integers; # · ARRIVING · $i = x_i$ indicates that x_i people are entering at the station at the present moment.

STATION · i ($i = 1, 2$)

· WAITING · i—with range the nonnegative integers; # · WAITING · $i = q_i$ indicates that q_i people are currently waiting in STATION · i for the BUS.

BUS

· IN · BUS—with range the nonnegative integers; # · IN · BUS = q_b indicates that q_b people are currently passengers in the BUS.

TRIP · TIME—a random variable (see Appendix C) with range the positive reals; TRIP · TIME $= s$ means that it will take s time units for the BUS to travel from the present station to the next.

PASSENGERS · OFF—a random variable with range the nonnegative integers; PASSENGERS · OFF $= n$ means that n passengers will leave the BUS at a station.

PARAMETERS

CAPACITY—with range the positive integers; specifies the maximum number of passengers the bus can hold.

p_i ($i = 1, 2$)—the probability that a passenger leaves the bus at STATION · i.

MEAN (SIGMA)—with range the positive reals; mean and standard deviation of the TRIP · TIME between stations.

K_{on} (K_{off})—with range the positive reals; the time it takes for a passenger to get on (off) the BUS.

Component Interaction

1. BUS shuttles from STATION · i to STATION · j, the time of arrival at STATION · j being determined by sampling from TRIP · TIME (normally distributed with parameters MEAN and SIGMA).

2. On arriving at STATION · j the BUS
    (a) Releases passengers desiring to leave—this number is sampled from PASSENGERS · OFF (a binomial distribution with probability parameter p_i and number parameter equal to the current value of # · IN · BUS).
    (b) Acquires passengers at STATION · j until STATION · j is empty (# · WAITING · $i = 0$) or the BUS is full (# · IN · BUS = CAPACITY).

The BUS waiting time is the maximum of the time taken for processes a and b. The time for process a (and b, respectively) is just the number of passengers leaving (entering) multiplied by K_{off} (K_{on}).

Assumptions

Since no record is kept of the identity of a passenger by the model, it is being assumed in effect that personal characteristics such as the number of round trips already made by the passenger and family or friendship relation to other passengers, which may contribute to the traffic pattern in reality, do not play a major role in determining the model characteristics relevant to the question asked by the bus company. (This was: what is the income lost over some appropriate accounting period due to the lax control policy adopted?)

Other assumptions are left to the reader to ponder.

1.3.2 A Suggested Format for Informal Model Description

To help remember the concepts illustrated in the last examples and to provide a working definition for them, we present a format for informal model description.

Components

COMPONENT · A

COMPONENT · B
    ⋮   Some general description linking the com-
                         ponents to conceptual parts of the real system.
COMPONENT · Z

Descriptive Variables

COMPONENT A

   VARIABLE · A1
    ⋮
   VARIABLE · A2

   VARIABLE · An   Range of each variable (the values it can
                                          take on); a symbol to stand for an arbitrary
COMPONENT B   member of this set (if used later in the formal
                                          description); the role of the variable in
   VARIABLE · B1   describing its associated component briefly
    ⋮   indicated.
   VARIABLE · Bn

COMPONENT Z

   VARIABLE · Z1
    ⋮
   VARIABLE Zn

PARAMETERS

   PARAMETER · 1   Range of each parameter; a symbol to stand
                                          for an arbitrary member of the range set (if
   PARAMETER · 2   later used); the role of the parameter in
    ⋮   specifying the structure of the model.
   PARAMETER · m

Component Interaction

{The effect, influence, or action of components on each other and/or their communication with each other informally described by way of rules, postulates, laws, etc.}

Diagram

{The components displayed as boxes labeled by component names and the fact of influence of component *A* on component *B* represented by an arrow directed from box *A* to box *B*.}

This diagram communicates the set of causal pathways of the model—an important aspect of model structure (see Chapter 9).

1.3.3 Summary: Informal Model Description

In the development stage, a clear but not overly detailed description of the model helps the modeller to better deal with the testing and modification that characterize this phase of modelling activity. Moreover, once a public presentation stage is achieved, models have to be effectively described if they are to achieve their proper impact.

The informal description of a model consists of the specification of components, descriptive variables including parameters, component interaction, and presentation of the (major) assumptions implied by the specification of interest. This description also provides a basis for the other aspects of model communication, namely, formal description, program description, validation, and relation to other models.

1.4 INTRODUCTION TO FORMAL MODEL DESCRIPTION

We turn next to the communication aspect concerning formal model description. Although an informal model description may communicate the essential nature of a model, it is open to certain intrinsic problems: incompleteness, inconsistency, and ambiguity.

A model may be *incomplete* because the modeller did not think of all the relevant situations that might arise and did not provide a complete description. Or, if he did consider all possibilities, he may have intended that the rules should apply to distinct sets of situations, whereas in fact one or more rules apply to the same situation. If they prescribe contradictory actions, the model is rendered *inconsistent*, since no action is actually possible in this situation. Finally, a model may be *ambiguous* because two or more possibilities are suggested in a particular situation, but it is not clear which one the modeller intended.

In formalizing his model, the modeller is forced to consider more of the relevant possibilities. Even if he does not carry the process out completely, his informal description is likely to reflect this effort, which renders it less open to the bugaboos just mentioned. However, a fully formalized version has the added advantage that it is possible in some cases to mechanically check whether omissions, inconsistencies, or ambiguities exist.

Full understanding of formalization requires the mathematical developments of later chapters. We begin here to lay the groundwork in informal conceptual terms. We set the stage by considering the basic categories into which models fall and then consider models as shorthand means of specifying dynamic objects called systems.

1.4.1   Categories of Models

The model examples given in this chapter illustrate some fundamental categories in which models may be placed.

Perhaps the most basic categorization relates to the *time base* on which model events occur. A model is a *continuous time* model if time is specified to flow continuously—the model clock advances smoothly through the real numbers toward ever-increasing values. A model is a *discrete time* model if, in contrast, time flows in jumps—the model clock advances periodically, jumping from one integer to the next (the integers represent multiples of some specified time unit).

Examples 1, 2, and 4 are discrete time models; 3 and 5 are continuous time models.

A second category relates to the range sets of a model's descriptive variables. The model is a *discrete state* model if its variables assume a discrete set of values; it is *continuous state* if their ranges can be represented by the real numbers (or intervals thereof), and *mixed state* if both kinds of variables are present. Examples 2 and 5 are *discrete state* models, Example 3 is a continuous state model, and Examples 1 and 4 are mixed.

Continuous time models can be further divided into *discrete event* and *differential equation* classes. A differential equation specified model is a continuous time–continuous state model in which state changes are continuous; thus the time derivatives (rates of change) are governed by the differential equations. Example 3 is such a model. In a discrete event model such as Example 5, even though time flows continuously, state changes can occur only in discontinuous jumps. A jump can be thought of as triggered by an event, and (since time is continuous) these events can occur arbitrarily separated from each other. No more than a finite number, though, can occur in a finite time interval.

A third category incorporates random variables in the model description. In a *deterministic* model no such random variables appear. A *probabilistic* or *stochastic* model contains at least one such variable. (From the point of view of this book, this distinction centers on the interpretation of model behavior rather than on its structural description.) Example 5 is a probabilistic model; all others are deterministic.

A fourth way of categorizing models relates to the manner in which the model considers the real system to interact with its environment. If the real system is assumed by the model to be cut off from all influences of its environment, the model is said to be *autonomous*. A *nonautonomous* model, then, allows for the influence of the environment. It has variables called input variables whose values are not controlled by the model but to which it must respond. Examples 1, 2, and 3 are autonomous models; 4 and 5 are nonautonomous. Example 4 illustrates that a nonautonomous model can be made autonomous by sufficiently expanding its scope. As presented, the CAI system is considered to be part of the environment of the student. But if we expand our real system to incorporate both the student and the CAI system, we must augment the student model with a model of the CAI system. Connecting them together as in Figure 7, we would have an autonomous model of the student–CAI combination. Each of the individual models, however, is nonautonomous.

A fifth category relates to whether the rules of interaction of a model explicitly depend on time. A model is *time invariant* if the rules of interaction are stated entirely in terms of the values that the descriptive variables can assume. In a *time varying* model, on the other hand, time may enter explicitly as an argument of the rules of interaction, which may thus appear to be different at different times.

A sixth category of models relates to whether their responses are or are not influenced by past history.[†] The emphasis in this book is on models with such memory, and all the given examples are of this kind. The concept is explained further in the next section.

1.4.2   Models as System Specifications

We have indicated that a model is basically a set of instructions for generating behavioral data. When a model is realized as a computer program, these instructions are explicitly expressed by statements of the language in which the program is written. But there is another way of expressing the instructions of a model which is independent of any particular programming language. This is achieved by converting the informal description of a model into a formal object called a *system specification*.

A *system* (as defined in Chapter 9) is a mathematical concept consisting of a time base, a number of sets that characterize all possible input stimuli and output responses, and two functions that determine the output behaviors

---

† Actually time variance and memory are related concepts. A time varying model can be expressed without time dependance by incorporating time as a descriptive variable.

generated in response to particular input stimuli. The sets just mentioned are referred to as the *static* structure of the system; the functions constitute its *dynamic* structure. A system specification is a shorthand way of specifying the elements of a system. When a model, informally described, is formalized as a system specification, its components and their descriptive variables specify the static structure, and its component interaction and influence diagram specify the dynamic structure. The way in which the dynamic structure is specified by a model is the formal equivalent of the way in which a computer generates the model's behavior based on the set of model instructions.

Each of the discrete time, discrete event, and differential equation classes of models have corresponding shorthand conventions for specifying systems. These conventions are called system specification or model *formalisms*.

The heart of the concept of system is the *state* set, one of the sets in the static structure. The states (elements of the state set) characterize the *memory* possibilities of the system—what information it can retain from its past stimuli to affect its response to future stimuli. A system is a *memoryless* if its state set has only one element (thus can be ignored altogether). For such a system, present and future responses cannot be affected in any way by past input stimuli. Such systems are also called *instantaneous*, since their response at any time is a function only of the stimulus received at that time. On the other hand, a system that has two or more states may respond differently to present and future inputs depending on the history of its past input stimuli.

System specifications derived from informal model descriptions often take the form of *networks* of interconnected systems—the influence diagram indicates the manner in which the component systems are interconnected. Often such networks consist of fairly complex memoryless systems and fairly simple systems with memory. Indeed, consider the *delay elements*—systems whose output lags one time step behind the input. When interconnected by instantaneous elements, these memory systems are sufficiently powerful to specify any discrete time system. Likewise, networks of instantaneous elements and memory elements called *integrators*—whose present output is the time integral of the past input—can represent any differential equation specified system.

When a system is specified by a network, its structure is given in more detail than would be used if the same system were specified more abstractly. Indeed, there is a hierarchy of levels at which systems can be specified, higher levels asserting more about the system structure than lower levels. This hierarchy becomes essential when we attempt to ascertain the degrees to which a model may represent the internal working of a real system. Indeed, the increasing strength of replicative, predictive, and structural validity parallels the hierarchy of system specification levels.

1.4.3   A Comment on Our Starting Point

The existence of a hierarchy of levels of system specification suggests that on logical grounds, informal model description need not take the form of components, descriptive variables, and component interactions advocated earlier. However, there are good reasons for starting out as we have done.

1. As a matter of fact, the descriptions normally employed by modellers usually run along the lines we take here.
2. This way of thinking may best coincide with the "world model" structure discussed earlier. (Indeed we may hypothesize reason 2 as the explanation for reason 1!)
3. Later discussion makes apparent the relative advantages afforded by dealing with system specifications at the higher levels of the hierarchy, and ultimately, at the network level to which our informal description paradigm corresponds.

1.4.4   Summary: Formal Model Description

Formal model description helps to detect omissions and inconsistencies, and to resolve ambiguities inherent in informal description. Thus as a communications medium it has the virtue of clarity and conciseness, while sacrificing the natural interfacing with the reader's intuition afforded by informal description.

A formalized model can be considered to be a shorthand means of specifying a system.

1.5   SOURCES

The importance of communication in modelling and simulation is stressed by McLeod.[1] Blalock[2] gives a good introduction to dynamic modelling in the social sciences. An exposition of the world model is furnished in Forrester's book.[3] The student model is based on that of Osin.[4] Many other models are described in such journals as *Simulation* and *Simuletter* and in the annual proceedings of the *Summer Computer Simulation Conference* and the *Pittsburgh Modelling and Simulation Conference*. Klir's book[5] may be consulted for background in general systems concepts. Computer simulation languages and techniques are the subject of many books.[6-10]

1. J. McLeod, "Simulation: From Art to Science for Society," *Simulation*, **18** (20), 1974, 77–80.
2. H. Blalock, *Theory Construction: From Verbal to Mathematical Formulations*. Prentice-Hall, Englewood Cliffs, N.J., 1969.

3. J. W. Forrester, *World Dynamics*. Wright-Allen Press, Cambridge, Mass., 1972.

4. L. Osin, "A Model of a Teacher and his Students," in *Proceedings of the Sixth Annual Pittsburgh Conference on Modelling and Simulation*. University of Pittsburgh, Pittsburgh, Pa., 1975.

5. G. J. Klir, *An Approach to General Systems Theory*. Van Nostrand Reinhold, New York, 1969.

6. J. H. Mize and J. G. Cox, *Essentials of Simulation*. Prentice-Hall, Englewood Cliffs, N.J., 1968.

7. G. W. Evans, II, G. F. Wallace, and G. L. Sutherland, *Simulation Using Digital Computers*. Prentice-Hall, Englewood Cliffs, N.J., 1967.

8. G. Gordon, *System Simulation*. Prentice-Hall, Englewood Cliffs, N.J., 1969.

9. T. H. Naylor, J. L. Balintfy, D. S. Burdick, and K. Chu, *Computer Simulation Techniques*, Wiley, New York, 1966.

10. G. S. Fishman, *Concepts and Methods in Discrete Event Digital Simulation*. Wiley, New York, 1973.

Chapter Two

The Five Elements

In this chapter we introduce the five elements that constitute the basic approach of this book to modelling and simulation. These elements are:

—the real system
—the experimental frame
—the base model
—the lumped model
—the computer

The elements represent distinctly different conceptual aspects of modelling and simulation. Although they may not come isolated and neatly labeled in a modeller's description of his simulation, keeping the distinctions they embody in mind will greatly enhance our ability to deal with the subject area at hand.

After the elements have been introduced, two exemplary modelling contexts are given in which the elements, except the computer, are explicitly recognizable. Then we describe some general procedures employed by modellers to arrive at relatively simple models.

In Appendix A we describe a "quasisimulation" in which all elements appear and many of the problems involved in modelling and simulation are exemplified. We return often to this quasisimulation to concretize a general concept. I recommend that the reader skim through Appendix A after reading this chapter to acquire some familiarity with the case study discussed there.

2.1   THE REAL SYSTEM: BEHAVIOR

The *real system* refers to nothing more or less than a source of observable data. The system may be a *natural* one, such as a biological or ecological system, an *artificial* one, such as a computer operating system, or a *mixed* one involving both natural and artificial elements such as transportation, urban, or world systems. The important characteristic is the identification of a segment of reality and the distinguishing of it from the rest, permitting measurements and other observations to be made on it.

We can visualize a real system, as in Figure 1 where the small circles represent *descriptive variables* thought to be significant for the understanding, description, and/or control of the system. A variable can be thought of as a meter that is capable of registering a reading. For example, a gas pump meter in a gas station registers the amount of gas transferred to the gas tank of each car. We use the term "meter" both to mean the usual "quantitative" meter (i.e., one that produces numerical measurements) and also "qualitative" meters, such as a microscope that enables observations not necessarily numerical in form. Thus the *range* of the variable, which refers to its set of possible readings, may take many forms.

The descriptive variables of a real system can be classified as *observable* or *nonobservable*. The observable variables are those corresponding to meters now in existence. The nonobservable variables are those that cannot at present be measured directly; that is, no meter, or measurement apparatus, currently exists which corresponds to such a variable, although perhaps conceivably one might be built. These variables are introduced because often, even though they cannot be measured directly, they may play essential roles in determining system activity (or, as we say after Chapter 3, they are essential for representing the "state" of the system). Many modellers object to introducing nonobservable variables into their models. Indeed, their presence causes some difficulties (see Chapter 14). But we can come to

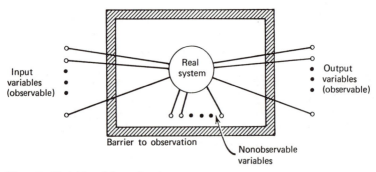

Figure 1   Variables of the real system.

understand how their presence may be necessary if a valid model is to be achieved.

The observable variables are further classified as *input* or *output* variables. Input variables are those considered to perturb, influence, or affect the system from outside. An input variable may also be under the experimenter's control; that is, he may be able to dictate or choose the actual value of the variable at points in time. Output variables are those considered to take on values as a result of the values assumed by the input variables. In other words, input variables are considered to be *causes* and output variables are *effects*.

Referring to Figure 2, suppose that at the points in time indicated, the values of all observable variables are recorded (the set is discrete for

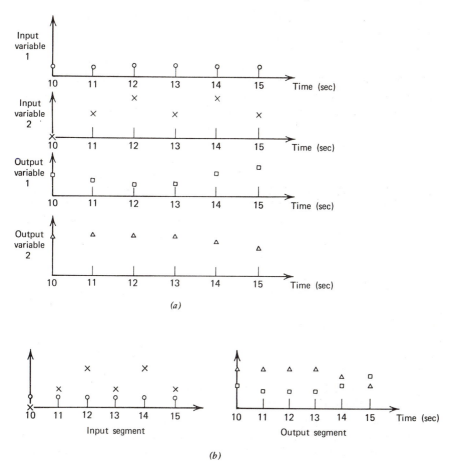

(a)

(b)

Figure 2   Chart of variables (a) observed at intervals of one second from 3:20:10 to 3:20:15 PM, April 2, 1973, (b) construed as an input-output segment pair.

illustrative purposes, but it could be continuous). Grouping together all the input variable charts, we call the result an *input segment*. "*Trajectory*" is often used interchangeably with "segment." Similarly, grouping together the output variable charts we obtain the associated output segment. The two form an input-output (I/O) segment pair. The set of all possible experimentally obtainable input-output segment pairs is called the *input-output behavior* of the real system. As indicated earlier, this constitutes **all that can be directly known about the real system.**

2.2 THE EXPERIMENTAL FRAME: VALIDITY

The *experimental frame* characterizes a limited set of circumstances under which the real system is to be observed or experimented with. Thus associated with an experimental frame is a subset of the input-output behavior of the real system. Indeed, there may be many possible experimental frames, and the input-output behavior of the real system is the union of the subsets associated with these frames.

Since an experimental frame puts constraints on the possible observation of the real system, it is possible for a relatively simple model to produce input-output pairs that agree, within some standard of comparison, with all the input-output pairs of the frame. When this happens, we say that the model is *valid* for that experimental frame. It is not surprising then to learn that a model may be valid in one experimental frame but invalid in another. Thus there may be many valid models (at least as many as experimental frames). We see that **the validity of a model is relative to an experimental frame and the criterion by which agreement of input-output pairs is gauged.**

2.3 BASE MODEL: HYPOTHETICAL COMPLETE EXPLANATION

The *base model* is a model capable of accounting for all the input-output behavior of the real system. In other words, it is valid in all the allowable experimental frames. In any realistic modelling and simulation area, **the base model description can never be fully known**, although certain aspects of its description may be accepted as known. Since **the base model provides a complete explanation of the behavior of a real system, it may be expected to comprise many, many components and interactions.** Because of this plethora of components and interactions, the complexity of the base model, as measured by the computational resources required to construct and simulate it, is likely to be extremely great.

2.4   LUMPED MODEL: SIMPLIFICATION

In realistic cases, the great complexity of the base model precludes its consideration as a possible simulation model. Fortunately, having specified the experimental frame of current interest, a modeller is likely to find it possible to construct a relatively simple model that will be valid in that frame.

Such a relatively simple model is called a *lumped model*, because often the model is constructed from the base model, or the experimenter's image of the real system, by lumping together components and simplifying interactions accordingly.

2.5   THE COMPUTER: COMPLEXITY

The *computer* is the computational device with whose help the input-output pairs of the lumped model are generated. Sometimes these trajectories or their properties can be worked out analytically using brain, paper, and pencil. Usually, however, trajectories must be worked out step by step, from one simulated time instant to the next. This process is often called *simulation*. The instructions for carrying out the *step-by-step* (also called *iterative recursive*, or *inductive*) simulation process are supplied by the lumped model. The computer must faithfully carry out these instructions, which constitute its *program*. Humans are not well suited to such a repetitive and boring job, but in special circumstances a modeller may still trace through parts of his model's trajectories (this is called *hand simulation*). The job is carried out with much more speed and efficiency by the electronic computer. Indeed, computer simulation made possible the consideration of models of complexity undreamed of in prior eras.

There are nontheless limits to the resources available both of the computer and the modeller (electronic computers have arisen and improved, but humans remain humans after all). These resources can be measured along a number of dimensions:

1. The *time* it takes to simulate one model time step (hence the cumulative time required to simulate a many step trajectory).
2. The *space* the program requires in the computer to represent the model structure and to store the values of the state variables.
3. The *overhead* associated with converting the model into its representing program, including translation, compiling, and/or assembling from higher level language to machine language, and with moving the program between short-term (core) and long-term storage locations.

4. The *time and effort* involved in debugging the program, adjusting parameters, and otherwise validating the model with respect to both the program (computer) and the experimental frame (real system).

As one can imagine there are usually constraints on the time, space, and other resources that can be allotted to a model building effort. Indeed, the dimensions described ultimately reduce to dollar costs—charged by computer facility and/or paid to the modelling staff—and the constraints then take the form of a limitation on the dollars allotted to the project budget. For a given modelling staff and computer facility, the cost of developing and simulating a model can be traced to characteristics of the model itself. For example, a model with many components may require more running time and storage space than a model with fewer components. Thus the complexity of model can be measured in terms of the extent of the resources it needs for development and simulation, and this complexity is often simply related to structural properties of the model. A model whose complexity exceeds the limits imposed by the project budget is useless even if it is valid in some desired experimental frame.

2.6   DISTINCTIONS TO KEEP IN MIND

1. The real system is simply a source of observable data. Often people refer to **structural** properties of a real system relating to its components and their interactions. But in our approach, all such properties are to be considered as referring to the base model of the real system, the modeler has in mind, not to the system itself. For example, it may be said that a brain consists of certain kinds of cells called neurons. What really has happened is as follows: neurophysiologists have made a number of microscopic observations and chemical analyses—these are part of the real system—and based on their conclusions, it is advisable, or at least accepted, to consider neuronlike components for any base model of a brain.
2. The base and lumped models differ in that the structure of the lumped model is **completely** known to the modeller but that of the base model is at most **partially** known to him. Indeed, he may be attempting to validate the lumped model in order to use its known structure to infer what the structure of the base model is like.
3. The computer program realizing a model should not be identified with the model itself. Different programming languages encode the same model in different ways. It is important that structural features, introduced in the program in order to simulate the model, be distinguished

from those of the model in its pure unrealized form. This is why good program-independent means of model description are necessary.

Exercise. Discuss other distinctions that come to mind in distinguishing the five elements.

2.7 EXAMPLES

2.7.1 The *E. coli* (Baterial) Cell

Bacterial cells have been studied at various levels. Their chemical constituents have been identified by means of chemical analyses, thus providing the basis for selecting universally agreed on components for a base model. At a much higher experimental level, cells have been placed in environments supplying varying kinds and amounts of food (for bacteria), and the growth of the cells given these diets is observed. A lumped model aimed at accounting for the observed growth behavior was constructed, and we briefly describe the situation as follows.

Real System

The kinds of data available include the following:

1. Chemical analysis giving evidence on the kinds of chemicals found in the cell.
2. Electronic microscopic and crystallographic observations giving evidence of the structure and composition of biochemical molecules.
3. Laboratory "simulations" of specific reactions and processes thought to occur in the real cell.
4. Tracer studies of the flow of biochemicals through a cell.
5. Records of the growth and multiplication behavior of cells placed in various nutritive environments and their adaptation to sudden changes in these environments.

Experimental Frame

The behavior that the lumped model must account for is that of kind 5.

Base Model

The data of kinds 1 to 4 are instrumental in defining the components of the base model and the form of the interactions. Whether these components suffice is unknown, as are some of the specific characteristics of their interactions.

The components, thought to number at least 3000, are called MOLE-
CULES. Each MOLECULE is described by a single real variable—its
concentration in the cell. These MOLECULES are engaged in the following
kinds of processes:

(a) *Metabolism*—converting external nutrients (foods) into material for
     building and maintenance of internal cell structures.
(b) *Energy production*—driving the metabolic processes.
(c) *Catalysis by enzymes*—selecting which of many possible metabolic
     processes are to take place is determined by the presence or absence
     of certain enzymes.
(d) *Genetic control of enzymes*—the presence or absence of enzymes is
     controlled by the cell genes in response to the external environment.
(e) *Replication of the genes and division of the cell.*
(f) *Material flow through the cell wall*—taking in nutrients and excreting
     wastes.

The complexity of interaction involved is apparent in Figure 3a.

Lumped Model

The components of the lumped model correspond to disjoint sets of molecule
types called "POOLS." The partition is illustrated in Figure 3a. There are
31 POOLS (as compared to the 3000 components of the base model); the
POOLS appear in Figure 3b). For example, all 20 different amino acids in
the base model appear as one undifferentiated pool in the lumped model;
all MOLECULES relating to the production of energy by breakdown of
nutrient sugar are lumped together in a single pool called GLUCOSE; all
4 nucleotides appear as a single pool; DNA, however, appears as the only
element of a pool.

In attempting to construct a valid lumped model, the interaction of the
POOLS was chosen to preserve the interaction thought to be characteristic
of the base model components. Thus the processes *a* to *f* of the base model
also appear in the lumped model. In the base model, a typical chemical
reaction might involve, say three MOLECULES. In the lumped model, a
"reaction" involving three POOLS is intended to represent, in actuality,
base model reactions involving the 300 or so component MOLECULES.
Now each POOL is described solely by a single real variable—its concentration in the cell, which in a valid model would equal the sum of the concentrations of its constituent molecule types. It is thus clear that a lumped model
"reaction" can only be a simplified version of the compounded effects of all

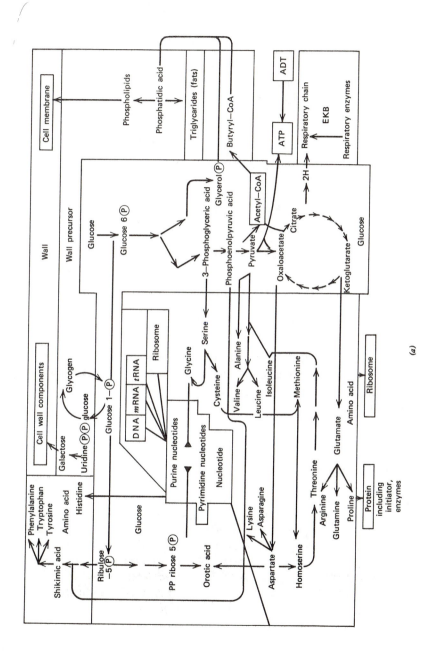

(a)

35

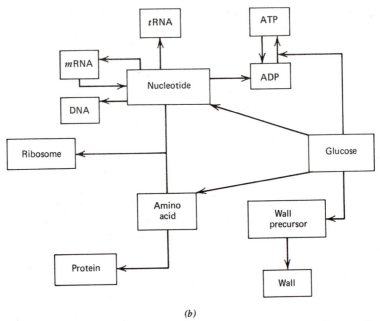

(b)

Figure 3 (a) Base model influence diagram. (b) Lumped model influence diagram. (Source: Reference 1, Figures 1, 2, pp. 37, 38.)

the base model reactions involved. The question we have to understand in modelling is: when can simplification such as this succeed in the construction of lumped models that validly account for the behavior of interest—(the experimental frame, as we have called it)?

The lumped model was subjected to stiff tests against laboratory data on the growth of cell cultures, and rather good agreement was obtained.

2.7.2 Building–Elevator System

The following is based on a simulation done in GPSS for a term project. The object was to approach the problem of designing an elevator system for an administration building by first modelling the building, including its present elevator system. Once such a model had been validated (this was beyond the scope of the project), different elevator systems could be substituted and their effects could be more confidently predicted by the simulation. The statistical simplification techniques used are illustrative of those employed in many discrete event simulation models.

The Real System

The kinds of data available include the following:

1. Structural data on the building and elevator layouts, floor plans, room sizes, and so on.
2. Data on the nature of the activities carried out in each office of the building.
3. Data on the flow of information (memos, telephone calls) between offices.
4. Data on the personal characteristics of the clients and of the office staff.
5. Data on the time a person spends waiting to see an officer, the time he spends with the officer, which office he goes to next, and how long he spends waiting for, and in, the elevator.

Experimental Frame

The behavior of interest is related to demand for elevator service—for example, the maximum number of people waiting at each floor, the traffic between pairs of floors. This represents statistical aggregation of the data of kind 5.

Base Model

The components of the base model include some that are called "OFFICES." Each OFFICE has a RECEPTIONIST and a set of OFFICERS. The OFFICES are partitioned into disjoint sets called FLOORS labeled 0, 1, 2, . . . , N. The other components are the ELEVATOR and the INPUT · SET whose elements are called PERSONS. Each PERSON has a FILE containing a personal characteristic description.

The FILE designates the first OFFICE a person is to go to. Entering at the bottom FLOOR (labeled 0), the PERSON goes to his designated OFFICE, calling for, waiting for, and taking the ELEVATOR, if necessary. At the OFFICE, the PERSON is assigned an OFFICER on the basis of his FILE by the RECEPTIONIST, and he waits in a line until his turn to see the OFFICER arrives. The PERSON spends some time with the OFFICER and is either finished and leaves the building, taking the ELEVATOR if necessary, or is directed to a next OFFICE where the same procedure is once again initiated. The times spent with the OFFICER and at the next destination are determined by the FILE and the OFFICER.

The ELEVATOR always goes from the bottom to the top FLOOR and back down. It stops at a FLOOR only if some PERSON wants to get on or get off at that FLOOR. Stopping at a FLOOR, the ELEVATOR waits for those getting off to leave its confines. It then waits for those getting on, until all who want to are aboard, or until the ELEVATOR is full. It then continues.

Data of kinds 1 and 2 are employed in defining the components. Data of kinds 3 to 5, *if they were completely obtainable*, would be instrumental in determining the form of the interactions.

Exercise. Why must such data be considered to be only partially obtainable? Give examples of how such data would be used in the model construction.

The Lumped Model

The lumped model includes components corresponding to the FLOORS of the base model. Each FLOOR has a SERVER. The other components correspond to INPUT · SET and the ELEVATOR. The elements of the lumped INPUT · SET correspond to PERSONS, but these do not have FILES; the ELEVATOR is unchanged in the lumped model.

A lumped model PERSON enters the bottom FLOOR and heads for a FLOOR determined by a random variable. After passing through the ELEVATOR as before, he waits in line at the FLOOR. When his turn comes, another random variable determines the time he is to engage the SERVER, and another random variable determines his next designation (FLOOR or out).

There are two kinds of simplification involved here. The first, like that of the *E. coli* case, involves lumping together of components (OFFICES) to form larger, compound, undifferentiated components (FLOORS). The second simplification technique is that of dropping entirely a descriptive variable and trying to account for the effect by probabilistic means (i.e., by substitution of random variables). In the base model, a PERSON's FILE enables a deterministic choice of his service time and next destination, whereas in the lumped model, these quantities are chosen according to probability distributions.

How would one go about selecting such distributions? From data of kinds 2 to 5 it may well be possible to logically enumerate the possibilities that would ensue when a PERSON with given FILE characteristics meets a given OFFICER. For example, a PERSON coming to claim an article sent by mail from a foreign country (this condition would be represented in his FILE) would see a claims OFFICER, who might send him to obtain proof of residential status and/or evidence of the article's value, and then to pay the cashier, before he received the article. By considering the various logical possibilities for PERSONS of all possible FILE characteristics appearing at an OFFICE, and combining them with an estimate of the distribution of FILE characteristics appearing at that OFFICE, an estimate of the next destination distribution for that OFFICE can be made.

Again the question arises: under what circumstances can such lumpings result in valid lumped models?

Exercise.   The experimental frame plays a major role in determining whether a lumped model is valid. Given the experimental frame and the statistical lumping technique of this example, do you think a valid lumped model is possible?

2.8   SIMPLIFICATION PROCEDURES

The last two examples illustrate two of the most fundamental gambits chosen by modellers in seeking to achieve valid, simplified models. In this section we enumerate a few of the common procedures of this kind. It should be understood that these procedures do not necessarily produce valid models or even simpler models when measured according to objective criteria such as those discussed in Section 2.5, even though one often feels that conceptually simpler models have been obtained. (In Chapter 14 we address the conditions under which true simplification can be achieved. As already mentioned, we consider in Chapters 8 and 12 the conditions that may be necessary and/or sufficient to guarantee that a lumped model, however constructed, is valid within an experimental frame.)

We discuss the procedures in terms of operations to be performed on the structural description of a base model. That is, suppose we have available a base model specified by its components, descriptive variables, component interaction rules, and influence diagram. We want to derive a lumped model by modifying one or more parts of this description. Some fundamental operations are as follows:

1. Dropping of one or more components, descriptive variables and/or interaction rules.
2. Replacing one or more deterministically controlled variables by random variables.
3. Coarsening the range set of one or more descriptive variables.
4. Grouping components together in blocks and aggregating the descriptive variables within blocks.

We briefly discuss each of these operations and provide some examples.

2.8.1   Dropping of One or More Components, Descriptive Variables and/or Interaction Rules

Underlying this approach is the premise that not all factors are equally important in determining a result. There may be a relatively small number of factors whose contribution is most significant, and a larger number with moderate to minor effects. In engineering terminology, the major effects are called "first-order" effects and the minor effects are "second-order" ones. Modellers often decide to neglect or ignore minor factors on the premise that retaining them would not significantly alter the overall model behavior and would unnecessarily complicate the modelling and simulation process. In engineering, this is called working within a "first-order approximation."

Phrased in our conceptual framework, the premise is as follows: it may be possible to construct a valid lumped model in which relatively few components, descriptive variables, and/or interaction rules are represented. A more refined base model could be hypothesized that would contain many more components variables and/or rules not contained in the lumped model. These additional entities, however, would only "insignificantly" affect the base model behavior *within the experimental frame of interest*. Of course the meaning of "insignificantly" would have to be specified relative to goodness of fit criteria by which the input-output pairs of the model and real system are compared.

Since one seldom knows beforehand in any particular instance whether the simplification process will work, it is best to regard it as a hypothesis about the base model—namely, that the omitted entities are relatively insignificant in the experimental frame of interest. This hypothesis is confirmed if the lumped model proves to be valid by empirical comparison with the real system and is rejected otherwise. In case of rejection, the obvious next step is to decide which base model entities might be added to the lumped model to increase its validity.

Dropping of certain entities may require dropping or modification of others. Thus dropping a component implies dropping all its descriptive variables as well. Dropping a descriptive variable will necessitate dropping or at least modifying interaction rules referencing that variable. On the other hand, dropping or modification of interaction rules is usually accomplished within an unmodified framework of components and descriptive variables.

The effect of dropping a component (or variable) on the interaction rules can be understood with the help of Figure 4. Components A, B, and C influence the to-be-dropped component V, which in turn influences components X, Y, and Z. In general one may think of a component as a channel for the transmission of effects from its influencers to its influencees. Dropping the component then necessitates modifying this influence flow. The effect of its influencers is easily handled—in Figure 4, removing V implies removal of all rules of interaction specifying the effect on V of the influencer variables A, B, and C (these are no longer necessary). The effect of removal of V on its influencees is the nontrivial aspect. In Figure 4, dropping V will leave a "hole" every place in the rules of interaction that the variables of V

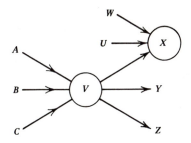

Figure 4 Effect of dropping a component.

appeared—specifically, the rules determining the values that variables of X, Y, and Z will assume on the basis of values that those of V may assume. These holes must be filled one way or another. The following example illustrates.

Example. Dropping a Descriptive Variable. Conside the "Dynamics of Government–People Relations" model (Example 2, Chapter 1). A modeller might hypothesize that the political tendency (PARTY) of the GOVERN-MENT might have little to do with its reaction to civil unrest. Thus taking Example 2 as his base model, he would construct a lumped model by dropping the descriptive variable PARTY from those describing the GOVERNMENT. This omission has ramifications in the choice of interaction rules. Postulates P4 and P5 assert differing GOVERNMENTAL action on the basis of PARTY distinction. These rules must be modified to make no such distinc-tion. For example, P4 and P5 may be replaced by:

P4′. If CIVIL STRIFE is HIGH, the government will in the next year adopt a PERMISSIVE POLICY.
P5′. If CIVIL STRIFE is LOW, the government does not change its POLICY.

Postulate P3 provides the conditions under which the PARTY in power has succeeded the PARTY of opposing ideology. This rule is dropped entirely in the lumped model, since no PARTY variable appears. This is an example of the "dropping of an interaction rule" simplification procedure.

Another common situation is the following.

Example. Dropping of an Interaction Term. Often the interaction between a set of numerically valued variables expressed in the form of a Taylor's series expansion. For example, one might have the relation

$$y = a_1 x_1 + a_2 x_2 + b_1 x_1^2 + b_2 x_2^2 + b_3 x_1 x_2 + c_1 x_1^3 + \cdots$$

where y is the value of a variable Y at any time t and x_1, x_2 are the values of variables X_1, X_2 at some time, t' preceding t. On the hypothesis that the values assumed by X_1 and X_2 are always likely to be less than one and that the coefficients b_1, b_2, b_3, c_1, ... are small in comparison to a_1 and a_2, the terms involving second or higher powers of the X's will be omitted in the lumped model. This retention of only first-order terms gives rise to the designation "first-order approximation." The lumped model rule then is $y = a_1x_1 + a_2x_2$.

2.8.2   Replacing Deterministic Variables by Random Variables

Example 2.7.2 exemplified the "replacement of deterministic variables by random variables" approach. In general, one hypothesizes a deterministic base model in which the rules of interaction deterministically control the values of all descriptive variables. A probabilistic lumped model is then derived by replacing some of the rules of interaction by probability mechanisms, thus converting the affected variables to random variables. (However, these probability mechanisms are realized by deterministically described random number generators, which means that only the form of the model and, essentially, the interpretation of its behavior have changed. See Chapter 6.)

As in Example 2.7.2 this procedure is often a follow-up to the dropping of descriptive variables. Referring again to Figure 4, we see that the dropping of component V will result in a nonunique choice in the values of the variables of components X, Y, Z. Rather than supply rules of interaction that will again uniquely specify these values, one may convert the variables affected into random variables. For example, if a variable of X is also influenced in the base model by variables U and W, in the lumped model it may be assigned a probability distribution conditioned by U and W.

Exercise.   Referring to the assumptions given in Example 5 of Chapter 1, provide a base model in which the identity of a passenger is retained in a personal FILE that uniquely determines the station at which he will leave the BUS. Presumably the FILE will include the station at which a passenger boards the BUS. Construct a lumped model in which the identity variable is dropped and the probability that a passenger disembarks at a station is conditioned by the station of embarkation. How might this probability be estimated?

2.8.3   Coarsening the Ranges of Descriptive Variables

Recall that a descriptive variable is a way of describing the condition of a model component. A value that the variable can assume represents a possible condition the component may be found in at any time. The range set of a variable is the set of all values it may assume.

"Coarsening of the ranges of descriptive variables" is a simplification procedure in which the lumped model components and descriptive variables are the same (i.e., in one-to-one correspondence) as those of the base model, but the range set of some or all of the lumped variables are smaller than the range sets of the same base variables. This means that the lumped model variables can describe relatively few of the conditions that the base model components can be found in. Thus a value in the range of a lumped variable may represent many values in range of the same base variable. Stated in another way, distinct values of the base range set may become identified or indistinguishable in the lumped model. In effect, the base model range set, hence its descriptive power, has been coarsened by the simplification procedure.

Example. Round Off. Balances of customer accounts in a certain base model of a bank are recorded in terms of dollars and cents, whereas in a corresponding lumped model only whole dollar units are used. Let BALANCE $\cdot$ OF $\cdot$ A be the descriptive variable for the account of customer A. Then the range of BALANCE $\cdot$ OF $\cdot$ A is the set of values of the form $d_1d_2d_3d_4d_5d_6 \, . \, d_7d_8$, where each d is a digit, that is, an element of the set $\{0, 1, 2, \ldots, 9\}$. For instance, 000345.12 represents \$345.12 (thus balances are limited to the range zero to one cent less than a million dollars). Since lumped model keeps track to within dollar units, for it BALANCE $\cdot$ OF $\cdot$ A is the set of all values of the form $d_1d_2d_3d_4d_5d_6$. There are 10^8 possible elements in the base range and only 10^6 possible elements in the lumped range; therefore some, perhaps all, of the lumped range values represent more than one value of the base range. Indeed, suppose we choose the rule whereby $d_1 \cdots d_6 \, . \, d_7d_8$ is represented by $d_1 \cdots d_6$; then the 100 base elements $d_1 \cdots d_6 \, . \, 00, d_1 \cdots d_6 \, . \, 01, \ldots, d_1 \cdots d_6 \, . \, 99$ are all represented by the single lumped value $d_1 \cdots d_6$. For example, \$345.12 is represented by \$345, but so are \$345.00, \$345.50, \$345.99, and so on.

Exercise. The given rule rounds balances *down* to the nearest dollar unit. Another rule would be to round *down* or *up* to the nearest dollar unit, whichever is closest (e.g., \$345.49 is represented by \$345, but \$345.51 is represented by \$346; use the convention that represents \$345.50 by \$346 as well). Describe the rule for a typical element $d_1 \cdots d_6 \, . \, d_7d_8$. Is it the case, as in the "always round down" rule, that every lumped range value represents the same number of base range values?

Example. Classification and Nonuniform Coarsening. The contents of the lumped model ELEVATOR of Example 2.7.2 are described by the PERSONS currently in it. Let this variable be called CONTENTS and suppose that the model concerns 26 alphabetically named PERSONS $a, b, c, \ldots, x, y, z$. Suppose, too, that the elevator capacity (the maximum number of passengers allowed at any time) is 10. Then the range of CONTENTS is the set of all subsets of the English alphabet, of size less than or equal to 10. For example, $\varnothing$ (the empty set), $\{a\}$ (only a is in the ELEVATOR), $\{a, b\}$ (a and b in the ELEVATOR) are values of CONTENTS.

Suppose that a further lumping is made in which the new lumped model recognizes PERSONS of only two types, TYPE · 1 and TYPE · 2. Call this lumped model 2, then in the new lumped model CONTENTS has as range the set of all pairs (i, j), where i and j range over the integers $0, 1, \ldots, 10$ such that $i + j$ is less than or equal to 10.

Continuing to coarsen the variable CONTENTS, let lumped model 3 be such that PERSONal identity is disregarded totally and just the number of PERSONS is recorded. (This is the same as recognizing only one type of PERSON). Then the range of CONTENTS in this case is the set $\{0, 1, \ldots, 10\}$.

Finally, in lumped model 4, only the condition of whether the ELEVATOR is empty is recorded. CONTENTS, then, has a binary valued range {EMPTY, NOT · EMPTY}.

Exercise. Fill in Table 1, assuming that TYPE · 1 and TYPE · 2 divide the alphabet into two equal parts of 13 letters each, say TYPE · 1 = $\{a, b, \ldots, 1, m\}$ and TYPE · 2 = $\{n, o, \ldots, y, z\}$.

Table 1   Exercise in Coarsening of Range Sets

Condition of ELEVATOR	Value of CONTENTS in			
	Model 1	Model 2	Model 3	Model 4
Empty				
a, b, c, x, y, z are in the ELEVATOR		(3, 3)		
e, l, e, v, a, t, o, r are in the ELEVATOR			8	

This example illustrates the dramatic effect of the coarsening procedure in reducing the descriptive power of a variable. A computer realization of lumped model 1 would have to represent any one of about 10 million possible conditions of the ELEVATOR. However, in lumped model 2, only 55 values of CONTENTS represent the 10 million model 1 conditions. Proceeding to model 4, only two values of CONTENTS represent the 10 million ELEVATOR conditions.

Note, also, that lumped values need not represent the same number of base model values. For example, the value EMPTY represents only one of the model 1 conditions, whereas NOT · EMPTY represents all 10 million or so other values.

Exercise.   Find the number of model 2 and model 1 values represented by the typical model 3 value k. If k PERSONS are in the elevator, how many possible ways are there of dividing the PERSONS into two classes, TYPE · 1 and TYPE · 2 (model 2) and into 26 classes (model 1)?

Let $C_i(k)$ be the number of values represented in model i by the model 3 value k. As k increases from 0 to 10, does $C_i(k)$ always increase, always decrease or increase first and then decrease?

Of course, we can readily simplify by coarsening descriptive variables, but we face the danger of "oversimplifying," that is, trying to construct a lumped model in which the descriptive power available is not sufficient to express the requisite base model dynamic behavior. Phrased in our framework, given an experimental frame, it may be possible to construct a valid lumped model by coarsening the descriptive values up to a certain point but not beyond.

Intuitively, in our example, if the experimental frame concerns the volume of traffic through the elevator, it may be possible to use model 3 (CONTENTS range–the number of PERSONS in ELEVATOR), but the model 4 CONTENTS (EMPTY/NOT EMPTY) would be too coarse for this frame. Whether a valid lumped model at the level of model 3 can in fact be constructed, however, depends on whether the lumped model has to know the identities of the PERSONS in the ELEVATOR to correctly reproduce the behavior of the base model. If the PERSONS identities must be known, no model at the level of model 3 can be valid. **Clearly whether a descriptive variable can be coarsened depends on whether enough information has been retained both for external reporting (i.e., the output of the model) and for internal use (i.e., the component interaction).** We return to this problem in Chapter 8.

2.8.4   Grouping Components and Aggregating Variables

Example 2.7.1 was a case of "grouping components and aggregating variables." In general, base model components are grouped into blocks that are identified with lumped model components. In the example, the 3000 base components are grouped into 30-odd lumped components. A descriptive variable for a lumped component is obtained by aggregating descriptive variables of the base components represented by the lumped component. This aggregation process can be viewed as first compounding without loss of information the component variables, then coarsening the resultant compound range.

In our example suppose we group 20 MOLECULES $A, B, C, \ldots, Z$ into a block called a POOL. Since each molecule is described by its concentration, we have a list of 26 variables $[A], [B], \ldots, [Z]$, where $[A]$ is the standard chemical notation for the descriptive variable CONCENTRATION · OF · A, which takes on positive (with 0) real values. The aggregation of these variables into the descriptive variable $[POOL]$ of the corresponding lumped component POOL is a simple summation: if $C_A, C_B, \ldots, C_Z$ are particular values of concentrations, then $C_A + C_B + \cdots + C_Z$ is the associated value of the lumped POOL concentration.

Exercise. Show that many conditions $(C_A, C_D, \ldots, C_Z)$ of the base model block are represented by a single lumped descriptive variable value.

This form of numerical aggregation appears pervasively in many model domains. Table 2 illustrates a few cases. In each case, the descriptive variable

Table 2   Aggregation of Variables

Field	Base Components Grouped into Blocks	Descriptive Variable of Each Component	Block Name
Chemistry	Molecules	Concentration	Pools
Ecology	Individuals	Biomass	Compartments
Economics	Enterprises	Capital	Sectors

of a component represents an amount of a particular resource it "owns." Grouping components into blocks, it is natural to associate the amount of the particular resource "owned" by a block as the sum of the individual amounts "owned." In the economic case, each enterprise owns capital, and a sector composed of enterprises owns the total capital. In the ecology case, each individual of a compartment represents or "owns" a certain amount of biomass, whose sum represents the compartment's biomass. In the chemistry case, each component "owns" a number of individuals of the molecular type it represents; thus the pool "owns" the sum of all these individuals.

A more general form of aggregation is the following: let $\alpha_1, \ldots, \alpha_N$ be base model components of a given block. Let $V_{\alpha_1}, \ldots, V_{\alpha_N}$ be a list of associated descriptive variables (one for each component), and suppose that the range set of each variable is the same set $S = \{s_1, \ldots, s_i, \ldots, s_m\}$. Then the descriptive variable of the lumped block will record for each s_i, the number of components having the value s_i. Thus let this variable be called NUMBER · HAVING · EACH · VALUE, and let its range be the set of vectors $(n_1, \ldots, n_i, \ldots, n_m)$, where each n_i lies between 0 and N and the sum of all the n_i's is N. Then, more formally, the aggregation is one which for a given list of base component values $s_{\alpha_1}, \ldots, s_{\alpha_N}$ produces a vector $(n_1, \ldots, n_i, \ldots, n_m)$, where for each i, n_i is the number of times the value s_i appears in the list $s_{\alpha_1}, \ldots, s_{\alpha_n}$.

The neuron net example of Appendix A illustrates this aggregation procedure. In Chapter 12, we show that there are "reasonable" constraints on the base model which enable such aggregation procedures to work.

2.9 SUMMARY

In this chapter we have introduced and illustrated a framework involving five key elements in modelling and simulation. In Figure 5, the elements are depicted in a way that suggests their interrelationships. We have also employed the framework to describe and illustrate a number of procedures very commonly appealed to for simplifying models. In Appendix A a "quasi-simulation" case study illustrates in a unified way framework and problem areas discussed in this book.

Exercise. List all the relations depicted in Figure 5.

2.10 SOURCES

The model of the E. coli cell was originated by Weinberg.[1, 2] Compartment models in ecology appear in Reference 3. Aggregation in economic models is surveyed by Ijiri.[4] Theory of measurement is discussed in Reference 5. A condensed version of this chapter appeared in Reference 6.

1. B. P. Zeigler and R. Weinberg, "System Theoretic Analysis of Models: Computer Simulation of a Living Cell," *Journal of Theoretical Biology*, **29** (1), 1970, 35–56.

2. E. Goodman, "Adaptive Behavior of Simulated Bacterial Cells Subjected to Nutritional Shifts." Doctoral dissertation, University of Michigan, Ann Arbor, 1972.

3. B. C. Patten (Ed.), *Systems Analysis and Simulation in Ecology*, Vols. 1–. Academic Press, New York 1971–.

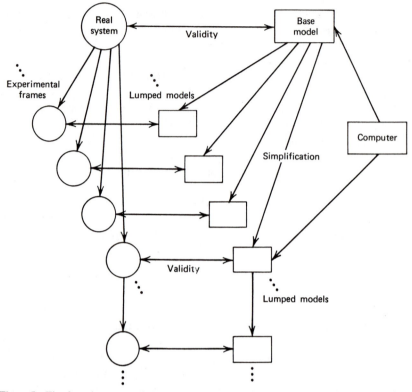

Figure 5 The five elements and their interrelationships. Squares indicate model structures; circles indicate sets of input-output behaviors. An arrow from *A* to *B* means *A*'s behavior includes that of *B*s.

4. Y. Ijiri, "Fundamental Queries in Aggregation Theory," *Journal of the American Statistical Association*, **66** (36), 1971, 766–782.

5. J. Pfanzagl, *Theory of Measurement*. Wiley, New York, 1968.

6. B. P. Zeigler, "Introduction to a Theory of Modelling and Simulation," in *Proceeding of the Sixth Annual Pittsburg Conference on Modelling and Simulation*, University of Pittsburgh, Pittsburgh, Pa., 1975.

PROBLEMS

1. For each of the following pairs, compare and contrast the paired elements; that is, state an important shared characteristic and an important distinguishing characteristic:

base model—lumped model
base model—real system
formal model—simulation program

2. (a) "Modelling is an attempt to replicate the way in which a real system works."

(b) "Modelling is an attempt at valid simplification of a real system."

State whether you basically agree or disagree with each of these "definitions" of modelling. Defend your position employing the concepts introduced (real system, base model, lumped model, experimental frame, computer).

3. Two modellers, Mr. A and Ms. B, are working on models of the same real system. A claims his model is better because it is more detailed, hence more valid. B disagrees that detail necessarily implies validity, and in addition claims superiority for her model on the basis of its simplicity. Judge the worthiness of the claims and counterclaims.

Chapter Three

Prototype Simulation and Formal Model Specification

We have thus far focused on the *modelling* aspect of "modelling and simulation." In terms of the five elements, this aspect has to do with the construction of a lumped model that is valid with respect to the real system in the context of an experimental frame. The *simulation* aspect, on the other hand, has to do with the construction of a computer program that will faithfully generate the behavior of a model.

Our discussion thus far has also relied on the informal description of models. When we come to consider computer simulation, however, we are naturally led into the area of formal model description. The computer is, after all, a rule-obeying device, and we must therefore phrase the model description in rulelike terms. The rules sometimes take the form of the program that implements the model. This program is written in some particular simulation language. There is, however, a more abstract form of specifying the rules, which we call *formal model description*. This form characterizes the model mathematically, that is, in the language of set theory. It has the advantage of being able to specify the model in its "pure" form rather than in the implemented form provided by a program description.

Our approach is as follows. We discuss a procedure that represents the essential features of a discrete time simulation, that is, any program that generates the behavior of a model in a step-by-step way, each step representing the passage of a constant amount of model time. We introduce a working definition for the state variable concept and concretize the properties of state variables in terms of some very desirable features of a simulation program. This leads naturally to the formalization of model descriptions and behaviors in system theoretic terms.

3.1 THE CONCEPT OF STATE

We have seen that the components of a model are described by a set of descriptive variables. The rules specifying the component interaction determine the manner in which these descriptive variables change over time. For a computer to be able to simulate the model, it must "know" these rules of interaction. It may also have to keep track of past values of the descriptive variables in order to compute their future values, since the rules of interaction are functions of these values. But it does not follow that the computer must keep a record of *all* past values of *all* descriptive variables. In fact, in many models it is possible to designate a small subset of all the descriptive variables such that only the *present* values of these variables have to be available to the computer for it to be able to compute the future values of *all* descriptive variables. Not counting the input variables, such a set is called a set of *state variables*. We can gain an understanding of the essential concepts by considering the case of autonomous models—models with no input variables. Later (Section 3.6) it will not be hard to understand how the presence of input variables affects the situation.

Consider then a model with descriptive variables $\alpha_1, \alpha_2, \ldots, \alpha_n$. We say that the values of these variables are $y_1, y_2, \ldots, y_n$ at any time t, if variable α_1 has the value y_1, variable α_2 has the value $y_2, \ldots$, at time t. We call a model *well described* if the rules of component interaction determine for any future t', (greater than t) a unique set of values $y'_1, y'_2, \ldots, y'_n$ given the values $y_1, y_2, \ldots, y_n$ at time t. Figure 1 illustrates this assumption. We further assume that the computer is ideal in the sense of being able to carry out with full precision the rules of interaction. Thus given the values $y_1, \ldots, y_n$ at time t, the computer produces the exact values $y'_1, \ldots, y'_n$ at time t'. The times t, t' are model times not actual computer times. To illustrate the difference, suppose that on December 21, 1973, at 4:10 PM the computer was given the values $y_1, \ldots, y_n$ and on the same day produced the values $y'_1, \ldots, y'_n$ at 4:11 PM. Then December 21, 1973, 4:10 PM, and December 21, 1973, 4:11 PM, are the computer times corresponding to the model times t and t'. The computer took one minute to make the computation, but the difference $t' - t$, the elapsed *model* time, may be an unrelated positive number.

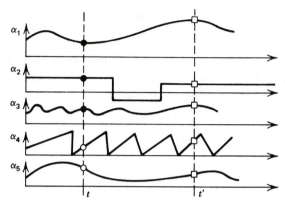

Figure 1   A model with five descriptive variables $\alpha_1, \alpha_2, \alpha_3, \alpha_4, \alpha_5$. If the model is well described, the values represented by circles uniquely determine the values represented by squares. If $\alpha_1, \alpha_2, \alpha_3$ form a state variable set, the solid circle values alone suffice for this purpose.

We say that a subset of the descriptive variable set is a *state variable set* if the values of these variables *alone* at any time t determine uniquely the values of *all* the descriptive variables at any future time t'. If a model is well described, $\alpha_1, \ldots, \alpha_n$ is such a set! But there may be proper subsets also. Suppose there is a state variable set with m variables and we order all the variables so that these m appear first; thus $\alpha_1, \alpha_2, \ldots, \alpha_m$ are the state variable set of interest, and $\alpha_{m+1}, \ldots, \alpha_n$ are the remaining descriptive variables. Since $\alpha_1, \ldots, \alpha_m$ are state variables, we are assured that given $y_1, \ldots, y_m$ at time t, the computer can compute $y'_1, \ldots, y'_m$ *and* $y'_{m+1}, \ldots, y'_n$ at time t' for any t, t' such that $t' > t$.

Exercise.   (*a*)   Show that a model is well described if and only if it has a state variable set. (*b*)   Show that if a model is well described, it cannot be inconsistent, incomplete, or ambiguous.

Example 1.   A Whale of a Courtship.   Two whales, a MALE and a FE-MALE, are attempting to find each other in an ocean. Each whale creates a low honking sound that radiates outward in all directions. When picked up by the other whale, this sound will be interpreted as a signal indicating the direction in which the signaling whale can be found.

Imagine a meter that faithfully models the response of a whale to an incoming honk. Imagine also that a grid has been established and a pair of honk meters has been placed at each point of the grid; one of the meters responds to the MALE and the other to the FEMALE. The list of readings of these meters at any time t, describes the distribution of signals emanating from MALE and FEMALE throughout the ocean at that time. At any grid point P, we shall refer to the pair of variables corresponding to its pair of meters as SIGNAL · AT · P · DUE · TO · MALE and SIGNAL · AT · P · DUE · TO · FEMALE.

When a whale picks up a honk, it heads in the apparent direction indicated at a constant rate. Let the locations of the whales be described by the variables LOCATION · OF · MALE and LOCATION · OF · FEMALE. We can now see that the latter two locations constitute a set of state variables.

For simplicity, we consider a one-dimensional ocean of width $2L$ with grid points $\{-L, -L + 1, \ldots, -1, 0, 1, \ldots, L - 1, L\}$ = GRID POINTS (see Figure 2).

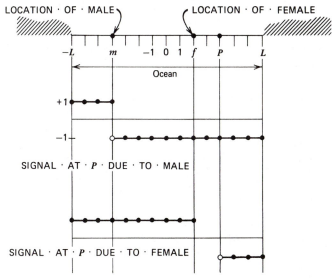

Figure 2   Readings of honk meters distributed in the ocean at some particular instant when MALE is a position m and FEMALE at position f.

Components

MALE, FEMALE, GRID · POINTS

Descriptive Variables

Describing MALE:
   LOCATION · OF · MALE—with range GRID · POINTS.
Describing FEMALE:
   LOCATION · OF · FEMALE—with range GRID · POINTS.
For each P in GRID · POINTS
Describing GRID · POINT P:
   SIGNAL · AT · P · DUE · TO · MALE—with range $\{1, -1\}$,
   SIGNAL · AT · P · DUE · TO · FEMALE—with range $\{1, -1\}$.

Component Interaction

The time base is discrete with values . . . , $-h$, 0, h, $2h$, ... The interaction is given by:

(a) The value of SIGNAL · AT · P · DUE · TO · MALE at time $t = D$ ((the LOCATION · OF · MALE at time t) $- P$) where $D(x)$ is 1 if $x \geq 0$ and is -1 if $x < 0$.

(b) The value of SIGNAL · AT · P · DUE · TO · FEMALE at time $t = D$ ((the LOCATION · OF · FEMALE at time t) $- P$).

(c) The LOCATION · OF · MALE at time $t+h =$ [the LOCATION · OF · MALE at time t] + [the value of the SIGNAL · AT · (LOCATION · OF · MALE at time t) · DUE · TO · FEMALE at time t].

(d) The LOCATION · OF · FEMALE at time $t+h =$ [the LOCATION · OF · FEMALE at time t] + [the value of the SIGNAL · AT · (LOCATION · OF · FEMALE at time t) · DUE · TO · MALE at time t].

Exercise. Check that the component interaction description agrees with the preceding text.

We now check that LOCATION · OF · MALE and LOCATION · OF · FEMALE are state variables as follows. Suppose that the values of LOCATION · OF · MALE and LOCATION · OF · FEMALE are known at time t. Calling these values m and f, respectively, we show how to compute the values of all descriptive variables at time $t + h$.

From (a) we have for every GRID · POINT P: the value of SIGNAL · AT · P · DUE · TO · MALE at time $t = D(m - P)$.

Similarly: the value of SIGNAL · AT · P · DUE · TO · FEMALE at time $t = D(f - P)$.

In particular for GRID · POINT m (the LOCATION · OF · MALE)

SIGNAL · AT · m · DUE · TO · MALE at time $t = D(m - m) = 1$

SIGNAL · AT · m · DUE · TO · FEMALE at time $t = D(f - m)$ (1)

Exercise. Compute the signals at GRID · POINT f at t.

From (c) we have

LOCATION · OF · MALE at time $t + h$
$$= m + \text{SIGNAL} \cdot \text{AT} \cdot m \cdot \text{DUE} \cdot \text{TO} \cdot \text{FEMALE at } t$$
$$= m + D(f - m) \text{ [using Eq. 1]} \tag{2}$$

Exercise. Compute the LOCATION · OF · FEMALE at time $t + h$.

Using (a) again we have

SIGNAL · AT · P · DUE · TO · MALE at time $t + h$

$$= D \, ((\text{LOCATION} \cdot \text{OF} \cdot \text{MALE at time } t + h) - P)$$

$$= D(m + D(f - m) - P) \, [\text{using Eq. 2}] \tag{3}$$

Exercise.   Compute the SIGNAL · AT · P · DUE · TO · FEMALE at time $t + h$.

From Equations 2, 3, and the exercises, we see that the values of all the descriptive variables at time $t + h$ are expressed in terms of m and f, the values of LOCATION · OF · MALE and LOCATION · OF · FEMALE at time t. We shall soon see that this implies that we can compute the values of all descriptive variables at times $t + h, t + 2h, t + 3h, \ldots$, knowing only the values m and f at time t. Thus restricting our time base to the instants $\{\ldots, -h, 0, h, 2h, \ldots\}$, we see that {LOCATION · OF · MALE, LOCA-TION · OF · FEMALE} is a state variable set.

Exercise.   Show that this set is *minimal*; that is, that no proper subset is also a state variable set.

3.2   STATE VARIABLE PROPERTIES

Imagine that the simulation of a well-described model is to be carried out by a program that has access to a number of storage locations, including those corresponding to the descriptive variables $\alpha_1, \ldots, \alpha_n$. The following properties give some insight into the meaning of the state concept as well as its usefulness.

1. *Program initialization.*   Suppose that the program is given the task of computing the values $y_1', \ldots, y_n'$ at t' given the values $y_1, \ldots, y_n$ at t. Then only the storage locations associated with the state variables need to be initialized (i.e., specified initially). Why?

2. *Repeating a run.*   Suppose we want to repeat the computation of the values $y_1', \ldots, y_n'$ at t' given the values $y_1, \ldots, y_n$ at t, say, because we have lost the record of a first simulation run. The two runs may be made on different computers at different (computer) times, yet the results will be the same, provided the locations associated with the state variables are initialized to the same values $y_1, \ldots, y_m$. Why?

3. *Program interruption, and restart.*   Suppose that after computing the values $y_1', \ldots, y_n'$ at t', we arrange to interrupt the program. For example, suppose the values of all the variables are put out onto tape for analysis.

The program itself is stored in a file; thus at some (actual) time later (e.g., after we have interpreted the results of the previous simulation run) it can be restarted. Suppose we want to be able to restart the program in such a way that it can compute the values $y'_1, \ldots, y'_n$ of all the variables at (model) time t'' with the same results it would have obtained if it had never been interrupted ($t'' > t'$). In other words, the program should be able to resume from the same point it stopped at and compute the same end results. We need only arrange to save the values in the storage locations associated with $\alpha_1, \ldots, \alpha_m$ at the moment that the program was interrupted, along with the program. Why?

4. *Program recovery.* Suppose that a failure occurs in the computer while the program is being executed. When the computer is repaired we want to proceed with the simulation, but we hope to avoid having to initialize the program to its beginning condition. Reinitialization would ultimately produce the same results but would be wasteful compared to restarting the program from the point at which it left off. This recovery is indeed possible if the failure did not affect the contents of the state variable locations. Why?

We now see how the computer can make the computations required for a simulation run in an *iterative* manner (see Section 2.5 for an introductory definition). Suppose that we want it to compute the descriptive values $y'_1, \ldots, y'_n$ at t' given the state values $y_1, \ldots, y_m$ at t. Now suppose that the rules of interaction are such that they can be translated into a program, which for a limited set of times $t_1, t_2, t_3, \ldots, t_i, t_{i+1}, \ldots$, can do the following.

Given any set of state values $y^i_1, \ldots, y^i_m$ at t_i, the program computes the unique descriptive values $y^{i+1}_1, \ldots, y^{i+1}_{m+1}, \ldots, y^{i+1}_n$ at t_{i+1} specified by the rules of interaction. When this is true we say that the program can compute or simulate the *model transition* from t_i to t_{i+1}. [This holds for any of the pairs of times (t_i, t_{i+1}).]

Let us call the set $\{t_1, t_2, \ldots\}$ the *computation instants*. These are the model times at which the program can produce a set of model description values. Often these times are successive multiples of some step size h, so that $t_{i+1} - t_i = h$ (e.g., with $h = 1$, we may have $0, 1, 2, \ldots$). We call this a *discrete time simulation*. Assume that the rules of interaction do not depend on the time but only on the state values $y_1, \ldots, y_m$; that is, the model is *time invariant*.

Exercise. In the time invariant, discrete time case, the program consists only of a set of rules which, given state values $y_1, \ldots, y_m$, computes descriptive values $y_1, \ldots, y_n$. Show that if it computes the correct model transition from time $t = 0$ to $t = h$, it computes the correct transition for any pair (t_i, t_{i+1}).

3.3   PROTOTYPE PROCEDURE FOR DISCRETE TIME SIMULATION OF TIME INVARIANT MODELS

Let us continue the problem of computing the descriptive values at t' given the state values $y_1, \ldots, y_m$ at t. Suppose that $t = t_M$ and $t' = t_{M+N}$, where t_M and t_{M+N} are computation instants so that $t_M, t_{M+1}, \ldots, t_{M+N}$ is the subset of computation instants between (and including) t and t'. We consider the discrete time, time invariant case. The program goes through the following iterative procedure to do the computation.

Step 1.   Initialize the locations associated with state variables $\alpha_1, \ldots, \alpha_m$ to $y_1, \ldots, y_m$. Call these locations $\bar{\alpha}_1, \ldots, \bar{\alpha}_m$.

Step 2.   Initialize the clock to t_M. (The clock $\bar{T}$ will record *model* time.)

Step 3.   Apply the rules of interaction to the contents of the state variable locations $\bar{\alpha}_1, \ldots, \bar{\alpha}_m$ to produce a new contents for $\bar{\alpha}_1, \ldots, \bar{\alpha}_m$ as well as new contents for the remaining descriptive variable locations $\bar{\alpha}_{m+1}, \ldots, \bar{\alpha}_n$.

Step 4.   Advance the clock by adding h to its current contents.

Step 5.   Check if the clock contents exceed $t_M + Nh$. If yes, stop the computation. If no, go to step 3.

To see how this procedure works we note that if the program executes step 2 and then repeats step 5 until it halts, it will produce the sequence $t_M + h, \ldots, t_M + Nh$, which is the sequence of computation instants beginning with t and ending with t' for the discrete time case with step size h. Step 1 places $y_1, \ldots, y_m$ in the state locations $\bar{\alpha}_1, \ldots, \bar{\alpha}_m$. Step 3 then computes successive model transitions $(t_M, t_M + h)$, $(t_M + h, t_M + 2h)$, ... These can be shown to be the correct transitions undergone by the model. Two kinds of proof can be given for this statement—the *informal* and the *formal*. In the informal kind we convince ourselves that the computer carries out a correct simulation, but we do not bind our argument to strict rules of logic and we may not consider every aspect of the situation. In formal proofs we attempt to put everything down and to adhere to strict rules of inference. In informal argument we are often essentially right, especially if we have built up a good intuition about the problem; but we are sometimes catastrophically wrong because we overlooked some aspect or did not fully trace through the implications of our premises. By undertaking formal *proofs* we hope to avoid these traps, but success in complex situations usually remains a goal rather than an achievement.

In this chapter, we give only informal proofs of our assertions. Chapters 10 and 16 provide the basis for a more formal approach.

An informal proof that the procedure correctly simulates the model is as follows. In step 1 the correct state values $y_1, \ldots, y_m$ for time t are placed in the locations $\bar{\alpha}_1, \ldots, \bar{\alpha}_m$. In step 2 the beginning model time t is stored in the $\bar{T}$ location. In step 3 the model rules of interaction are applied to the values $y_1, \ldots, y_m$ to produce a set of descriptive values $y'_1, \ldots, y'_m, y'_{m+1}, \ldots, y'_n$. These values are the correct model values at time $t + h$, and since the rules of interaction are those for the transition $(0, h)$, the model is time invariant and the computer carries out the rules exactly (all these rules being assumptions we have already made). In step 4 we increment the model time by h so that it now is $t + h$. We then continue to go around the loop— steps 3, 4, and 5—until, we reach the model time t', which is $t_{M+N} = t_M + Nh$. At that stage the correct descriptive values will appear in the $\bar{\alpha}_1, \ldots, \bar{\alpha}_m, \bar{\alpha}_{m+1}, \ldots, \bar{\alpha}_n$ locations, since at every pass through the loop the correct state variables continue to be updated in the $\bar{\alpha}_1, \ldots, \bar{\alpha}_m$ locations.

Let us summarize several features of the procedure just outlined.

It is *prototypical* (i.e., represents the essential characteristics) of discrete time simulations. The instants at which the model's descriptive values are computed comprise a sequence of the form $t, t + h, \ldots$. The step size h is a parameter we may be able to manipulate. The smaller h is, the better view we get of the model behavior; but the number of iterations needed to simulate the behavior between t and t' is $(t' - t)/h$, and since for each iteration the program must execute the loop (steps 3, 4, and 5), the smaller h is, the larger the computation time will be (assuming, as we often must, that the computer time required to execute the loop remains constant). In the prototype procedure step 4 is the crucial one because it embodies the rules of interaction of the model. This step must be further broken down into steps that simulate the actions of each of the model components that together make up a model transition. We return to this problem in Chapter 4. In the remainder of this chapter we pause to capture in formal terms what we have just developed.

Exercise.   The time required to execute the loop depends on the particular model rules of interaction and the step size h. Assuming that the total time required to compute the values at t', given those at t, can be expressed as $\tau_i + \tau_h \times (t' - t)/h$, identify the terms in this expression.

The procedure correctly simulates the model if the computation of the one step transition $(0, h)$ is exact. Often, however, the rules of interaction can be realized only *approximately* by the computer, and the accuracy of the approximation may depend on h. Such is the case for rules of interaction specified in differential equation form (see Chapter 5). If there is some error introduced at each iteration, even a small amount, we must be concerned with the possible accumulation of errors over many steps (see Chapter 13).

The procedure is *sequential*. It directs the computer to carry out a sequence of actions, one after another. The procedure is *iterative* because this sequence of actions involves a sequence of actions repeated over and over again— the loop of steps 3, 4, and 5.

Exercise. Modify the procedure to simulate a model that is not time invariant.

Exercise. Check directly that the procedure has the four properties discussed in Section 3.2.

3.4 FORMAL SPECIFICATION OF MODELS

Let us note the form of step 4. It consists of a subprogram that accepts a list of state values as input and produces a list of descriptive values as output. The subprogram thus can be thought of as carrying out a mapping f whose domain is the set of possible lists of state values and whose range is the set of possible lists of descriptive values. Then

$$f(y_1, \ldots, y_m) = (y'_1, \ldots, y'_m, y'_{m+1}, \ldots, y'_n)$$

represents the situation wherein the subprogram receives a list $y_1, \ldots, y_m$ and produces a list $y'_1, \ldots, y'_n$. Now f can be thought of as consisting of two functions: when given the list $(y_1, \ldots, y_m)$, one function returns the list $(y'_1, \ldots, y'_m)$, and the other takes in the lists $y_1, \ldots, y_m$ and $y'_1, \ldots, y'_m$ and produces the list $y'_1, \ldots, y'_i, \ldots, y'_m, y'_{m+1}, \ldots, y'_n$ (the $y'_1, \ldots, y'_m$ values are merely copied). Call these functions δ and λ, respectively. Then

$$\delta(y_1, \ldots, y_m) = (y'_1, \ldots, y'_m)$$

and

$$\lambda((y_1, \ldots, y_m), (y'_1, \ldots, y'_m)) = (y'_1, \ldots, y'_m, y'_{m+1}, \ldots, y'_n)$$

and we can write

$$f(y_1, \ldots, y_m) = \lambda((y_1, \ldots, y_m), \delta(y_1, \ldots, y_m))$$

Pictorially we have

$$y_1, \ldots, y_m \longrightarrow \boxed{f} \longrightarrow y'_1, \ldots, y'_m, y'_{m+1}, \ldots, y'_n$$

which can be replaced by

$$y_1, \ldots, y_m \longrightarrow \boxed{\delta} \longrightarrow y'_1, \ldots, y'_m \longrightarrow \boxed{\lambda} \longrightarrow y'_1, \ldots, y'_n$$

Often the function λ does not depend on the values $y_1, \ldots, y_m$, making possible an even simpler form:

$$\delta(y_1, \ldots, y_m) = (y_1', \ldots, y_m')$$
$$\lambda(y_1', \ldots, y_m') = (y_1', \ldots, y_n')$$
$$f(y_1, \ldots, y_m) = \lambda(\delta(y_1, \ldots, y_m))$$

Pictorially, f is replaced by

$$y_1, \ldots, y_m \longrightarrow \boxed{\delta} \longrightarrow y_1', \ldots, y_m' \longrightarrow \boxed{\lambda} \longrightarrow y_1', \ldots, y_n'$$

We call this simplified form the *normal form*, and we learn that for many models, a set of state variables can be chosen that will bring about the normal form. What does this normal form mean? The map δ is called the *state transition function*: it takes a list of values of the model state variables at time t_i and produces a list of values for the model state variables at time t_{i+1}.

Exercise. Actually δ is a mapping that takes the contents of the state variable locations just before step 4 is executed into the contents of these locations just after step 4 is executed. Explain how we can identify the "before" and "after" contents with the model state values at times t_i and t_{i+1}.

In other words, δ takes the state in which the model finds itself at the present computation instant and produces the state in which the model will be at the next future computation instant.

Exercise. The function δ should really be represented by notation δ_h, indicating dependence on the step size h. Why?

The map λ is called the *output* function; it takes a list of values of the state variables at a computation instant and produces the list of values of the descriptive variables at the *same* instant.

Exercise. Justify the foregoing statement.

In other words, λ takes the present state of the model and produces the total description of the model in the present state.

As we have seen, we may be interested only in observing a subset of the descriptive variables we call the model *output* variables. What this set actually consists of will depend on the circumstances: if we want to check the internal working of the model, the output set may consist of part or all of the state variables; if we are interested in validating the model with respect to a real system, only certain descriptive variables (those which correspond to observable real system variables in the experimental frame we are working in) will be called output variables. Therefore, given a choice of output variables, we can modify the output function λ so that it produces only the present values of the output variables, thus only a partial description of the model in its present state.

We have just slipped in some important concepts that should now be clarified. What exactly do we mean by the state of the model? its output? the transition function? the output function? To define these concepts precisely, we are led to use the formalism of systems theory.

Let DESCRIPTIVE · VARIABLES be the set of model descriptive variables and let STATE · VARIABLES and OUTPUT · VARIABLES be subsets of DESCRIPTIVE · VARIABLES representing choices of state and output variables, respectively. For each STATE · VARIABLE β, let RANGE · β denote the range set of β (the set of possible values β can assume). Similarly, for each OUTPUT · VARIABLE γ let RANGE · γ be the range set of γ. (We later introduce the INPUT · VARIABLES for which α is a typical member and RANGE · α its range set.)

Let $\beta_1, \beta_2, \ldots, \beta_i, \ldots$, be the STATE · VARIABLES listed in some convenient order. Similarly, let $\gamma_1, \gamma_2, \ldots, \gamma_j, \ldots$, be a list of the OUTPUT · VARIABLES. A STATE of the model is an assignment of a value to each of the STATE · VARIABLES from its range set. We denote a typical STATE by the notation $(y_{\beta_1}, y_{\beta_2}, \ldots, y_{\beta_i}, \ldots,)$ where y_{β_1} belongs to RANGE · β_1, y_{β_2} belongs to RANGE · β_2, and so on. [The term $(y_{\beta_1}, y_{\beta_2}, \ldots, y_{\beta_i}, \ldots,)$ corresponds to the list of state values $y_{\beta_1}, y_{\beta_2}, ,,,, y_{\beta_i}, \ldots$, we referred to before, except that the sandwiching parentheses bestow on it the status of standard mathematical notation.] Mathematics (or, more properly, set theory) gives us a way of denoting the set of all possible legal assignments of values to the STATE · VARIABLES. This set is called the CROSS · PRODUCT of the RANGE sets of the STATE · VARIABLES and often denoted by

$$\times_{\beta \in \text{STATE} \cdot \text{VARIABLES}} \text{RANGE} \cdot \beta$$

or by

$$\text{RANGE} \cdot \beta_1 \times \text{RANGE} \cdot \beta_2 \times \cdots \times \text{RANGE} \cdot \beta_i \cdots,$$

where the symbol $\in$ denotes "is a member of". By definition this is the set

$$\{(y_{\beta_1}, y_{\beta_2}, \ldots, y_{\beta_i}, \ldots) | y_{\beta_i} \in \text{RANGE} \cdot \beta_i$$
$$\text{for each } \beta_i \in \text{STATE} \cdot \text{VARIABLES}\}$$

The model need not deal with all possible state variable assignments. Instead often one specifies a subset, called the STATE set of the model which is relevant to it. Thus in set notation we have

$$\text{STATES} \subseteq \times_{\beta \in \text{STATE} \cdot \text{VARIABLES}} \text{RANGE} \cdot \beta$$

Recapping, a STATE is a member of STATES and is a parenthesized list of state values $(y_{\beta_1}, y_{\beta_2}, \ldots, y_{\beta_i}, \ldots)$, where y_{β_i} is a member of the possible values that can be assumed by STATE $\cdot$ VARIABLE β_i.

Similarly, for the output of the model we have a set OUTPUTS which is a subset of the CROSS $\cdot$ PRODUCT of the RANGE sets of the OUTPUT $\cdot$ VARIABLES. An OUTPUT is a typical element of the OUTPUTS and is a parenthesized list of OUTPUT $\cdot$ VARIABLE values.

Exercise. Express OUTPUTS in set theoretic notation.

So far we have the means for static model description—we know what "state" and "output" signify. The transition and output functions tell us how the model description changes with (model) time. In the case of a time invariant model and discrete time step h (which we have been examining), the normal form of these functions can be expressed simply in set notation:

$$\delta_h : \text{STATES} \to \text{STATES} \qquad \text{and} \qquad \lambda : \text{STATES} \to \text{OUTPUTS}$$

That is, for every STATE in STATES, $\delta_h(\text{STATE})$ is a member of STATES and $\lambda(\text{STATE})$ is a member of OUTPUTS. If δ_h, and λ, correctly represent the rules of interaction of the model, we have the following interpretation: if STATE is the state of the model at computation instant t_i, then $\delta_h(\text{STATE})$ is the model's state at $t_i + h$ and $\lambda(\text{STATE})$ is the output of the model at time t_i.

Exercise. Check to see that the foregoing statements agree with the previous definitions of δ and λ.

Example.   Formal Model of Whale Courtship.   We saw in Example 1 that LOCATION $\cdot$ OF $\cdot$ MALE and LOCATION $\cdot$ OF $\cdot$ FEMALE constitute a state variable set. Since each variable has range GRID $\cdot$ POINTS, we write

$$\text{STATES} = \text{GRID} \cdot \text{POINTS} \times \text{GRID} \cdot \text{POINTS}$$

and a typical STATE is of the form (m, f) where $m \in \text{GRID} \cdot \text{POINTS}$ and $f \in \text{GRID} \cdot \text{POINTS}$.

From Example 1 we also know how to compute the STATE at time $t + h$, given the STATE at time t. Thus we can write the transition function as

$$\delta_h : \text{STATES} \to \text{STATES}$$

such that for each $(m, f) \in$ STATES

$$\delta_h(m, f) = (m + D(f - m) \quad , \quad f + D(m - f))$$

Note that $m + D(f - m)$, $f + D(m - f)$ are the values of LOCATION · OF · MALE and LOCATION · OF · FEMALE at time $t + h$, as given by Equation 2 of Example 1.

Now suppose that observation stations have been set up at the ocean shores (i.e., GRID POINTS L and $-L$). The output variables are to give the honk meter readings at these points. Thus the OUTPUT · VARIABLES are SIGNAL · AT · L · DUE · TO · MALE, SIGNAL · AT · L · DUE · TO · FEMALE, SIGNAL · AT · $(-L)$ · DUE · TO · MALE, and SIGNAL · AT · $(-L)$ · DUE · TO · FEMALE. Since each variable has range $\{1, -1\}$, we have

$$\text{OUTPUTS} = \{1, -1\} \times \{1, -1\} \times \{1, -1\} \times \{1, -1\}$$

Looking at the calculations in Example 1, we can see that the honk meter readings at time t are completely determined by the MALE and FEMALE locations at time t. This means that our formal model can take the normal form with the output function

$$\lambda : \text{STATES} \rightarrow \text{OUTPUTS}$$

such that for each $(m, f) \in$ STATES,

$$\lambda(m, f) = (D(m - L), D(f - L), D(m + L), D(f + L))$$

Exercise.   Justify the definition of λ.

3.5   STRUCTURE AND BEHAVIOR

The quadruple $\langle$STATES, OUTPUTS, δ_h, $\lambda\rangle$ forms what is called a *discrete time system specification* (often referred to as an automaton or sequential machine). More specifically, it is an autonomous system, since no input set has been named. The quadruple is a formal representation of the informal description of a model we have been using until now. The quadruple itself serves a specification of an even more general object, called a *system*. The process is summarized in Figure 3. In Chapter 9, we consider the various possibilities for system specifications and their elaboration into systems. For the present, we note that the system specification gives a formal, precise way of indicating how to simulate the model, just as the rules of interaction served the same purpose informally and less precisely. The *result* of simulating

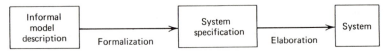

Figure 3   Formalization and elaboration of models.

the model is its behavior over time, and this is what is captured in a uniform way by the system concept.

In the present case of discrete time system specification, we can define "behavior" directly. Suppose we start the model at some model time t and simulate it until some time t'. We call the interval $[t, t']$ an *observation interval*. Let $t_M, \ldots, t_M + Nh$ be the sequence of computation instants contained in the observation interval, so that $t = t_M$ and $t' = t_M + Nh$: with every STATE q and observation interval $[t, t']$, we associate a sequence of STATES $q_M, q_{M+1}, \ldots, q_{M+N}$. This sequence represents the successive STATES the model goes through when it is started in STATE q at time t and runs until time t'. Since it starts in STATE q, we must have $q_M = q$. From then on the sequence is generated by the model transition function, and we indicate this by saying that for each i from 1 to N, $q_{M+i} = \delta_h(q_{M+i-1})$. This is a recursive or iterative formula—it does not give the sequence explicitly but tells us (or the computer—indeed, anyone who "knows" δ_h) how to compute the successive entries, given the first. Thus given $q_M = q$, with $i = 1$, we can compute, $q_{M+1} = \delta_h(q_M)$; then knowing q_{M+1} we use the formula with $i = 2$, to obtain $q_{M+2} = \delta_h(q_{M+1})$, and so on.

Exercise. Convince yourself that the procedure of Section 3.3 computes the sequence associated with STATE q and interval $[t, t']$ if its state variable locations are initialized to $y_1, \ldots, y_m$, where $q = (y_1, \ldots, y_m)$.

The sequence $q_M, q_{M+1}, \ldots, q_{M+N}$ tells us what STATES are generated and in what order, but it does not tell us the times at which the model passes through these states. To do this we introduce a function, called the *state trajectory associated with STATE q and observation interval* $[t, t']$ which we denote by $\text{STRAJ}_{q, [t, t']}$. The function definition is simply that $\text{STRAJ}_{q, [t, t']}$ maps $\{t_M, t_M + h, \ldots, t_M + Nh\}$ into STATES in such a way that

$$\text{STRAJ}_{q, [t, t']}(t_M + ih) = q_{M+i} \qquad \text{for} \qquad 0 \le i \le N$$

This says that at the ith computation instant, $t_M + ih$, the state of the model is q_{M+i} (the ith member of the sequence). Thus $\text{STRAJ}_{q, [t, t']}$ can be represented by a table as in Figure 4a or by a graph as in Figure 4b.

Corresponding to the sequence of STATES $q_M, q_{M+1}, \ldots, q_{M+N}$ is the sequence of OUTPUTS $\lambda(q_M), \lambda(q_{M+1}), \ldots, \lambda(q_{M+N})$ generated by the model.

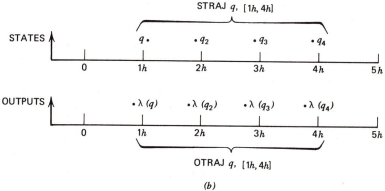

Figure 4   State and output trajectories.

Again to relate OUTPUTS to the times at which they appear, we introduce the function $\text{OTRAJ}_{q,\,[t,\,t']}: \{t_M, t_M + h, \ldots, t_M + Nh\} \to \text{OUTPUTS}$ called the *output trajectory associated with STATE q and interval* $[t, t']$. As would be natural,

$$\text{OTRAJ}_{q,\,[t,\,t']}(t_M + ih) = \lambda(q_{M+i}) \qquad \text{for} \qquad 0 \le i \le N$$

Exercise.   Interpret the definition of $\text{OTRAJ}_{q,\,[t,\,t']}$.

As with the state trajectory, $\text{OTRAJ}_{q,\,[t,\,t']}$ can be represented by a table as in Figure 4a or by a graph as in Figure 4b.

The set of all state trajectories is called the *state behavior* of the model. The set of all output trajectories is its *output behavior*.

3.6   THE CASE OF NONAUTONOMOUS MODELS

We now consider the formal specification of discrete time models having input variables. Let DESCRIPTIVE · VARIABLES be the set of descriptive variables, and let a subset INPUT · VARIABLES be the input variables, the variables whose values are determined externally to the model. The remaining variables NON · INPUT · VARIABLES = DESCRIPTIVE · VARIABLES–INPUT · VARIABLES are thus at least partially under the model's control.

We say that a model is *well described* if the values of the NON · INPUT · VARIABLES at any time t and the trajectory of values of the INPUT · VARIABLES over the interval $[t, t']$, where $t' > t$, uniquely determine the values of the NON · INPUT · VARIABLES at time t'.

A subset of NON · INPUT · VARIABLES is called a *state variable* set if the values of these variables at any time t and the trajectory of values of the INPUT · VARIABLES over the interval $[t, t']$, where $t' > t$, uniquely determine the values of the NON · INPUT · VARIABLES at time t'.

Thus as in the autonomous case, a model is well described if and only if it has a state variable set.

We now restrict our attention to discrete time, time invariant models. Just as in the autonomous case, we can construct a protypical procedure that uses the state variables in an iterative manner to simulate the model. The operation of this program suggests the following assertion: a subset of NON · INPUT · VARIABLES is a state variable set if and only if the values of these variables at any time t and the values of the INPUT · VARIABLES at times t and $t + h$ uniquely determine the values of the NON · INPUT · VARIABLES at time $t + h$.

Exercise.   Use an induction argument to prove the foregoing assertion.

Now let STATE · VARIABLES be a state variable set. We say that the model is in *normal form* if the values of the INPUT · VARIABLES and the STATE · VARIABLES at any time t uniquely determine the values of the NON · INPUT · VARIABLES at time t and the STATE · VARIABLES at time $t + h$ (see Figure 5).

Exercise.   Show that in a normal form model, the INPUT · VARIABLES at time $t + h$ do not influence the STATE · VARIABLES at time $t + h$ and the INPUT · VARIABLES at time t do not directly influence the NON · STATE · VARIABLES at time $t + h$.

Exercise.   Show that the definitions for state variables and normal form reduce to those in the autonomous case when input variables are absent.

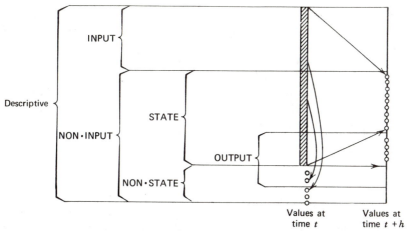

Figure 5   Normal form state variables. Values of solid variables determine values of variables represented by circles.

Let OUTPUT · VARIABLES be a subset of NON · INPUT · VARI-ABLES. From Figure 4, it is clear that the values of the INPUT · VARI-ABLES and the STATE · VARIABLES at time t uniquely determine the values of the OUTPUT · VARIABLES at time t and the STATE · VARI-ABLES at time $t + h$.

Just as before, this leads to the definition of a *sequential machine*, which now takes the form ⟨INPUTS, STATES, OUTPUTS, δ_h, λ⟩ where INPUTS, STATES, and OUTPUTS are subsets, respectively, of the cross product of the range sets of INPUT ·, STATE ·, and OUTPUT · VARIABLES; δ_h is the state *transition function*

$$\delta_h : \text{STATES} \times \text{INPUTS} \rightarrow \text{STATES}$$

and λ is the output function

$$\lambda : \text{STATES} \times \text{INPUTS} \rightarrow \text{OUTPUTS}$$

Exercise.   If q is a member of STATES and x is a member of INPUTS, explain the meaning of $\delta_h(q, x)$ and $\lambda(q, x)$.

Just as in the autonomous case, we can define the state and output trajectories generated by the sequential machine. Now however, both the input trajectory and the initial state must be specified if unique state and output trajectories are to result.

The *state sequence associated with STATE q and INPUT* sequence $x_M, x_{M+1}, \ldots, x_{M+N}$ is the sequence $q_M, q_{M+1}, \ldots, q_{M+N}$, where $q_M = q$ and for $i = 0, 1, \ldots, N - 1, q_{M+i+1} = \delta_h(q_{M+i}, x_i)$.

The *output sequence associated with q and* $x_M, \ldots, x_{M+N}$ is $y_M, \ldots, y_{M+N}$, where for $i = 0, 1, \ldots, N, y_{M+i} = \lambda(q_{M+i}, x_{M+i})$.

Also, analogously to the autonomous case, input, state, and output trajectories can be defined which explicitly place the sequence elements in their proper locations in time.

Exercise.   Define input, state, and output trajectories over a time interval $[t_M, t_{M+Nh}]$.

An input trajectory paired with an associated state trajectory is called *input-state trajectory pair*. The set of all such pairs is called the *state behavior* of the model. Similarly, a *input-output trajectory pair* consists of an input trajectory paired with an associated output trajectory. The *input-output behavior* of the model is the set of all such pairs.

Exercise.   Suppose that in a particular model the values of the OUTPUT · VARI-ABLES at any time t are determined by the values of the STATE · VARIABLES at time t. Show that the output function takes the form

$$\lambda: \text{STATES} \rightarrow \text{OUTPUTS}$$

This also has an effect on the definition of output trajectories. Provide appropriate modifications.

Example.   The Neuron.   Neurons, cells of the brain, were early targets for formalization as researchers sought to find ways to express the logical processing these cells can perform. The following model, slightly elaborated, will serve as the basic component for our discussion neural net simplication (Chapter 12).

The neuron then is modelled by a sequential machine:

$$M = \langle X, Q, Y, \delta, \lambda \rangle$$
$$X = R \quad \text{(the reals)}$$
$$Q = N \quad \text{(the nonnegative integers)}$$
$$Y = \{0, 1\}$$
$$\delta: N \times R \rightarrow N$$

$$\delta(n, x) = \begin{cases} 0 \text{ if } x \geq \text{THRESHOLD}(n) & (1) \\ n + 1 \text{ otherwise} & (2) \end{cases}$$

$$\lambda: N \rightarrow \{0, 1\}$$

$$\lambda(n) = \begin{cases} 1 & \text{if } n = 0 & (3) \\ 0 & \text{otherwise} & (4) \end{cases}$$

Interpretation

$x \in X \equiv$ strength of the input, for example, measured in millivolts.

$n \in Q \equiv$ time elapsed since the neuron last fired; n is set to zero when the neuron fires and is increased by one each time step that it does not fire.

$y \in Y \equiv$ signal of whether the neuron has just fired: $y = 1$ means firing (i.e., a pulse is put out); $y = 0$ means not firing (no pulse).

Explanation of Transition Function

For any state n, if the input strength x is great enough (i.e., surpasses the threshold for state n) the neuron fires; otherwise it does not fire, and the elapsed time increases by 1. A typical threshold function

$$\text{THRESHOLD}: N \rightarrow R$$

appears in Figure 6.

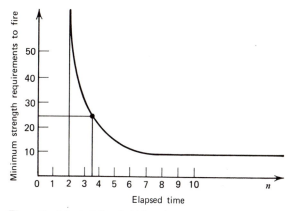

Figure 6   A typical threshold function.

Explanation of Output Function

In state $n = 0$ the neuron emits a one, indicating it has just fired on the last time step; otherwise it signals no firing by putting out a zero.

Figure 7a presents the neuron model subjected to an input sequence in which it receives three pulses of strength 25 spaced 7 time steps apart. Starting in state 2, the associated state sequence is shown below the input sequence, and the associated output sequence appears below the state sequence.

This is an example of the response to low-frequency excitation, where the input pulses are separated enough to permit the neuron always to fire when a pulse arrives. In contrast, Figure 7b shows a high-frequency excitation,

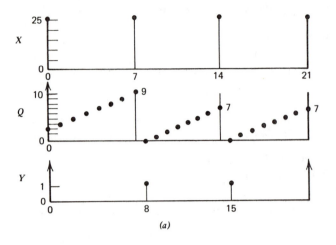

(a)

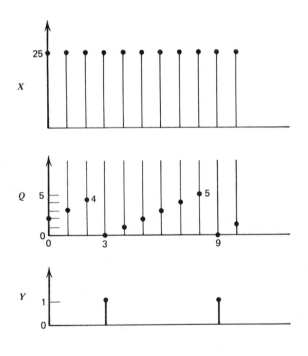

(b)

Figure 7   Neuron input, state, and output trajectories.

where the neuron can only fire every 5 time steps even though it receives inputs every time step.

Exercise. Draw state and output trajectories for periodic input pulses of height 50 and period 2; height 50 and period 5; height 5 and arbitrary period p.

Exercise. Verify that the state and output trajectories shown are correct.

3.7 PSEUDORANDOM NUMBER GENERATORS

Simulation programs often require the generation of random numbers. Subroutines that produce sequences of such numbers actually employ deterministic rules and accordingly are sometimes called pseudorandom number generators.

Indeed, such generators are nicely modelled as autonomous sequential machines. For example, let a typical sequence produced be $r_0, r_1, r_2, \ldots, r_i, \ldots$. Then a commonly used generator works according to the following rule:

(a)   Let s_0 be an integer in the range $[0, p)$.[†]

(b)   Given s_i, $i = 0, 1, 2, \ldots$, generate s_{i+1} by the rule $s_{i+1} = (as_i + b)$ mod p.

(c)   and $r_i = \dfrac{s_i}{p}$.

This is called the *linear congruential* generator and has as parameters the integers p, a, and b, where a and b are in the range $[0, p)$.

The modulo p operation is defined as follows: any integer x can be uniquely expressed by the formula

$$x = np + y$$

where y is in the range $[0, p)$ and n is an integer; by definition, x mod $p = y$.

Normally $p = 2^m$ for some positive integer m and the numbers in $[0, p)$ are represented as m bit binary numbers. The modulo operation then is realized by retaining the m least significant bits in the binary representation of an integer.

Exercise. Give an algorithm to compute y, given an arbitrary x.

The integers $\{s_i\}$ are called seeds; s_0 is called the *initial* seed and may be set by the user.

[†] $[0, p)$ is the set $\{0, 1, \ldots, p - 1\}$.

Exercise. Given $p = 3$, $a = 2$, $b = 1$, generate the sequence of seeds and "random" numbers starting from $s_0 = 2$.

The linear congruential generator is modelled by an autonomous sequential machine $M = \langle Q, Y, \delta, \lambda \rangle$ where Q is the state set $[0, p)$; Y is the output set $[0, 1)$; δ is the transition function, $\delta: Q \to Q$, given by the rule $\delta(q) = (aq' + b) \bmod p$ for all $q \in Q$; and λ is the output function $\lambda: Q \to Y$ given by the rule $\lambda(q) = q/p$.

Exercise. Show that the output sequence of length n generated by M from state $q = s_0$ is exactly the sequence $r_0, r_1, \ldots, r_n$ produced by the rules a through c.

3.7.1 State Representation of Lagged Variables

There are other rules that use previous seeds in addition to the one just generated to produce the next seed. For example, the following rule uses the third- and fifth-last-produced seeds:

(a) Let $s_{-5}, s_{-4}, s_{-3}, s_{-2}, s_{-1}$ be integers in the range $[0, p)$ (i.e., initial chosen seeds).

(b) Given $s_{i-3}, s_{i-5}, i = 0, 1, 2, \ldots$, generate s_{i+1} by the rule

$$s_{i+1} = (as_{i-3} + bs_{i-5}) \bmod p$$

$$r_i = \frac{s_i}{p}.$$

To formulate this rule as a sequential machine, we notice that five past seeds must be retained at all times to compute the next seed. This means that the proper state space Q is the set of all 5-tuples (u, v, w, x, y), where each element comes from $[0, p)$. Here u represents the last-generated seed; v the second last, and so on. In representing rule b, the transition $(u, v, w, x, y) \to (u', v', w', x', y')$ is carried out where $u' = (aw + by) \bmod p$, $v' = u$, $w' = v$, $x' = w$, and $y' = x$.

Exercise. Use the foregoing idea to formulate the sequential machine $M = \langle Q, Y, \delta, \lambda \rangle$ where $Q = [0, p)^5$ and $Y = [0, 1)$.

Models often employ past values of a variable in the computation of new values of this or other variables. If the last n values of a variable must be retained in this computation, n additional variables must be added to the model to render it well described and to determine the appropriate state set as illustrated previously.

3.7.2   Randomness of Random Numbers

Since pseudorandom number generators are, in effect, autonomous sequential machines, it is clear that the sequences they produce are not random in the dictionary sense of being left to chance. In fact from the properties of state variables (Section 3.2) we know that these sequences are repeatable at will by reinitializing the state variable seeds. Also a generator that employs n past seeds in the range $[0, p)$ has a state set of size p^n and therefore according to Problem 2, must begin to repeat the numbers it produces in cyclic fashion after p^n steps.

Any randomness of such sequences is therefore a matter of appearance rather than fact. (Actually, it is arguable whether there is a "factual" notion of randomness.) One is therefore led to pragmatic criteria for randomness— a sequence is "random" if it passes certain tests deemed appropriate for the occasion. One basic test is that the numbers produced are sufficiently uniformly distributed over the range $[0, 1]$. Another is that the average serial correlation between successive numbers is sufficiently small. A random number generator is good, then, to the extent that it produces sequences that are random in the sense just indicated in a relatively inexpensive way.[3] See also Problem 3 of Chapter 6.

3.8   GATHERING UP THE STRANDS

We have seen that it may be possible to choose a set of state variables $\alpha_1, \ldots,$ α_m for an autonomous model such that knowing the values of these variables at time t, it is possible to compute the values of *all* descriptive variables at any future t'. This leads naturally to a prototypical procedure for carrying out this computation in an efficient, step-by-step (iterative) manner. The usefulness of identifying a set of model state variables for any such simulation program is manifested in the properties of program initiation, rerun, interruption/restart, and recovery. These properties of state variables should be remembered and employed in the organization and execution of simulation studies. Their exploitation may lead to great savings in storage and computation time—the larger the model size and the greater the number of simulation runs to be done, the more important will such savings be. From an entirely different perspective, we learn that these properties correspond to the basic postulates forming the formal definition of a system (Chapter 9).

We have seen that we can abstract two mappings from the prototypical procedure—the state transition function and the output function. Every time the procedure simulates a model time step, it in effect computes these functions. Moreover, the state and output functions are characteristic of the model and in fact constitute its formal description, along with the characterization of the input, state, and output sets.

The prototypical procedure in effect computes the state and output functions, but it may not be doing this in an optimal manner. In other words, it may be possible to achieve increased efficiency, better program organization, and better understandability by exploiting explicit knowledge of the forms of these functions. Here we see a gap—we must be able to translate an informal model definition into its formal counterpart, with the aim of displaying the characterizing functions explicitly. Although the state of the art is meager in this regard, some simulation languages carry out a translation process that is very much in this spirit. Other languages force and help the user to explicitly structure his program along the lines of the formal model definition. Still others ignore this state concept entirely. In the last case, no user or translator effort is required, but on the other hand, any advantages that could be gained are lost. We examine the translation process in Chapter 5.

Finally we have been restricting our consideration to the case of the model that has been constructed to ensure that its descriptive variables form a state variable set (but not necessarily a set of smallest size). Is it always possible to do so? We take up this question in Chapter 14. Also, since we have been discussing discrete time simulations, we have been ignoring the very important class—discrete event simulations—which can be understood by allowing the computation instant set more freedom. This subject is treated in Chapter 6.

3.9 SOURCES

An exposition of finite state sequential machines is given by Booth.[1] Networks of formal neurons are discussed by Minsky.[2] Knuth[3] provides an extensive discussion of random number generators and randomness tests.

1. T. L. Booth, *Sequential Machines and Automata Theory*. Wiley, New York, 1967.
2. M. L. Minsky, *Computation: Finite and Infinite Machines*. Prentice-Hall, Englewood Cliffs, N.J., 1967.
3. D. E. Knuth, *The Art of Computer Programming*. Vol. 2, *Seminumerical Algorithms*. Addison-Wesley, Reading, Mass., 1969.

PROBLEMS

1.   For each of Examples 1, 2, and 4 of Chapter 1 find a minimal set of state variables and formalize the model as a sequential machine.

2. For each of your models of Problem 1 generate typical state and output trajectories.

3. A sequence $x_1 x_2 x_3 \cdots x_i, \ldots$ is *ultimately periodic* if there exist integers i and j such that $x_{i+k} = x_{i+j+k}$ for all $k = 0, 1, 2, \ldots$. The least i for which this is true is called the *index r* and the least j for which it is true is called the *period p*.

   Explanation. The sequence has the appearance $x_1 x_2 x_3 \cdots x_{r-1} \underbrace{y_1 y_2 \cdots y_p}$ $\underbrace{y_1 y_2 \cdots y_p} \underbrace{y_1 y_2 \cdots y_p} \cdots$. Let $M = \langle Q, Y, \delta, \lambda \rangle$ be an autonomous machine with a finite number of states $|Q| = n$. Show that every state trajectory is *ultimately periodic* with index r and period p such that $r + p < n$. Conclude that every output trajectory has the same property (that it is ultimately periodic with $r + p < n$). *But* is it necessarily the case that the output trajectory and the state trajectory associated with the same state q have the same r and p?

4. Show that the response of the neuron of Section 3.6 is ultimately periodic to periodic inputs of the kind discussed there. More formally, for any state q and input segment of the form $0^{p-1} x 0^{p-1} x \cdots$, the associated output trajectory is ultimately periodic with index r' and period p'. Characterize r' and p' as functions of p and x.

Chapter Four

Simulation of
Cell-Space-Like Models

In Chapter 3, we presented a prototypical procedure for discrete time simulation. Now we want to elaborate this procedure to reveal in more detail the workings of actual simulation systems. We may think of the procedure as having three main phases: initialization, one-step state transition computation, and time advancement.

Exercise.   Identify each of the phases with a step or steps in the prototypical procedure.

The initialization phase is in general conceptually straightforward. When the model (to be simulated) operates in discrete time, the time advancement phase is simply the advancement of model time by one unit. Thus the one-step state transition computation is of primary interest in this case. We now consider a class of discrete time models called cell space models and a simulation system geared to this class which illustrates the basic idea. From this basis we can generalize to see how an arbitrary discrete time model can be simulated. First, however, we clarify the distinction between sequential and parallel processing and its importance for simulation. Then we discuss program models to prepare ourselves for the simulation programs to be presented.

4.1   SEQUENTIAL AND PARALLEL PROCESSING

We have seen that a model can be viewed as a set of components that interact. The interaction of the components is most generally of a *parallel* nature as opposed to a *sequential* one. We can think of a sequential interaction as the case where only one action is taking place at any time—the present action is followed by a unique next action, and so on.

Parallel interaction, on the other hand, may involve many actions occurring simultaneously. In general, some or all of the components of a model may be considered to be simultaneously active, hence the parallel nature of the interaction.[†]

Exercise.   Review the models described in Chapter 1: which do you think are characterized more by parallel than by sequential operation?

Although most models are largely parallel, present-day computers are basically sequential processors. Thus one of the essential tasks of current simulation languages is to enable the computer, which acts sequentially, ponderously, one step at a time, to faithfully generate the behavior of a parallel acting model. Note the key word here is "faithfully"—the computer-generated behavior cannot exactly replicate that of the model in a strict time correspondence. This is true because simultaneous actions in the model must be spread out in a one-at-a-time fashion in the computer. Thus by "faithfully" we have to mean something less than full, but nevertheless, significant, behavior preservation. In this chapter we examine the basic features found in current simulation languages which enable them to carry out the "parallel to sequential conversion" task.

The astute reader will notice the qualification "current" and "present-day," in the above. The reason is that future computers are likely to be much more parallel operating, the goal naturally being to speed up significantly the simulation of parallel-type models.

Exercise.   Suppose a model involves n simultaneous actions, all of which would be over in t_m seconds if the real system were to perform them. Simulated by a computer, each action requires t_c seconds. Compare the respective times taken by a sequential computer and a fully parallel computer in carrying out the n actions, assuming the same t_c for both. For what values of n, t_m, and t_c could the computers operate as predictors of future real system behavior? Plug in some representative numbers in the case of the brain models of Appendix A.

Still much of what we are about to say will continue to apply in the future because a simulation language must coordinate and control actions specified by a model in such a way that they can be executed in proper phase by a computer. In present-day computers this coordination and control must be

[†] "Sequential" and "parallel" are descriptive terms that convey a general feeling about the operation of a system but do not lend themselves to precise definition.

reduced to a strict one-at-a-time sequencing. Future computers may be less strait-jacketted, but understanding the basic problems in coordination and control currently encountered will help to prepare one for assignments to be tackled with the tools of the future.

4.2   INFORMAL MODELS OF PROGRAMS AND SEQUENTIAL COMPUTERS

We begin with a rather simple-minded idea of what a program is. A *program* consists of (1) a set of variables $\alpha_1, \ldots, \alpha_n$ and (2) a list of instructions that, when executed by a computer, can cause an action of one of the following kinds:

(a)   A change in the values of one or more of the variables—called a *memory operation.*

(b)   A change in the order of which instruction to execute next—called a *transfer instruction.*

(c)   A termination of program execution—called a *halt instruction.*

The computer starts executing the program by examining the first instruction on the list. If a memory operation is called for, this is performed and the machine goes on to the second instruction. If the second instruction also calls for a memory operation this will be carried out, and the third instruction will be examined. In general, whenever an instruction calls for a memory operation, it is carried out and the next instruction examined is the next instruction on the list. Whenever a transfer instruction is encountered, no change in the values of the variables $\alpha_1, \ldots, \alpha_n$ takes place, but the instruction may cause the computer to examine an instruction other than the one next on the list. Execution proceeds from the new instruction in the usual way. When a halt instruction is encountered, the computer stops executing the program.

A programming language provides a set of instructions from which to fashion a program. We call these the *primitive* instructions. If the user does not find a primitive instruction for an action he wants carried out, he must write a sequence of primitive instructions whose effect, when executed, will be to carry out the intended action. Most languages have facilities (macros, subroutines, etc.) enabling the user to give a name to a sequence of instructions. Instead of writing the sequence of primitives every time a given action is required, he may merely write the name of the sequence, and the computer will behave as if this actual sequence appears in the program wherever the name appears. In effect the user is able, by means of such facilities, to add instructions to the primitives that will carry out new actions—actions that are compounds of elementary actions.

In the following we are very free with our instruction types—if an action is required we sometimes assume we have an instruction to implement it, or, if we want to be more explicit, we may express the action as a series of more basic actions for which instructions are assumed to exist.

Fortunately, in the sequential processing mode, the time taken to carry out a compound action can be obtained as the sum of the times taken by each of its constituent actions. Thus even though we allow ourselves arbitrary instruction types, we can realistically estimate the time it takes to run a program if we can realistically estimate the time it takes to execute its component instructions.

Example.   The following program adds two nonnegative numbers x and y by successively subtracting 1 from x and adding 1 to y until x becomes 0.

1.   If $X = 0$, go to 5.
2.   Set X to $X - 1$.
3.   Set Y to $Y + 1$.
4.   Go to 1.
5.   Stop.

We are considering "set X to $X - 1$" and "set Y to $Y + 1$" to be instruction types, and they are both memory operations; "if $X = 0$, go to 5" is a transfer instruction that will cause instruction 5 to be executed instead of instruction 2, if and when X becomes 0; "go to 1" is a transfer instruction that always causes 1 to be the next instruction executed.

Exercise.   If the ith instruction ($1 \leq i \leq 5$) takes t_i seconds to execute (this includes the action it invokes plus the time to jump to the next instruction), what is the time taken to run the program? Is this time a function of the input x? y?

4.3   MODELS OF COMPUTERS AND PROGRAMS

Just as we may construct a model for any real system, we can make a model for a real-life computer. We have some additional help that we seldom receive, however, if we know the computer is executing a known program. For if the program is being correctly executed, we know that the computer must be carrying out the actions required by the program in the sequence it lays down. Of course, we do not know everything about the computer, since two computers can be carrying out the *same* sequence of actions; but the *way* in which these actions are realized by each machine may be quite different. Nevertheless, by looking at the program we can, construct a model of any computer that correctly executes it. This is a model in the true sense that although something is being preserved, much is being abstracted—indeed, in the terminology of Chapter 2, we can regard the program model as a lumped model relative to a base model of a computer that is correctly executing it. In this spirit, we now present a means of writing an informal model description for a program. We often use this program model to represent the computer, which is one of the basic elements of our formulation of a simulation (Chapter 2). When a more refined computer model is required, we can extend the relations established between the other elements and the program model to the more refined computer model.

Exercise.   Discuss the following occasions for considering a more refined computer model using the notions of base model, lumped model, and experimental frame: (*a*) when the times required to carry out program actions are to be estimated, and (*b*) when it is not known whether a computer is carrying out a known program correctly.

Consider a **PROGRAM** with variables $\alpha_1, \ldots, \alpha_n$ and instruction sequence INSTRUCTION $\cdot$ 1, INSTRUCTION $\cdot$ 2, $\ldots$, INSTRUCTION $\cdot$ *M*. We construct an informal description of the **PROGRAM** $\cdot$ **MODEL** as follows.

Components
  MEMORY, CONTROL, HALT $\cdot$ REGISTER
Descriptive Variables
  MEMORY
    $\alpha_1, \ldots, \alpha_n$
  CONTROL
    CURRENT $\cdot$ INSTRUCTION—with range $\{1, 2, \ldots, M\}$;
    CURRENT $\cdot$ INSTRUCTION $= i$ means that the computer, currently executing INSTRUCTION $\cdot$ *i*.

  HALT $\cdot$ REGISTER
    INDICATOR—with range $\{ON, OFF\}$; ON means execution continuing, OFF means program halted.
Component Interaction
At time t, let $v_1, \ldots v_n$ be the list of values of MEMORY variables $\alpha_1, \ldots, \alpha_n$; let CURRENT $\cdot$ INSTRUCTION $= i$ ($i \in \{1, \ldots, M\}$) and let INDICATOR $= j$ ($j \in \{ON, OFF\}$).

If $j = $ OFF, then at time $t + 1$ the values of variables are the same as those at time t (program has halted).

If $j = $ ON, and INSTRUCTION $\cdot$ *i* is a halt instruction, then at time $t + 1$ INDICATOR $=$ OFF and all other variables are unchanged (program is being stopped).

If j = ON, and INSTRUCTION $\cdot$ i is a transfer instruction of the form "if condition C, go to k," then if condition C is true of the values $v_1, \ldots, v_n$, then at time t + 1, CURRENT $\cdot$ INSTRUCTION = k; otherwise it is i + 1. All other variables are unchanged.

If j = ON and INSTRUCTION $\cdot$ i is a memory instruction of the form "set the variables $\beta_1, \ldots, \beta_p$ to values determined by applying a function f to variables $\gamma_1, \ldots, \gamma_q$," then at time t + 1 CURRENT $\cdot$ INSTRUCTION = i + 1, the values of $\beta_1, \ldots, \beta_p$ are equal to those given by $f(v_{\gamma_1}, \ldots, v_{\gamma_q})$, where $v_{\gamma_1}, \ldots, v_{\gamma_q}$ is the list of current values of the variables $\gamma_1, \ldots, \gamma_q$, and all other variables are unchanged.

Exercise. Show that the set of all descriptive variables is a set of state variables but the set of memory variables alone is not.

Note that the description implies discrete time operation with equal time units (h = 1) for each state transition. Thus this model would have to be extended to account for the time taken to perform an instruction (see Chapter 16).

Exercise. Convert the informal program model description to an autonomous sequential machine without outputs (see Chapter 16).

4.4   CELL SPACE MODELS AND SIMULATORS

A cell space model consists of an infinite set of geometrically located cells, each cell containing the same computational apparatus as all other cells and connected to other cells in a uniform way. Figure 1 illustrates the subclass of such models that is most easily visualized. The cells are located at the lattice points of an infinite two-dimensional plane. The cells feeding inputs to a particular cell, called its neighborhood, are often chosen to be the cells nearest to it in the geometrical sense. For a cell located at the origin $(0, 0)$, the nearest neighbors would be those located at: $(0, 0)$ distance 0 away (itself); $(0, 1)$ $(1, 0)$ $(0, -1)$ $(-1, 0)$—the cells that are distance 1 away orthogonally and $(1, 1), (-1, 1), (-1, -1) (1, -1)$ which are distance 1 away diagonally. Since every cell is identical and has a uniform neighborhood, this means that the neighborhood of a cell at (i, j) would be $\{(i + \Delta_1, j + \Delta_2)|\Delta_1, \Delta_2 \in \{-1, 0, 1\}\}$—consisting of itself and the cells immediately adjacent to it.

A remarkable game called the Game of Life is framed within a two-dimensional cell space structure, and its presentation in *Scientific American*[1] can serve as a fascinating introduction to the ideas involved. We briefly look at the game as an example. Cell space models are the bases of many models of real systems which are viewed as homogeneous media, having

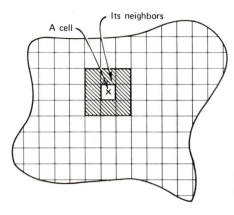

Figure 1 A finite portion of a two-dimensional cell space.

uniform interactive properties and being compartmentalized into discrete cells. Often the modeller writes his own simulation program for such a model. This tends to be true when the model interactions are described by partial differential equations. But one can take advantage of the homogeneity and uniformity of structure in a general way, and this has been attempted in the design of CESL (cell space simulation language).[2]

4.5 INFORMAL DESCRIPTION OF A CELL SPACE MODEL

We first provide a description of a general two-dimensional cell space model with nearest neighbor interaction.

Components

CELLS = $\{CELL(i, j) | i, j \in \text{integers}\}$

Descriptive Variables

For each CELL(i, j)

STATE $\cdot$ OF(i, j)—with range S (a set).

STATE $\cdot$ OF$(i, j) = s_{i, j}$ means that CELL(i, j) is in state $s_{i, j} \in S$.

Component Interaction

Suppose that at time t, for each CELL(i, j), the STATE $\cdot$ OF(i, j) is $s_{i, j}$; at time $t + 1$ let STATE $\cdot$ OF(i, j) be $s'_{i, j}$. Then

$$s'_{i, j} = \tau(s_{i, j}, s_{i, j+1}, s_{i+1, j}, s_{i, j-1}, s_{i-1, j}, s_{i+1, j+1}, s_{i-1, j+1}, s_{i+1, j-1}, s_{i-1, j-1})$$

where τ is a function called the *local* or *component* transition function. In other words for each CELL(i, j), its state at time $t + 1$ is a function of the states of its nine nearest neighbors at time t.

Example.   Conway's Game of Life.   In the Game of Life, each CELL can be in two states—ALIVE or DEAD. Thus for each CELL(i, j), the range of STATE $\cdot$ OF(i, j) is {ALIVE, DEAD} (i.e., $S =$ {ALIVE, DEAD}). The local transition function τ is given by

$$\tau(s_{0,\,0},\, s_{0,\,1},\, s_{1,\,0},\, s_{0,\,-1},\, s_{-1,\,0},\, s_{1,\,1},\, s_{-1,\,1},\, s_{1,\,-1},\, s_{-1,\,-1})$$

ALIVE   if $s_{0,\,0} =$ ALIVE and there are either 2 or 3 ALIVE values
             in the list $s_{0,\,1} \cdots,\, s_{-1,\,-1}$

$=$ ALIVE   if $s_{0,\,0} =$ DEAD and there are exactly 3 ALIVE values in the
             list $s_{0,\,1},\, \ldots,\, s_{-1,\,-1}$

DEAD   otherwise

This function is a formalization of the following rules informally given in Reference 1:

1. Survivals. Every counter with two or three neighboring counters survives for the next generation.
2. Deaths. Each counter with four or more neighbors dies (is removed) from over-population. Every counter with one neighbor or none dies from isolation.
3. Births. Each empty cell adjacent to exactly three neighbors—no more, no fewer—is a birth cell. A counter is placed on it at the next move.

Exercise.   Check to see that the formalization has been carried out correctly.
    Note that from the informal description, the set of all variables STATE $\cdot$ OF(i, j) constitutes a set of state variables. Why?

Exercise.   Convert the informal description into an autonomous sequential machine. Call the states of this machine GLOBAL $\cdot$ STATES, to distinguish them from the local or cell STATES.

Note also that all CELLS are assumed to be active simultaneously—this is a parallel system par excellence. But there is a very important constraint on the simultaneous activity of the CELLS: they all change state, if at all, at regular instants $t,\, t + 1,\, t + 2,\, \ldots$ This, indeed, is the essence of a discrete time model. With this constraint, the simulation program does not have to worry about scheduling the activities of the CELLS in the proper time sequence. It can handle the simultaneity in a rather simple way, as we soon see.
    But there is another problem that is insurmountable as things now stand—the number of CELLS in the space is infinite. If, in fact, all these CELLS change state in one time step, it would take a sequential computer (which must carry out each of the CELL actions one at a time) an infinite amount of time just to simulate this time step. Indeed, such cell models are called

nonalgorithmic because they can accomplish tasks not considered doable by real computers.[†] Thus in any model that can be simulated, only a finite number of CELLS can change states at any time step. The simplest way of achieving this is to limit the model to a finite area in the plane, hence to a finite number of CELLS. In the following we consider this area to be a square array centered about the origin containing L^2 CELLS. Later we see how this restriction can be removed while at the same time improving the efficiency of the simulation.

[The restriction to a finite array introduces a possible inhomogeneity in the model: what do we do about the cells at the edges of the array, which have been robbed of some of their natural neighbors? This problem can be handled in a number of ways—for example, by specifying externally the states of the missing neighbors for the edge CELLS (analogous to boundary condition in partial differential equation described models), or by "wrapping" the array around into a torus so that oppositive edges are joined. This procedure is not of central interest to us now].

4.6 SIMULATION PROGRAM FOR BOUNDED CELL SPACE

The program has the following variables: two arrays of dimension $L \times L$, call them FLIP and FLOP, a one-dimensional array of dimension 9 called NEIGHBOR · STATES, a one-dimensional array of dimension one (ordinary variable) called NEXT · STATE, a binary variable with range {FLIP, FLOP} called FLIP · FLOP, and an integer variable called CLOCK.

FLIP and FLOP are indexed by $\{(i, j)| -L/2 < i, j < L/2\}$ (for simplicity, let L be odd), such that FLIP(i, j) and FLOP(i, j) hold—at different times—the STATE · OF(i, j). NEIGHBOR · STATES are used to hold, temporarily, the list of current states of the nine neighbors of a cell whose state transition is being simulated, the result being stored temporarily in NEXT · STATE. The FLIP · FLOP enables storing a GLOBAL · STATE of the model in FLIP and its successor in FLOP, and vice versa.

The program:
*   INITIALIZATION
1. Initialize the FLIP · FLOP to FLOP.
2. Initialize the FLIP array to the desired initial GLOBAL · STATE of the model (i.e., assign a value to each location FLIP(i, j) corresponding to the initial STATE · OF(i, j).

[†] Such models violate Church's thesis that whatever can realistically be computed by a computer can be computed by a Turing machine.

3. Initialize CLOCK to the desired starting time t.
*   STATE · TRANSITION · COMPUTATION
4. Complement the FLIP · FLOP; that is, if FLIP · FLOP is FLIP, change it to FLOP; if it is FLOP, change it to FLIP.
5. If FLIP · FLOP is FLIP, let FLIP be called by the name FROM and let FLOP be called by the name TO; if FLIP · FLOP is FLOP, call FLOP by FROM and FLIP by TO.
*   SCANNING SEQUENCE
6. Scan the FROM array in some particular order (e.g., along the top row, then along the second row, etc.) until all the L^2 pairs have been treated; let the current pair be called (i, j); then go to 11.
7. Retrieve the nine values {FROM(i, j), FROM$(i, j + 1)$, ..., FROM$(i - 1, j - 1)$} and store them in NEIGHBOR · STATES.
8. Apply the function τ to NEIGHBOR · STATES and place the result in NEXT · STATE.
9. Store NEXT · STATE in TO(i, j).
10. Return to 6.
*   TIME ADVANCEMENT
11. Increment CLOCK by 1 unit.
12. If CLOCK $< t'$ (the desired end of run time), go to 4.
13. Stop.

Exercise.   In the Game of Life, the GLOBAL · STATE of Figure 2a generates the successor, shown in Figure 2b (here the black dot indicates an ALIVE CELL, and a blank is a DEAD CELL; boundary CELLS are assumed to have DEAD neighbors).

First check that the successor is correct according to both the informal and formal transition rules.

The simulation of this transition by the program just given would require 121 ($= 11 \times 11$) executions of instructions 4 through 10.

Scanning from left to right along the top row, then the second row, and so on, describe the contents of the FROM, TO, NEIGHBOR · STATES, and NEXT · STATE arrays after each instruction is executed. For example, after 27 CELLS been simulated and the next state of CELL(3, 8) is about to be computed, verify that the simulator state is as it appears in Figure 2c, and after 41 iterations and looking at CELL(5, 2), it is as shown in Figure 2d.

This program fits the prototypical procedure, with the state transition phase carried out by instructions 4 through 10. We now give an informal proof that this phase is correctly carried out. Suppose that the FLIP array holds the correct model GLOBAL · STATE at time t, and instruction 4 is about to be executed. The execution of 4 and then of 5 will cause FLOP to become the TO array, and FLIP to become the FROM array. The next state computation proceeds by taking for each (i, j) the states of CELL(i, j)'s

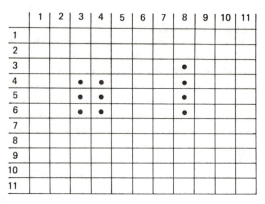

(a)

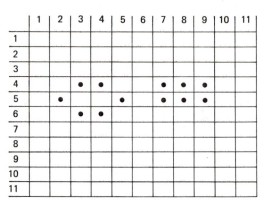

(b)

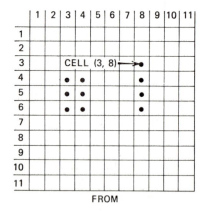

FROM

Not yet
computed for
this step

TO

NEIGHBOR
STATES

NEXT
STATE

(c)

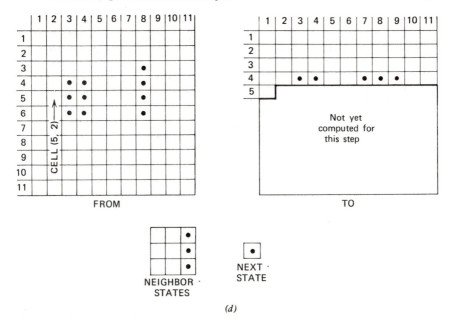

(d)

Figure 2   Computation of a GLOBAL · STATE transition.

neighbors in the FROM array (by assumption these are correctly represented by FLIP), computing the next STATE · OF(i, j) using τ, and storing it in the TO array. After all CELLS have been simulated, TO holds the correct GLOBAL · STATE of the model at time $t + 1$. But since FLOP is really the TO array, we have succeeded in taking the GLOBAL · STATE of the model found in FLIP at time t and placing its successor GLOBAL · STATE in FLOP.

Exercise.   Now after executing instructions 11, 12, 4, and 5, the roles of FLIP and FLOP will be reversed, with FLOP acting as the FROM array and FLIP as the TO array. Complete the proof of correct simulation.

Exercise.   When the simulation has halted, the correct GLOBAL · STATE at time t' is found in either FLIP or FLOP. How does the computer know which?

Why are copies of the cell space array being kept in the simulation, with the correct GLOBAL · STATE of the model being shuttled betweem them. To see that one copy will not suffice, consider computing the next states of CELLS(0, 0) and (0, 1). Note that CELL(0, 0) is in the neighborhood of CELL(0, 1) and that conversely, CELL(0, 1) is in CELL(0, 0)'s neighborhood.

No matter which order we choose to scan the array, we will come to one of the two CELLS before the other, say CELL(0, 0) is simulated first and then CELL(0, 1) (because of the symmetry of their interaction, the same argument will apply in the opposite case). If we have only one copy of the cell space array, say FLIP, we will have to store CELL(0, 0)'s next state in FLIP(0, 0). But now when we come to compute CELL(0, 1)'s next state, we will have at least one incorrect argument in its NEIGHBOR · STATES list—FLIP(0, 0) will not represent the present STATE · OF(0, 0) as it should. Applying the function τ to the wrong set of values is not a good way to correctly compute the next STATE · OF(0, 1)! (Another view of the same problem is given in Reference 1.)

This argument shows that for any two CELLS A and B, if A directly influences B, the computation of the new state of A requires that its old state be saved if we are to be able to compute the new state of B. It does not show that the old states of *all* CELLS must be saved in order to compute their new states as our program does. We return to consider this question in Problem 2.

4.7 DISCRETE TIME STRUCTURED MODELS†

The cell space model we have considered can be transformed by removing its homogeneity and uniformity, and adding input variables so that it represents any discrete time model described by components and their interactions. Correspondingly, the simulation program can be transformed to simulate such a model. The base model neuron net and the lumped model of Appendix A are examples of such discrete time models.

First of all, we have seen that the neighbors of a CELL(0, 0) need not consist of the nearest ones geometrically but can be made of any finite subset of CELLS. Call this set INTERNAL · NEIGHBORS · OF(0, 0); some examples are given in Figure 3. Uniformity then requires that the INTERNAL · NEIGHBORS · OF(i, j) for any CELL(i, j) be simply related to INTERNAL · NEIGHBORS · OF(0, 0). In fact, thinking of INTERNAL · NEIGHBORS · OF(0, 0) as a template, we get the INTERNAL · NEIGHBORS · OF(i, j) by translating the template without rotating it ensuring that the (0, 0) point lies on (i, j).

Exercise. Show that the uniformity enables a simple computation of the internal neighbors of any cell—namely, INTERNAL · NEIGHBORS(i, j) is the set $\{(k + i, l + j)|(k, l) \in$ INTERNAL · NEIGHBORS(0, 0)}—thus we have only to store INTERNAL · NEIGHBORS(0, 0) and compute INTERNAL · NEIGHBORS(i, j) "on the fly."

---

† This section may be omitted in an introductory course.

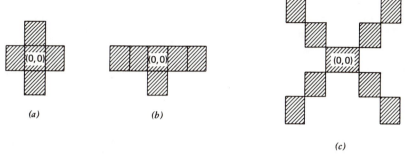

Figure 3   Some neighborhood templates.

Now if we drop the uniformity, the INTERNAL · NEIGHBORS set must be specified individually for each CELL.

To allow external inputs to the model, we specify for each cell its EXTERNAL · NEIGHBORS, and we must generate values for these variables at each time step, to provide the external simulation desired.

If we drop the homogeneity requirement, CELLS are no longer alike in their internal characteristics. This means that a single set S will no longer characterize the state set of each CELL, and a single local transition function τ will no longer suffice to compute the next state of each of the CELLS. Thus we must specify for each CELL its own state set and local transition function.

Having accomplished the foregoing preliminaries, we arrive at a *structured discrete time model.* Its general form is as follows.

Components

INPUT · WIRES $= \{\alpha_1, \ldots, \alpha_m\}$,
LOCAL · COMPONENTS $= \{\beta_1, \ldots, \beta_n\}$

Descriptive Variables

For each INPUT · WIRE α
STATE · OF · α—with range X_α.
For each LOCAL · COMPONENT β
STATE · OF · β—with range S_β.

PARAMETERS: for each LOCAL · COMPONENT β
EXTERNAL · NEIGHBORS · OF · β—a subset of INPUT · WIRES.
INTERNAL · NEIGHBORS · OF · β—a subset of LOCAL · COMPONENTS.

Component Interaction

Suppose that at time t, for each LOCAL · COMPONENT β, the STATE · OF · β is s_β. At time $t + 1$, let STATE · OF · β be s'_β. Then we write

$$s'_\beta = \delta_\beta(s_{\beta_1}, s_{\beta_2}, \ldots, s_{\beta_{n_j}}, x_{\alpha_1}, x_{\alpha_2}, \ldots, x_{\alpha_{m_j}})$$

where $s_{\beta_1}, s_{\beta_2}, \ldots, s_{\beta_{n_j}}$ is the list of STATE · OF · β values for $\beta_1, \beta_2, \ldots,$ β_{n_j} — the INTERNAL · NEIGHBORS of β; $x_{\alpha_1}, x_{\alpha_2}, \ldots, x_{\alpha_{m_j}}$ is the list of STATE · OF · α values for $\alpha_1, \alpha_2, \ldots, \alpha_{m_j}$ — the EXTERNAL · NEIGHBORS · OF · β.

The function δ_β is called the *local transition* function for LOCAL · COMPONENT β.

Exercise.   Convert the informal description to a sequential machine (see Chapter 9).

We can now indicate which changes must be made in the program (for simulating a cell space model) to simulate a general structured discrete time model. The modifications are essentially as follows:

(a)   In instruction 6 we no longer have L^2 pairs (i, j) but some number, n say, of indices $\beta_1, \beta_2, \ldots, \beta_n$ representing the LOCAL · COMPONENTS.

(b)   In instruction 7 we retrieve the list of values FROM$(\beta_1), \ldots,$ FROM(β_{n_j}), where $\beta_1, \ldots, \beta_{n_j}$ are the INTERNAL · NEIGHBORS · OF β; obtain the list of STATE · OF · α values for the EXTERNAL · NEIGHBORS · OF $\cdots \beta$ (which must be supplied externally to the model); and store all these in NEIGHBOR · STATES.

(c)   In instruction 8 we apply the function δ_β to NEIGHBOR · STATES and place the result in NEXT · STATE.

(d)   In instruction 9 we store NEXT · STATE in TO(β).

Exercise.   Rewrite the program (both variables and instructions) to account for the modifications just given.

4.8   A STEP TOWARD DISCRETE EVENT SIMULATION

In the Game of Life example the program often goes through the motions of computing the next state of a CELL even though the CELL does not eventually change its state—in the example, 111 of the 121 CELLS did not change their states. Is there any way of detecting beforehand whether a CELL will change state? There is; but doing the detecting may turn out to be no simpler than computing the next state, and by comparison seeing whether a change has occurred. It is much easier to detect whether *a CELL cannot possibly change its state*. The criterion is simple—a CELL cannot possibly change its state in the next transition if none of its NEIGHBORS (INTERNAL and EXTERNAL) have changed theirs in the current transition. This follows because the next state of a CELL is a function of the current states of its NEIGHBORS. If the states of the NEIGHBORS are the same at times $t - 1$ and t, the state of CELL must be the same at times t and $t + 1$.

Exercise.   Expand the foregoing argument into a complete proof.

For example, in Figure 2, the NEIGHBORS (including itself, of course) of CELL(3, 3) have not changed in the simulated GLOBAL · STATE transition. (Verify this.) Thus in the next transition CELL(3, 3)'s state will be unchanged; the same is true for CELL(3, 4) but not for CELL(3, 5) (although it will not change state because of the particular transition function).

Indeed, let us call an instance of a (nonidentical) state change at a CELL, an *event* at that CELL. For example, there are exactly two events in the Game of Life: a BIRTH event (the CELL state changes from DEAD to ALIVE) and a DEATH event (change from ALIVE to DEAD). When an event occurs at a CELL, the CELL undergoes a state change which we can call an *action*.

Now we can say that in a cell space model events may be actually occurring at only relatively small number of CELLS (even though it may be *possible* for events to occur at all the CELLS simultaneously). Whether an event can occur next at a CELL is determined by whether any events have occurred at its NEIGHBORS—if no actions have been carried out by them, the CELL will not carry out an action.

How should we make use of this situation? We should try to avoid processing all CELLS at which no events will occur. Suppose we keep a LAST · EVENTS list that at time t contains just those CELLS at which events occurred at time t. From what has been said, given the LAST · EVENTS list, it is possible to determine precisely those CELLS at which an event can occur at time $t + 1$, and these constitute the NEXT · EVENTS list. (We consider how to do this efficiently in a moment.) Using the same simulation program as before—but not scanning all CELLS, just those on the NEXT · EVENTS list—we compute the next states of each of the latter CELLS. After we have simulated each (of these) CELL's transition, we check to see if a true state change has occurred; if so we put the CELL on the LAST · EVENTS list for time $t + 1$.

How do we start up such a procedure? If we wish to start the simulation at model time t we must somehow specify the NEXT · EVENTS list at time $t + 1$, but if we have never computed the prior transition, the actual CELLS on this list are not known to us. There are two solutions:

1. For a finite model with a finite number of CELLS we can put all the CELLS on the initial NEXT · EVENTS list. (We may be doing a lot of useless simulation on the first GLOBAL · STATE transition, but we will not lose anything on the second such transition.)

2. We can do better: if there is a so-called *quiescent* state, an element s of S (the CELL state set) such that if a CELL and all its NEIGHBORS

are in state s at time t, the CELL will remain in state s at time $t + 1$. [Equivalently the local transition function τ is such that $\tau(s, \ldots, s) = s$.] For example, in the Game of Life, the DEAD state is a quiescent state. (Verify this.)

Then only those CELLS not in the quiescent state and the CELLS they directly influence need be put on the initial NEXT · EVENTS list. Why?

Exercise. What would the initial NEXT · EVENT list be in Figure 2?

Notice that now it is possible for a sequential computer to simulate a CELL space model with an infinite number of CELLS, provided only a finite number of CELLS are initially nonquiescent and every CELL can directly influence only a finite number of CELLS.

Exercise. Show that if the NEXT · EVENTS list is finite at time t, it is also finite at times $t + 1, t + 2, \ldots$, that is, at any future time t'.

Exercise. As model time advances, it may take longer and longer for the computer to simulate a GLOBAL · STATE transition. Under what circumstances can this happen?

We have seen that the component interaction in a cell space model (or more generally in a discrete time model) is specified for each CELL (or LOCAL · COMPONENT) by giving its NEIGHBORS and the local transition function that specifies the *influence of the NEIGHBORS on the CELL*

Another point of view that can be taken in discrete event models is to specify for each component the *components that it influences and the actual effect it exerts on them when it carries out an action*. We are seeing here a half-way transition between these differing model structures.

Let us call the CELLS directly influencing a CELL its INFLUENCERS, and the CELLS it directly influences its INFLUENCEES. Then in a cell space specification, the NEIGHBORS are precisely the INFLUENCERS. Given the INFLUENCERS of each CELL, it is possible to easily determine the INFLUENCEES of each CELL—the INFLUENCEES of a CELL α are precisely those CELLS β such that α is one of the INFLUENCERS of β. The situation is best visualized with the help of the diagram of component interaction (introduced in Chapter 1). The diagram is a directed graph (digraph) such that the points of the graph are the CELLS and there is a line with an arrow from CELL α to CELL β if α directly influences β. Then the INFLUENCERS of a CELL are precisely the CELLS sending arrows directly into it, and the INFLUENCEES of a CELL are precisely the CELLS it sends arrows directly to.

Exercise.   Give for each point in the graph of Figure 4 its INFLUENC*ERS* and its INFLUENC*EES*.

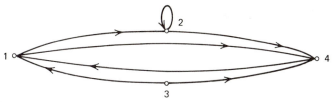

Figure 4   An interaction graph.

Exercise.   Give a procedure to go from a specification giving for each CELL its INFLUENC*EES* to a one giving for each CELL its INFLUENC*ERS*, and conversely.

Show that in a uniform cell space INFLUENC*ERS* · OF · (0, 0) is the mirror image of INFLUENC*EES* · OF · (0, 0). Find the INFLUENC*EES* · OF · (0, 0) for each of the templates in Figure 3.

The graph of component interaction is *symmetric* if for every arrow from one point to another, there is also an arrow in the reverse direction. (Newton was stating that interactions graphs of mechanical systems are symmetric when he said, "For every action there is an equal and opposite reaction.")

Exercise.   Show that the interaction graph of the Game of Life is symmetric.

Show that an interaction graph is symmetric if and only if, for each CELL its IN-FLUENC*ERS* are the same as its INFLUENC*EES*.

Now we can see how to efficiently determine the NEXT · EVENTS list at time $t + 1$ given the LAST · EVENTS list at time t: namely, we scan down the LAST · EVENTS list and add the INFLUENC*EES* of each CELL we encounter to the NEXT · EVENTS list (which starts out empty). In other words, the NEXT · EVENTS list is just the union of all the INFLUENC*EES* of the LAST · EVENTS list.

Exercise.   Rewrite the discrete time model simulation program to carry out the "next event simulation" strategy just discussed. Give the LAST · EVENTS list for the transition of Figure 2*b* and the subsequent NEXT · EVENTS list.

We were led to develop the next event simulation procedure because we wished to avoid unnecessary computation (beyond any desire to simulate an infinite cell space). But under certain circumstances, for finite models, the extra list processing required may not be worth any savings made. For a model in which all CELLS are carrying out actions at all times, for example, we would do better not to employ the next event strategy. Clearly then the cost/benefit analysis must take into account the *activity level* of the model—the ratio of CELLS at which events are occurring to the total number of CELLS. The activity level is, in fact, a measure of the parallelism of the model, and all other things being equal, it is around low to moderate levels—where some CELLS but not all CELLS are simultaneously active—that the next event strategy comes into its own. In Chapter 16 we consider this question again in our treatment of model complexity.

Exercise.   What other factors should be taken into account in the cost benefit analysis?

4.9   SOURCES

Conway's Game of Life is described by Martin Gardner[1] in his column "Mathematical Games." CESL is described in Reference 2. The cellular space concept was originated by Von Neumann and surveys of papers employing this concept in biological modelling have appeared.[3-5]

1.   M. Gardner, "The Fantastic Combinations of John Conway's New Solitaire Game 'Life'." *Scientific American*, **23** (4), 1970, 120–123.
2.   R. F. Brender, "*A Programming System for the Simulation of Cellular Spaces.*" Doctoral Dissertation, University of Michigan, Ann Arbor, 1970.
3.   A. W. Burks (Ed.), *Essays on Cellular Automata.* University of Illinois Press, Urbana, 1970.
4.   V. Aladyev, "Survey of Research in the Theory of Homogeneous Structures and Their Applications." Mathematical *Biosciences*, **22** (1), 1974, 121–154.
5.   G. Herman and G. Rosenberg (Eds.) *Developmental Systems and Languages.* North-Holland, Amsterdam, 1975.
6.   A. Aho and J. Hopcroft, *The Design and Analysis of Computer Algorithms.* Addison-Wesley, Reading, Mass., 1974.

PROBLEMS

1.   An inhomogeneous cell space model is the same concept as a homogeneous cell space except that the CELLS need not all be the same type. Here is an example.

   We have an infinite checkerboard in which each square is marked N, E, S, W, or B as in the Figure 5. As in the Game of Life, an initial configuration is obtained by placing a finite number of counters on the board.

7	S	S	N	N	W	W	W	W	W
6	S	S	N	N	W	W	W	W	W
5	S	S	N	E	E	E	E	E	E
4	S	S	N	E	E	E	E	E	E
3	S	.S	N	N	B	B	B	B	B
2	S	S	N	N	B	B	B	B	B
1	S	S	N	N	B	B	B	B	B
	1	2	3	4	5	6	7	8	9

Figure 5 An inhomogeneous cell space.

A counter on a B square does not move. A counter on an N square moves north one square, a counter on an E square moves east one square, and so on. Two or more counters that crash (move to the same square) annihilate each other.

(a) Assuming the neighborhood template is the same for every CELL, give the INFLUENCERS and INFLUENCEES of an arbitrary CELL.

(b) Give the local transition function τ, again assuming it takes the same form for every CELL.

(c) Show that the LAST · EVENTS · LIST consists of the CELLS that have just received a counter, together with those that have just lost a counter. Describe the NEXT · EVENTS · LIST.

(d) The local transition function obtained in b seems to be an awkward way of specifying what is essentially a simple model. This is because the "world view" of a cell space is one in which CELLS respond to the influence of their neighbors. In this example, the more natural description is in terms of the converse—the way a CELL influences its neighbors. This also shows up in the relative inefficiency of the NEXT · EVENT–LAST · EVENT strategy, which places CELLS that have just lost a counter on the LAST · EVENTS list to no real purpose. Provide a more efficient simulation strategy that will work in this case.

2. In this problem we consider the question of memory requirements for simulation.

(a) We indicated in Section 4.6 that it may not be necessary to save a complete copy of the current GLOBAL · STATE while computing the next GLOBAL · STATE. We can state the following principle: if a LOCAL · COMPONENT is scanned before any of its IN-FLUENCEES (other than itself), its current STATE must be saved.

Thus in Figure 6*a* there is a scanning sequence requiring that *no* component's state be saved. In Figure 6*b* there is a scanning sequence in which only one component's state must be saved. Provide such scanning sequences.

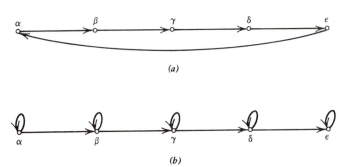

(*a*)

(*b*)

Figure 6   Directed graphs.

(*b*)   Clearly, the number of components whose state must be saved depends on the structure of the model's component interaction graph.

Prove the following

Proposition.   Given an interaction graph, let V be a subset of points whose removal from the graph, together with all their incoming and outgoing lines, causes the resulting graph to be acyclic (i.e., having no cycles). Then only the present STATES of the LOCAL COMPONENTS represented by points in V need be saved for an appropriate scanning sequence (see Chapter 16).

A set V is called a break-cycle set. Clearly one measure of the complexity required to simulate a model is the minimum size of all its break-cycle sets. Unfortunately, there is not likely to be an efficient algorithm that, given an arbitrary interaction graph, finds a minimum size break-cycle set. This is true because the problem is known to be NP-complete.[6]

This, of course, does not rule out efficient algorithms for special classes or for finding small but not necessarily minimal break-cycle sets.

(*c*)   Now the present STATES of the LOCAL · COMPONENTS of a minimum break-cycle set must be saved during the simulation of a global state transition. But it does not follow that all these STATES must be saved at the same time. Explain.

(d) Obtain a lower bound on the break-cycle sizes of regular symmetric graphs by considering that every point removed requires that all its neighbors be retained.

(e) Since the nearest neighbor two-dimensional cell space has a symmetric regular graph, the result of (d) applies. But show that for a finite $N \times N$ array, only the present STATES of $N + 1$ CELLS need be saved at any time for an appropriate scanning sequence.

Chapter Five

Simulation of Discrete and Continuous Time Models

We have thus far discussed prototypical procedures for simulation of discrete time models. The essential ideas remain valid when we deal with computer simulation of models specified by differential equations. However, first we must consider how one can more conveniently describe a model in a form readily interpretable by the computer. We shall soon introduce a model description language very much like that employed by common differential equation simulation packages, such as CSMP[1] and DYNAMO.[2] This language allows one to specify a model as a network of components. Since networks of arbitrarily high complexity (in terms of number of components and richness of connections) can be described, it is necessary to understand how to convert such a network into a form compatible with the prototypical simulation procedures we have already seen.

5.1 FROM NET DESCRIPTION TO SYSTEM SPECIFICATION

In Chapter 3 we raised the problem of obtaining a description of the abstract functions required in the formal description of models starting from an informal description. In the context of discrete time simulation we can see this more concretely. Our simulation procedure presupposes explicit specification of the component transition functions. For a cell space model, this is the function τ, which specifies the next state of a cell as a function of the current states of its neighbors. In the Game of Life, this turns out to be a very simple function, but in general it may be far less easy to describe this function or to obtain it from an informal description.

Certain systems, such as CSMP, allow the modeller to describe his model in a kind of descriptive language, which is automatically translated into a simulation program. Such systems carry out a translation that is very much parallel to the derivation of the formal model description from the informal one.

Let us consider a concrete example to show how this works. In Figure 1 we have a simplified representation of Forrester's World Model given in World Dynamics.[3] This model is intended to make predictions concerning, for example, the effect of pollution and natural resource depletion on population size and quality of human life. It is a highly aggregated model (thus we would consider it to be a lumped model relative to almost any imaginable base model of the earth). Nevertheless, it is sufficiently complex for illustrative purposes. Each of the circles and boxes of Figure 1 represents a function that takes a list of values of its input variables and produces a value for its output variable. There are 40-odd circles and boxes, thus 40-odd descriptive variables to the model. But there is actually a set of state variables of size 5, and these are outputs of the boxes. Also shown in Figure 1 are three output variables of the model—outputs of the double circles. (All eight variables are assumed to be directly measurable, although at least one criticism of the model attacks the truth of this assumption.)

The circles represent *instantaneous* functions,[†] that is, functions yielding an output at model time t which is determined by the input values at time t. The graphs in Figure 2, represent instantaneous functions of one argument; for example, the function of Figure 2a establishes that if at time t, the value of variable CIR (capital investment ratio) is 3, the value, also at time t, of POLCM (pollution from capital investment multiplier) will be 5.4. The graph embodies the hypothesis that the greater the level of capital investment, the greater the rate of pollution generated. The function itself is called POLCMT (pollution from capital investment multiplier table). If at time t, CIR has value x, and POLCM has value y, then $y = \text{POLCMT}(x)$; this is often denoted in shorthand notation[‡] by $\text{POLCM}(t) = \text{POLCMT}(\text{CIR}(t))$.

[†] The outputs of instantaneous functions are called A (auxilliary) and R (rate) variables in DYNAMO.

[‡] This strictly speaking is incorrect because, for example, CIR is the name of a variable and is not a function CIR($\cdot$). To correctly state the functional relation, we must refer to an arbitrary state trajectory as in Section 3.5 and the values of CIR and POLCM assumed in such a trajectory.

100

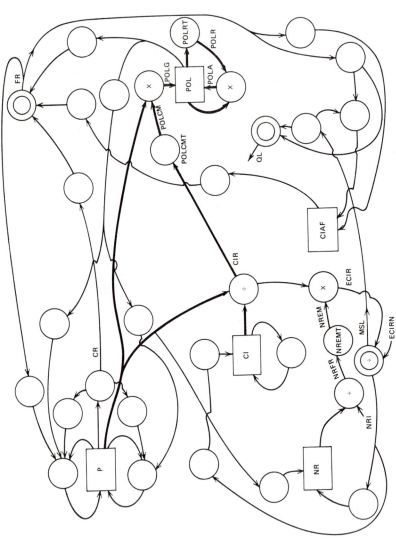

Figure 1 A simplified diagram of the world model. Heavy lines indicate paths traced out in tracing back from POL. POP = population, CR = crowding ratio, FR = food ratio, POLG = polution generation, POLRT = polution ratio table, POLR = polution ratio, POLA = polution absorption, QL = quality of life, CIAF = Capital Investment in Agricultural Fraction, ECIR = Effective Capital Investment Ratio, MSL = Material Standard of Living, ECIRN = Effective Capital Investment Normal, NRI = Natural Resources Initial, NR = Natural Resources, CI = Capital Investment, CIR = Capital Investment Ratio, POLC MT = Pollution from Capital Multiplier Table, NRFR = Natural Resources Fraction Remaining, NREMT = Natural Resources Extration Multiplier Table, NREM = Natural Resources Extration Multiplier. (After Reference 3, Figure 2.1, Figure 2.1, pp. 20, 21; Reprinted with

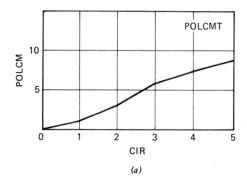

(a)

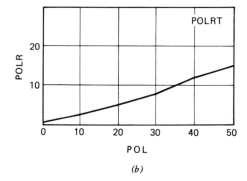

(b)

Figure 2   Some instantaneous functions. (After Reference 3, Figures 3.14, 3.15, pp. 56, 57; Reprinted with permission from *World Dynamics* Second Edition, by Jay W. Forrester. Copyright © 1973 Wright-Allen Press, Inc., Cambridge, Mass. 02142 USA.)

The squares represent *memory* or *noninstantaneous* functions.[†] In this particular model, as in a large class of models specified by differential equations, the squares represent either integrators or their discrete time analogs—depending on whether the model is to be viewed as essentially a continuous time or a discrete time one. We take the discrete time view for now, since it is easier to see how to derive the formal model description in this case.

Consider POL (pollution), one of the chosen state variables. As a memory function output its current value is not just a function of its current input values at time t; in fact, in shorthand notation we write

$$POL(t + h) = POL(t) + [POLG(t) - POLA(t)]h$$

which says that the POLlution at time $t + h$ (h being the discrete time step, e.g., 1 year) is equal to the POLlution at time t plus $POLG(t)h$, the POLlution Generated at time t, minus $POLA(t)h$, the POLlution Absorbed at time t.

[†] The outputs of memory functions are called L (level) variables in DYNAMO.

In other words, $[POLG(t) - POLA(t)]h$ is the net amount of pollution generated in the period $(t, t + h)$, and this is to be added to $POL(t)$, the pollution prevailing at the beginning of the period, to obtain $POL(t + h)$, the amount prevailing at the end of the period; $(POLG(t) - POLA(t))$ is thus the *net rate* of pollution generated (and approximates the *derivative* of POLlution in a continuous time model).

To obtain the state transition function, we have to be able to express $POL(t + h)$ as a function of the values of the state variables at time t. To do this, we trace back from POLG and POLA against the arrows, skipping over instantaneous functions and stopping when we have reached a state variable. The paths traced out by such a process are shown in Figure 1. When we remove this portion of the network and "lay it out flat," we obtain Figure 3. The process is also described by the (shorthand) equations:

$$POL(t + h) = POL(t) + [POLG(t) - POLA(t)]h$$
$$POLG(t) = P(t) \times POLCM(t)$$
$$POLCM(t) = POLCMT(CIR(t))$$
$$CIR(t) = \frac{CI(t)}{P(t)}$$

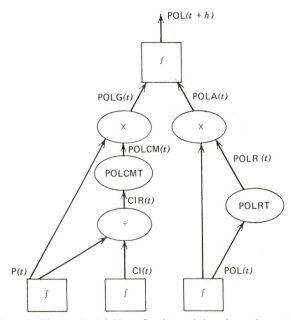

Figure 3   The traceback laid out flat; integral signs denote integrators.

$$\text{POLA}(t) = \text{POL}(t) \times \text{POLR}(t)$$
$$\text{POLR}(t) = \text{POLRT}(\text{POL}(t))$$

The end result is that POLlution at time $t + h$ is expressible as a function of the values at time t of the state variables POLlution, CI (capital investment), and Population, that is,

$$\text{POL}(t + h)$$

$$= \text{POL}(t) + \left[P(t) \times \text{POLCMT}\left(\frac{\text{CI}(t)}{P(t)}\right) - \text{POL}(t) \times \text{POLRT}(\text{POL}(t)) \right] h$$

More formally, the component transition function for state variable POL is given by

$$\text{NEIGHBORS} \cdot \text{OF} \cdot \text{POL} = \{\text{POL, CI, P}\}$$

and

$$\delta_{\text{POL}}(pol, ci, p) = pol + \left[p \times \text{POLCMT}\left(\frac{ci}{p}\right) - pol \times \text{POLRT}(pol) \right] h$$

with the interpretation that if at time t, POL, CI, and P have values pol, ci, and p, then at $t + h$, POL has value $\delta_{\text{POL}}(pol, ci, p)$.

We can go through the same process for each of the remaining state variables to complete the transition function specification; likewise we can do the same for each of the additional output variables. For example for material standard of living, (MSL; see Figure 1), we have

$$\text{MSL}(t) = \frac{\text{ECIR}(t)}{\text{ECIRN}}$$

$$\text{ECIR}(t) = \text{NREM}(t) \times \text{CIR}(t)$$

$$\text{NREM}(t) = \text{NREMT}(\text{NRFR}(t))$$

$$\text{NRFR}(t) = \frac{\text{NR}(t)}{\text{NRI}}$$

$$\text{CIR}(t) = \frac{\text{CI}(t)}{P(t)}$$

Thus $\text{MSL}(t) = \dfrac{\text{NREMT}(\text{NR}(t)/\text{NRI}) \times [\text{CI}(t)/P(t)]}{\text{ECIRN}}$ or more formally, the component output function associated with MSL is given by

$$\text{NEIGHBORS} \cdot \text{OF} \cdot \text{MSL} = \{\text{NR, CI, P}\}$$

$$\lambda_{\text{MSL}}(nr, ci, p) = \frac{\text{NREMT}(nr/\text{NRI}) \times (ci/p)}{\text{ECIRN}}$$

In the end, we can obtain a formal, structured model description (Section 4.7) shown in Table 1.

Table 1   The World Model

All variables have range R^+ (the positive real numbers).

State variables

  P (population)
  NR (natural resources)
  CI (capital investment)
  CIAF (capital investment in agriculture fraction)
  POL (pollution)

Output variables

  P, NR, CI, CIAF, POL
  MSL (material standard of living)
  QL (quality of life)
  FR (food ratio)

Transition Function

State Variable	NEIGHBORS	Local Transition Function
P	P, NR, CI, CIAF, POL	$\delta_P(p, nr, ci, ciaf, pol) = \cdots$
NR	P, NR, CI	$\delta^{NR}(p, nr, ci) = \cdots$
CI	P, NR, CI, CIAF	$\delta_{CI}(p, nr, ciaf) = \cdots$
CIAF	P, NR, CI, POL, CIAF	$\delta_{CIAF}(p, nr, ci, pol, ciaf) = \cdots$
POL	POL, CI, P	$\delta_{POL}(pol, ci, p) = \cdots$

Output Function

Output Variable	NEIGHBORS	Local Output Function
P	P	$\lambda_P(p) = p$
NR	NR	Identity
CI	CI	$\vdots$ Functions
CIAF	CIAF	
POL	POL	$\lambda_{POL}(pol) = pol$
MSL	P, NR, CI	$\lambda_{MSL}(p, nr, ci) = \cdots$
QL	P, NR, CI, POL, CIAF	$\lambda_{QL}(p, nr, ci, pol, ciaf) = \cdots$
FR	P, CI, POL	$\lambda_{FR}(p, ci, pol) = \cdots$

Exercise.   Obtain the actual expressions for δ_{NR} and λ_{QL} by referring to the network on pages 20 and 21 of Forrester's book.[3]

The process discussed here applies to a general network description of a model. Such a description, besides being presentable in diagram form (as in Figure 1) can also be accepted by certain simulation languages, such as DYNAMO (in which the present model is simulated) or CSMP, as a list of statements describing the instantaneous and memory functions involved and their input and output variables. DYNAMO and CSMP will sort these statements into an order that can be carried out by a sequential program, thus in effect, translating the net description into a formal structured model specification.

The sorting routine may reject a modeller's network description when it finds that no sequence of statements leads to a consistent computation. The primary cause of a contradictory description is the existence of a cycle consisting entirely of instantaneous functions. If this is the case, the model may not be well described (see Section 3.1) and there is no formal system specification corresponding to it.

Exercise.   A cycle is traced out by starting at a function and traveling around a series of arrows, from one function to a next one, until one returns to the original function. Demonstrate some cycles in Figure 1. What would go wrong if one of these did not go through a memory function?

Once we have specified the state transition and output function, the simulation of a discrete time model can be carried out as indicated in Chapter 4. In the prototype described there, the state variables are scanned in some fixed order, and for each variable the associated local transition is computed to obtain its next state. But in some models, such as the World Model we have been examining, a more efficient procedure may be advisable. Here instantaneous functions play a role in determining more than one variable's transition function, or output function. For example, CR (crowding ratio) must be computed for the next states of P and CIAF and the outputs FR and QL. Is there a way to avoid recomputing such a function more than once (at each time step)? We want to find an ordering of the computation of instantaneous functions which makes this possible.

To do this, we present a model description language, very similar to that used by CSMP. Then we describe a procedure for ordering the model description statements so that an efficient sequential interpretation results. The procedure is a mathematical equivalent of the trace back process described in the last section.

5.2   A MODEL DESCRIPTION LANGUAGE

There are just three kinds of statements in the language:

(a)   Denoting instantaneous functions
$$Y_1, Y_2, \ldots, Y_m = \text{INSTANT} \cdot \text{FUNCT}(X_1, X_2, \ldots, X_n)$$

(b)   Denoting input time functions

$$X_1, X_2, \ldots, X_m = \text{TIME} \cdot \text{FUNCT}$$

(c)   Denoting memory functions

$$Y_1, Y_2, \ldots, Y_m = \text{MEM} \cdot \text{FUNCT}(Q_1, \ldots, Q_n; X_1, \ldots, X_p)$$

The meaning of each statement is given next.

(a)   If the values of variables $X_1, X_2, \ldots, X_n$ are $x_1, x_2, \ldots, x_n$ at time t, the values of $Y_1, Y_2, \ldots, Y_n$ at time t are given by $y_1, y_2, \ldots, y_m = \text{INSTANT} \cdot \text{FUNCT}(x_1, x_2, \ldots, x_n)$. See the preceding section for examples.

(b)   The TIME $\cdot$ FUNCT statements generate the input trajectories for the model. Thus at time t, the values of $X_1, X_2, \ldots, X_m$ are given by

$$x_1, x_2, \ldots, x_m = \text{TIME} \cdot \text{FUNCT}(t)$$

For example

$$X_1, X_2 = \text{SIN}, \text{COS}$$

would produce the input trajectory $(\sin(t), \cos(t))$ for the variables X_1, X_2.

(c)   The MEM $\cdot$ FUNCT declares itself to have state variables $Q_1, \ldots, Q_n$ whose values must be set at the beginning of a run. Internally, it has a state transition function that determines the trajectories of these variables as influenced by the trajectories of its input variables $X_1, \ldots, X_p$, and an output function that determines the trajectories of its output variables $Y_1, \ldots, Y_m$.

For now we deal with only two types of memory functions. The statement

$$Y = \text{INTGRL}(IY; YRT)$$

denotes an integrator[†] whose output Y is the time integral of its input YRT plus its initial state IY. Of course in a discrete time simulation, this function can only be approximated; we gave an example of how this is done in the last section. We discuss other methods in Section 5.6.

The integrator constitutes the basic primitive for differential equation specified systems. Models whose only memory functions are integrators are exactly those which can described by a system of ordinary first-order differential equations (see Chapter 9).

Correspondingly, for discrete time models, the basic primitive is the delay element

$$Y = \text{DELAY}(IY; YP).$$

[†] IY is the initial value of Y, YRT is the rate of change of Y, and YP is the previous value of Y.

For a DELAY with discrete time steps, the output trajectory $Y(\cdot)$ lags one step behind the input trajectory $YP(\cdot)$; its initial value is given by IY. We provide a formal definition in Section 5.4.

Every discrete time model can be described with recourse to just DELAY type statements (see Chapter 9).

A *model description* in this language is a list of statements $S_1, S_2, \ldots, S_n$, where each S_i is of the kind a, b, or c just given.

Associated with such a model description is a *net* of the kind appearing in Figure 1. The rules for going from description to net (and back) are obvious, and we do not give them formally. An example clarifies the matter:

Example. Consider the following model description:

Description 1

$$Y2 = \text{DELAY}(IY2; Y2P)$$
$$U = \text{PROD}(Y1, Y2)$$
$$Y1P = \text{SUM}(X1, U)$$
$$Y2P = \text{SUM}(X2, U)$$
$$X1, X2 = \text{SIN}, \text{COS}$$
$$Y1 = \text{DELAY}(IY1; Y1P)$$

Here PROD and SUM are instantaneous functions (standing for product and sum, respectively); SIN, COS is a time function; and DELAY is a memory function. The corresponding net is shown in Figure 4.

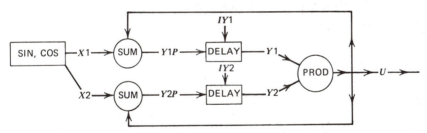

Figure 4 An example net.

To understand how the net is derived from the description, notice, for example, that the instantaneous function PROD has two input wires labeled $Y1$ and $Y2$ and an output wire labeled U, corresponding to the statement "$U = \text{PROD}(Y1, Y2)$"; $Y1$ also labels the output wire of a DELAY function corresponding to the statement $Y1 = \text{DELAY}(IY1; Y1P)$; thus the outputs of the two DELAY boxes are directly fed as the inputs to PROD.

Exercise. Trace through the net to assure yourself that it corresponds exactly to Description 1.

Exercise. Formalize the rules for converting between description and net.

Now note that the order of the statements in the description sequence is not relevant to the description: one obtains the same net from the sequence $S_1, S_2, \ldots, S_n$ in any of its permutations.

Example. The net also corresponds to

Description 2

$$X1, X2 = \text{SIN, COS}$$
$$U = \text{PROD}(Y_1, Y_2)$$
$$Y1P = \text{SUM}(X1, U)$$
$$Y2P = \text{SUM}(X2, U)$$
$$Y1 = \text{DELAY}(IY1; Y1P)$$
$$Y2 = \text{DELAY}(IY2; Y2P)$$

Order does not count because the statements describe a parallel model in which actions occur simultaneously—each statement describes such an action.

But whereas order does not count in the treatment of a model description, it is highly significant when the statements are interpreted as actions to be carried out by a sequential computer. These actions must be carried out in a correct order if a valid simulation is to result. Moreover, we reemphasize that for efficient simulation, the same action should not be carried out more than once.

5.3 SORTING PROCEDURE

Imagine now that a list of statements $S_1, S_2, \ldots, S_n$ is given as input to a computer program. First the list should check that the description makes sense; it can do this as follows.

$\boxed{1}$ Check if any variable appears on the left side of two distinct statements. If yes, reject the description as invalid.

For example, if the statements

$$Y = \text{SUM}(X, Z) \quad \text{and} \quad Y = \text{INTGRL}(IY; YRT)$$

appear anywhere in the list, the description is invalid because by the semantics of the language, the value of Y at time t is to be determined in two distinct ways—as the output of the SUM and INTGRL function. Which value should be used as the true one? (Would the real value of Y please stand up.) The computer has no way of knowing what the modeller intended.

In the corresponding net, the corresponding situation is one in which output wires of two distinct function blocks converge to a single wire, for example as shown in Figure 5.

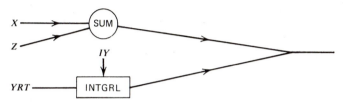

Figure 5 Outputs of SUM and INTGRL converge to the same wire.

$\boxed{2}$ Remove all TIME · FUNCT and MEM · FUNCT statement types from the list. (The program must, of course, be told the types of each statement.) The list now consists only of the INSTANT · FUNCT type of statement.

$\boxed{3}$ Define a precedence relation on the variables mentioned in the (new) list as follows.

U *precedes* V whenever U is an input variable and V is an output variable of some instantaneous function, that is, whenever there is a statement $Y_1, Y_2, \ldots, Y_m = \text{INSTANT} \cdot \text{FUNCT}(X_1, X_2, \ldots, X_n)$ such that U is one of the X_i and V is one of the Y_j.

If U *precedes* V, the value of U at time t must be known to the computer before it can compute the value of V at time t. But this does not account for all variables subjected to this constraint. The complete set is determined as follows

$\boxed{4}$ Generate the transitive closure *precedes** of *precedes*: *precedes** is a relation on the variables defined as follows: U *precedes** V if and only if there is a sequence of variables $W_0, W_1, \ldots, W_n$ such that $W_0 = U$, $W_n = V$, and each W_i *precedes* W_{i+1}.

Example. In Description 1 (or 2), removing the memory and time functions we obtain

$$U = \text{PROD}(Y1, Y2)$$
$$Y1P = \text{SUM}(X1, U)$$
$$Y2P = \text{SUM}(X2, U)$$

We obtain the precedence relation: $Y1$ *precedes* U, $Y2$ *precedes* U, $X1$ *precedes* $Y1P$, U *precedes* $Y1P$, $X2$ *precedes* $Y2P$, U *precedes* $Y2P$.

Then transitive closure contains all the pairs just named and in addition: $Y1$ *precedes*[*] $Y1P$ (since $Y1$ *precedes* U and U *precedes* $Y1P$), $Y1$ *precedes*[*] $Y2P$, $Y2$ *precedes*[*] $Y1P$, and $Y2$ *precedes*[*] $Y2P$.

U *precedes*[*] V precisely when there is a path going along the arrows in the net from U to V. If U *precedes*[*] V because U *precedes* W_1 *precedes* W_2 *precedes* $\cdots$ W_{n-1} *precedes* V, there is a path from U to V traversing $n-1$ instantaneous functions. In the net example, there is a path from Y through PROD and SUM to $Y1P$ and indeed Y *precedes*[*] $Y1P$.

[5] Check to see if any variable V is such that V *precedes*[*] V; if so, reject the description as invalid.

Exercise. Show that if V *precedes** V, there is a cycle in the net not containing any memory function. What is wrong with this situation? Compare with [1] above.

If a description surves this far, its statements can be arranged in a computationally correct and efficient sequence as follows.

[6] Assign to each of the variables a nonnegative integer called its *level* as follows:

(a) All variables that appear only on the left-hand side of the *precedes* relation have level 0; that is, if U *precedes* V for some V and there is no W such that W *precedes* U, then *level* $(U) = 0$.
(b) The level of any (other) variable is the length of the longest path in the net to it from any of the level 0 variables; that is, if U *precedes*[*] V, *level* $(U) = 0$, and n is the largest number such that U *precedes* W_1 *precedes* $W_3 \cdots$ *precedes* W_{n-1} *precedes* V, then *level* $(V) = n - 1$.

In our example, we obtain the following table:

Variable	Level
$Y1$	0
$Y2$	0
$X1$	0
$X2$	0
U	1
$Y1P$	2
$Y2P$	2

It is easiest to visualize the level assignment by redrawing the net, putting all variables at the same level in a line, as in Figure 6.

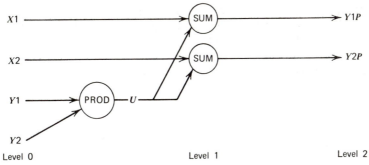

Level 0   Level 1   Level 2

Figure 6   The net of Figure 4 redrawn by level.

Exercise. Design a procedure that generates the level assignment by starting with level 0 variables, then obtains all level 1 variables, all level 2 variables, and so on.

It should be clear by now that the level of a variable is the greatest lower bound on the number of instantaneous functions required to compute the value of that variable at time t, given the values of all level 0 variables at time t. For example, $Y1P$ is at level 2 because two instantaneous functions in a row must be computed to obtain its value.

Exercise. But *level V* is not necessarily the total number of instantaneous functions that must be computed to obtain V's value. Why?

⌐7⌐ Having a level for each variable, we can assign a level to each of the statements as follows: For $S_i: Y_1,\ldots, Y_m = \text{INSTANT} \cdot \text{FUNCT}(X_1,\ldots, X_n)$, the level of S_i is the largest of the levels of the X_j; that is, level $(S_i) = \max \{\text{level } (X_j)\}, j = 1, \ldots, n$.

The function denoted by $\text{INSTANT} \cdot \text{FUNCT}$ cannot be computed until each of its arguments have been computed, and this explains the level assignment for S_i.

In our example:

    level $[U = \text{PROD}(Y1, Y2)] = \max \{level\,(Y1),\ level\,(Y2)\} = 0$
    level $[Y1P = \text{SUM}(X1, U)] = level\,(U) = 1$
    level $[Y2P = \text{SUM}(X2, U)] = level\,(U) = 1$

⌐8⌐ Check that all level 0 variables are outputs of either time functions or memory functions. If not, reject the description as invalid because some input variable to the model is not generated externally by a time function nor is its value available from the previous time step.

⌐9⌐ Order the statements by level; the order within a level does not matter. That is, if $S_1, S_2, \ldots, S_n$ is the *new* sequence, then level $(S_i) \leq$ level (S_{i+1}) for each i.

10 Now place all the time function type statements at the beginning of the list, and the memory function type statements at the end of the list (again the internal order does not matter).

The final sequence then has the appearance:

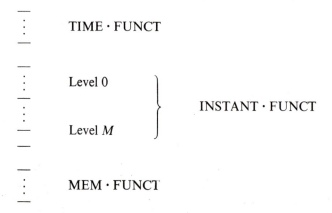

where M is the maximum of the levels of the statements. Call such a sequence a *final sequence*.

Description 2 of our example is a final sequence by these rules, but Description 1 is not.

Given a final sequence, we can imagine it transformed into a subprogram as follows: the TIME · FUNCT and INSTANT · FUNCT statements are treated as memory operation instruction types (recall Chapter 4). Then executing the TIME · FUNCT and INSTANT · FUNCT statements in sequence will carry out the computation of the values of all descriptive variables at time t, starting from the values of the outputs of the memory functions at time t. The values at time t of two important subsets are thus computed—the model output variables, and the input variables to the memory functions.

In our example, the sequence

$$X1, X2 = \text{SIN, COS}$$
$$U = \text{PROD}(Y1, Y2)$$
$$Y1P = \text{SUM}(X1, U)$$
$$Y2P = \text{SUM}(X2, U)$$

computes the values at time t of the output variable U and the integrator inputs $Y1P$ and $Y2P$ given the values at time t of the integrator outputs variables $Y1, Y2$.

Simulation of the memory functions is discussed in the discrete time context first. The differential equation case appears in Section 5.5.

5.4 DISCRETE TIME MODELS

When model descriptions contain only DELAY memory function statements, the DELAY output variables can be selected to constitute the state variables of the model. Thus each $Y = \text{DELAY}(IY, X)$ statement can be interpreted as follows: in the initialization phase, set Y equal to IY; in the state transition phase set the value of Y at time $t_i + h$ to the value of X at time t_i.

Exercise. Show that a DELAY element can be modelled by a sequential machine whose transition function takes the form $\delta(q, x) = x$.

In our example, Description 2 would be translated as follows.

0. Initialize the clock T to desired initial time t.
1. Set $Y1$ to $IY1$.
2. Set $Y2$ to $IY2$.
3. Set $X1$, $X2$ to SIN (T), COS (T).
4. Set U to PROD($Y1$, $Y2$).
5. Set $Y1P$ to SUM($X1$, U).
6. Set $Y2P$ to SUM($X2$, U).
7. Set $Y1$ to $Y1P$.
8. Set $Y2$ to $Y2P$.
9. Set T to $T + h$.
10. If T is less then the finish time, go to 3.
11. Stop.

Exercise. Generalizing the example, describe the program interpretation of an arbitrary final sequence with DELAY memory functions. Be sure to indicate explicitly the variables of the program.

This program appears to differ from the simulation procedure of Section 4.6. To get a clear idea of the difference, we now show how to produce a program that is more in the spirit of the original strategy.

Let $S_1, \ldots, S_m$ be a final sequence and let

$$Y1 = \text{DELAY}(IY1; Y1P)$$
$$\vdots$$
$$Yn = \text{DELAY}(IYn; YnP)$$

be the MEM · FUNCT statements. For each delay input variable YiP let PRIOR · VARIABLES$_i$ be the set of all variables relevant to computing YiP; that is, PRIOR · VARIABLES$_i$ is the set of variables V such that V precedes* YiP. Now let $S_{i_1}, S_{i_2}, \ldots, S_{i_m}$ be the subsequence of the final sequence relevant to computing YiP, that is, each S_j^i contains either YiP and/or at least one variable in PRIOR · VARIABLES$_i$.

Exercise. Show that $S_{i_1}, S_{i_2}, \ldots, S_{i_m}$ is exactly the computation sequence one would obtain by the traceback process of Section 5.1 for computing the transition function associated with state variable Yi (remember to *reverse* the order of the statements obtained by tracing back).

Now form the sequence:

$$
\left.
\begin{array}{l}
\overline{} \\
\vdots \\
\overline{}
\end{array}
\right\} Y1P\text{---relevant sequence} \\
Y1 = \text{DELAY}(IY1; Y1P)
$$
$$
\left.\vphantom{\begin{array}{l}a\\b\\c\\d\end{array}}\right\} \text{Transition function for } Y1
$$

$$
\left.
\begin{array}{l}
\overline{} \\
\vdots \\
\overline{}
\end{array}
\right\} Y2P\text{---relevant sequence} \\
Y2 = \text{DELAY}(IY2; Y2P)
$$
$$
\left.\vphantom{\begin{array}{l}a\\b\\c\\d\end{array}}\right\} \text{Transition function for } Y2
$$

$$\vdots$$

$$
\left.
\begin{array}{l}
\overline{} \\
\vdots \\
\overline{}
\end{array}
\right\} YnP\text{---relevant sequence} \\
Yn = \text{DELAY}(IYn; YnP)
$$
$$
\left.\vphantom{\begin{array}{l}a\\b\\c\\d\end{array}}\right\} \text{Transition function for } Yn
$$

$$
\left.
\begin{array}{l}
\overline{} \\
\vdots \\
\overline{}
\end{array}
\right\} \text{Remaining statements}
$$
$$
\left.\vphantom{\begin{array}{l}a\\b\\c\end{array}}\right\} \text{Output functions}
$$

Call this the *normal form* sequence.

In our example, the normal form sequence is

$$
\begin{aligned}
X1, X2 &= \text{SIN, COS} \\
U &= \text{PROD}(Y1, Y2) \\
Y1P &= \text{SUM}(X1, U) \\
Y1 &= \text{DELAY}(IY1; Y1P) \\
X1, X2 &= \text{SIN, COS} \\
U &= \text{PROD}(Y1, Y2) \\
Y2P &= \text{SUM}(X2, U) \\
Y2 &= \text{DELAY}(IY2; Y2P)
\end{aligned}
$$

To interpret the normal form sequence as a simulation program, we interpret the TIME $\cdot$ FUNCT and INSTANT $\cdot$ FUNCT statements the same as before. Then we see that the normal form sequence will fit the format of the simulation program of Section 4.6 in that each state variable is scanned and its next state computed. In fact the YiP relevant sequence computes the transition function for Yi. Just as before we will need to keep (in general) a second copy of the state variable array so that the interpretation of $Yi = \text{DELAY}(IYi, YiP)$ is now for the state transition phase: set the Yi value in the TO array to YiP.

Exercise. Check whether this would actually be required in the example.

But note also that the normal form sequence may require much more computation time than the final sequence. As we indicated earlier, this is because of the repeated computation of the same statement if it is relevant to the transition functions of more than one state variable. For example, both $X1, X2 = \text{SIN, COS}$ and $U = \text{PROD}(Y1, Y2)$ are computed twice in the normal form program as opposed to just once in the final sequence program.

Exercise. Show (*a*) that a final sequence yields a correct simulation of the model (i.e., the statements are executed in the correct order, and a valid computation of the transition and output functions is carried out) and (*b*) that relative to all possible sequences of the given description statements that produce valid simulation programs, it is an *optimal* sequence in the sense of requiring the least time to carry out.

Exercise. The foregoing is immediately generalizable to the discrete time model in which each memory function is itself a discrete time specified system. Underlying each statement $Y_1, Y_2, \ldots, Y_m = \text{MEM} \cdot \text{FUNCT}(Q_1, \ldots, Q_n; X_1, \ldots, X_p)$ is a sequential machine of the form:

$$\text{INPUTS} = X_1 \times X_2 \times \cdots \times X_p$$
$$\text{STATES} = Q_1 \times Q_2 \times \cdots \times Q_n$$
$$\text{OUTPUTS} = Y_1 \times Y_2 \times \cdots \times Y_m$$
$$\text{transition function} = \delta : \text{STATES} \times \text{INPUTS} \to \text{STATES}$$
$$\text{output function} = \lambda : \text{STATES} \to \text{OUTPUTS}.$$

Interpret the MEM · FUNCT statement as follows: in the initialization phase, set the values of $Q_1, Q_2, \ldots, Q_n$ to desired values $\bar{q}_1, \bar{q}_2, \ldots, \bar{q}_n$; in the state transition phase set the values of $Q_1, Q_2, \ldots, Q_n$ at time $t + h$ to $\delta(q_1, q_2, \ldots, q_n, x_1, \ldots, x_p)$ where $q_1, q_2, \ldots, q_n$ and $x_1, \ldots, x_p$ are the values of the $Q_1, \ldots, Q_n, X_1, \ldots, X_p$ at time t; set the values of $Y_1, Y_2, \ldots, Y_m$ at time t to $\lambda(q_1, q_2, \ldots, q_n)$.

Given a model description consisting of TIME · FUNCT, INSTANT · FUNCT, and MEM · FUNCT statements, we can reorder the statements to create a final sequence as demonstrated. Choose a set of state variables for the model described.

Show how to translate the sequence just given into a program that correctly simulates the model.

5.5 DIFFERENTIAL EQUATION SPECIFIED MODELS

When the memory function statements consist of INTGRL statements, the list of statements can be interpreted as an analog net or as a differential equation specified system (Chapter 9). The INTGRL output variables can be selected to constitute the state variables of the model. This becomes understandable once we make the following substitutions in the normal form sequence of Section 5.4: (a) $YiRT$ for YiP, and (b) "$Yi = $ INTGRL(IYi, $YiRT$)" for "$Yi = $ DELAY(IYi, YiP)" for each $i = 1, \ldots, n$.

Now the integrator "$Y = $ INTGRL(IY, YRT)" establishes the relation

$$\frac{dY(t)}{dt} = YRT(t)$$

between the values assumed by its input YRT and output Y (in shorthand notation). In other words, YRT is the *rate of change* of Y or the derivative of Y with respect to time.

Thus we obtain the following sequence of first-order differential equations:

$$\frac{dY_1}{dt} = f_1(Y_1, \ldots, Y_n, X_1, \ldots, X_m)$$
$$\vdots$$
$$\frac{dY_n}{dt} = f_n(Y_1, \ldots, Y_n, X_1, \ldots, X_m) \tag{1}$$

where for each $i = 1, \ldots, n$, f_i is the function computed by the $YiRT$ relevant sequence. Note that each f_i is a function of the integrator output variables $Y_1, \ldots, Y_n$ and the input variables $X_1, \ldots, X_m$ (outputs of the TIME · FUNCT statements), although not all these variables need actually influence it.

For example, returning to Section 5.1 we have

$$\frac{d \, \text{POL}}{dt} = f_{\text{POL}}(pol, ci, p)$$

where

$$f_{\text{POL}}(pol, ci, p) = p \times \text{POLCMT} \left(\frac{ci}{p} \right) - pol \times \text{POLRT}(pol)$$

In Chapter 9 we show how Equation set 1 can serve as a system specification which we call a *differential equation system specification* (DESS). A DESS specifies a continuous time system in the same way that a sequential machine specifies a discrete time system.

For now, we can understand how the integrator output variables can serve as a set of state variables by noting how they are employed by integration methods to compute successive values of the descriptive variables.

5.6   INTEGRATION METHODS

In the simplest integration technique, known as the Euler or rectangular method, the statement $Y = \text{INTGRL}(IY; X)$ is interpreted as follows: in the initialization phase, set Y equal to IY; in the state transition phase set the value of Y at time $t + h$ to $y + hx$, where y and x are the values of Y and X at time t (recall Section 5.1).

Exercise.   Write a model description for the analog net of Figure 7. Sort your original sequence of statements into final form and convert this sequence into a simulation program using the Euler integration method.

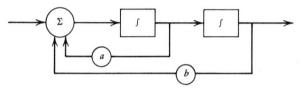

Figure 7   An analog net. The Σ function adds its inputs together; the @ function multiplies its input by a constant a.

The idea underlying the Euler method is that for a perfect integrator

$$\frac{dY(t)}{dt} = \lim_{h \to 0} \frac{Y(t + h) - Y(t)}{h} = X(t)$$

thus for small enough h, the approximation

$$Y(t + h) = Y(t) + h \cdot X(t)$$

ought to be employable. As we have learned (Section 4.6), the smaller the step size h, the greater the computation time required for a given length of run. In view of this limitation on the size of h, much effort has been put into developing integration methods that can produce acceptable accuracy within acceptable costs.

A whole literature deals with construction and analysis of the integration methods currently employed.[4, 5] Here we try only to provide an insight into the operation, accuracy, and complexity of these methods from a broader systems theoretic perspective.

The basic idea is easily stated: an integration method employs estimated past and/or future values of output and derivative in an effort to better estimate their present values. Thus in interpreting the statement $Y = \text{INTGRL}(IY; X)$, the computation of the value Y at time t_i may involve computed values of Y and X at prior computation instants $t_{i-1}, t_{i-2}, \ldots$, and/or subsequent instants $t_{i+1}, t_{i+2}, \ldots$. Notice that the values of the output Y and the derivative X are mutually interdependent—the integrator itself causes a dependence of Y on X, and the feedback of integrator outputs through the network of instantaneous functions transmits a dependence of X on Y. This situation sets up an inherent difficulty that must be faced by every approximation method—namely, *the propagation of error*. Error arises from two sources, that introduced at each step by the approximation and that accumulated through the effect of prior error propagating through the system. In the case of integration methods, the first source of error exists because even if the values of X and Y at time t are correct, the program cannot (in general) employ the values of X and Y over continuous interval $(t, t + h)$ which it requires to correctly compute the value of Y at time $t + h$. Thus, what is computed is likely to be in error because the computation is based on incomplete data. The second source of error is due to the mutual dependence of Y and X just mentioned. An error in Y is transmitted to X, where it may further affect Y. An integration method may tend to amplify or dampen the effect of error feedback. All other things being equal, a so-called *stable method* (one that dampens error propagation) is preferable to one that amplifies the error propagation. But the error propagation does not only depend on the method, it also depends on the nature of the model—whether it tends to amplify deviations (e.g., whether trajectories emerging from initial states close together tend to remain close together). From this we can see that the choice of integration method for a given model is not an easy one. In Chapter 13, we discuss more formally the concepts relevant to error propagation.

We now briefly describe the principles of some frequently employed integration methods. We can distinguish methods according to whether they employ estimated future values of variables to compute their present values. We call a method *causal* if it employs only values of Y and X at prior computation instants $t_{i-1}, t_{i-2}, \ldots$, and the value of X, at time t_i, to compute the value of Y at time t_i. A method is *noncausal* if in addition to prior values it employs estimated values of Y and X at instants $t_{i+1}, t_{i+2}, \ldots$.

The *order* of a method is the number of pairs of derivative-output values it employs to compute the value of Y at t_i. For example, a method employing the pairs (X_{i-3}, Y_{i-3}), (X_{i-2}, Y_{i-2}), (X_{i-1}, Y_{i-1}), and X_i (where X_j is the value of X at time t_j) is causal of order 3. A causal method of order d is characterized by a function f; the method sets Y_i (the value of Y at t_i) to $f(X_{i-d}, \ldots, X_{i-1}, X_i, Y_{i-d}, \ldots, Y_{i-1})$. The function is often a linear combination of the arguments, with coefficients chosen to minimize the error introduced in the value of Y at time t_i. Usually the basis of the derivation of the coefficients is that the input and output trajectories are smooth enough to be approximatable by a dth order polynomial. Of course often it is not known beforehand whether the requisite smoothness indeed obtains, especially for the output trajectory.

Example. The Adams method can be described by

$$Y_{t+h} = Y_t + h(3X_t - X_{t-h})$$

Exercise. What is the order of the Adams method? of the rectangular method? What is the function f, underlying each method?

5.6.1 Causal Methods

To implement a causal method of order d, a program must save the d past values of the model derivative and state (integrator input and output) variables. Thus the simulation program must retain more past history about the model than the model itself specifies. Thinking in terms of the model of the program, it will *have a larger number of state variables than does the model itself.* We have here an example of a general phenomenon that is treated in Chapter 16—the relation between computer and lumped model is very similar to that between base model and lumped model. In both cases, when valid relations are established, the computer or base model has a larger state space than does the lumped model, but relative to the output variables of interest, the same input-output behavior is generated.

The program implementation of a model description begins as before. The final form sequence is first obtained. Then each "$Y = \text{INTGRL}(IY, X)$" statement is translated as a program segment, which implements the integration method chosen for that statement (in some situations one may want to employ differential integration methods for different integrators).

The program segment that implements the integration method can be viewed as simulating a discrete time model that formally describes the method.

Let us denote this model by the statement:

$$Y = \text{INT} \cdot \text{METHOD}(P1Y, P2Y, \ldots, PdY, P1X, \ldots, PdX, X)$$

Then the transition and output functions associated with this statement can be defined by Table 2.

Exercise.
(a) Show that the state variables represent the d past values of Y and X by examining the operation of the transition function.
(b) Write a program for simulating the sequential machine specified in Table 2. Instead of saving two copies of the state variables, use only

Table 2   Causal Integration Methods

State Variable	Value at Time t_{i-1}	Values of State Variables at Time t_i if the Value of X (derivative at time t_i) is x	Value of Y (output) at Time t_{i-1}
$P1Y$	y_{i-1}	$f(x_{i-1}, \ldots, x_{i-d},$ $x, y_{i-1}, \ldots, y_{i-d})$	y_{i-1}
$P2Y$	y_{i-2}	y_{i-1}	
$\vdots$	$\vdots$	$\vdots$	
PdY	y_{i-d}	$y_{i-(d-1)}$	
$P1X$	x_{i-1}	x	
$P2X$	x_{i-2}	x_{i-1}	
$\vdots$	$\vdots$	$\vdots$	
PdX	x_{i-d}	$x_{i-(d-1)}$	

one copy and a single temporary cell (see Problems, Chapter 4). What problem arises in the initiation phase?

(c) Write a program for simulating the model of Description 1 with all DELAY statements replaced by INTGRL statements and employing the Adams method. [*Remark.* The sequential machine described in the table is an instance of the class of finite memory systems (see Chap 14).]

5.6.2   Noncausal Methods

As we have indicated, the noncausal integration methods make use of "future" values of derivatives and outputs. Clearly, the only way of obtaining "future" values is to run the simulation out past the present model time, calculate and store the needed values, and use these data to estimate the present values. Thus the values at the present time may be computed twice— tentatively, during the initial "predictor" phase when the future is simulated, and once again during the "corrector" phase when the final value is computed. In some methods, called *variable step methods*, the difference between the two computed values is compared with a criterion level; if it is too large, the step size is decreased and the predictor—corrector cycle repeated until a step size is found for which the difference between predicted and corrected values is below the criterion level. Of course, if output trajectory is not sufficiently smooth, no finite step size may be found for which the divergence is sufficiently small, and the simulation will drive to a grinding, expensive, halt.

As before, a noncausal method is characterized by a function g which receives the derivative-output pairs as arguments. Thus we have

$$Y_i = g(X_{i-d}, \ldots, X_{i-1}, \bar{X}_i, \bar{X}_{i+1}, \ldots, \bar{X}_{i+e}, Y_{i-d}, \ldots, Y_{i-1}, \bar{Y}_i, \bar{Y}_{i+1}, \ldots, \bar{Y}_{i+e})$$

where $(X_{i-d}, Y_{i-d}), \ldots, (X_{i-1}, Y_{i-1})$ are the already computed past value pairs, $(\bar{X}_i, \bar{Y}_i)(\bar{X}_{i+1}, \bar{Y}_{i+1}) \cdots (\bar{X}_{i+e}, \bar{Y}_{i+e})$ are the predicted present and future pairs, and Y_i is the final estimate of Y at t_i. Here the order is $d + e + 1$. The $e + 1$ present and future values are computed using a causal method characterized by a function f.

Example. A simple predictor-corrector method is as follows:

$$\bar{Y}_t = Y_{t-h} + hX_{t-h}$$

$$Y_t = Y_{t-h} + \frac{h}{2}(\bar{X}_t + X_{t-h}).$$

Exercise. Describe the function g for the method just presented and the function for its causal component.

The implementation of a noncausal method can be described as follows: employing the causal method f, simulate the model for $e + 1$ instants t_i, $t_{i+1}, \ldots, t_{i+e}$. Store the pairs $(\bar{X}_i, \bar{Y}_i), (\bar{X}_{i+1}, \bar{Y}_{i+1}), \ldots, (\bar{X}_{i+e}, \bar{Y}_{i+e})$ obtained. Then apply the function g to these values and the d past values $(X_{i-d}, Y_{i-d}), \ldots, (X_{i-1}, Y_{i-1})$ to obtain the estimated final value Y_i for the output variable Y at time t_i.

Exercise. Write a program to implement the foregoing description.

The initial values required by a causal method are often obtained by beginning with a noncausal method for which $d = 1$; that is, only the past value Y_{i-1} (which is the initial value of the output given by IY) is used.

5.7 THE GENERAL CASE: THE PROBLEM OF "BRIDGING THE GAP"

Consider now the case where the memory functions are arbitrary continuous time systems. The integrator is an example of such a system, and the simulation problems encountered there continue to apply to the general case.

The central problem can be stated as follows. Let the memory function be denoted by the statement $Y_1, \ldots, Y_m = \text{MEM} \cdot \text{FUNCT} (Q_1, \ldots, Q_n; X_1, \ldots, X_p)$. Let $y_1, \ldots, y_m$, and $q_1, \ldots, q_n$ be the lists of output and state variable values at computation instant t_i. If for each MEM · FUNCT these values are known, feedback through the instantaneous functions will determine the list $x_1, \ldots, x_p$ of input variable values at time t_i (these values are computed by executing the program associated with the final sequence). In digital simulation, there is necessarily a next computation instant t_{i+1} and a nonzero interval $[t_i, t_{i+1}]$. The model is supposed to be operating in continuous time over this interval, and the input, state, and output variables of each memory function may be continually changing during this period. The computer program has available only the values at t_i, and from these it must estimate the values at t_{i+1} *without* knowledge of what has happened in the gaps between t_i and t_{i+1}, that is, without having computed the input, state, and output trajectories associated with the interval $[t_i, t_{i+1})$.

Figure 8 may help clarify the problem. Suppose we have a model having three memory functions, each with a single state variable Q_i ($i = 1, 2, 3$). Since Q_1, Q_2, Q_3 is a state variable set, the values of the variables q'_1, q'_2, q'_3 at time t_{i+1} are uniquely determined by the values q_1, q_2, q_3 at time t_i. Thus if the computer "knew" the transition function, it could compute the transition $[t_i, t_{i+1}]$ precisely. However, the computer has only knowledge of the individual memory functions.

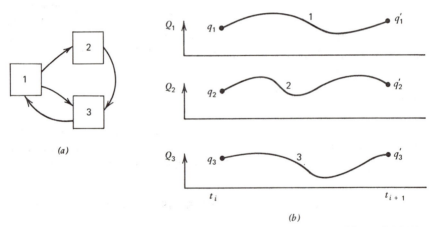

(a)

(b)

Figure 8   (a) A network consisting of MEM · FUNCT$_1$, MEM · FUNCT$_2$, and MEM FUNCT$_3$. (b) A trajectory over $[t_i, t_{i+1}]$.

Suppose that the connecting instantaneous functions form a feedback loop, as in Figure 8a. To compute the value q'_3 using MEM · FUNCT$_3$, the computer requires the value q_3 and also the state trajectories 1 and 2.

But these trajectories are not available, and the machine cannot compute them because to compute trajectory 1, it would have to first compute trajectory 3, which it could not do without prior knowledge of q'_3.

Exercise. Argue that if a simulation is not to take an infinite amount of time, there must always be a gap like the one just described, even if a look-ahead predictor technique is used to estimate intermediate values. Why does this problem fail to arise for discrete time models?

The problem then is how to bridge the gap. In the case of INTGRL statements, integration methods employ an extrapolation technique for causal methods, or an interpolation technique (for noncausal methods), to fill the gap. In effect, it is assumed that the state variable trajectories in the $[t_i, t_{i+1}]$ interval are time polynomials whose coefficients can be estimated from observations at adjacent computation instants. Very little is known at present about how to handle the general situation, and this is an area for fruitful research. (We suggest an approach in Chapter 9.)

In addition to the discrete time and differential equation cases already discussed, we have the *discrete event* models in which the "bridging the gap" problem has been solved ... *by assuming that nothing happens in the gap!* In effect, models in this large class specify that all trajectories are piecewise constant. Moreover, computation instants can be "scheduled" to occur at the discontinuities of the trajectories. Thus having computed the values of all variables at time t_i and having determined the next scheduled instant t_{i+1}, the program can determine the new values at time t_{i+1}. How this is done is the subject of the next chapter.

5.8 SUMMARY

In this chapter we introduced a model description language. A list of statements in this language describes a model in network form. Each statement describes the action carried out by a component of the model, and since parallelism is assumed, there is no inherent order to the list (really, a set). By appropriately sorting the statements and interpreting them, however, an efficient simulation program for a sequential acting digital computer is obtained.

In the discrete time case, the validity of the program can be proved, but in the continuous time case, fundamental "bridging the gap" problems arise in which a weaker notion of validity, allowing for error introduction, is appropriate.

It was also shown how the sorting process corresponds to the process of model description formalization (i.e., the selecting of input, output, and state variables and the specification of the component transition and output functions).

5.9 SOURCES

1. *System 1360 Continuous System Modelling Program* (CSMP), User's Manual. IBM Publication H20-0367, 1967.
2. A. L. Pugh, *DYNAMO II User's Manual.* MIT Press, Cambridge, Mass., 1973.
3. J. W. Forrester, *World Dynamics.* Wright-Allen Press, Cambridge, Mass., 1972.
4. R. W. Hamming, *Numerical Methods for Scientists and Engineers.* McGraw-Hill, New York, 1973.
5. Y. Chu, *Digital Simulation of Continuous Systems.* McGraw-Hill, New York, 1969.

Chapter Six

Introduction to Discrete Event Models

We have seen how the discrete time, prototypical simulation procedure, which we introduced in Section 3.3, leads naturally to the formulation of discrete time models that are appropriate to this kind of simulation. We indicated in Section 4.8 that it may be advantageous to augment the prototypical procedure with a next event selection mechanism that restricts the simulator's attention to the components that can change states at the next time step. The next logical development is to free the simulator from a fixed time step regimen. This is the discrete event philosophy.

In the discrete event mode, the simulator is driven by a next events list that contains the next clock times at which components are scheduled to undergo an (internally determined) state change. Let us call the time at which such an event is scheduled its *hatching* time.

The essence of the discrete event philosophy is the presumption that the hatching times of some events are *predictable* on the basis of the results of the occurrence (i.e., hatching) of other events. When the simulator can predict the next hatching time of a component, it can schedule it on the next event list. A second necessary presumption is that if the next hatching time of a component *cannot* be predicted in advance, it will not undergo a state change *until* and *unless* such a change is caused by a state transition of a component that *has* been prescheduled. When these presumptions hold, a valid simulation can be achieved in which the simulator successively advances the model clock to the closest hatching time on its list and carries out the component actions prescribed for that time. Thus the sequence of computation instants (at which model states are computed) is not confined to integer multiples of a basic step, as in the discrete time case. By advancing the clock in jumps, the simulator in effect pays no attention to the model between the jumps. As indicated at the end of Chapter 5, the model can be ignored at these points because it is claimed that *nothing significant happens in the gaps.*

Exercise. Show that the foregoing presumptions justify the claim that nothing significant happens in the gaps.

Under the same conditions, however, a discrete time simulator would have to chug along in fixed time steps, checking at each one, whether the hatching time of any component on its next event list had arrived. For the steps falling between the hatching times, of course, the simulator would find nothing of significance to do.

Exercise. Assuming finite precision for time representation, you are given a finite sequence of computation instants generated by a discrete event simulator. What is the largest step size a discrete time simulator can employ if it is not to be late for the hatching of any component? What is the maximum number of successive nonsignificant time steps it would encounter with this step size?

We see from the presumptions given earlier that a rather special class of models will be appropriate to discrete event simulation. Chapter 1 informally described such a model (Example 5). Many more are available in the literature. (See Section 1.5.) As with discrete time models there is a formalism appropriate for describing discrete event models. In Chapter 9 we develop the intuitive basis for this formalism. Before the full presentation, however, an example can serve the basis for further discussion.

6.1 DISCRETE EVENT MODEL EXAMPLE

The grocery store represented in Figure 1 is considered to have an EN-TRANCE where a customer enters the shopping area (SHOP · AREA) and selects his groceries. When he is finished shopping, he goes to a checkout counter (CHECKOUT), where he waits in LINE until served by a cashier. After paying the cashier, the customer leaves the store by way of the EXIT.

Before providing an informal description of this model, we present some new notation. By R we mean the set of all real numbers; R^+ is the set of positive real numbers; R_0^+ is R^+ with zero included (the nonnegative reals) $R_{0,\infty}^+$ is R_0^+ with the addition of the infinity element (∞). We make use of a well-known property of ∞, namely, that $\infty + r = \infty$ for every finite real number r.

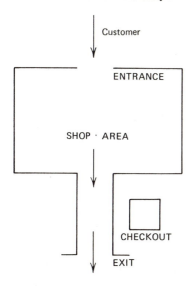

Figure 1   Schematic of a grocery store.

Given a set A, we denote by A^* the set of all finite sequences of elements of A. A typical sequence in A^* takes the form $a_1, a_2, \ldots, a_n$ where each $a_i \in A$. This sequence is said to have *length n*. When $n = 0$, we have the *empty sequence*, or the sequence of zero length, which we all denote by Λ.

The grocery store model is an example of a *queueing* model. The customers entering the store are given *identities* or *names* from the set $\{a, b, c, \ldots\}$ (the lowercase alphabet). The customers waiting to be served by the cashier form a *queue*. A typical configuration of the queue is denoted by a sequence from $\{a, b, \ldots\}^*$.

Informal Description of Grocery Store Model

Components

ENTRANCE, SHOP $\cdot$ AREA, CHECKOUT, EXIT

Descriptive Variables

1. Describing ENTRANCE

    HELLO—with range $\{\phi, a, b, c, \ldots\}$; HELLO = ϕ means no customer in ENTRANCE, HELLO = x means customer named x is in ENTRANCE.

2. Describing SHOP $\cdot$ AREA

    SHOPPING $\cdot$ TIME—with range R^+; a random variable (rv) giving the elapsed time a customer will spend in SHOP $\cdot$ AREA.

    TIME $\cdot$ LEFT $\cdot$ LIST—with range $(\{a, b, \ldots\} \times R^+)^*$; (x_1, τ_1) $(x_2, \tau_2) \cdots (x_n, \tau_n)$ means customer x_i will leave SHOP $\cdot$ AREA in time τ_i from now.

3. Describing CHECKOUT

    LINE—with range $\{a, b, \ldots\}^*$; LINE $= x_1, x_2, \ldots, x_n$ means x_1 is first in line, x_2 second, $\ldots$, to get checked out (first in, first out—FIFO—queue).

    SERVICE $\cdot$ TIME—with range R^+; an rv assigning time it will take customer now first in line to be processed.

    SERVICE $\cdot$ TIME $\cdot$ LEFT—with range R^+; SERVICE $\cdot$ TIME. LEFT $= \sigma$ means that customer being processed will leave CHECKOUT in σ from now.

    BUSY—with range $\{YES, NO\}$; indicates whether CHECKOUT is serving a customer.

4. Describing EXIT

    BYE $\cdot$ BYE—with range $\{\phi, a, b, \ldots\}$; BYE $\cdot$ BYE $= \phi$ means no customer, BYE $\cdot$ BYE $= x$ means customer x is leaving.

Component Interaction

A customer in ENTRANCE at clock time t is signaled by HELLO $= x$ (his name); he immediately enters SHOP $\cdot$ AREA (HELLO becomes ϕ) and after sampling SHOPPING $\cdot$ TIME, he gets a time τ. Thus (x, τ) is added to TIME $\cdot$ LEFT $\cdot$ LIST. As clock time advances (x, τ) will be decremented until $(x, 0)$ is on list; at this point customer x will leave SHOP $\cdot$ AREA, immediately joining the back of the CHECKOUT $\cdot$ LINE. As prior customers in LINE are processed, he advances to the front of LINE. When he is first in LINE, he samples SERVICE $\cdot$ TIME to get a time σ, and SERVICE $\cdot$ TIME $\cdot$ LEFT is set to σ. Customer x waits at the head of the LINE until SERVICE $\cdot$ TIME $\cdot$ LEFT becomes 0; then his departure by way of EXIT is signaled by BYE $\cdot$ BYE $= x$. The component-influence diagram appears in Figure 2.

In a typical trajectory of the descriptive variables (Figure 3), the observation interval is $[t, t']$. At time t the store is empty; this is reflected by the fact that the TIME $\cdot$ LEFT $\cdot$ LIST is empty (no one in SHOP $\cdot$ AREA), the CHECKOUT $\cdot$ LINE is empty, SERVICE $\cdot$ TIME $\cdot$ LEFT $= 0$, and BUSY $= NO$ (no one is being served).

At time t_a customer a arrives as shown in the HELLO trace. Customer a samples a SHOPPING $\cdot$ TIME so that at time t_a, the TIME $\cdot$ LEFT $\cdot$ LIST becomes (a, τ_a).

At time $t_a + \tau_a$, a leaves the SHOP $\cdot$ AREA and becomes the only person in LINE; thus LINE $= a$. Being first in LINE, a is immediately served; he samples a SERVICE $\cdot$ TIME σ_a, his bill is totaled and paid in the interval $[t_a + \tau_a, t_a + \tau_a + \sigma_a]$, and during this time the cashier is engaged, as shown by BUSY $= YES$. EXIT becomes a at the time $t_a + \tau_a + \sigma_a$ when a leaves the store.

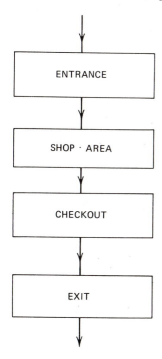

Figure 2 Grocery store influence diagram.

Just as a is leaving, customer b arrives. Sampling SHOPPING · TIME τ_b, b will leave the SHOP · AREA at time $t_b + \tau_b$. While b is shopping, however, c arrives at time t_c and samples SHOPPING · TIME τ_c. Having less shopping to do (i.e., $\tau_c < \tau_b$), c leaves the SHOP · AREA before b does. This is shown by the TIME · LEFT · LIST, which at t_b is (b, τ_b), at t_c is $(b, \tau_b - [t_b - t_c])(c, \tau_c)$ and at time $t_c + \tau_c$ is $(b, \tau_b - [(t_b - t_c) + \tau_c])$.

At time $t_c + \tau_c$, c enters the CHECKOUT and is immediately served; after sampling SERVICE · TIME, he is scheduled to leave at $t_c + \tau_c + \sigma_c$.

While c is still in LINE, b joins him at time $t_b + \tau_b$ and then LINE $= cb$. Now b waits until c leaves the CHECKOUT and at that time $(t_c + \tau_c + \sigma_c)$ b becomes the first in LINE (LINE $= b$) and samples from SERVICE · TIME · LEFT.

Note that the cashier is engaged while serving c and then b; that is, BUSY $=$ YES in the interval $[t_c + \tau_c, t_c + \tau_c + \sigma_c + \sigma_b]$.

All this English language description of the behavior is implicit within the trajectories portrayed in Figure 3, which for each descriptive variable Y and each time t depicts the value assumed by Y at time t. The behavior is a consequence of the incoming stream of customers, the initial conditions assumed (store is empty), and the rules given for component interaction.

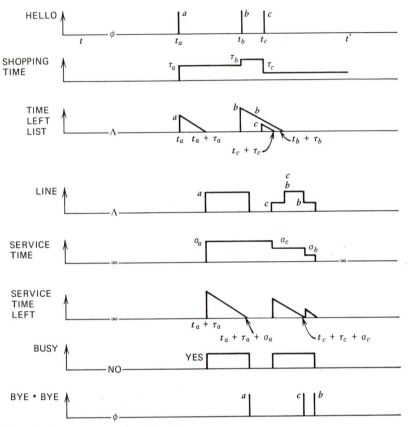

Figure 3 Grocery store model trajectories.

As we indicated in Chapter 3, these rules must be translated into a computer program for the computer to be able to generate the behavior. Many authors apparently believe that for discrete event models, no rigorous, elegant description is possible other than the program itself. However, by following the approach to discrete time models of Chapter 3, we are led to just such a descriptive formalism.

Again, we first consider the autonomous case (where there are no input variables). Of course, in Example 1, there *is* an input variable, namely, HELLO, the variable that records the arrival of customers.

Exercise.   Recalling that an input variable is one whose behavior is generated externally (i.e., not influenced by the model), argue that HELLO is the one and only input variable of the model.

To consider the case of no input variables, imagine that the grocery store has been operating normally for some time since opening and then shuts its ENTRANCE. The subsequent behavior is generated by a model without input variables. We want to determine whether our descriptive variables can serve as a set of state variables, that is, whether the model is well described.

Most variables remain constant and change only at certain times—the hatching times referred to in the previous section. We call these *piecewise constant* variables. The hatching times are determined by the other variables, which are essentially *countdown clocks*. In our example, SHOPPING · TIME, LINE, SERVICE · TIME, BUSY, and EXIT remain constant and change (if at all) when one or more of the countdown clocks on TIME · LEFT · LIST or SERVICE · TIME · LEFT reaches zero.

Assume for the moment that at a hatching time the new values of the piecewise constant variables are determined as a function of the immediately previous values of these variables, the countdown clocks that have reached zero, and the values of the countdown clock variables that have not yet reached zero. Also, assume that the countdown clocks are reset on the same basis. Then under these conditions, the descriptive variables form a set of state variables. Reason—at any time t_i, the countdown clock variables determine the next hatching time, t_{i+1}. Until t_{i+1} is reached, all noncountdown variables remain constant and all countdown variables decay linearly. At t_{i+1}, the values of all descriptive variables are determined by their immediately preceding values. After this updating, the next hatching time is uniquely determined; thus by an induction argument, all future values of the descriptive variables are determined.

6.2   DETERMINISTIC REPRESENTATION OF PROBABILISTIC MODELS

In Chapters 1 and 2, we noted that many models are probabilistic; that is, their descriptive variable set includes random variables. This is especially true of discrete event models. Indeed our grocery store example has two random variables: SHOPPING · TIME and SERVICE · TIME. Such variables do not satisfy the assumption just made—that their values are determined uniquely by other variables. However, we can provide a simple way of transforming any probabilistic model into an equivalent deterministic model to which the foregoing assumptions apply.

To do this we must understand how random variables are generated in the computer.

The generation process is composed of a serial connection of two subprocess, as in Figure 4. The first process is a *pseudorandom number generator*.

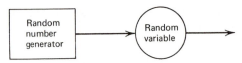

Figure 4   Random variable generation.

Every time this subroutine is called, it returns a different real number in the interval $[0, 1]$. A call for this subroutine is made whenever the simulation program desires to sample a random variable. The random variable is actually a function realized by the second process, which takes the number given to it by the number generator and produces an output in the range set of the variable. The output constitutes the desired sample of the random variable.

Appendix C provides an introduction to probability theory, random variables, and their computer realization. In the following development we assume that the reader has acquired this background.

We have seen (Section 3.7) that the random number generator can be thought of as an autonomous sequential machine. The mapping that takes the output of the sequential machine and converts it to a value of the random variable can be treated an instantaneous function. Thus once the initial state of the generator is specified, the sequence of values sampled from the random variable is uniquely determined. This suggests that to the list of descriptive variables, we should add a state variable for each random number generator that would be required to simulate the model. These new variables would be piecewise constant variables, since they would change values only when random variables are sampled. We must assume that such sampling is to be triggered only at the event hatching times and that the decision to sample a particular variable at such a time is a function of the immediately previous values of the piecewise constant variables and the countdown clock variables. The random generator state variables would then behave just like ordinary piecewise constant variables, and a well-described model would result.

Notice that an autonomous sequential machine model of the random number generator is now not fully descriptive of the situation. When it makes a transition, the next state is completely determined by the previous state, but the times at which transitions occur are no longer necessarily integer multiples of a fixed time step. Problem 2 at end of the chapter indicates how to provide a more appropriate formulation in our discrete event formalism.

Recall that we are seeking to provide program-independent means of model description. Thus the decision of whether to include descriptions of the actual random generators employed in simulating a model will depend on whether we consider these generators to be parts of the program or parts of the model. We might want to regard them as integral to the model when we wish to study the effect of generators with different characteristics on the model's behavior. Recall that practical generators do not produce truly random sequences, thus may well have differential effects on model behavior. In this chapter, however, we formulate a notion of an "ideal" random number generator and employ this generic concept to represent the appearance of an actual generator anywhere in the model.

Our *ideal* generator has as its state set the interval $[0, 1]$ and has a transition function of the form $\Gamma : [0, 1] \rightarrow [0, 1]$. Thus the sequence of length n associated with an initial seed r is $r_0, r_1, \ldots, r_{n-1}$, where $r_0 = r$ and for $i = 0, 1, \ldots, n - 1$, $r_{i+1} = \Gamma(r_i)$.

Exercise. A rule of this form is $\Gamma(r) = (ar + b) \bmod 1$, where $x \bmod 1$ is the difference between x and the largest integer just less than or equal to x. Show how this is an idealization of the linear-congruential generators of Section 3.7.

We want our generator to be ideal in the sense that whenever it is sampled, it appears to produce numbers uniformly distributed in the interval $[0, 1]$ and independent of all numbers previously sampled. Problem 3 shows how to formulate this requirement in formal terms.

Appendix C demonstrates that any independent random variable can be represented by a so-called *standard random variable*. A standard random variable takes the form of function mapping $[0, 1]$ into the real numbers (or a subset thereof). Let $Y : [0, 1] \rightarrow R$ be such a random variable as appearing in the informal description of a model. Then, following the lines of our earlier discussion, to put a model in deterministic form, we add a variable to the list of descriptive variables whose range is the state set of the random number generator on whose outputs Y operates. Thus using our ideal generator, we add a variable, call it $Y \cdot \text{SEED}$ with range $[0, 1]$. Whenever the rules of interaction call for sampling the variable Y, we rewrite them to indicate that if r is the present value of $Y \cdot \text{SEED}$, then $Y(r)$ is the sampled value received, and the next value of $Y \cdot \text{SEED}$ is to be $\Gamma(r)$.

For example, consider our grocery store model. Among the descriptive variables, we have the random variables SHOPPING $\cdot$ TIME and SERVICE $\cdot$ TIME. We replace these by the variables SHOPPING $\cdot$ TIME $\cdot$ SEED and SERVICE $\cdot$ TIME $\cdot$ SEED, each having range $[0, 1]$ and typical values r_1 and r_2, respectively.

In the component interaction rules, whenever the phrase "sample a SHOPPING · TIME τ" appears we replace it by:

1. Apply the map SHOPPING · TIME to the current value r_1 of SHOPPING · TIME · SEED, obtaining a result τ, called the sampled SHOPPING · TIME.
2. Apply Γ to r_1 to obtain a next value r_1' of SHOPPING · TIME · SEED.

An analogous substitution is made for SERVICE · TIME and indeed for every independent random variable.

[For a set of jointly distributed random variables $Y_1, \ldots, Y_n$, we take the common sample space to be represented by $[0, 1]^n$ with uniform probability, and a variable $Y_1, \ldots, Y_n$ · SEED with range $[0, 1]^n$ appears. The generator is modelled by Γ_n, where $\Gamma_n(r_1, \ldots, r_n) = (\Gamma(r_1), \ldots, \Gamma(r_n))$. The current sampled value of Y_i used in the model description then is $Y_i(r_1, \ldots, r_n)$, where $(r_1, \ldots, r_n)$ is the current value of $Y_1, \ldots, Y_n$ · SEED].

Having made the conversion, we can see that the model operates deterministically and satisfies the assumptions made in Section 6.1. Thus the new set of descriptive variables is a state variable set, and the model is well described.

Exercise. Verify the previous statement.

Of course, given a descriptive variable set that is a state variable set, we may look for a smaller or, if possible, a smallest state variable set, using such a set to specify (in the autonomous condition) the model transition function. To illustrate this idea, let us once more turn to the grocery store example.

6.3 TOWARD FORMALIZATION OF THE GROCERY STORE MODEL

After converting all random variables to proper form, we have the descriptive variables: SHOPPING · TIME · SEED, TIME · LEFT · LIST, LINE, SERVICE · TIME · SEED, SERVICE · TIME · LEFT, BUSY, and BYE · BYE. These variables form a state variable set. We do not have to show this directly. It will follow if we can pick out a smaller state variable set. Such a set, indeed, the smallest such set, is obtained by omitting BUSY and BYE · BYE, both of which can be instantaneously determined from SERVICE · TIME · LEFT.

Exercise. Express the value of BUSY at time t as a function of the value of SERVICE · TIME · LEFT at time t. Do the same for BYE · BYE.

The remaining variables are as follows:

SHOPPING · TIME · SEED   with typical value r_1
TIME · LEFT · LIST   with typical value $(x_1, \tau_1) \cdots (x_n, \tau_n)$
LINE   with typical value $y_1 \cdots y_m$
SERVICE · TIME · SEED   with typical value r_2
SERVICE · TIME · LEFT   with typical value σ

A typical (global) state is a list of values of the state variables; let us say

$$\begin{aligned} s = (r_1, &(x_1, \tau_1), \ y_1, \ r_2, \ \sigma) \\ &(x_2, \tau_2) \ \ y_2 \\ &\quad \vdots \qquad \vdots \\ &(x_n, \tau_n) \ \ y_m \end{aligned}$$

is such a state.

Recall that this state describes the following situation: there are customers $x_1, x_2, \ldots, x_n$ in the SHOP · AREA; each customer x_i has a time τ_i remaining to shop; there are customers $y_1, y_2, \ldots, y_m$ in the LINE at the checkout; customer y_1 is being served and has a time σ remaining before leaving. The next sampled SHOPPING · TIME and SERVICE · TIME will be determined by the seeds r_1 and r_2, respectively.

According to the previous discussion, if we do indeed have a state variable set, we ought to be able to compute the next hatching time, knowing only the state s of the model at time t_i. Let t_{i+i} be this next hatching time and write

$$t_{i+i} = \begin{array}{lll} t_i + \sigma & \text{if} \quad \sigma < \min\{\tau_1, \ldots, \tau_n\} & (1) \\ t_i + \sigma & \text{if} \quad \sigma = \min\{\tau_1, \ldots, \tau_n\} & (2) \\ t_i + \min\{\tau_1, \ldots, \tau_n\} & \text{if} \quad \sigma > \min\{\tau_1, \ldots, \tau_n\} & (3) \end{array}$$

Exercise. In shorter notation, $t_{i+i} = t_i + \min\{\tau_1, \ldots, \tau_n, \sigma\}$.

We have purposely separated out Cases 1, 2, and 3. Each case corresponds to an event occurring in the SHOP · AREA or the CHECKOUT or both, simultaneously. By way of explanation, at time t_i, customer y_1 has SERVICE · TIME · LEFT $= \sigma$ at the CHECKOUT; also, each customer x_i ($i = 1, 2, \ldots, n$) has a time τ_i left in the SHOP · AREA. Customer y_1 will be checked out at time $t_i + \sigma$. A customer x_i will leave the SHOP · AREA at time $t_i + \tau_i$. Thus the next event time t_{i+i} is the minimum of the hatching times $\{t_i + \tau_1, t_i + \tau_2, \ldots, t_i + \tau_n, t_i + \sigma\}$ or equivalently $t_{i+1} = t_i + \min\{\tau_1, \ldots, \tau_n, \sigma\}$.

In Case 1, since σ is smaller than all of the τ_i's, the next event is a CHECKOUT · EVENT. The rules of interaction indicate that a customer

y_1 (at the head of the LINE) should leave the LINE; if there is a second customer y_2 in LINE ($y_2, \ldots, y_m$ is not empty), the SERVICE $\cdot$ TIME $\cdot$ LEFT clock is reset to SERVICE $\cdot$ TIME(r_2); if not, no next CHECKOUT event is to be scheduled.

This is formalized by letting s' be the state obtaining just after t_{i+i} and writing

$$
s' = \begin{cases}
(r_1, (x_1, \tau_1 - \sigma), y_2, \Gamma(r_2), \text{SERVICE} \cdot \text{TIME}(r_2)) & \text{if } m \geq 2 \\
\quad (x_2, \tau_2 - \sigma), y_3 \\
\qquad \vdots \qquad \quad \vdots \\
\quad (x_n, \tau_n - \sigma), y_m \\
(r_1, (x_1, \tau_1 - \sigma), \Lambda, r_2, \infty) & \text{if } m \leq 1 \\
\quad (x_2, \tau_2 - \sigma) \\
\qquad \vdots \\
\quad (x_n, \tau_n - \sigma)
\end{cases}
$$

Recall that the symbol Λ means the empty sequence.

Exercise. Why are all the τ_i's decremented by σ? How does the setting SERVICE $\cdot$ TIME $\cdot$ LEFT $= \infty$ ensure that no next CHECKOUT event is scheduled?

Consider Case 3, where the smallest of the τ_i's is less than σ. This means that one or more of the customers (having the smallest SHOPPING $\cdot$ TIME $\cdot$ LEFT) will leave the SHOP $\cdot$ AREA and join the LINE.

Let us first suppose that only one customer will leave the SHOP $\cdot$ AREA; that is, there is only one i, call it i^*, such that $\tau_{i^*} = \min \{\tau_1, \ldots, \tau_n\}$. Then the state achieved just after the SHOP $\cdot$ AREA event takes place is

$$
\begin{aligned}
s' = (r_1, &(x_1, \tau_1 - \tau_{i^*}), & y_1, r_2, \sigma - \tau_{i^*}) \\
&(x_2, \tau_2 - \tau_{i^*}), & y_2 \\
& & y_m \\
& & x_{i^*} \\
&(x_{i^*-1}, \tau_{i^*-1} - \tau_{i^*}) \\
&(x_{i^*+1}, \tau_{i^*+1} - \tau_{i^*}) \\
&(x_n, \tau_n - \tau_{i^*})
\end{aligned}
$$

Notice that customer x_{i^*} (who is *the one customer* next scheduled to leave the SHOP $\cdot$ AREA) joins the end of the LINE. This describes the "first in, first out" (FIFO) queue discipline. Other disciplines could have been employed in the model. Specifying such disciplines involves the considerations brought out in the next section.

6.4 SIMULTANEOUS EVENTS

Now consider what happens when more than one customer will leave simultaneously; that is, there is more than one τ_i that equals the minimum value. For the next state s' to be unique, we will have to specify the order in which such a group of customers joins the LINE.

Suppose, for example, that we have the TIME · LEFT · LIST: $(a, 3)(b, 2)$ $(c, 2)(d, 4)(e, 2)(f, 5)$. Then $2 = \min \{3, 2, 4, 5\}$ so that at time $t_i + 2$, customers b, c, and e are scheduled to leave the SHOP · AREA and join the LINE. There are $3! = 6$ possible permutations in which they can join the LINE; bce is one possibility. According to the FIFO queue discipline, the new LINE would become $y_1 y_2, \ldots, y_m bce$. The rules must specify which permutation to select, based on the state variables of the model.

For example, one selection rule[†] is: join the LINE in the same order as on the TIME · LEFT · LIST. This would result in the order bce in our example. Specifying the reverse order to that on the TIME · LEFT · LIST would also work with the state variables available. On the other hand, a selection rule based on the size of the customer's grocery order would not be possible with the present set of state variables; to employ such a rule would require enlarging the state variable set.

Exercise. How would a "choose at random" rule be defined?

Using the first selection rule mentioned, we can describe the state s' achieved just after the SHOP · AREA event as

$$
s' = (r_1, \overline{(x_1, \tau_1 - \tau^*)}, y_1, \quad r_2, \sigma - \tau^*) \\
\overline{(x_2, \tau_2 - \tau^*)}, y_2 \\
\vdots \qquad \vdots \\
\overline{(x_n, \tau_n - \tau^*)} \quad y_m \\
\overline{\overline{(x_1, \tau_1 - \tau^*)}} \\
\overline{\overline{(x_2, \tau_2 - \tau^*)}} \\
\vdots \\
\overline{\overline{(x_n, \tau_n - \tau^*)}}
$$

where $\tau^* = \min \{\tau_1, \tau_2, \ldots, \tau_n\}$ and the following table defines the bar ($^-$) and double bar ($^=$) functions:

	$\overline{(x_i, e)}$	$\overline{\overline{(x_i, e)}}$
If $e > 0$	(x_i, e)	Λ
If $e = 0$	Λ	x_i

[†] This rule is employed by the GPSS simulator when no priority is specified.

We are using the property of the empty list that $x\Lambda = \Lambda x = x$. For example, $(a, \overline{3-2})(b, \overline{2-2})(c, \overline{2-2})(\overline{d, 4-2})(e, \overline{2-2})(\overline{f, 5-2}) = (a, 1)\Lambda\Lambda(d, 2)\Lambda(f, 3) = (a, 1)(d, 2)(f, 3)$; and $(\overline{a, 3-2})(\overline{b, 2-2})(\overline{c, 2-2})$ $(\overline{d, 4-2})(e, \overline{2-2})(\overline{f, 5-2}) = \Lambda bc\Lambda e\Lambda = bce$.

Finally consider Case 2, involving a simultaneous scheduling of a SHOP · AREA event and a CHECKOUT event. There are two approaches to specifying the results of such a compound event:

Approach 1.   Specify the state s' achieved after the compound event directly. In our example we would have $\tau^* = \min \{\tau_1, \ldots, \tau_n\} = \sigma$ and

$$
\begin{aligned}
s' = (r_1, &(\overline{x_1, \tau_1 - \tau^*}), y_2, \quad r_2', \sigma') \\
&(\overline{x_2, \tau_2 - \tau^*}), y_3 \\
&\quad \vdots \qquad\qquad \vdots \\
&(\overline{x_n, \tau_n - \tau^*}), y_m \\
&\qquad\qquad\quad \overline{(x_1, \tau_1 - \tau^*)} \\
&\qquad\qquad\quad \overline{(x_2, \tau_2 - \tau^*)} \\
&\qquad\qquad\quad\quad \vdots \\
&\qquad\qquad\quad \overline{(x_n, \tau_n - \tau^*)}
\end{aligned}
$$

$$
r_2' = \begin{cases} \Gamma(r_2) & \text{if} \quad m \geq 2 \\ r_2 & \text{otherwise} \end{cases}
$$

$$
\sigma' = \begin{cases} \text{SERVICE} \cdot \text{TIME}(r_2) & \text{if} \quad m \geq 2 \\ \infty & \text{otherwise} \end{cases}
$$

Approach 2.   Specify tie-breaking rules that select a unique event to occur from those *imminent* (next scheduled to occur). In our example, when both a SHOP · AREA event and a CHECKOUT event are imminent, we might specify that a CHECKOUT event will in fact occur. Use of the transition rules given in Cases 1 and 3, now completely determines the resultant state s'. This can be seen as follows. Starting with

$$
\begin{aligned}
s = (r_1, &(x_1, \tau_1), y_1, r_2, \sigma) \\
&(x_2, \tau_2), y_2 \\
&\quad \vdots \qquad \vdots \\
&(x_n, \tau_n) \; y_m
\end{aligned}
$$

with the situation $\tau^* = \sigma = \min \{\tau_1, \ldots, \tau_n\}$ so that CHECKOUT and SHOP · AREA events are both imminent, the tie-breaking rule orders us to carry out the CHECKOUT transition (Case 1) to get

$$s^{(1)} = (r_1, (x_1, \tau_1 - \sigma), y_2, r_2', \sigma_2')$$
$$(x_2, \tau_2 - \sigma) \ y_3$$
$$\vdots \qquad \vdots$$
$$(x_n, \tau_n - \sigma) \ y_m$$

where r_2' and σ_2' are as defined earlier.

This transition is scheduled for time $t_{i+1} = t_i + \tau^*$ as before. *But* it is not *the final transition* that will occur at t_{i+1}. For now note that min $\{\tau_1 - \sigma, \tau_2 - \sigma, \ldots, \tau_n - \sigma, \sigma_2'\} = 0$, since at least one $\tau_i = \sigma$. Moreover, since we have restricted the range of SERVICE $\cdot$ TIME to positive values or ∞, the next imminent event must now be a SHOP $\cdot$ AREA event.[†] Thus the next hatching time is

$$t_{i+2} = t_{i+1} + 0 = t_{i+1}$$

and carrying out the SHOP $\cdot$ AREA transition (Case 3) from $s^{(1)}$ we obtain

$$s^{(2)} = (r_1, \overline{(x_1, \tau_1 - \sigma - 0)}, y_2, \quad r_2', \sigma_2' - 0)$$
$$(x_2, \tau_2 - \sigma - 0) \ y_3$$
$$\vdots \qquad \vdots$$
$$y_m$$
$$(x_n, \tau_n - \sigma - 0) \ \overline{(x_1, \tau_1 - \sigma - 0)}$$
$$\vdots$$
$$\overline{\overline{(x_n, \tau_n - \sigma - 0)}}$$

By inspection we see that $s^{(2)}$ of Approach 2 is the same as s' of Approach 1.

Current discrete event simulation languages provide means for specifying tie-breaking rules and, without apparent exception, force the programmer to use them. Approach 2 is thus the dominant mode of handling simultaneous events. This is natural in view of the necessity for converting multiple simultaneous actions into a sequence of individual actions, which is the theme of digital simulation we introduced in Chapter 4. Approach 2 has the advantage of simplicity in that only individual events need be defined and the tie-breaking rules automatically sequence the simulator. But Approach 2 is not always the most natural and appropriate one to use from the model standpoint. Approach 1 enables us to specify a *global* state transition that may not be built up by a series of independent actions of components. Our structured discrete time model (Chapter 4) is an alternate way of specifying such a transition. Discrete event languages do not readily accept global state transition specifications of this type (although such a

---

[†] Allowing zero could get the model into an infinite loop. This is discussed in Chapter 9.

capability usually can be built in, ad hoc). This is another area calling for more research. In what follows, we remain with the traditional Approach 2.

6.5   SPECIFYING THE EFFECT OF INPUT VARIABLES

We have been treating the grocery store in the autonomous mode (as if the ENTRANCE were shut and there were no arriving customers). The same specification will continue to hold *between* customer arrivals even when the ENTRANCE is open. For example, in Figure 3, if we know the state of the model just after customer *a* enters, by applying the transition rules for the autonomous case we can compute the model's behavior until customer *b* arrives. This will tell us the state obtaining just before *b* arrives, and now all we need specify is the effect that *b*'s arrival has on the state. This will give us the state obtaining just after *b*'s arrival, and we can then apply the autonomous rules until *c* arrives, and so on.

According to the informal component interaction, when a customer arrives he immediately samples SHOPPING · TIME and joins the TIME · LEFT · LIST. This accounts for part of the new state obtaining just after his arrival; the other part relates to the values of the countdown clock variables.

Suppose that at time t_i the state of the model is

$$s = (r_1, (x_1, \tau_1), y_1, r_2, \sigma)$$
$$\begin{matrix} \vdots & y_2 \\ (x_n, \tau_n) & \vdots \\ & y_m \end{matrix}$$

Then the next *internal* event is scheduled to occur at $t_i + \min \{\sigma, \tau_1, \ldots, \tau_n\}$. If no *external* events (a customer arrival) occur in the interim, that is, in the interval $[t_i, t_i + \min \{\sigma, \tau_1, \ldots, \tau_n\}]$, the autonomous rules will determine the behavior in this period. However, suppose that at some time in this period $t_i + e$ (where $0 \le e < \min \{\sigma, \tau_1, \ldots, \tau_n\}$), customer *x* arrives (HELLO is ϕ until $t_i + e$ and then becomes *x* instantaneously). Then the state just after *x*'s arrival is

$$s' = (\Gamma(r_1), (x_1, \tau_1 - e), \qquad\qquad y_1, r_2, \sigma - e)$$
$$\begin{matrix} \vdots & y_2 \\ (x_n, \tau_n - e) & \vdots \\ (x, \text{SHOPPING} \cdot \text{TIME}(r_1)) & y_m \end{matrix}$$

Note that we have placed $(x, \text{SHOPPING} \cdot \text{TIME}(r_1))$ at the tail of the TIME · LEFT · LIST. This represents another situation of choice from a number of possibilities. The choice, which forces customers to appear on the list in the order of their arrival in the SHOP $\cdot$ AREA, could play a role in the model if the LIST order is used as a basis for determining the order in which simultaneously emerging customers will join the LINE (Section 6.4).

6.6   ABSTRACT DISCRETE EVENT SYSTEM SPECIFICATION

In Chapter 3 we obtain an abstract system specification from an informally described discrete time model. We can do the same in the discrete event case. Instead of the sequential machine we now obtain a similar object called a *discrete event system specification* (DEVS).

Suppose we have a well-described discrete event model with input variables $\alpha_1, \alpha_2, \ldots, \alpha_n$, state variables $\beta_1, \beta_2, \ldots, \beta_m$, and output variables $\gamma_1, \gamma_2, \ldots, \gamma_n$. Forming the cross products of the ranges of the input, state, and output variables, we obtain the INPUTS, STATES, and OUTPUTS sets, respectively.

A subset of the state variables consists, as we have seen, of countdown clock variables. Let $\sigma_1, \sigma_2, \ldots, \sigma_c$ be the list of values of the clock variables at model time t_i. Then the next hatching time is $t_i + \min \{\sigma_i | \sigma_i \geq 0\}$.[†] In abstract terms, this means we can associate with every STATE a quantity specifying the *incremental time to the next hatching time*. Let t: STATES $\rightarrow R^+_{0,\infty}$ denote this function, called the *time advance function*. Thus if the model is in STATE s at time t_i, it will remain in s until $t_i + t(s)$ where $t(s) = \min \{\sigma_i | \sigma_i \geq 0\}$.

The transition function consists of two parts: one describing the model's state transitions in the absence of external events, and one for the case of an external event occurring.

For the first part, we have a function δ_ϕ: STATES $\rightarrow$ STATES (the ϕ represents the nonexternal event condition). The interpretation is that if the model has just entered a STATE s at time t, at time $t + t(s)$ it will enter state $\delta_\phi(s)$ if no external events occur in the interim $[t, t + t(s)]$. Recall the interpretation that the piecewise constant variables remain constant in this period while the clock variables count down linearly.

For the second part we have a function δ_{ex}: $Q \times$ INPUTS $\rightarrow$ STATES. Here Q is the set of all pairs of the form (s, e), where s is a STATE and e is a real number between (and including) zero and $t(s)$. The pair (s, e) represents the condition of e time units having elapsed since the model entered state s. Since a transition dictated by $\delta_\phi(s)$ will take place when time $t(s)$ has elapsed, the elapsed time e must lie in $[0, t(s)]$ as required. The interpretation is that if the model is in STATE s at time t, and if an INPUT x arrives at time

---

[†] The meaning of a negative σ_i is clarified in Chapter 7.

$t + e$, then the STATE just after the external event will be $\delta_{ex}(s, e, x)$. It is presumed that no external events have occurred in the interim $[t, t + e]$.

Finally, we have an output function $\lambda: Q \to$ OUTPUTS with the same interpretation as the discrete time case.

The 6-tuple $\langle$INPUTS, STATES, OUTPUTS, δ, λ, $t\rangle$ (where δ consists of the parts δ_ϕ and δ_{ex}) constitutes the DEVS, or abstract specification for discrete event systems. The formal development is continued in Chapter 9.

Exercise. Using the development of the last section, specify the objects of a DEVS for the grocery store model. Check your answer with that given in Section 8.1.

6.7 SOURCES

The formal approach to discrete event model description developed here is based on the informal approach taken by Tocher.[1] Probabilistic models are discussed in Reference 2.

1. K. D. Tocher, *The Art of Simulation.* Van Nostrand, Princeton, N.J., 1963.
2. H. Maisel and G. Gnugnoli, *Simulation of Discrete Stochastic Systems.* Scientific Research Associates, Chicago, 1972.
3. P. Billingsley, *Ergodic Theory and Information.* Wiley, New York, 1965.

PROBLEMS

1. Provide a DEVS formalization of the model of Example 5, Chapter 1, and of the examples in Section 2.7.2.

2. Consider a random number generator to have an input variable with range $\{0, 1\}$, where a 1 occurring at any time causes an immediate state transition to a new state (determined uniquely by the previous state) and 0 means no such external event is occurring. Formalize the generator as a DEVS.

3. An *ergodic* system is a structure $(S, \mathscr{F}, P, \tau)$, where S is a set of states, $\mathscr{F}$ a σ-algebra over S, P a probability function on $\mathscr{F}$, and $\tau: S \to S$ is a transition function with the following properties:

    (a) $\tau(A) = A \to P(A) = 0$ or   1
    (b) $P(\tau^{-1}(A)) = P(A)$ for all $A \in \mathscr{F}$

    Property a asserts that the only sets closed under τ are those measure equivalent to the empty set or the whole space S. Property b asserts that τ is measure preserving. Ergodic systems are discussed by Billingsley.[3]

A random generator can be formulated as an ergodic system with $S = [0, 1]$, $\mathscr{F} = $ the σ-algebra generated by the subintervals of $[0, 1]$, P the uniform distribution on $[0, 1]$, and $\tau = \Gamma$, the transition function.

Let $([0, 1], \mathscr{F}, P, \Gamma)$ be an ergodic system and Y be a standard random variable. The combination of Figure 4 can be regarded as a sequential machine with transition function Γ and output function Y. Let $y_0 y_1 \cdots y_n$ be an output sequence of this machine. The probability that $y_{n+1} = y$ is given by $P(\Gamma(S_n) \cap Y^{-1}(y))$, where $S_n = \{r_n | r_0 r_1 \cdots r_n$ is a state sequence for which $Y(r_0) Y(r_1) \cdots Y(r_n) = y_0 y_1 \cdots y_n\}$.

We say that Γ *is ideal for* Y if for every output sequence $y_0 y_1 \cdots y_n$, $P(\Gamma(S_n) \cap Y^{-1}(y)) = P(Y^{-1}(y))$.

(a) Show that the rule $\Gamma(x) = ax \bmod 1$ satisfies the ergodic properties.

(b) Show that given any standard random variable Y with a discrete finite distribution, there is a rule $\Gamma(x) = ax \bmod 1$ which is ideal for Y.

Chapter Seven

Discrete Event
Simulation Strategies
and Models

We gave in the preceding chapter an abstract specification for discrete event models. Just as in the discrete time case (Chapter 4), we usually deal with models built up from interconnection of components. So we are not given the abstract specification explicitly but must construct it from a specification of the components and their interactions. Such a specification is called a *structured model*. As in the discrete time case, structured models fall into different classes depending on the kinds of restrictions placed on their construction. In the discrete event case, these restrictions arise from the simulation strategies employed by simulation languages. There are three common types—the event scheduling, activity scanning, and process interaction (a combination of the first two) strategies. Each strategy, and language employing it, implicitly embodies a "world view." The world view of a strategy makes certain forms of model description more naturally expressible and efficiently processable than others. It seems to be true also that in their "pure" forms some of these strategies are not universal (i.e., able to simulate every discrete event model). Although there are some studies of the relative efficiencies of simulation strategies, there has been very little analysis of basic limitations; thus the universality of the strategies appears to be an open question.

In this chapter we consider three forms of structured model specification appropriate to the simulation strategies just mentioned, describing each strategy and showing how it can validly simulate a model specified in the appropriate form. Again, for simplicity's sake, we treat only the autonomous model cases.

We present the "pure" forms of these strategies, that is, the forms in which only the features inherent to the basic conception are employed. We can identify the pure form as the first historically attempted strategy of its type. As experience has accumulated and limitations have been perceived, language designers have naturally tended to incorporate features of other strategies. As a result, the lines are blurred between the more recent forms of different strategically based languages. We briefly analyze some of the most common languages—SIMSCRIPT, SIMULA, GPSS—from the perspective we have developed.

7.1   EVENT ORIENTED MODEL SPECIFICATIONS

The event oriented strategy emphasizes *the prescheduling of all events*. In the pure form, this means that no provision is made for activating a state change by tests on the global model state; if a state change is to occur, it must occur by explicit scheduling. The structured description for models naturally associated with such a strategy appears as follows.

7.1.1   Structured Event Oriented Model

Components

    A set $D = \{\alpha_1, \alpha_2, \ldots, \alpha_n\}$ divided into ACTIVE and PASSIVE types. The ACTIVE types are denoted by $\{\alpha_1, \ldots, \alpha_A\}$ and the PASSIVE types by $\{\alpha_{A+1}, \ldots, \alpha_n\}$.

Descriptive Variables

    For each ACTIVE component, $\alpha \in D$

        STATE $\cdot$ OF $\cdot$ α—with range S_α (a set) and typical value s_α.

        $\alpha \cdot$ TIME $\cdot$ LEFT $\cdot$ IN $\cdot$ STATE—with range $R_\alpha = R_{0,\infty}^+$ (the nonnegative reals numbers with ∞) and typical value σ_α.

    For each PASSIVE component $\alpha \in D$

        STATE $\cdot$ OF $\cdot$ α—with range S_α and typical value s_α.

    PARAMETERS

        For each ACTIVE $\alpha \in D$: INFLUENCEES $\cdot$ OF $\cdot$ α—a subset of D with typical value $\{\beta_1, \beta_2, \ldots, \beta_m\}$ (α is usually included as one of the β_i's).

A function SELECT that given a nonempty subset of ACTIVE type components, selects a member from it. (SELECT incorporates the tie-breaking rules required by Approach 2, Section 6.4.)

Component Interaction

For each ACTIVE component $\alpha \in D$, a local transition function δ_α is specified which maps the set of state assignments of the INFLUENCEES $\cdot$ OF $\cdot \alpha$ into itself. The interpretation is as follows: suppose α is selected by SELECT as the next component at which an event is to occur. Let $((\mathit{s}_{\beta_1}, \sigma_{\beta_1}),$ $(\mathit{s}_{\beta_2}, \sigma_{\beta_2}), \ldots, (\mathit{s}_{\beta_A}, \sigma_{\beta_A}), \mathit{s}_{\beta_{A+1}}, \ldots, \mathit{s}_{\beta_m})$ be the list of descriptive values of the INFLUENCEES $\cdot$ OF $\cdot \alpha$ just before α is to become active, then $((\mathit{s}'_{\beta_1}, \sigma'_{\beta_1}), (\mathit{s}'_{\beta_2}, \sigma'_{\beta_2}), \ldots, \mathit{s}'_{\beta_m}) = \delta_\alpha((\mathit{s}_{\beta_1}, \sigma_{\beta_1}), \ldots, \mathit{s}_{\beta_m})$ is the list of descriptive values of the INFLUENCEES $\cdot$ OF $\cdot \alpha$ pertaining just after the event at α has occurred.

Note that in contrast to the discrete time model structure specification, the set of components influenced by an ACTIVE type α (INFLUENCEES $\cdot$ OF $\cdot \alpha$) and its effect on them (δ_α) is specified in the discrete event case. Thus rather than viewing each component as *passive* (being acted on by its neighbors), we regard each ACTIVE type component as capable of *acting* on its neighbors. The PASSIVE type components, however, can never undertake such action— if a state change occurs at a PASSIVE component, it is caused by the activity of some ACTIVE component of which it is an INFLUENCEE. Examples of PASSIVE types are memory registers and queues, which will retain their states indefinitely unless acted on externally. In GPSS (see Section 7.8), the transactions can be viewed as the ACTIVE components while the equipment (facilities, storages, save values locations, logic switches) are all PASSIVE type. (Often in model descriptions, PASSIVE type elements serve as "owned" subcomponents for ACTIVE components.)

7.1.2 Event Oriented DEVS[†]

Given a structured model description, we can associate with it a DEVS as follows. The set of STATES is the cross product of the ACTIVE range sets (typically of the form $S_\alpha \times R_\alpha$) and the PASSIVE range sets (typically of the form S_α). A typical STATE

$$s = ((\mathit{s}_{\alpha_1}, \sigma_{\alpha_1}), (\mathit{s}_{\alpha_2}, \sigma_{\alpha_2}), \ldots, (\mathit{s}_{\alpha_A}, \sigma_{\alpha_A}), \mathit{s}_{\alpha_{A+1}}, \ldots, \mathit{s}_{\alpha_n})$$

where $\alpha_1, \alpha_2, \ldots, \alpha_A$ are the ACTIVE types and $\alpha_{A+1}, \ldots, \alpha_n$ are the PASSIVE types. The time advance function t: STATES $\to R_{0,\infty}^+$ is defined by

$$t((\mathit{s}_{\alpha_1}, \sigma_{\alpha_1}), \ldots, (\mathit{s}_{\alpha_A}, \sigma_{\alpha_A}), \mathit{s}_{\alpha_{A+1}}, \ldots, \mathit{s}_{\alpha_n}) = \min \{\sigma_{\alpha_i} | i = 1, \ldots, A\}$$

(In the event oriented case each $\sigma_{\alpha_i} \geq 0$.)

Only the autonomous part of the transition function has been specified and this is defined as follows: δ_ϕ : STATES $\to$ STATES

[†] This section may be omitted in an introductory course.

Let $\text{IMMINENT}(s) = \{\alpha \mid \sigma_\alpha = t(s)\}$, where $\text{IMMINENT}(s)$ is the subset of ACTIVE type components scheduled to change state at the next event time [if t is the current time, $t + t(s)$ is the next event time; if $t(s) = 0$, because one or more of the $\sigma_{\alpha_i} = 0$, the clock is not advanced].

Applying the SELECT function yields a unique component among those vying to become active next; let this be called $\bar{\alpha}(s)$, that is,

$$\bar{\alpha}(s) = \text{SELECT}(\text{IMMINENT}(s))$$

(Clearly $\bar{\alpha}(s)$ is one of the ACTIVE types.) The state $s' = \delta_\phi(s)$ pertaining just after the event at $\bar{\alpha}(s)$ has occurred is given by letting

$$\delta_{\bar{\alpha}(s)}((\Delta_{\beta_1}, \sigma_{\beta_1}), \ldots, (\Delta_{\beta_A}, \sigma_{\beta_A}), \Delta_{\beta_{A+1}}, \ldots, \Delta_{\beta_m})$$
$$= ((\Delta''_{\beta_1}, \sigma''_{\beta_1}), \ldots, (\Delta''_{\beta_A}, \sigma''_{\beta_A}), \Delta''_{\beta_{A+1}}, \ldots, \Delta''_{\beta_m})$$

where $\beta_1, \ldots, \beta_A$ are the ACTIVE $\cdot$ INFLUENCEES $\cdot$ OF $\cdot$ $\bar{\alpha}(s)$, and $\beta_{A+1}, \ldots, \beta_m$ are the PASSIVE $\cdot$ INFLUENCEES $\cdot$ OF $\cdot$ $\bar{\alpha}(s)$. Then $s' = ((\Delta'_{\alpha_1}, \sigma'_{\alpha_1}), \ldots, (\Delta'_{\alpha_A}, \sigma'_{\alpha_A}), \Delta'_{\alpha_{A+1}}, \ldots, \Delta'_{\alpha_n})$ is given by its value for ACTIVE types:

$$(\Delta'_\beta, \sigma'_\beta) = \begin{cases} (\Delta''_\beta, \sigma''_\beta) & \text{if } \beta \in \text{ACTIVE} \cdot \text{INFLUENCEES} \cdot \text{OF} \cdot \bar{\alpha}(s) \quad (1) \\ (\Delta_\beta, \sigma_\beta - t(s)) & \text{otherwise} \quad\quad\quad\quad\quad\quad\quad\quad\quad\quad\quad\quad (2) \end{cases}$$

and for PASSIVE types

$$\Delta'_\beta = \begin{cases} \Delta''_\beta & \text{if } \beta \in \text{PASSIVE} \cdot \text{INFLUENCESS} \cdot \text{OF} \cdot \bar{\alpha}(s) \\ \Delta_\beta & \text{otherwise} \end{cases}$$

Exercise. Explain how line 2) implements the conception of the TIME $\cdot$ LEFT $\cdot$ IN $\cdot$ STATE variables as the output of a countdown clock. Line 1) allows $\bar{\alpha}(s)$ to act on the clock of an INFLUENCEE β. Explain how the following interpretations arise:

$$\sigma''_\beta = \begin{cases} 0 & \text{activate } \beta \text{ immediately} \\ \infty & \text{passivate (make passive or cancel) } \beta \end{cases}$$

$$\sigma''_\beta \neq \sigma_\beta - t(s) \quad \text{and} \quad \begin{array}{ll} \sigma_\beta = \infty & \text{schedule } \beta \\ \sigma_\beta < \infty & \text{reschedule } \beta \end{array}$$

7.2 COMMENTS ON THE "SELECT" FUNCTION

The SELECT function must select from each nonempty set of ACTIVE type components a member of that set. If there are N ACTIVE types, there are $2^N - 1$ nonempty subsets; thus the complexity required to specify the SELECT function may grow rapidly. Ordinarily, a very simple solution to the problem is employed. The ACTIVE types are assigned a unique *priority level*. Given a subset, SELECT chooses the element with highest priority in the subset. Sometimes the priority level is not specified directly but is built up from a number of partial priority orderings, which individually do not assign unique levels to the elements. *Lexicographical ordering*, the process of combining these orderings is exemplified by the listing of words in a dictionary. Of two words having different first letters, the one nearest the beginning of the alphabet comes first. If two words have the same first letter, the decision is based on the first succeeding position in which the words differ. Here the ordering of the alphabet $a, b, c, \ldots, z$ serves as a priority order for words that differ in the first position. It also serves as a priority order for words that agree in the first position but disagree in the second position, and so on.

The following example illustrates such a lexicographical definition for SELECT.

Exercise. Define a SELECT function for the set $\{\alpha, \beta, \gamma\}$ which is not determined by any unique priority assignment.

7.3 COMPUTER–USER MODEL

We now describe a model of computer-user interaction. The model is first expressed in event oriented form. Later it is rephrased to conform to the other strategies considered.

Informal Description

Components
  Active types: USER1, . . . , USER99, COMPUTER, CLERK
  Passive types: USER · QUEUE, BATCH · QUEUE
Descriptive Variables
  Describing USERi $(i = 1, \ldots, 99)$
    STATE · OF · USERi—with range $\{0, 1, 2\}$ $(\measuredangle_i)$.
    i · TIME · LEFT · IN · STATE—with range $R_{0,\,\infty}^{+}$ (σ_i).
    WRITE · TIME—an rv determined by TYPE of USERi.
    WAIT · TIME—an rv determined by TYPE of USERi.
  Describing COMPUTER
    STATE · OF · CPU—with range $\{0, 1\}$ $(\measuredangle_{\mathrm{CPU}})$.
    CPU · TIME · LEFT—with range $R_{0,\,\infty}^{+}$ (σ_{CPU}).
  Describing CLERK
    TIME · LEFT · TO · NEXT · BATCH · RELEASE—with range $R_{0,\,\infty}^{+}$ (σ_{CL}).
  Describing USER · QUEUE
    Q-LINE—with range $\{0, 1, \ldots, 0, 99\}^{*}$ $(\measuredangle_{\mathrm{UQ}})$.

Describing BATCH · QUEUE

B-LINE—with range the subsets of $\{0, 1, \ldots, 99\}$ ($\mathcal{A}_{BQ}$).

PARAMETER

TYPE—a function that classifies USERS.

Component Interaction

USER*i*

   0. Writes (debugs) a program, takes time WRITE · TIME.

   1. Submits program called *i*, which waits in USER · QUEUE until processed by COMPUTER with service time WAIT · TIME.

   2. Waits in BATCH · QUEUE until released by CLERK, then goes to step 0.

COMPUTER

Receives a USER program; if CPU is free (state 0), processes the program and puts it in BATCH · QUEUE; if CPU is busy (state 1), puts program at end of USER · QUEUE; if CPU is free and USER · QUEUE is empty, it checks every 0.1 minute to see whether a USER program has arrived.

CLERK

Every 8 hours takes all programs out of BATCH · QUEUE and gives them to USERS at the same time.

TIE–BREAKING RULES

CPU first, then USER by low user number, then CLERK.

The time unit is taken to be 1 minute.

The structured specification is given by the following.

1. *Tie-breaking rules*

For any nonempty subset $D' \subseteq D$

$$\mathrm{SELECT}(D') = \begin{cases} \mathrm{CPU} & \text{if}\;\; \mathrm{CPU} \in D' \\ i & \text{if}\;\; \mathrm{CPU} \notin D' \text{ and } i = \min\{j | j \in D'\} \\ \mathrm{CL} & \text{otherwise} \end{cases}$$

2. *Influencees*

We use the following INFLUENCEES:

THE INFLUENCEES · OF · USER*i* are USER · QUEUE, BATCH · QUEUE, and USER*i* himself.

The INFLUENCEES · OF · COMPUTER are all the users USER1,..., USER99, the USER · QUEUE, and the COMPUTER itself.

The INFLUENCEES · OF · CLERK are the users USER1, ..., USER99, BATCH · QUEUE, and the CLERK himself.

The corresponding influence diagram appears in Figure 1.

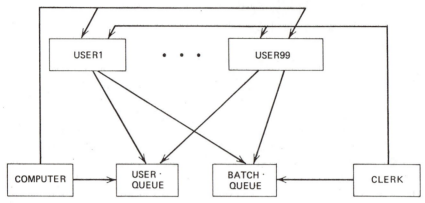

Figure 1 The COMPUTER–USER influence diagram.

3. *Local transition functions*

As state variables we have chosen the following:

For each USERi:STATE $\cdot$ OF $\cdot$ USERi; $i \cdot$ TIME $\cdot$ LEFT $\cdot$ IN $\cdot$ STATE; WRITE $\cdot$ TIME $\cdot$ SEED; WAIT $\cdot$ TIME $\cdot$ SEED with typical value assignment $(s_i, \sigma_i, r_{i,1}, r_{i,2})$.

For COMPUTER: STATE $\cdot$ OF $\cdot$ CPU; CPU $\cdot$ TIME $\cdot$ LEFT with typical value assignment (s_{CPU}, σ_{CPU}).

For CLERK: TIME $\cdot$ LEFT $\cdot$ TO $\cdot$ NEXT $\cdot$ BATCH $\cdot$ RELEASE with typical value σ_{CL}.

For USER $\cdot$ QUEUE: Q-LINE with typical value s_{UQ}.

For BATCH $\cdot$ QUEUE: B-LINE with typical value s_{BQ}.

For the local transition function of USERi, $i = 1, \ldots, 99$, we have

$$\delta_i(s_i, \sigma_i, r_{i,1}, r_{i,2}, s_{UQ}, s_{BQ}) = (s_i', \sigma_i', r_{i,1}', r_{i,2}', s_{UQ}', s_{BQ}')$$

where $\quad s_i' = (s_i + 1) \bmod 3$

$$\sigma_i' = \begin{cases} \text{WRITE} \cdot \text{TIME}(\text{TYPE}(i), r_{i,1}) & \text{if } s_i = 0 \\ \infty & \text{otherwise} \end{cases}$$

$$r_{i,1}' = \Gamma(r_{i,1})$$

$$r_{i,2}' = r_{i,2}$$

$$s_{UQ}' = \begin{cases} s_{UQ}i & \text{if } s_i = 1 \\ s_{UQ} & \text{otherwise} \end{cases}$$

$$s_{BQ}' = \begin{cases} s_{BQ} \cup \{i\} & \text{if } s_i = 2 \\ s_{BQ} & \text{otherwise} \end{cases}$$

Note that WRITE $\cdot$ TIME is a function of the output of its random number generator WRITE · TIME · SEED as well as the TYPE assigned to USERi.

The transition function for COMPUTER is given by

$$\delta_C(\measuredangle_1, \sigma_1, r_{1,1}, r_{1,2}, \ldots, \measuredangle_{99}, \sigma_{99}, r_{99,1}, r_{99,2}, \measuredangle_{CPU}, \sigma_{CPU}, \measuredangle_{UQ})$$
$$= (\measuredangle'_1, \sigma'_1, r'_{1,1}, r'_{1,2}, \ldots, r'_{99,2}, \measuredangle'_{CPU}, \sigma'_{CPU}, \measuredangle'_{UQ})$$

where $\qquad \measuredangle'_i = \measuredangle_i \qquad$ for $\quad i = 1, \ldots, 99$

$$\sigma'_i = \begin{cases} 0 & \text{if } i = \text{top}(\measuredangle_{UQ}) \quad \text{and} \quad \measuredangle_{CPU} = 1 \\ \sigma_i - t(s) & \text{otherwise} \end{cases}$$

$$\measuredangle'_{CPU} = \begin{cases} 1 & \text{if } \measuredangle_{CPU} = 0 \quad \text{and} \quad \measuredangle_{UQ} \neq \Lambda \\ 0 & \text{otherwise} \end{cases}$$

$$\sigma'_{CPU} = \begin{cases} 0.1 & \text{if } \measuredangle_{CPU} = 0 \quad \text{and} \quad \measuredangle_{UQ} = \Lambda \\ \text{WAIT} \cdot \text{TIME(TYPE(top}(\measuredangle_{UQ})), r_{\text{top}(\measuredangle_{UQ}),2}) \\ \qquad \text{if } \measuredangle_{CPU} = 0 \quad \text{and} \quad \measuredangle_{UQ} \neq \Lambda \\ 0 & \text{otherwise} \end{cases}$$

$$\measuredangle'_{UQ} = \begin{cases} \text{rest}(\measuredangle_{UQ}) & \text{if } \measuredangle_{CPU} = 1 \\ \measuredangle_{UQ} & \text{otherwise} \end{cases}$$

$$r'_{i,1} = r_{i,1} \qquad \text{for} \quad i = 1, \ldots, 99$$

$$r'_{i,2} = \begin{cases} \Gamma(r_{i,2}) & \text{if } i = \text{top}(\measuredangle_{UQ}) \quad \text{and} \quad \measuredangle_{CPU} = 0 \\ r_{i,2} & \text{otherwise} \end{cases}$$

We have employed the string operations *top* and *rest* defined by top $(a_1 a_2 \cdots a_n) = a_1$ and rest $(a_1 a_2 \cdots a_n) = a_2 \cdots a_n$.

Exercise.   Write the local transition function for CLERK.

7.4 EVENT SCHEDULING SIMULATION STRATEGY

In a prototypical procedure for event-driven simulation appropriate to the model structure presented in Section 7.1, we assume that the state sets of all the ACTIVE type components are finite. Thus for a typical α we can rename the state set as $S_\alpha = \{0, 1, \ldots, m - 1\}$, where α has m states. The transition function δ_α splits into m functions $\{\delta^i_\alpha\}$, each describing the activity of component α if it is started in one of its states i. In event-based simulation, each of the δ^i_α is coded separately as a program or routine, and these routines are scheduled and executed by the simulator. Formally, the function δ^i_α is obtained by fixing the STATE · OF · α argument of δ_α at i and allowing the other variables to go free; that is,

$$\delta^i_\alpha(\sigma_\alpha, \ldots) = \delta_\alpha((i, \sigma_\alpha), \ldots)$$

For example, in the user-computer model, the STATE $\cdot$ OF $\cdot$ COMPUTER has range $\{0, 1\}$. There are thus two functions δ_C^0 and δ_C^1.

Exercise. Using the definition for δ_C given in Section 7.3, define δ_C^0 and δ_C^1.

In the simulation procedure, we call the routine coding δ_α^i, the "EVENT $\cdot$ $i \cdot$ OF $\cdot \alpha$".[†] For comparison, we can consider a SIMSCRIPT[1] simulation program of the user-computer model. The implementations of EVENT $\cdot$ 0 $\cdot$ OF $\cdot$ COMPUTER and EVENT $\cdot$ 1 $\cdot$ OF $\cdot$ COMPUTER (Figure 2) can be compared with their logical versions just defined.

EVENT 0 $\cdot$ OF $\cdot$ COMPUTER $\cdot$ <u>SAVING</u> <u>THE</u> <u>EVENT</u> <u>NOTICE</u>

<u>IF</u> USER $\cdot$ QUEUE <u>IS</u> <u>EMPTY</u>
  <u>SCHEDULE</u> <u>THE</u> <u>ABOVE</u> 0 $\cdot$ OF $\cdot$ COMPUTER <u>IN</u> <u>TIME</u> $\cdot$ V + 0.1 <u>MINUTE</u>
  <u>RETURN</u>
<u>OTHERWISE</u>
  <u>CREATE</u> 1 $\cdot$ OF $\cdot$ COMPUTER
  <u>SCHEDULE</u> <u>THIS</u> 1 $\cdot$ OF $\cdot$ COMPUTER <u>IN</u> <u>TIME</u> $\cdot$ V + <u>EXPONENTIAL</u> $\cdot$ F (WAIT $\cdot$
    TIME (TYPE (<u>F</u> $\cdot$ USER $\cdot$ QUEUE), 2) <u>MINUTES</u>
  <u>DESTROY</u> <u>THE</u> <u>ABOVE</u> 0 $\cdot$ OF $\cdot$ COMPUTER
  <u>RETURN</u>
  <u>END</u>

EVENT 1 $\cdot$ OF $\cdot$ COMPUTER

<u>REMOVE</u> <u>THE</u> <u>FIRST</u> 2 $\cdot$ OF $\cdot$ USER <u>FROM</u> <u>THE</u> USER $\cdot$ QUEUE
<u>SCHEDULE</u> 2 $\cdot$ OF $\cdot$ USER <u>IN</u> <u>TIME</u> $\cdot$ V <u>MINUTES</u>
<u>CREATE</u> 0 $\cdot$ OF $\cdot$ COMPUTER
<u>SCHEDULE</u> <u>THIS</u> 0 $\cdot$ OF $\cdot$ COMPUTER <u>IN</u> <u>TIME</u> $\cdot$ V <u>MINUTES</u>
<u>RETURN</u>
<u>END</u>

Figure 2 SIMSCRIPT routines implementing the COMPUTER local transition function.

7.4.1   Next Event Simulation Prototype

As usual the next event procedure employs variables $\bar{S}_{\alpha_1}, \bar{S}_{\alpha_2}, \ldots, \bar{S}_{\alpha_n}$ for holding the present states of the components $\alpha_1, \alpha_2, \ldots, \alpha_n$ of the model, and a CLOCK to schedule the activity. It employs a NEXT $\cdot$ EVENTS $\cdot$

[†] We proceed as if "EVENT $\cdot$ $i \cdot$ OF $\cdot \alpha$" is decodable to the pair (i, α) (i.e., the map $\delta_\alpha^i \rightarrow$ EVENT $\cdot$ $i \cdot$ OF $\cdot \alpha$ is one-to-one). In practice, different model components may share event routines, and the identification with components is made via parameter settings on entry.

LIST containing pairs of the form (EVENT · NAME, TIME). The pairs are initially ordered by low TIME (the pair or pairs with the smallest TIME value come first, those with the second smallest TIME follow, etc.). This ordering is maintained dynamically as the list evolves.

Thus a typical NEXT · EVENTS · LIST might resemble that in Figure 3. The simulator will assume that a pair (EVENT · i · OF · α, t_α) on the list, means that the routine called EVENT · i · OF · α is scheduled to be executed when the simulation CLOCK reaches time t_α. If more than one EVENT is scheduled to be executed (e.g., $t_\alpha = t_\beta$ in the foregoing example), the tie-breaking rules specified by the SELECT function will determine the EVENT actually executed.

EVENT · i · OF · α	t_α
EVENT · j · OF · β	t_β
EVENT · k · OF · γ	t_γ
EVENT · l · OF · ε	t_ε

Figure 3 Typical NEXT · EVENTS · LIST representing components α, β, γ, ε, where $t_\alpha \leq t_\beta \leq t_\gamma \leq t_\varepsilon$

The procedure is as follows.

*   INITIALIZATION

1.   Set CLOCK to desired initial model time t_0

2.   Set variables $\overline{S}_{\alpha_1}, \ldots, \overline{S}_{\alpha_n}$ to the corresponding initial values ($\mathit{s}_{\alpha_1}, \ldots, \mathit{s}_{\alpha_n}$) of the STATE · OF · α variables.

3.   For each ACTIVE type component α, place the pair (EVENTS · s_α · OF · α, $t_0 + \sigma_\alpha$) on the NEXT · EVENTS · LIST, where s_α is as in step 2 and σ_α is the initial value of the α · TIME · LEFT · IN · STATE (if $\sigma_\alpha = \infty$, omit the pair); order the list by low TIME as explained previously.

*   TIME ADVANCE

4.   Set the CLOCK to the time of the first pair on the NEXT · EVENTS · LIST and call this the NEW · EVENT · TIME. Save present time t.

*   TIE–BREAKING

5.   Let IMMINENT · COMPONENTS denote the components with events scheduled at the NEW · EVENT · TIME (i.e., $\{\alpha | (\text{EVENT} \cdot i \cdot \text{OF} \cdot \alpha,$ $t_\alpha)$ is on the list with $i \in S_\alpha$ and $t_\alpha = $ NEW · EVENT · TIME$\}$). Apply SELECT to IMMINENT · COMPONENTS to obtain the winning component $\overline{\alpha}$.

*   STATE TRANSITION

6.   Remove (EVENT · $\mathit{s}_{\overline{\alpha}}$ · OF · $\overline{\alpha}$, $t_{\overline{\alpha}}$) from the list. (If more than one such

pair involving $\bar{\alpha}$ appears, stop the simulation in ERROR! If a well-described model is being simulated, more than one pair should never appear. Why?)

7. Execute the routine called EVENT $\cdot$ $\mathit{s}_{\bar{\alpha}}$ $\cdot$ OF $\cdot$ $\bar{\alpha}$. Assuming this routine correctly implements $\delta_{\bar{\alpha}}^{+\bar{\alpha}}$, this execution should involve the following:

    (a) For each INFLUENCEE $\cdot$ β of $\bar{\alpha}$, retrieve the current value of $\bar{S}_{\beta}$. For each ACTIVE $\cdot$ INFLUENCEE $\cdot$ β of $\bar{\alpha}$, check if a pair involving β is on the NEXT $\cdot$ EVENTS $\cdot$ LIST. If there is such a pair (EVENT $\cdot$ s_{β} $\cdot$ OF $\cdot$ β, t_{β}), remove and save it. From the information so obtained construct the list

    $$((\mathit{s}_{\beta_1}, \sigma_{\beta_1}), (\mathit{s}_{\beta_2}, \sigma_{\beta_2}), \ldots, (\mathit{s}_{\beta_A}, \sigma_{\beta_A}), \mathit{s}_{\beta_{A+1}}, \ldots, \mathit{s}_{\beta_m})$$

    where $\beta_1, \beta_2, \ldots, \beta_A$ are the ACTIVE and $\beta_{A+1}, \ldots, \beta_m$ are the PASSIVE $\cdot$ INFLUENCEES of $\bar{\alpha}$, respectively, s_{β_i} is the current value of $\bar{S}_{\beta_i}$ (which should be the current value of STATE $\cdot$ OF $\cdot$ β_i), and

    $$\sigma_{\beta_i} = \begin{cases} t_{\beta_i} - t & \text{if } (\text{EVENT} \cdot \mathit{s}_{\beta_i} \cdot \text{OF} \cdot \beta_i, t_{\beta_i}) \text{ was} \\ & \text{removed from the NEXT} \cdot \text{EVENTS} \cdot \text{LIST} \\ \infty & \text{otherwise} \end{cases}$$

    (Note that $t_{\beta_i} - t$ should be the current value of $\beta_i \cdot$ TIME $\cdot$ LEFT $\cdot$ IN $\cdot$ STATE.)

    (b) Let $\delta_{\bar{\alpha}}((\mathit{s}_{\beta_1}, \sigma_{\beta_1}), \ldots, \mathit{s}_{\beta_m}) = ((\mathit{s}'_{\beta_1}, \sigma'_{\beta_1}), \ldots, \mathit{s}'_{\beta_m})$. Then for each $\beta \in$ INFLUENCEES $\cdot$ OF $\cdot$ $\bar{\alpha}$, set $\bar{S}_{\beta}$ to s'_{β}; in addition, if β is an ACTIVE type and $\sigma'_{\beta} < \infty$, place (EVENT $\cdot$ s'_{β} $\cdot$ OF $\cdot$ β, NEW $\cdot$ EVENT $\cdot$ TIME $+$ σ'_{β}) in its proper place on the NEXT $\cdot$ EVENTS $\cdot$ LIST.

*   ANY EVENTS LEFT TO PROCESS AT THIS TIME?

8. If the NEW $\cdot$ EVENT $\cdot$ TIME (for the current NEXT $\cdot$ EVENTS $\cdot$ LIST) equals the CLOCK time, go to 5.

*   TERMINATION TEST

9. If NEW $\cdot$ EVENT $\cdot$ TIME exceeds the desired finish time t_1, STOP; otherwise go to 4. (Start the scanning phase.)

In step 6, note that $\bar{\alpha}$ may be one of its own INFLUENCEES, which means that execution of the routine for state $\mathit{s}_{\bar{\alpha}}$ will schedule the routine for the successor state $\mathit{s}'_{\bar{\alpha}}$.

Exercise. Provide an informal proof that the simulation procedure is valid as follows.
Suppose that at model time t_i the model is in state $((\mathit{s}_{\alpha_1}, \sigma_{\alpha_1}), (\mathit{s}_{\alpha_2}, \sigma_{\alpha_2}), \ldots, \mathit{s}_{\alpha_{A+1}}, \ldots, \mathit{s}_{\alpha_n})$ and at time $t_{i+1} = t_i + \min \{\sigma_{\alpha_i}\}$ the state is $((\mathit{s}'_{\alpha_1}, \sigma'_{\alpha_1}), \ldots, \mathit{s}'_{\alpha_n})$. Suppose on entry to step 4, CLOCK $= t_i$, the variables $\bar{S}_{\alpha_1}, \ldots, \bar{S}_{\alpha_n}$ have values $(\mathit{s}_{\alpha_1}, \ldots, \mathit{s}_{\alpha_n})$ and the NEXT $\cdot$

EVENTS · LIST represents the set $\{(\mathcal{A}_{\alpha_1}, t_i + \sigma_{\alpha_1}), \ldots, (\mathcal{A}_{\alpha_A}, t_i + \sigma_A)\}$, ordered by low TIME. Show that on exit from step 9, CLOCK $= t_i + \min\{\sigma_{\alpha_i}\}$, the variables $\bar{S}_{\alpha}, \ldots, \bar{S}_{\alpha_n}$ have values $(\mathcal{A}'_{\alpha_1}, \ldots, \mathcal{A}'_{\alpha_n})$ and the NEXT · EVENTS · LIST represents the set $(\mathcal{A}'_{\alpha_1}, t_{i+1} + \sigma'_{\alpha_1}), \ldots, (\mathcal{A}'_{\alpha_A}, t_{i+1} + \sigma'_{\alpha_A})$ ordered by low TIME (in both cases pairs $(-, \infty)$ are omitted).

7.5   COMBINED EVENT ORIENTED—ACTIVITY SCANNING MODEL SPECIFICATION

We now augment the event oriented scheme of Section 7.1 to allow for activating components by means of contingency tests. Referring to Figure 4, we can understand the additional model description power attained by these means. Suppose that at time t component α is in state $\mathcal{A}_{\alpha}$ (STATE · OF · α = $\mathcal{A}_{\alpha}$), with its countdown clock set at σ_{α} (α · TIME · LEFT · IN · STATE $= \sigma_{\alpha}$). If α is not affected externally, it will be activated at time $t + \sigma_{\alpha}$. In the event scheduling format this activation must eventually result in a resetting of α's countdown clock; for if α · TIME · LEFT remains zero, the model time will not advance. Why?

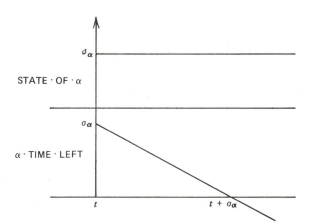

Figure 4   The meaning of negative α · TIME · LEFT.

In the activity scanning format, however, we may allow the countdown clock to continue running into the negative region. The interpretation is that when α · TIME · LEFT is zero or negative, component α is ready to start its activity, provided the conditions given in its specification are satisfied. As stated in Chapter 6, however, a well-described discrete event model does not allow activation to occur between hatching times; checking of the activation conditions, therefore, can take place only at these times.

Thus at any time t there may be many components α in the "ready" or "due" condition (i.e., $\alpha \cdot \text{TIME} \cdot \text{LEFT} \leq 0$); $\alpha \cdot \text{TIME} \cdot \text{LEFT}$ is then the time elapsed since α was last due to become activated.

By suitably extending the scheme of Section 7.1 we arrive at structured combined models.

7.5.1 Structured Combined Models

Components

A set $D = \{\alpha_1, \ldots, \alpha_n\}$ divided into ACTIVE and PASSIVE types.

Descriptive Variables

For each ACTIVE component, $\alpha \in D$

STATE $\cdot$ OF $\cdot$ α—with range S_α and typical value $\measuredangle_\alpha$.

$\alpha \cdot \text{TIME} \cdot \text{LEFT} \cdot \text{IN} \cdot \text{STATE}$—with range $R_\infty = R \cup \{\infty\}$ (reals with ∞) and typical value σ_α.

For each PASSIVE component $\alpha \in D$

STATE $\cdot$ OF $\cdot$ α—with range S_α and typical value $\measuredangle_\alpha$.

PARAMETERS for each ACTIVE $\alpha \in D$

INFLUENCEES $\cdot$ OF $\cdot$ α—a subset of D with typical value $\{\beta_1, \ldots, \beta_m\}$.

INFLUENCERS $\cdot$ OF $\cdot$ α—a subset of D with typical value $\{\bar{\beta}_1, \ldots, \bar{\beta}_m\}$.

The α is usually a member of both sets (recall Section 4.7). A function SELECT as in Section 7.1.1.

Component Interaction

For each ACTIVE component $\alpha \in D$, a local transition function δ_α, which takes a list of values for the INFLUENCERS $\cdot$ OF $\cdot$ α and the INFLUENCEES $\cdot$ OF $\cdot$ α and produces a list of values for the INFLUENCEES $\cdot$ OF $\cdot$ α.

In interpreting such a model, suppose α is selected by SELECT as the next component to be checked for activation. Let $\bar{s}$ be the state assignment to the union of the INFLUENCEES $\cdot$ OF $\cdot$ α and the INFLUENCERS $\cdot$ OF $\cdot$ α just before α is to be tested for activation. Then $\delta_\alpha(\bar{s})$ is the state assigned to the INFLUENCEES $\cdot$ OF $\cdot$ α just after α has been tested and activated. To explicitly display the activation conditions, we provide further structure for the function δ_α.

Let C_α be a predicate on the state assignments to the INFLUENCERS $\cdot$ OF $\cdot$ α; that is, for every state $((\measuredangle_{\bar{\beta}_1}, \sigma_{\bar{\beta}_1}), \ldots, \measuredangle_{\bar{\beta}_{\bar{m}}})$, $C_\alpha((\measuredangle_{\bar{\beta}_1}, \sigma_{\bar{\beta}_1}), \ldots, \measuredangle_{\bar{\beta}_m})$ is either TRUE or FALSE (but not both). This predicate represents the conditions to be tested.

Let f_α have the same domain and range as δ_α. This function represents the action to be taken by α on its INFLUENCEES, if α is activated.

Then

$$\delta_\alpha((\textit{\textbf{s}}_{\beta_1}, \sigma_{\beta_1}), \ldots, \textit{\textbf{s}}_{\beta_m}, (\textit{\textbf{s}}_{\bar\beta_1}, \sigma_{\bar\beta_1}), \ldots, \textit{\textbf{s}}_{\bar\beta_{\bar m}})$$

$$= \begin{cases} f_\alpha((\textit{\textbf{s}}_{\beta_1}, \sigma_{\beta_1}), \ldots, \textit{\textbf{s}}_{\beta_m}, (\textit{\textbf{s}}_{\bar\beta_1}, \sigma_{\bar\beta_1}), \ldots, \textit{\textbf{s}}_{\bar\beta_{\bar m}}) & \text{if } C_\alpha((\textit{\textbf{s}}_{\bar\beta_1}, \sigma_{\bar\beta_1}), \ldots, \textit{\textbf{s}}_{\bar\beta_{\bar m}}) = \text{TRUE} \\ ((\textit{\textbf{s}}_{\beta_1}, \sigma_{\beta_1} - t(s)), \ldots, \textit{\textbf{s}}_{\beta_m}) & \text{otherwise} \end{cases}$$

That is, if C_α is TRUE, f_α is applied to obtain the next states of the INFLUENCEES $\cdot$ OF $\cdot \alpha$; if C_α is FALSE, no action is taken, except to update the countdown clocks.

7.5.2 Example

In an alternate, activity scanning oriented realization of the COMPUTER – USER model, the COMPUTER is a PASSIVE component, recording only whether the CPU is FREE or BUSY. USERS continually check to see whether they have attained the head of the USER $\cdot$ QUEUE, and when they reach this position they schedule themselves for a processing period.

Also, upon emerging from the CPU, USERS are held at a GATE which is operated by the CLERK. BATCH $\cdot$ QUEUE forms when the GATE is CLOSED and is emptied as the USERS pass through the OPEN $\cdot$ GATE (which they continually check). Note that the continued checking by the USERS of the USER $\cdot$ QUEUE and GATE constitutes activity scanning. The control of the GATE by the CLERK is also an example of activity scanning.

Components

　ACTIVE types
　　USER1, . . . , USER99, CLERK
　PASSIVE types
　　USER $\cdot$ QUEUE, BATCH $\cdot$ QUEUE, COMPUTER, GATE

Descriptive Variables

Same as in Section 7.3 except:
　Describing USERi
　　STATE $\cdot$ OF $\cdot$ USERi with range $\{0, 1, 2, 3, 4\}$ (σ_i)
　Describing COMPUTER
　　STATE $\cdot$ OF $\cdot$ CPU with range $\{\text{FREE, BUSY}\}$ $(\textit{\textbf{s}}_{\text{CPU}})$
　Describing CLERK
　　STATE $\cdot$ OF $\cdot$ CLERK—with range $\{0, 1\}$ $(\textit{\textbf{s}}_{\text{CL}})$.
　　CLERK $\cdot$ TIME $\cdot$ LEFT $\cdot$ IN $\cdot$ STATE—with range $R(\sigma_{\text{CL}})$.
(All $\alpha \cdot$ TIME $\cdot$ LEFT $\cdot$ IN $\cdot$ STATE variables have new range R.)
　Describing GATE
　　GATE $\cdot$ POSITION—with range $\{\text{OPEN, CLOSED}\}$ $(\textit{\textbf{s}}_G)$.

Component Interaction

USERi

0. Writes (debugs) a program, takes time WRITE · TIME.
1. Submits program called i, which is placed in USER · QUEUE.
2. While program i waits in USER · QUEUE, USERi waits until it has reached the top; if it has and if CPU is free, program i is processed with service time WAIT · TIME.
3. When finished processing, USERi goes to GATE (joins BATCH · QUEUE).
4. Waits until GATE is open, when OPEN, goes to step 0.

CLERK

0. Waits 8 hours, then opens GATE.
1. Waits until BATCH · QUEUE is empty, then closes GATE and goes to step 0.

TIE–BREAKING RULES

USER by low number, then CLERK.

The time unit is 1 minute.

Most of the formalization of the model is left to the reader as an exercise. To illustrate the specification of the local transition functions, we work out the one for the CLERK.

The INFLUENCERS · OF · CLERK are BATCH · QUEUE and CLERK; the INFLUENCEES · OF · CLERK are GATE and CLERK.

The activating conditions for CLERK are given by

$$C_{CL}(s_{BQ}, s_{CL}) \equiv (s_{CL} = 0) \quad \text{or} \quad (s_{CL} = 1 \text{ and } s_{BQ} = \Lambda)$$

Thus once chosen by SELECT, CLERK will be activated if he is in state 0, or if he is in state 1 and the BATCH · QUEUE is empty.

The action carried out by the CLERK is given by

$$f_{CL}(s_{BQ}, s_G, s_{CL}, \sigma_{CL}) = (s'_G, s'_{CL}, \sigma'_{CL})$$

where

$$s'_G = \begin{cases} \text{OPEN} & \text{if } s_{CL} = 0 \\ \text{CLOSED} & \text{if } s_{CL} = 1 \end{cases}$$

$$s'_{CL} = (s_{CL} + 1) \bmod 2$$

$$\sigma'_{CL} = \begin{cases} 0 & \text{if } s_{CL} = 0 \\ 480 & \text{if } s_{CL} = 1 \end{cases}$$

Note that the action f_α is conditional. This is because if the conditions for action C_α are satisfied, *some* action must be taken, but what this should be must be further decided. A more elegant description ought to be possible if tests for action/nonaction in a particular "situation" are associated with action to be taken in the same "situation." This is done in the process—interaction formulation treated in Section 7.6.

7.5.3   Combined Event–Activity DEVS [†]

As in Section 7.12 we may associate a DEVS with the structure specification. The STATES are as before, a typical state $s = ((\mathit{4}_{\alpha_1}, \sigma_{\alpha_1}), \ldots, (\mathit{4}_{\alpha_A}, \sigma_{\alpha_A}), \mathit{4}_{A+1}, \ldots, \mathit{4}_n) \in$ STATES.

In this case, however, we must distinguish the ACTIVE type components according to their clock readings. Let

$$\text{FUTURE}(s) = \{\alpha | \sigma_\alpha > 0\}$$
$$\text{PRESENT}(s) = \{\alpha | \sigma_\alpha = 0\}$$
$$\text{PAST}(s) = \{\alpha | \sigma_\alpha < 0\}$$

We now identify the PRESENT(s) and PAST(s) components that can be activated because their activation conditions are satisfiable:

ACTIVATABLE(s) = $\{\alpha | C_\alpha(s) = \text{TRUE and } \alpha \in \text{PRESENT}(s) \cup \text{PAST}(s)\}$.

Next the time advance function is defined as follows.

Case 1.   ACTIVATABLE(s) is not empty:
$t(s) = 0$

Case 2.   ACTIVATABLE(s) is empty and FUTURE(s) is not empty:
$t(s) = \min \{\sigma_\alpha | \alpha \in \text{FUTURE}(s)\}$

Case 3.   ACTIVATABLE(s) is empty and FUTURE(s) is empty:
$t(s) = \infty$

Since Case 1 contains a component that can be activated at the present time, time should not advance. In Case 2, no activatable components are left (perhaps because all previously activated ones have indeed been activated); thus time should be advanced to the most imminent future event time. No components are activatable in Case 3, and none are scheduled in the future; therefore the state of the model will remain unchanged for all future time.

We select the component to be activated as follows.

Case 1. $\bar{\alpha}(s) = \text{SELECT(ACTIVATABLE}(s))$

Case 2. $\bar{\alpha}(s) = \text{SELECT(IMMINENT}(s))$
where, as before, IMMINENT(s) = $\{\alpha | \sigma_\alpha = t(s)\}$.

[†] This section may be omitted in an introductory course.

In Case 1, one of the ACTIVATABLE(s) is chosen for activation. In Case 2, since no components can be activated, time is advanced and one of the imminent future events is selected for activation.

To define the global transition function δ_ϕ:STATES $\rightarrow$ STATES we note that in Case 3, $\delta_\phi(s) = s$. In Cases 1 and 2, the next state $s' = \delta_\phi(s)$ is defined in exactly the manner of Section 7.1.2, as the result of activating the SELECTed component.

7.5.4 Activity Scanning Simulation Prototype

In our activity scanning prototype we suppose that each component transition function δ_α is correctly implemented as a routine for f_α (call it ACTIVITY $\cdot$ ROUTINE $\cdot$ FOR $\cdot$ α) and a routine for C_α (CONDITIONS $\cdot$ ROUTINE $\cdot$ FOR $\cdot$ α). The state component STATE $\cdot$ OF $\cdot$ α is represented by the variable (or variables) $\bar{S}_\alpha$. In addition, ACTIVE components have an associated time cell T_α, which will represent $\alpha \cdot$ TIME $\cdot$ LEFT $\cdot$ IN $\cdot$ STATE in the sense that the contents t_α is treated as the time of the next, or the last, scheduled activation of α. Thus if the simulation is valid, $t_\alpha = t + \sigma_\alpha$ at any time t.

We suppose that the SELECT function is derived from a fixed priority listing $\alpha_1, \alpha_2, \ldots, \alpha_A$ of the ACTIVE components. This is implemented in the procedure by a scan pointer called SCAN, which moves down the list of names from TOP to BOTTOM. We also suppose that the routines for checking the activating conditions are paired with the components on the list, which we call the CONDITIONS list, which appears as in Figure 5. The procedure is as follows.

*   INITIALIZATION
1.   Set CLOCK to desired initial model time t_0.
2.   Set variables $\bar{S}_{\alpha}, \ldots, \bar{S}_{\alpha_n}$ to the corresponding initial values $(\mathcal{A}_{\alpha_1}, \ldots, \mathcal{A}_{\alpha_n})$ of the STATE $\cdot$ OF $\cdot$ α variables.

TOP

	α_1	CONDITIONS $\cdot$ ROUTINE $\cdot$ FOR $\cdot$ α
SCAN →	α_2	CONDITIONS $\cdot$ ROUTINE $\cdot$ FOR $\cdot$ α_2
	α_3	CONDITIONS $\cdot$ ROUTINE $\cdot$ FOR $\cdot$ α_3
		$\vdots$
	α_A	CONDITIONS $\cdot$ ROUTINE $\cdot$ FOR $\cdot$ α_A

BOTTOM

Figure 5   The CONDITIONS LIST.

3. Set the time cells $T_{\alpha_1}, \ldots, T_{\alpha_A}$ to represent the initial values $(\sigma_{\alpha_1}, \ldots, \sigma_{\alpha_A})$ of the $\alpha \cdot \text{TIME} \cdot \text{LEFT} \cdot \text{IN} \cdot \text{STATE}$ variable (i.e., $t_\alpha = t_0 + \sigma_\alpha$).
* ACTIVITY SCANNING
4. Set the SCAN to TOP of CONDITIONS · LIST.
5. Move the SCAN down until the first activatable $\bar\alpha$ is found, that is, α such that $t_\alpha \leq t$, and the CONDITIONS · ROUTINE · FOR · α returns TRUE when applied to $((\mathcal{A}_{\bar\beta_1}, t_{\bar\beta_1} - t), (\mathcal{A}_{\bar\beta_2}, t_{\bar\beta_2} - t), \ldots, \mathcal{A}_{\bar\beta_{\bar m}})$, where $\bar\beta_1, \bar\beta_2, \ldots, \bar\beta_{\bar m}$ are the INFLUENCERS · OF · α, t_α is the content of T_α, and t is the current CLOCK time.
* STATE TRANSITION
6. Execute the ACTIVITY · ROUTINE · FOR · $\bar\alpha$.
* TEST FOR END OF SCANNING PHASE
7. If the SCAN has not reached the BOTTOM of the CONDITIONS · LIST, go to 4 (repeat scanning).
* TIME ADVANCE
8. Advance the CLOCK to the time of the next event; that is, set the CLOCK to min $\{t_\alpha | t_\alpha \geq t\}$, where t_α is the current contents of T_α and t is the current reading of the CLOCK.
* TERMINATION TEST
9. If the CLOCK exceeds the desired finish time t_1, STOP; otherwise, go to 4.

Exercise.   Provide an informal proof to show that the prototype procedure validly simulates the combined structured model.

7.6   PROCESS INTERACTION SIMULATION

The process interaction simulation strategy is basically a combined event scheduling–activity scanning procedure. The distinguishing feature is that a model component description can be implemented as a unit rather than being separated into a number of unconnected events and activity routines. The advantage is that the program structure maintains a closer relation to the model structure, and by scanning the program text, the reader gets a better impression of the model structure. This can increase the likelihood of a correct implementation in the first place, as well as quicker debugging.

To understand how the strategy works, it is convenient to further refine the general model specification of Section 7.5.1. There the ACTIVE component transition function δ_α was characterized by two parts: the conditions predicate C_α and the action function f_α. We now wish to break each part into several pieces, just as we did in the event scheduling case of Section 7.1.1. However, rather than associate, each piece with a state (of S_α), we associate each one with a substate corresponding to the control state of the program implementing δ_α.

To do this we further structure STATE $\cdot$ OF $\cdot$ α by CONTROL $\cdot$ OF $\cdot$ α and MEMORY $\cdot$ OF $\cdot$ α components so that $S_\alpha = L_\alpha \times V_\alpha$, where L_α is a finite set $\{0, 1, 2, \ldots, M\}$. V_α is later identified with the local variables of the program representing α, and L_α with the current instruction number (or statement label).

If α is one of the INFLUENCEES $\cdot$ OF $\cdot$ α we define C_α^l by fixing the CONTROL component of α to value l in C_α; that is,

$$C_\alpha^l((v_\alpha, \sigma_\alpha), (l_{\bar\beta_2}, v_{\bar\beta_2}, \sigma_{\bar\beta_2}), \ldots, v_{\bar\beta_{\bar m}}) = C_\alpha((l, v_\alpha, \sigma_\alpha), (l_{\bar\beta_2}, v_{\bar\beta_2}, \sigma_{\bar\beta_2}), \ldots, v_{\bar\beta_{\bar m}}).$$

If α is not one of the INFLUENCEES $\cdot$ OF $\cdot$ α, $C_\alpha^l = C_\alpha$ for all $l \in L_\alpha$. Similarly,

$$f_\alpha^l((v_\alpha, \sigma_\alpha), \ldots, v_{\bar\beta_{\bar m}}) = f_\alpha((l, v_\alpha, \sigma_\alpha) \cdots v_{\bar\beta_{\bar m}})$$

Thus the C_α and f_α break into the sets $\{C_\alpha^l\}$ and $\{f_\alpha^l\}$. The transition function δ_α can be expressed by the scheme

In CONTROL state 0
    If C_α^0 is TRUE apply f_α^0, otherwise do nothing.

In CONTROL state 1
    If C_α^1 is TRUE apply f_α^1, otherwise do nothing.

$\vdots$

In CONTROL state l
    If C_α^l is TRUE apply f_α^l, otherwise do nothing.

$\vdots$

In CONTROL state M
    If C_α^M is TRUE apply f_α^M, otherwise do nothing.

Exercise.   Express the foregoing scheme formally as in Section 7.5.1.

7.6.1   Example

Using the computer-user model of Section 7.3, we have the following for the CLERK: CONTROL OF CLERK = $\{0, 1\}$. (We consider the CLERK states to involve only control, not memory.)

In CONTROL state 0
    Always OPEN the GATE, go to state 1, and retain activation.

In CONTROL state 1
    Wait until (i.e., "if") the BATCH $\cdot$ QUEUE is empty, CLOSE the GATE, schedule an activation in 8 hours, and go to state 0.

Formally, this is given by:

$$C^0_{CL}(\textit{s}_{BQ}) \equiv \text{TRUE}$$
$$f^0_{CL}(\textit{s}_{BQ}, \textit{s}_G, \sigma_{CL}) = (\textit{s}'_G, \textit{s}'_{CL}, \sigma'_{CL})$$

where

$$\textit{s}'_G = \text{OPEN}$$
$$\textit{s}'_{CL} = 1$$
$$\sigma'_{CL} = 0$$

$$C^1_{CL}(\textit{s}_{BQ}) \equiv (\textit{s}_{BQ} = \Lambda)$$
$$f^1_{CL}(\textit{s}_{BQ}, \textit{s}_G, \sigma_{CL}) = (\textit{s}'_G, \textit{s}'_{CL}, \sigma'_{CL})$$

where

$$\textit{s}'_G = \text{CLOSED}$$
$$\textit{s}'_{CL} = 0$$
$$\sigma'_{CL} = 480$$

Exercise.   Complete Table 1.

Table 1   Definition of Transition Function for USERi

l	C^l_i	f^l_i
0	TRUE	$\textit{s}'_i = 1$ $\sigma'_i = \text{WRITE} \cdot \text{TIME}\,(\text{TYPE}(i), r_{1,i})$ $\textit{s}'_{UQ} = \textit{s}_{UQ}$ $\textit{s}'_{BQ} = \textit{s}_{BQ}$ $r'_{1,i} = \Gamma(r_{1,i})$ $r'_{2,i} = r_{2,i}$
1	?	?
2	$i = \text{top}(\textit{s}_{UQ})$ $\textit{s}_{CPU} = \text{FREE}$	$\textit{s}'_i = 3$ $\sigma'_i = \text{WAIT} \cdot \text{TIME}\,(\text{TYPE}(i), r_{2,i})$ $\textit{s}'_{UQ} = \textit{s}_{UQ}$ $\textit{s}'_{BQ} = \textit{s}_{BQ}$ $r'_{1,i} = r_{1,i}$ $r'_{2,i} = \Gamma(r_{2,i})$
3	TRUE	$\textit{s}'_i = 4$ $\sigma'_i = 0$ $\textit{s}'_{UQ} = \text{rest}(\textit{s}_{UQ})$ $\textit{s}'_{BQ} = \textit{s}_{BQ} \cup \{1\}$ $r'_{1,i} = r_{1,i}$ $r'_{2,i} = r_{2,i}$
4	?	?

7.6.2 Process Interaction Prototype

Having for each ACTIVE type α, the sets $\{C_\alpha^l\}$ and $\{f_\alpha^l\}$ which define its transition function δ_α, we are in a position to translate this specification into a software routine, or *process*.

The PROCESS $\cdot$ FOR $\cdot$ α, is a sequence of statements divided into M segments (one for each CONTROL state), and each segment is itself a sequence of two segments: a CONDITIONS segment and an ACTION segment, as in Figure 6.

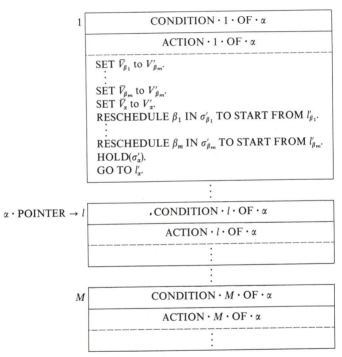

Figure 6 PROCESS $\cdot$ FOR $\cdot$ α.

If the PROCESS $\cdot$ FOR $\cdot$ α validly implements the component transition function δ_α, the ACTION segment can be represented in the form illustrated.

We assume that MEMORY variables $V_{\alpha_1}, \ldots, V_{\alpha_n}$ are represented by program variables $\bar{V}_{\alpha_1}, \ldots, \bar{V}_{\alpha_n}$. The CONTROL variable L_α (of an ACTIVE type component α) is represented by the position of a pointer that indicates the current statement of PROCESS · FOR · α being executed, if α is now active, or the next-to-be-executed statement, if α is now passive. By "activation" positions we mean the first lines of each of the segments of code constituting PROCESS · FOR · α. Thus, in contrast to the previous strategies, the execution of a process can begin at any one of the m activation points, say l_α. When the segment associated with l_α has been executed, execution will cease and the pointer will be set to the next activation point, which is either $l_\alpha + 1$, if no GO · TO statement appears, or l'_α if GO · TO · l'_α appears. One such control pointer, called α · POINTER, is associated with the PROCESS · FOR · α routine, for each ACTIVE type component α.

The simulator will maintain the FUTURE · ACTIVATIONS · LIST of triples of the form (PROCESS · NAME, STATEMENT · #, TIME). A typical triple $(\alpha, l_\alpha, t_\alpha)$ will be treated by the simulator as scheduling PROCESS · FOR · α to begin attempted execution from statement l_α at time t_α. The list is thus the functional equivalent of the NEXT · EVENTS · LIST of event scheduling (Section 7.4).

A second list, the CURRENT · ACTIVATIONS · LIST, consists of triples of the same form (PROCESS · NAME, STATEMENT · #, TIME) and is supposed to represent the components whose scheduled time has just arrived, or, if the scheduled time arrived in the past, the components' activation conditions at that time were not satisfied. The CURRENT · ACTIVATION · LIST is thus functionally similar to the CONDITIONS · LIST in activity scanning with the major difference that it does not represent components that have been scheduled for the future (these are on the FUTURE · ACTIVATIONS · LIST). As before, the list has a TOP, a BOTTOM, and a SCAN pointing to the triple presently being considered. Finally, we have the usual CLOCK.

As in activity scanning we assume that the SELECT function is determined by a strict priority ordering $\alpha_1, \alpha_2, \ldots, \alpha_A$ of ACTIVE type components. The process is as follows.

* INITIALIZATION
1. Set CLOCK to desired initial model time t_0.
2. Set variables $\bar{V}_{\alpha_1}, \ldots, \bar{V}_{\alpha_n}$ to the corresponding initial values $(v_{\alpha_1}, \ldots, v_{\alpha_n})$ of the MEMORY · OF · α variables.
3. For each ACTIVE type α, suppose l_α is the initial value of CONTROL · OF · α; if σ_α, the initial value of α · TIME · LEFT · IN · STATE, is positive, place the pair $(\alpha, l_\alpha, t_0 + \sigma_\alpha)$ on the FUTURE · ACTIVATIONS · LIST; order the list by low TIME; if the initial value σ_α is negative or zero, place $(\alpha, l_\alpha, t_0 + \sigma_\alpha)$ on the CURRENT · ACTIVATIONS · LIST; order the list by the priority on components characterizing the SELECT function (highest priority at the TOP, lowest at the BOTTOM).

* SCANNING PHASE
4. Set SCAN to TOP of CURRENT · ACTIVATION · LIST.
5. Move the SCAN down until $\bar{\alpha}$, the first activatable component, is found; that is, for each triple $(\alpha, l_\alpha, t_\alpha)$ scanned, execute the PROCESS · FOR · α beginning at the statement l_α; if CONDITION · l_α · OF · α so executed returns FALSE, move SCAN down one, otherwise α becomes $\bar{\alpha}$; remove $(\bar{\alpha}, l_{\bar{\alpha}}, t_{\bar{\alpha}})$ from the list.

* STATE TRANSITION
6. Continue executing the PROCESS · FOR · $\bar{\alpha}$ segment associated with activation point $l_{\bar{\alpha}}$, namely, ACTION · $l_{\bar{\alpha}}$ · OF · $\bar{\alpha}$. Assume that this segment correctly implements the action function $f_{\bar{\alpha}}^{l_{\bar{\alpha}}}$ and that for each $\beta \in$ INFLUENCEES · OF · $\bar{\alpha}$, $(v'_\beta, l'_\beta, \sigma'_\beta)$ is the state assigned to β by this function: set $\bar{V}_\beta$ to v'_β. In addition, if β is an ACTIVE type, remove the triple $(\beta, l_\beta, t_\beta)$ from its place, either on the FUTURE or the CURRENT · ACTIVATIONS · LIST; if σ'_β is positive, insert $(\beta, l'_\beta, t_\beta + \sigma'_\beta)$ in the FUTURE · ACTIVATIONS · LIST (in its place determined by $t + \sigma'_\beta$); if σ'_β is negative or zero, insert $(\beta, l'_\beta, t + \sigma'_\beta)$ in the CURRENT · ACTIVATIONS · LIST in a position appropriate to the priority level of β. In Figure 6, this is coded for $\beta \neq \alpha$ by the generic instruction RESCHEDULE β IN σ'_β TO START FROM l'_β; for $\bar{\alpha}$ it is coded by the instructions HOLD($\sigma'_{\bar{\alpha}}$) and GO TO $l'_{\bar{\alpha}}$.

* TEST FOR END OF SCANNING PHASE
7. If the SCAN has not reached the BOTTOM of the CURRENT · ACTIVATIONS · LIST, go to 5 (restart scanning).

* TIME ADVANCE
8. Advance the CLOCK to the time of the first triple on the FUTURE · ACTIVATIONS · LIST—call it the NEXT · EVENT · TIME.

* UPDATE OF CURRENT · ACTIVATIONS · LIST
9. Remove the imminent activations (triples whose time component = NEXT · EVENT · TIME) from the FUTURE · ACTIVATIONS · LIST and insert them in the CURRENT · ACTIVATIONS · LIST in the positions determined by their priority levels.

* TERMINATION TEST
10. If the NEXT · EVENT · TIME exceeds the desired finish time t_1, STOP; otherwise go to 5 (resume the scanning phase).

Exercise. As usual, the procedure has to be shown to be valid. Provide an informal proof.

Exercise. Compare and contrast the three strategies given in this chapter. How do they handle the processing of simultaneously scheduled events?

7.7 "SIMULA"

SIMULA[2] is a process interaction language based on ALGOL. In SIMULA, a "*process*" corresponds to what we have called "PROCESS · FOR · α," an "*activity*" is a scheme for defining a class of *processes*, any specific one of which is determined by fixing all the open parameters of the generic *activity*. An example, the activity for COMPUTER, is given in Figure 7. The structure of SIMULA is very similar to that of our prototype procedure. It is interesting to note, however, that SIMULA does not allow a process to directly alter another's pointer. Thus the "RESCHEDULE . . ." instruction of the prototype appears in its variants "ACTIVATE β," "PASSIVATE β," "SCHEDULE β IN σ_β," and so on, without the "TO START FROM l_β" ending. For finite σ_α, the prototype and SIMULA statements HOLD(σ_α) are equivalent, whereas for $\sigma_\alpha = \infty$ SIMULA employs the "WAIT(LIST)" statement, which is different in that the triple representing process α is removed from the equivalent of FUTURE · ACTIVATIONS · LIST and inserted into the designated LIST. The activation test segments "CONDITION · l · OF · α" in the prototype are represented in SIMULA by the "WAIT UNTIL C_α^l" statement. Indeed, execution of the process will wait at l until the condition C_α^l is satisfied.

```
ACTIVITY COMPUTER
BEGIN
START:   IF EMPTY (USER · QUEUE) THEN HOLD (0.1 minute)
         ELSE INSPECT FIRST (USER · QUEUE)
                 WHEN USER DO
         BEGIN
             REMOVE (FIRST (USER · QUEUE))
             HOLD (EXP (WAIT · TIME (TYPE), RANDNU))
             ACTIVATE USER
         END
         GO TO START
END OF ACTIVITY COMPUTER
```

Figure 7 A SIMULA version of PROCESS · FOR · COMPUTER. (After Reference 6, p. 97.)

7.8 GPSS

General Purpose Simulation System (GPSS) is a discrete event language oriented toward the philosophy of "model construction by interconnection of modules." A list of 40-odd "block description" statements is supplied. A

GPSS model description is obtained essentially by placing a selected set of these statements in a sequence. Each statement corresponds to a block in a GPSS diagram that resembles the flow chart of a conventional program. The flow of control, however, is much different; instead of the usual pointer moving from statement to statement, there may be many pointers, or "transactions."

Each "block statement" is actually a macroinstruction. When a transaction encounters a block, the associated macroinstruction code is executed. Usually the instruction involves first carrying out certain tests. If these are not satisfied, no further action can be taken and the transaction will remain at the block. If the conditions are satisfied, the action part of the instruction is carried out. Ultimately, the transaction goes on to the next block in sequence or is rerouted to another block by the instruction just executed.

Since many transactions are flowing through a GPSS block diagram, some overall control must exist for selecting which of several contending transactions should begin execution of its encountered block instruction. In addition, means must be available for introducing transactions and removing them from the flow. These are accomplished by distinguished blocks called GENERATE and TERMINATE. Now execution of a statement, and flow from one block to the next, take zero model time (the simulation clock is not advanced). Thus to introduce the flow of time and the associated scheduling of activities, a block called ADVANCE is used. This block, when encountered by a transaction, causes it to be delayed by specifiable amount before allowing it to proceed to the next block.

An excellent exposition of the GPSS language in both its model description and simulation aspects is given by Schriber, and we are assuming that readers are familiar with GPSS basics obtainable from his book or from the language manuals.[3, 4] The model description aspect is further considered in Chapter 9, where some of the GPSS blocks are formalized as DEVS components and the GPSS block diagram is seen as one example of a more general approach to model construction by interconnection of modules. As an example, the user-computer model is shown programmed in GPSS in Figure 8.

The surface structure of GPSS is designed to foster mental imagery in which objects (the transactions) flow through a network (the GPSS block diagram), entering at certain points and possibly emerging at other points. At some blocks in the network, the transactions meet with blockades and must wait in FIFO queues until their turn comes to be processed by the block. This view is clearly appropriate for establishing a straightforward correspondence between a model and its program implementation. If one understands how the block process transactions are routed from block to block, he can implement a network model without further understanding of the GPSS internal structure (i.e., how it actually processes the model

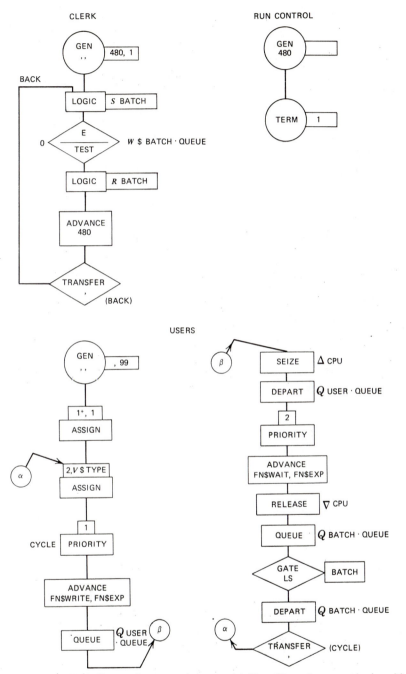

Figure 8 GPSS block diagram for user-computer model. Note that each segment begins with a GENERATE (GEN) block.

169

description). Unfortunately, the surface structure does not completely determine the underlying processing, and the model may be in fact processed in ways not intended or understood by the programmer who is not familiar with this processing. Moreover, the transaction imagery fostered by the GPSS designers may inhibit the employment of GPSS to its fullest potential. A basic understanding of the simulation strategy used by GPSS would be more valuable in this regard.

The GPSS strategy can, in fact, be simply described in terms of the process interaction prototype procedure just given, providing the proper correspondences are made. To avoid confusion before setting forth a model of the GPSS internal structure, we stress that this model does not reflect the structure of a model *programmed* in GPSS.

The correspondences between the prototype and GPSS simulation strategy are shown in Table 2. From an interval view of GPSS we have a picture in

Table 2   Correspondence Between Process Interaction Prototype and GPSS Simulator

Prototype	GPSS
Passive components	Equipment (facilities, storages, logic switches, save-value locations, explicit queues, user chains)
Process names $(\alpha_1, \alpha_2, \alpha_3, \ldots)$	Transaction numbers $(1, 2, 3, \ldots)$
PROCESS $\cdot$ FOR $\cdot$ α	GPSS program (the whole program can be associated with transaction i, or, better, that component to which it is confined)
MEMORY $\cdot$ OF $\cdot$ α	Parameters of transaction i
POINTER $\cdot$ OF $\cdot$ α	Next block attempted by transaction i (where it is located in "network")
FUTURE $\cdot$ ACTIVATIONS $\cdot$ LIST	FUTURE $\cdot$ EVENTS $\cdot$ CHAIN (FEC)
CURRENT $\cdot$ ACTIVATIONS $\cdot$ LIST	CURRENT $\cdot$ EVENTS $\cdot$ CHAIN (CEC)
Segment of PROCESS $\cdot$ FOR $\cdot$ α associated with activation point l	Interpretive code associated with BLOCK statement number l
CONDITION $\cdot$ l $\cdot$ OF $\cdot$ α	Test conditions for denying entry to a transaction at BLOCK l [e.g., SEIZE j involves testing whether facility j is 0 (free) or 1 (busy)]
ACTION $\cdot$ l $\cdot$ OF $\cdot$ α	Actions carried out by BLOCK l in processing the entering transaction x (e.g., in SEIZE j, if facility j is 0, it is set to 1)
HOLD(σ_α)	ADVANCE σ_α
GO TO l_α	TRANSFER l (various variants)

which several control pointers (the transactions) are attempting to execute a program from several possibly different points. To fit the prototype strategy, we associate a copy of the GPSS source program with each transaction.[†] Block statements in GPSS are macroinstructions of the form of the code segments in Figure 6. There are essentially three types.

Type 1.   Never deny entry to a transaction and never cause delay (e.g., ASSIGN i,j; RELEASE i; LEAVE i,j; LOGIC i,j; TRANSFER l). Except for TRANSFER, these blocks contain only the ACTION segment; TRANSFER contains only the GO · TO segment.

Type 2.   May deny entry to a transaction (e.g., SEIZE i; ENTER i, j; GATE i,j; TEST i, j, k). Except for GATE and TEST, these blocks contain the CONDITION and ACTION segments; GATE and TEST contain, in addition, the GO · TO segment.

Type 3.   Never deny entry but may delay a transaction (e.g., ADVANCE i,j). These blocks contain only the HOLD segment.

We can describe the block processing as shown in Table 3. As in the general scheme, processing proceeds in two phases. In the first, the most imminent transaction triples are removed from the FUTURE · EVENTS · CHAIN (FEC) and merged into the CURRENT · EVENTS · CHAIN (CEC) and, in the second, the CEC is scanned for possible movement of the transactions through the program according to the manner of Table 3. When all transactions are blocked (i.e., all the CONDITION segments return FALSE), the first phase begins again.

Several interesting observations arise from the perspective we have taken. GPSS is more limited in some ways than the prototype strategy, in which processes can in general directly modify the local variables of other processes. In GPSS, however, the transactions (which correspond to processes) cannot modify directly other transaction's parameters. Also the prototype permits a process to reschedule another process. In GPSS, however, there is no corresponding operation that a transaction can perform on the FEC. (The PREEMPT block does some restricted rescheduling.)

On the other hand, GPSS goes beyond the prototype in the following ways:

1.   Blocks exist to introduce new transactions into the simulation (GENERATE and SPLIT) and to remove transactions (TERMINATE).
2.   Blocks exist to cause resetting of the SCAN (BUFFER) and to alter the priority level of a transaction (PRIORITY).

[†] Actually, GPSS programs often consist of several disjoint, noncommunicating components, and we could take the component in which a transaction begins execution as the program segment to be associated with it.

Table 3   The Processing of GPSS Blocks

Type	Surface View	Internal View
1	Transaction XACT · # passes through block BLOCK · # in zero time.	(XACT · #, BLOCK · #, −) is pointed to by SCAN on the CEC, the ACTION macroinstruction is executed and the triple is replaced by (XACT · #, BLOCK · # + 1, −) [(XACT · #, l, −) if TRANSFER l] the CEC SCAN is returned to the TOP of CEC.
2	Transaction XACT · # is denied entry to block BLOCK · #.	The triple (XACT · #, BLOCK · #, −) is pointed to by SCAN on the CEC, the CONDITION section is executed and returns FALSE. The only effect is that SCAN is moved one down to next triple on CEC.
	(Entry not denied is same as Type 1 case except for CONDITION segment execution.)	
3	Transaction XACT · # is delayed in passing through block BLOCK · #	The triple (XACT · #, BLOCK · #, −) under SCAN on CEC is removed and the triple (XACT · #, BLOCK · # + 1, $t + \sigma$) is placed on the FEC (t is current clock time).

3. The ordering of transactions on the CEC goes beyond the simple priority employed in the prototype. Several transactions may have the same priority level, and to provide a total order, the CEC is ordered by high priority, then by low time of arrival on the CEC, and by low transaction number (See Section 7.2).

In fact, item 3 gives the reason that priority-ordered FIFO queues form automatically at Type 2 blocks. Consider the CEC chain in Figure 9. Transactions a, b, d, f, and g are attempting to enter the same block B_1; since a and b have the same priority level 3, they are placed above d with priority 2 and above f, g with priority 1. Within the pair $\{a, b\}$, a is placed higher because it has arrived first. Within $\{f, g\}$ both components have the same time of arrival but f has the lower number and therefore is placed first. Because the SCAN always begins at the top, transaction a will have the first chance to test the CONDITIONS segment of block B_1, then b, then d, and so on. Suppose the CONDITIONS are insensitive to the transaction parameters so that if b satisfies the conditions, so does a. Then we have, in

	Priority	Time of Arrival	Transaction Number	Block
a	3	100	—	B_1
b	3	110	—	B_1
c	—	—	—	B_2
d	2	—	—	B_1
e	—	—	—	B_3
f	1	50	5	B_1
g	1	50	6	B_1

(a)

$\Longrightarrow$

a	3	100	—
b	3	110	—
d	2	—	—
f	1	50	5
g	1	50	6

(b)

Figure 9 (a) Typical CEC Configuration. (b) Queue formed at B_1.

effect, a priority-ordered FIFO queue a, b, d, f, g waiting for service at block B_1.

Exercise.   The GPSS approach has the advantage of convenience, since transactions do not have to be explicitly linked into passive lists to create the desired queues (cf. the WAIT instruction of SIMULA). But it has the enormous disadvantage of being very inefficient to process.[†] Explain why.

The foregoing items 1 to 3 motivate the extension of the prototype in the following directions:

—facilities for simulating models with input
—facilities for expanding or contracting the set of model components
—facilities for changing the SELECT function dynamically and allowing it to be sensitive to time of arrival on the CURRENT · ACTIVATIONS · LIST

Exercise.   Show how to modify the structured model description and the process interaction prototype to make the desired extensions.

7.9   SOURCES

Expositions of SIMSCRIPT, SIMULA, and GPSS are available in books and manuals.[1–5] The computer-user model is based on a model given to

[†] This is somewhat mitigated by the delay chain concept in GPSS.

illustrate SIMULA.[6] Reviews of simulation languages and their world views are given in References 7 to 10.

1. P. J. Kiviat, R. Villanueva, and H. M. Markowitz, *The Simscript II Programming Language*. Prentice-Hall, Englewood Cliffs, N.J., 1968.

2. O. J. Dahl and K. Nygaard, "SIMULA—An ALGOL-Based Simulation Language." *Communications of the Association for Computer Machinery*, **9** (9), 1966, 671–678.

3. *General Purpose Simulation System 1360* (GPSS), *User's Manual*. IBM Publication H20-0326, 1967.

4. T. J. Schriber, *Simulation Using GPSS*. Wiley, New York, 1974.

5. A. Alan, B. Pritsker, and P. Kiviat, *Simulation with GASP II*. Prentice-Hall, Englewood Cliffs, N.J., 1969.

6. J. W. McCredie, "The Structure of Discrete Event Simulation Languages," in *Proceedings of the Summer Computer Simulation Conference*, AFIPS Press, Montvale, N.J., 1969, 88–97.

7. K. D. Tocher, "Simulation Languages," in *Progress in Operations Research*, J. Aronafsky (Ed.), Wiley, New York, 1969.

8. D. Teichroew, J. F. Dubin, and T. D. Truitt, "Discussion of Computer Simulation Techniques and Comparison of Languages," *Simulation*, **9**, 1967.

9. J. G. Laski, "On Time Structures in Monte Carlo Simulations," *Operational Research Quarterly*, **16** (3), 1965, 329–339.

10. P. Kiviat, "Simulation Languages," in *Computer Simulation Experiments with Models of Economic Systems*, T. H. Naylor (Ed.) Wiley, New York, 1971.

PROBLEMS

1. (a) The next event simulation strategy of Chapter 4 can be modified by adding an "activity scanning" phase that requires decomposing the local transition function δ_α into condition C_α and action f_α segments such that if C_α is TRUE, then f_α determines the next state of α; if C_α is FALSE, then α does not change state. The simulator then scans the NEXT $\cdot$ EVENTS $\cdot$ LIST checking for possible activations using the conditions C_α explicitly given. Modify the procedure of Chapter 4 to carry this out.

   (b) For the Game of Life, describe explicitly the conditions C under which a BIRTH or a DEATH occurs at a cell.

   (c) Provide a procedure that, given an arbitrary local transition function in a discrete time model, will express the function in the form of the set $\{(C_\alpha^{\pm}, f_\alpha^{\pm}) | \pm \in \text{STATE} \cdot \text{OF} \cdot \alpha\}$.

2. Model the life cycle of an organism using the process interaction format.

Chapter Eight

Introduction to Modelling Theory

This chapter introduces the theory of modelling as a prelude to the formal statement of postulates in Chapter 11. We work through an example relating to the grocery store model introduced in Chapter 6. We imagine experimenting with a real grocery store for which the model of Chapter 6 serves as a *base* model. In this context we first consider the concept of experimental frames. Then we construct a simplified lumped model and argue informally that it may be valid in one of the frames previously considered. Finally, we introduce the important concept of homomorphism and show how it enables us to formally verify the validity of the lumped model. At this point the reader is invited to reread the exposition parts of Chapter 2 dealing with the elements of modelling and simulation and basic simplification procedures.

8.1 GROCERY STORE—BASE MODEL AND REAL SYSTEM

The grocery store model of Chapter 6 is already relatively simple. Since we consider it to be a base model of a real store, however, it represents the internal structure of the real system—the grocery store. We first briefly review the informal description of the model, which is to be expressed in DEVS form.

Grocery Store Base Model

Components
ENTRANCE, SHOP · AREA, CHECKOUT, EXIT

Descriptive Variables

ENTRANCE
   HELLO $x \in \{\phi, a, b, c, \ldots\}$
SHOP $\cdot$ AREA
   SHOPPING $\cdot$ TIME $\cdot$ SEED $r_1 \in [0, 1]$
   TIME $\cdot$ LEFT $\cdot$ LIST $(x_1, \tau_1) \cdots (x_n, \tau_n) \in (\{a, b, \ldots\} \times R^+)^*$
CHECKOUT
   LINE $y_1 y_2 \cdots y_m \in \{a, b, \ldots\}^*$
   SERVICE $\cdot$ TIME $\cdot$ SEED $r_2 \in [0, 1]$
   SERVICE $\cdot$ TIME $\cdot$ LEFT $\sigma \in R_0^+$
   BUSY $\{$YES, NO$\}$
EXIT
   BYE $\cdot$ BYE $x \in \{\phi, a, b, \ldots\}$
PARAMETERS
   SHOPPING $\cdot$ TIME
   SERVICE $\cdot$ TIME
   functions of the form $Y : [0, 1] \to R^+$, representing random variables

Component Interaction

A customer enters at ENTRANCE, shops in the SHOP $\cdot$ AREA, pays at
the CHECKOUT, and leaves from the EXIT. The discussion of Chapter 6
leads to the formalization of the interaction as a DEVS, which we summarize
as follows.

Since HELLO is the only *input variable*, we have

$$\text{INPUTS} = \{\phi, a, b, c, \ldots\}$$

With the *state variables* selected as in Table 1, we have

$$\text{STATES} = \{s | s = (r_1, (x_1, \tau_1), y_1, r_2, \sigma)\}$$
$$(x_n, \tau_n) \quad y_m$$

Then the *time advance function*: $t : \text{STATES} \to R_{0,\infty}^+$ is such that for
$s \in \text{STATES}$, $t(s) = \min \{\tau_1, \ldots, \tau_n, \sigma\}$. Since we employ the *tie-breaking
rule* based on the priority of CHECKOUT over SHOP $\cdot$ AREA,

$$\text{SELECT}(\{\text{SHOP} \cdot \text{AREA}, \text{CHECKOUT}\}) = \text{CHECKOUT}$$

Otherwise $\text{SELECT}(\{x\}) = x$ (in the absence of ties).

The autonomous transition function $\delta_\phi : \text{STATES} \to \text{STATES}$ and the
external transition function δ_{ex} are described as follows.

Let $\qquad\qquad \text{IMMINENT}(s) = \{\alpha | \sigma_\alpha = t(s)\}$

where $\sigma_{\text{SHOP} \cdot \text{AREA}} = \min \{\tau_1, \ldots, \tau_n\}$ and $\sigma_{\text{CHECKOUT}} = \sigma$.

Table 1 The Base Model Transition Function.

$s \in$ STATES	$\delta_\phi(s)$ if $\overline{\alpha}(s) =$			$\delta_{ex}(s, e, x)$
	CHECKOUT		SHOP · AREA	$\Gamma(r_1)$
	$m \geq 2$	$m \leq 1$		
SHOPPING · TIME · SEED r_1	r_1	r_1	r_1	$\Gamma(r_1)$
TIME · LEFT · LIST $\begin{array}{c}(x_1, \tau_1)\\ \ldots \\ (x_n, \tau_n)\end{array}$	$\begin{array}{c}(x_1, \tau_1 - t(s))\\ \ldots \\ (x_n, \tau_n - t(s))\end{array}$	$\begin{array}{c}(x_1, \tau_1 - t(s))\\ \ldots \\ (x_n, \tau_n - t(s))\end{array}$	$\begin{array}{c}\overline{(x_1, \tau_1 - t(s))}^*\\ \ldots \\ \overline{(x_n, \tau_n - t(s))}\end{array}$	$\begin{array}{c}(x_1, \tau_1 - e)\\ \ldots \\ (x_n, \tau_n - e)\\ (x, \text{SHOPPING} \cdot \text{TIME}(r_1))\end{array}$
LINE $\begin{array}{c}y_1\\ \ldots \\ y_m\end{array}$	$\begin{array}{c}y_2\\ \ldots \\ y_m\end{array}$	Λ (empty)	$\begin{array}{c}y_1^*\\ \ldots \\ y_m\\ (x_1, \tau_1 - t(s))\\ \ldots \\ \overline{(x_n, \tau_n - t(s))}\end{array}$	$\begin{array}{c}y_1\\ \ldots \\ y_m\end{array}$
SERVICE · TIME · SEED r_2	$\Gamma(r_2)^{**}$	r_2	r_2	r_2
SERVICE · TIME · LEFT σ	$\text{SERVICE} \cdot \text{TIME}(r_2)$	∞	$\sigma - t(s)$	$\sigma - e$

* See Section 6.4 for definitions of $\overline{(x, e)}$ and $\overline{\overline{(x, e)}}$.

** $\Gamma : [0, 1] \to [0, 1]$ is the random number generator transition function.

177

Thus IMMINENT(s) is the set of components scheduled to undertake activity at the next hatching time.

Then $\bar{\alpha}(s) = $ SELECT(IMMINENT(s)) is the imminent component selected to first become active at the next hatching time. The next state if no external events occur, $\delta_\phi(s)$, is given by columns 2, 3, and 4 of the Table 1, and the state just after customer x arrives at elapsed time $e \in [0, t(s)]$ is given in column 5.

Exercise.   Explain in your own terms each column of Table 1.

Thus far we have a base model that represents, for us, the internal structure of the real grocery store. Actually we have a *class* of such models, since we have left the parameters SHOPPING · TIME and SERVICE · TIME unspecified. That is, each choice of a pair of functions—one for SHOPPING · TIME and one for SERVICE · TIME—will result in a completely specified model, which when given an input segment and an initial state will undergo a unique state trajectory.

8.2   EXPERIMENTAL FRAMES FOR GROCERY STORE

In Section 2.2 we informally defined a valid model. Validity was explained to be always relative to experimental frames and the behavior of the real system observable within them. We are now ready to attempt a more precise understanding of these concepts in the context of our grocery store example.

Suppose we have made an assignment of parameter values and therefore are considering a specific model M from the class of potential base models. Each of the experimental frames described by Table 2 specifies a set of output variables through which observation of the real system is permitted. No other restrictions are placed on the possible observations in these frames, although other kinds of restrictions are possible, as Chapter 11 indicates. In the base model each frame determines an output function, as shown in Table 3.

We have associated suggestive names with the given frames. Let us see how these names apply. In Frame 1 we are allowed to observe directly only the variable BYE · BYE, signaling the emergence of a customer from the store as seen by an outside observer who is not allowed to look into the store. The observer would have to limit his sightings to those he could see by watching the ENTRANCE and the EXIT. Thus all he saw would be a stream of customers entering and leaving the store. More than this, since HELLO and BYE · BYE take on a range of values corresponding to customer names, we are assuming that the observer can identify customers to a corresponding

Table 2 Some Experimental Frames for the Grocery Store Base Model

Experimental Frame	Associated Output Variables
1. Outsider's view	BYE · BYE
2. Customer satisfaction	BYE · BYE, LINE
3. CHECKOUT utilization	BUSY

Table 3 Output Functions Determined by Experimental Frames

Output Function Mapping STATES to OUTPUTS:
if $s = (r_1(x_1, \tau_1), y_1, r_2, \sigma)$
$$\vdots$$
$$(x_n, \tau_n), y_m$$

Experimental Frame and Output Variables	OUTPUTS	Then
1. BYE · BYE	$\{\phi, a, b, c, \ldots\}$	$\lambda_1(s) = \begin{cases} y_1 & \text{if } \sigma = 0 \\ \phi & \text{otherwise} \end{cases}$
2. BYE · BYE, LINE	$\{\phi, a, b, c, \ldots\} \times \{a, b, c, \ldots\}^*$	$\lambda_2(s) = (\lambda_1(s), y_1 \cdots y_m)$
3. BUSY	$\{\text{YES, NO}\}$	$\lambda_3(s) = \begin{cases} \text{YES} & \text{if } y_1 \cdots y_m \neq \Lambda \\ \text{NO} & \text{if } y_1 \cdots y_m = \Lambda \end{cases}$

degree of distinction (e.g., he might station himself by the door and ask the entering or leaving customers for their names).

Now imagine the following experiment. At some time t_0 the observer arrives at the store and begins taking the names of customers entering the ENTRANCE and leaving the EXIT. In a notebook, he records as raw data triples of the form [customer name, time of arrival, time of departure]. He continues his data gathering during a period $[t_0, t_1]$. He obtains an input-output (I/O) segment pair represented graphically in Figure 1.

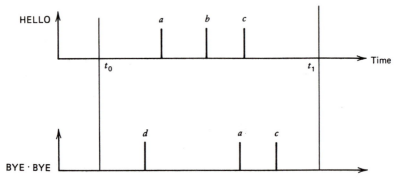

Figure 1 A typical I/O pair observed from the real store in Frame 1 of Table 3 showing customers a, b, and c entering and d, a, and c leaving.

Exercise. Explain why an I/O pair of the form of Figure 1 (customer d is observed to leave the store but not to enter it) is not an unlikely observation.

Now suppose he continues to perform this kind of experiment; for example, let him make hour-long observations beginning at randomly selected times over a six-month period. At the end of six months he will have collected a set of I/O pairs of the form of Figure 1 which will constitute his *acquired data* in Frame 1 as of the end of the six-month period. Necessarily, any set of acquired data is finite, consisting of a finite set of I/O pairs—one pair for each period of continuous observation. Each observation interval is also necessarily of finite length. We can imagine, however, that the data *potentially* acquirable comprise an infinite set of I/O pairs: such data consist of segment pairs over finite observation periods of ever-increasing lengths. The real grocery store in Frame 1 is *precisely the set of potentially acquirable I/O pairs of the form of Figure 1*. Recall that a real system is for us a set of input-output segment pairs.

Our specific base model M will also generate a set of I/O pairs of the form of Figure 1, as explained in Chapter 6. We assign an initial state to the model, at a beginning time t_0. We prescribe a specific input segment over an observation period $[t_0, t_1]$, and by iterating the transition function, we generate a corresponding state trajectory. By applying the output function, we generate a corresponding output segment. For example, in Figure 3 of Chapter 6 we start with an initial state in which the grocery store is empty—this is a state of the form $(r_1, \Lambda, \Lambda, r_2, \infty)$. Note that each pair of random number seeds (r_1, r_2) specifies a different state of this form. The input segment in Figure 2 is the HELLO trace at the top. In Frame 1 the output variable is BYE $\cdot$ BYE; thus the corresponding output segment is that at the bottom. Following this logic, we obtain from Figure 3 of Chapter 6 the pair in Figure 2.

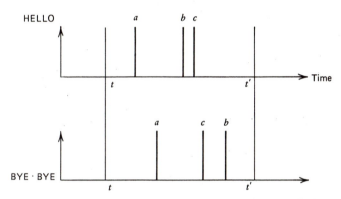

Figure 2 A typical I/O pair generated by the base model in Frame 1 of Table 2.

Now the *input-output behavior* of the base model M in Experimental Frame E is the set of all I/O segment pairs obtainable by assigning an initial state, selecting an input segment, and using M to generate the associated output segment.

Exercise. Provide an initial state for the base model that will enable it to generate the I/O pair of Figure 1. Is this a unique state, or are there many such states?

In line with our informal concepts, we say that a base model M is *valid in the Experimental Frame (E)* if its I/O behavior in Frame E is exactly the set of data potentially acquirable by observing the real system in Frame E.

Thus if M is valid in Frame 1, its I/O behavior—the infinite set of all input-output segment pairs it generates—characterizes for us the set of potentially acquirable data from the real system in Frame 1.

In other words, we postulate that the grocery store can be described structurally by a base model of the type specified in Table 1. Since certain parameters are left unspecified, we do not commit ourselves to a particular member of this class. However, we do make the assumption that at least one of the models in the class is valid in Experimental Frame 1. We can then visualize how the full set of potentially acquirable data in Frame 1 is generated by the real system. Namely, if the base model is subjected to an input segment over an observation interval $[t_0, t_1]$, it will undergo a state trajectory (uniquely determined by its transition function) beginning from the state it was in at time t_0 and will emit a corresponding output segment (determined by the output function appropriate for Frame 1).

Note that often people talk about the "state" of a real system. Since the real system is a set of data, it is incorrect to ascribe statehood to it. But we can speak of the state of a valid base model.

Exercise.   Do you think that "the state of a valid base model" adequately conveys what people have in mind when they speak about the state of the real system?

Frame 2 of Table 2 subtitled "customer satisfaction" to connote a particular behavior of interest: namely, how well is the customer treated by the store? In this frame, we could be asking, "How long does a customer remain in the store?" or "How long does a customer stand in line?" or "How long a line does he encounter when entering the check-out?" To answer such questions requires a greater access to the grocery store than is permitted by the outsider's view of Frame 1. It is true that the length of time spent in the store by a customer can be obtained in Frame 1—this is the difference in time between a successive entry and departure of a customer. These times are obtainable by observing HELLO and BYE · BYE in Frame 1 (see below). But we have no means of determining how long a customer spent in line by observing HELLO and BYE · BYE.

To understand this, we can think in terms of our base model, where the total time spent by a customer in the store is the sum of the time he spends shopping, waiting in the line, and being served. The total time spent may be divided arbitrarily between these three components; knowing the total, therefore, we cannot infer uniquely what any one component's value is.

Thus in Frame 2 we must be able to make additional observations over those permitted in Frame 1. What is the smallest number of additional descriptive variables that must be observed? The answer is one—LINE will do the trick.

Is LINE directly observable? Yes, if we place our observer *inside* the store, in an area corresponding to the CHECKOUT of the base model. We assume the observer can record at any time the names of the customers found in the area, listed in the order of increasing distance from the cashier. Thus we take Frame 2 to prescribe as output variables BYE · BYE and LINE.

Just as in Frame 1, we can collect input-output segment pairs by observing the real grocery store in Frame 2. Also, for any particular base model M, we can specify what constitutes its I/O behavior in Frame 2 by employing the transition function of Table 1 and the output function shown in Table 2. Then the base model will be valid in Frame 2 if its I/O behavior is exactly the potentially acquirable data of the real system in Frame 2. A typical I/O pair in Frame 2 appears in Figure 3; this segment is taken from Figure 3 of Chapter 6. Having this I/O pair, we can obtain the following:

The time spent by x (i.e., a, b, or c) in the store $=$ clock time when BYE · BYE $= x$ minus the clock time when HELLO $= x$.

The time spent by x in LINE not being served $=$ clock time when x becomes the head of the LINE minus the clock time when the LINE first contains x.

The length of the LINE encountered by $x =$ (number of element in the LINE when LINE first contains x) $- 1$.

Thus LINE and BYE · BYE form a sufficient set of output variables for the questions being asked in Frame 2. Actually for the base model being considered, LINE by itself forms a sufficient set (which is minimal), since the BYE · BYE trajectory can be determined from the LINE trajectory.

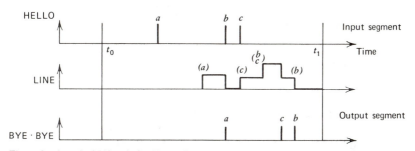

Figure 3 A typical I/O pair for Frame 2.

Exercise. Verify the foregoing assertion.

Of course, in general an observation period $[t_0, t_1]$ may not be long enough to permit the determination of the desired quantities for every customer. In Figure 1, customer d must have entered the store before the observer went on duty, and his total time cannot be determined. On the other hand, the observation period ended before customer *b* left the store; thus *b*'s total time is not determinable. For the customers entering and leaving during the observation period, however, it is possible to compound the quantities obtained for each, to compute statistics such as "average time in store" and "average waiting time in LINE."

Exercise. Show how to determine the times spent by a customer in SHOP · AREA and at the head of the LINE (i.e., being served) while still working within Frame 2.

Finally, Experimental Frame 3 is subtitled "CHECKOUT Utilization." In this frame, we are interested in how busy the cashier really is (i.e., what percentage of the cashier's time is spent serving customers). The descriptive variable BUSY is an appropriate choice for the output variable here. The corresponding output function is shown in Table 2 and a typical I/O pair in this frame would appear as in Figure 4 (taken from Figure 3 of Chapter 6.) *Utilization* of the CHECKOUT is then the ratio of the total YES period to the observation period, $t_1 - t_0$.

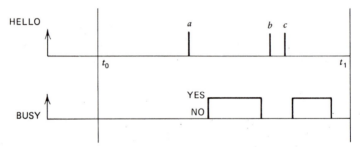

Figure 4   A typical I/O pair for Frame 3.

In the real grocery store, BUSY is directly observable by appropriately classifying the actions of the cashier. In the base model, BUSY can be determined as YES whenever the SERVICE · TIME · LEFT is not zero of infinity. We can also use the approach suggested in Table 2, however, considering that BUSY is YES whenever there is at least one customer standing in LINE. In the base model, a customer arriving at the head of the line is always attended to immediately (in contrast to reality?).

Now let us compare Frames 2 and 3. Since BUSY can be derived from LINE, any data collectable in Frame 3 can be derived from data collectable in Frame 2. In other words, we can observe anything in Frame 2 that we can observe in Frame 3. On the other hand, the converse situation does not hold. We cannot derive the contents of the LINE merely by knowing whether the cashier is BUSY. Thus the observational access allowed by Frame 3 is strictly less than that allowed by Frame 2. This situation suggests that base model simplification in Frame 3 may be possible, and this is confirmed in Section 8.7.

Exercise.   Show that it is not possible to determine any of the quantities (e.g., total time spent in store) of Frame 2 under the limitations of Frame 3, that is, by having available a HELLO–BUSY I/O pair.

8.3   CHOICE OF EXPERIMENTAL FRAMES AND OUTPUT VARIABLES

We have considered three experimental frames and associated output variables. We argued that LINE, BUSY, and BYE · BYE are directly observable descriptive variables. Now we argue that these are the only directly observable descriptive variables suitable for output purposes. In Chapter 2 we indicated that to be legitimate, an experimental frame must specify directly observable variables only. We thus conclude that no legitimate frames other than "combinations" of the three already considered, are possible for the base model chosen.

Why are there no other directly observable variables suitable for output? Excluding the input variable HELLO, and the mentioned three, the descriptive variables are of two kinds: (a) random variables and (b) countdown clock variables. In the case of random variables we must be able to determine directly, by observing the real system at any time t, what the seed of the associated random number generator is at time t. For example, by observing the store at time t we must be able to learn the value of SHOPPING · TIME · SEED at time t. Since nothing in the real grocery store corresponds to the random number generator, such a determination is not possible. In fact, inherent in the probabilistic framework is the definition of generator seeds (or sample spaces in general) as the ultimately nonobservable variables.

In the case of countdown clock variables, we must be able to measure directly TIME · LEFT · LIST and/or SERVICE · TIME · LEFT. In the case of SERVICE · TIME · LEFT, we must be able to determine, at any time t, the time in the future that the customer now being served will leave the CHECKOUT counter. This is intrinsically impossible because it calls for an infallible prediction about the future. Of course, an observer may be able to *estimate* the future time. For example, he may be able to measure the number of items in a customer's shopping cart at time t and, assuming a certain processing time per item, estimate the time left for checkout processing. But then the value assigned to SERVICE · TIME · LEFT at time t is heavily dependent for its accuracy on the truth of assumptions made in the estimate.[†]

Exercise. Consider the case of TIME · LEFT · LIST. Can the shopping time left for a customer be measured directly? How might it be estimated?

We conclude that in general, random variable seeds and countdown clock variables are instances of nondirectly observable variables. Still, as in the present case, such variables may be essential state variables. We take up the consequences of this situation in Chapter 14.

8.4   VALID SIMPLIFICATION

We have discussed three possible experimental frames in which the grocery store can be considered. We have seen that Frame 3 is a relatively restrictive frame in that it requires observation of the grocery store only to the extent required to determine whether the cashier is busy. From what was said in Chapter 2, we might expect that the base model could be simplified to yield a lumped model that is equally valid in Frame 3. In other words, as long as we are interested only in the question of "CHECKOUT Utilization," we may be able to find a relatively simple model that will provide as good an answer to this question as does the base model.

Indeed, this is the case. In Frame 3, the base model output variable BUSY is computed on the basis of whether the LINE is empty. The *identities* of the customers in LINE are irrelevant to this decision. This suggests that we try a lumped model, which unlike the base model does not keep track of customer names. Instead of the base variable LINE, we would have the lumped variable LINE · LENGTH'. If the resulting lumped model is valid, LINE · LENGTH' at time t will be the number of customers in LINE at time t. The correct value of BUSY at any t can then be computed by the lumped model according to whether LINE · LENGTH' is zero at time t.

But we have to be careful that customer identities are not used anywhere else in the base model in such a way that ignoring them will cause the lumped model to compute incorrect values for LINE · LENGTH' (hence for the desired output variable BUSY). For example, when a customer leaves the base model LINE, the lumped model must at the same time decrease LINE · LENGTH' by one. To do this, the lumped model must be able to determine the SERVICE · TIME of the customer at the head of the base model LINE *without* knowing the individual's identity. Fortunately, in the base model considered, the SERVICE · TIME of a customer is *not* dependent on his

---

[†] Thus it would be better to consider a base model in which the indicator variables (e.g., number of items in cart) appear explicitly, and the assumptions are formalized.

identity, and the lumped model does not have to know this identity in order to perform the subtraction at the right time.

Exercise. When a customer joins the base model LINE after leaving the SHOP · AREA, the lumped model must simultaneously add one to LINE · LENGTH'. Why can this be accomplished by the lumped model without knowing the identities of the customers in SHOP · AREA?

By such considerations we can convince ourselves that a lumped model can ignore customer identities and get away with it! But we would like to be able to establish this in a more clear-cut manner that can ultimately be justified by formally stated principles. To do this, we construct the lumped model we have in mind and establish that the proper structural correspondence exists between the base and lumped models, allowing them to produce the I/O behavior represented in Frame 3.

8.5 GROCERY STORE LUMPED MODEL

Components
  ENTRANCE, SHOP · AREA, CHECKOUT
Descriptive Variables
  For ENTRANCE
    HELLO: $x \in \{\phi, a, b, c, \ldots\}$.
  For SHOP · AREA
    SHOPPING · TIME · SEED': $r_1' \in [0, 1]$.
    TIME · LEFT · LIST': $(\tau_1, \ldots, \tau_n) \in (R^+)^*$.
  For CHECKOUT
    LINE · LENGTH': $m' \in \{0, 1, 2, \ldots\}$.
    SERVICE · TIME · SEED': $r_2' \in [0, 1]$.
    SERVICE · TIME · LEFT': $\sigma' \in R_{0, \infty}^+$.
    BUSY': {YES, NO}.
  PARAMETERS
    SHOPPING · TIME'
    SERVICE · TIME'

Component Interaction
A customer x enters the store at time t (signaled by HELLO $= x$) and without revealing his identity receives a value τ' sampled from a random variable SHOPPING · TIME', which is placed on the TIME · LEFT · LIST'. From this point, the model knows only that there is a customer of unknown identity who will emerge from the SHOP · AREA at time $t + \tau'$. When this time is reached, LINE · LENGTH' is increased by one and the associated entry

in TIME $\cdot$ LEFT $\cdot$ LIST is dropped. (This is the model's way of placing a customer of unknown identity in the CHECKOUT LINE).

When SERVICE $\cdot$ TIME $\cdot$ LEFT' becomes zero, LINE $\cdot$ LENGTH' is decreased by one (a customer has just finished the checkout process). If LINE $\cdot$ LENGTH' is not zero, a value σ' is sampled from SERVICE $\cdot$ TIME' and SERVICE $\cdot$ TIME $\cdot$ LEFT' is set to σ' (another customer service is initiated). If LINE $\cdot$ LENGTH' is zero, SERVICE $\cdot$ TIME $\cdot$ LEFT is set to infinity (no customers are waiting for service).

The lumped model is expressed more formally as a DEVS as follows:

With HELLO as the input variable,
    INPUTS' $= \{\phi, a, b, c, \ldots,\}$.
With the state variables given in Table 4 we have
    STATES' $= \{s'|s' = (r'_1, \tau'_1, m', r'_2, \sigma')\}$
$$\vdots$$
$$\tau'_n$$

The time advance function t':STATES' $\rightarrow R^+_{0,\,\infty}$ is such that for any $s' \in$ STATES'

$$t(s') = \min \{\tau'_1, \ldots, \tau'_n, \sigma'\}$$

The tie-breaking rule is the SELECT function of the base model.

The autonomous transition function δ'_ϕ:STATES' $\rightarrow$ STATES' and the external transition function δ'_{ex} are described as follows. Let $\bar{\alpha}(s')$ be the imminent component chosen by SELECT in STATE' s', then $\delta'_\phi(s')$, the next state if no external inputs occur, is given by columns 2, 3, and 4 of Table 4, and the state just after input x arrives at elapsed time $e' \in [0, t'(s')]$ is given in column 5. With BUSY the output variable, OUTPUTS' $= \{$YES, NO$\}$, and the output function λ':STATES' $\rightarrow$ OUTPUTS' is

$$\lambda(r'_1, \tau'_1, \ldots, \tau'_n, m', r'_2, \sigma') = \begin{array}{ll} \text{YES} & \text{if } m' \neq 0 \\ \text{NO} & \text{if } m' = 0 \end{array}$$

Exercise. Explain in your own terms each column in Table 4. Show that the process by which the lumped model was derived from the base model is an instance of the "coarsening the ranges of descriptive variables" simplification procedure (Section 2.8.3).

8.6 HOMOMORPHISM: CRITERION FOR VALID SIMPLIFICATION

Having constructed formal versions of both base and lumped models, we can apply a formal criterion for deciding whether the lumped model is a valid simplification of the base model. Our criterion is very basic and goes by the name "homomorphism," from the Greek "homo" meaning "similar" and

Table 4 The Lumped Model Transition Function

	$\delta'_\phi(s')$ if $\overline{\alpha}(s') =$			$\delta'_{ex}(s', e, x)$
	CHECKOUT		**SHOP · AREA**	
$s' \in$ STATES	$m' \geq 2$	$m' \leq 1$		
SHOPPING · TIME · SEED' r'_1	r'_1	r'_1	r'_1	$\Gamma'(r'_1)$
TIME · LEFT · LIST' τ'_1 ... τ'_n	$\tau'_1 - t'(s')$ ... $\tau'_n - t'(s')$	$\tau'_1 - t'(s)$ ... $\tau'_n - t'(s)$	$\overline{\tau'_1 - t'(s')}$† ... $\overline{\tau'_n - t'(s')}$	τ'_1 ... τ'_n
				SHOPPING · TIME'(r'_1)
LINE · LENGTH m'	$m' - 1$	0	$m' + \sum_{i=1}^n \overline{(\tau'_i - t'(s))}$†	m'
SERVICE · TIME · SEED' r'_2	$\Gamma'(r'_2)$	r'_2	r'_2	r'_2
SERVICE · TIME · LEFT' σ'	SERVICE · TIME'(r'_2)	∞	$\sigma' - t'(s')$	$\sigma' - e'$

†$\overline{e} = \begin{matrix} \Lambda & \text{if } e = 0 \\ e & \text{otherwise;} \end{matrix}$

$\overline{\overline{e}} = \begin{matrix} 0 & \text{if } e = 0 \\ 1 & \text{otherwise.} \end{matrix}$

189

"morph" meaning "structure"; the combined meaning pertains to establishing that the base and lumped models share a similar structure. As we have seen, however, the structure of models may be specified at different levels, and correspondingly there are different levels of "shared structure" or "homomorphism." This situation is more fully treated in Chapter 10. Yet regardless of the structural level considered, the tactic employed in using the homomorphism criterion is the same: show that the base–lumped model structures match up in a certain way and call on general theorems asserting that if the structures correspond as indicated, so will the behaviors.

The homomorphism we are interested in matches up the abstract DEVS specifications of the base and lumped models. That is, it involves a mapping of the STATES of the base model to the STATES' of lumped model, which preserves the transition, time advance, and output functions of the models.

If we can establish that such a mapping exists, a general theorem (proved in Chapter 10) allows us to conclude that the I/O behavior of the lumped model is exactly the same as the I/O behavior of the base model. Notice that the existence of such a homomorphism depends not only on the transition functions of the models, but on the output functions as well. Recall that the output function of the base model is determined by the experimental frame under consideration. Thus we see again that the validity of a lumped model cannot be considered in isolation but is always relative to a given experimental frame.

The general idea is as follows. If h is a mapping from the STATES of the base model *onto* the STATES' of the lumped model, for every base STATE s we have a corresponding lumped STATE' $h(s)$. We say that s and s' *correspond* if $h(s) = s'$.[†] Now consider the following conditions.

8.6.1   Preservation of Time Advance Function

Corresponding states must have the same maximum resting time. More precisely, if s and s' correspond under h, then $t(s) = t(s')$.

8.6.2   Preservation of Transition Functions

After an elementary transition, the successors, of corresponding states must also correspond. More precisely, let s and s' correspond and let $\tau = t(s) = t(s')$ be their respective common resting times. Suppose that at time t the base and lumped models have just entered states s and s', respectively. Then the base model is scheduled to enter the state $\delta_\phi(s)$ at time $t + \tau$, and the lumped model is scheduled to enter the state $\delta'_\phi(s')$ at the same time. For transition function preservation, it must be shown that $\delta_\phi(s)$ and $\delta'_\phi(s')$ also

---

[†] By insisting that the mapping be onto, we require that every lumped state "come from" a base state (i.e., has a base state that corresponds to it).

correspond under h. This can be schematized by the so-called commutative diagram:

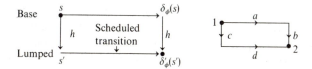

The adjective "commutative" means "any order." Starting at point 1 we can arrive at point 2 by applying the mapping h and the transition functions in "any order" and still obtain the same result. The path ab means apply the base transition function to reach a next base state, then apply the mapping h to get a corresponding lumped state. The result should be the same as that obtained by path cd (i.e., by first applying the map h to get a corresponding lumped state and then applying the lumped transition function to reach a next lumped state).

The same kind of consideration applies for an input x arriving at both models at the same time $t + e$, where the elapsed time $e \in [0, \tau]$. Then the base model will immediately enter state $\delta_{ex}(s, e, x)$ and the lumped model will enter $\delta'_{ex}(s', e, x)$. We require that $\delta_{ex}(s, e, x)$ and $\delta'_{ex}(s', e, x)$ correspond under h. Pictorially, we have

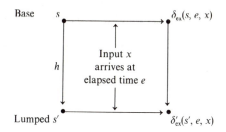

8.6.3   Preservation of Output Functions

Corresponding states must give the same outputs. More precisely, if s and s' correspond, then $\lambda_E(s) = \lambda'(s')$, where λ_E is the output function of the base model in Experimental Frame E. This can be represented as

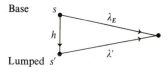

We say that the mapping h from the base STATES onto the lumped STATES' is a DEVS *homomorphism from the base model in Experimental*

Frame E onto the lumped model if the preservation requirements of Sections 8.6.1 to 8.6.3 are satisfied.

We say that the lumped model is *valid in Experimental Frame E* if its I/O behavior is the same as that of the base model in Frame E (i.e., if the two models generate exactly the same set of input-output segment pairs).

By Theorem 3 of Chapter 10, if we establish a homomorphism of the type just described, the lumped model is valid in Frame E. It follows that if the base model itself is valid with respect to the real system in Frame E, the lumped model is, too.

8.7 ESTABLISHING THE GROCERY STORE BASE—LUMPED HOMOMORPHISM

Our goal now should be to establish that a DEVS homomorphism does indeed relate the base and lumped models of the grocery store. We must set up the appropriate correspondence between the parameters and the states of the two models.

Given a base model with a fixed choice for the random variable maps SHOPPING $\cdot$ TIME and SERVICE $\cdot$ TIME, we consider a lumped model employing the same parameter values; that is, we set SHOPPING $\cdot$ TIME$'$ = SHOPPING $\cdot$ TIME and SERVICE $\cdot$ TIME$'$ = SERVICE $\cdot$ TIME. Moreover, we use the same random number generator in both models, so that $\Gamma = \Gamma'$.

The mapping h from base STATES onto lumped STATES$'$ is given in Table 5.

Table 5 asserts that the base STATE

$$s = (r_1, (x_1, \tau_1), y_1, r_2, \sigma)$$
$$\vdots \quad \vdots$$
$$(x_n, \tau_n) \ y_m$$

is mapped into the lumped STATE$'$

$$h(s) = (r_1, \tau_1, m, r_2, \sigma)$$
$$\vdots$$
$$\tau_n$$

In other words, imagine initializing the two models to corresponding states. Then the random number generator seeds of the two models must be set to the same values; the lumped model must represent the same number of customers in the SHOP $\cdot$ AREA scheduled to leave at the same times as in the base model; the same number of customers must be standing in line in both CHECKOUTs, and the lumped model must schedule its CHECKOUT event for the same time as does the base.

Table 5 The Mapping h

Base Model $s \in$ STATES		Lumped Model $h(s) \in$ STATES'	
SHOPPING · TIME · SEED	r_1	r_1	SHOPPING TIME SEED'
TIME · LEFT · LIST	$(x_1, \tau_1) \cdots (x_n, \tau_m)$	$\tau_1, \ldots, \tau_n$	TIME · LEFT · LIST'
LINE	$y_1 \cdots y_m$	m	LINE · LENGTH
SERVICE · TIME · SEED	r_2	r_2	SERVICE · TIME · SEED'
SERVICE · TIME · LEFT	σ	σ	SERVICE · TIME · LEFT'

Exercise. Convince yourself that the explanatory paragraph is consistent with the formal mapping.

Exercise. Show that the states $(.5, (a, 5), d, .6, 10)$ and $(.5, 5, 2, .6, 10)$ correspond under

$$(b, 3) \quad e \quad 3$$
$$(c, 7) \quad 7$$
$$\vdots$$

h but the states $(.5, \Lambda, d, .6, 10)$, $(.5, 8, 3, .6, 10)$ do not

$$e$$

Exercise. Show that the mapping h is onto; that is, give a base STATE corresponding to an arbitrary lumped STATE': $s' = (r_1', \tau_1', m', r_2', \sigma')$

$$\vdots$$
$$\tau_n$$

Is this base state unique?

1. *Time advance function preservation.* To see that the three preservation requirements for homomorphism hold, study the following diagram.

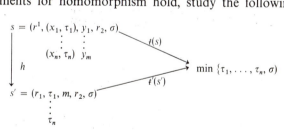

Corresponding states s and s' have the same values of the τ_i's and σ, and the time advance functions t and t' employ these values in the same way, so as shown, $t(s) = t'(s')$.

2. *Transition function preservation.* If the base and lumped states correspond initially, will they still correspond after an elementary transition? This is the crucial test. To find out, we compare the tables describing the transition functions (Tables 1 and 4). Applying the h map to the second base column $\delta_\phi(s)$, we obtain exactly the second lumped column $\delta_\phi'(s')$,

remembering that $t(s) = t'(s')$ (from the preservation of time advance functions already shown) and $\Gamma = \Gamma'$ and SERVICE $\cdot$ TIME = SERVICE $\cdot$ TIME' (by initial choice of random number generator and parameters).

Exercise. Show that columns 3, 4, and 5 of Tables 1 and 4 agree as stated.

Now we have to check that corresponding columns are used by both models in corresponding states. This means, for example, that if CHECKOUT is activated in STATE s in the base model, CHECKOUT must also be activated in the corresponding STATE' s' in the lumped model. To show this, note that using SELECT we have

$$\bar{\alpha}(s) = \begin{array}{ll} \text{CHECKOUT} & \text{if } \sigma \leq \min\{\tau_1, \ldots, \tau_n\} \\ \text{SHOP} \cdot \text{AREA} & \text{otherwise.} \end{array}$$

Since the lumped model also employs SELECT with the same values of σ and $\{\tau_1, \ldots, \tau_n\}$, we have $\bar{\alpha}(s') = \bar{\alpha}(s)$. The two columns within CHECKOUT are also applied in corresponding states, since $m' = m$ for corresponding states. In fact the tables are constructed in such a way that one can place the base model table over that of the lumped model. Then by applying the h mapping to all base model columns, full agreement with the lumped model table is obtained. The first columns represent corresponding states. The second columns are the successor states when the CHECKOUT is selected for the next event and there are at least two customers in LINE, and so on. Pictorially, considering the first and second columns:

r_1	r_1
(x_1, τ_1)	$(x_1, \tau_1 - t(s))$
$\vdots$	$\vdots$
(x_n, τ_n)	$(x_n, \tau_n - t(s))$
y_1	y_2
$\vdots$	$\vdots$
y_m	y_m
r_2	$\Gamma(r_2)$
σ	SERVICE $\cdot$ TIME(r_2)

r_1	r_1
τ_1	$\tau_1 - t'(s)$
$\vdots$	$\vdots$
τ_n	$\tau_n - t'(s)$
m	$m - 1$
r_2	$\Gamma'(r_2)$
σ	SERVICE $\cdot$ TIME'(r_2)

s ... $\delta_\phi(s)$

h ... h

s' ... $\delta'_\phi(s')$

3. *Output function preservation.* Preservation of the output function involves checking that corresponding states give the same output, in the experimental frame of interest. Using the output function λ_3 for Frame 3 (Table 3) of the base model, we have

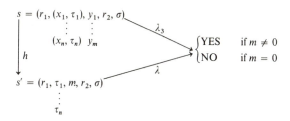

The corresponding states are such that if the LINE is empty (not empty) in the base model, $m' = 0$ $(m' \neq 0)$ in the lumped model. Thus both states report the same value of BUSY.

In conclusion, having shown that the mapping h satisfies the required conditions, we can assert it to be a homomorphism from the base model in Frame 3 onto the lumped model. By Theorem 3 of Chapter 10, we can further assert that the lumped model is a valid simplification of the base model in this particular experimental frame. Finally, if the base model is valid with respect to the real grocery store in Frame 3, so is the lumped model. In other words, the answers provided by the lumped model to the question of CHECKOUT utilization are the same as those of the base model. If we are only interested in this aspect of real system behavior, the relatively simple lumped model will suffice.

Exercise. Recall the discussion in Section 8.4 in which the basis for deriving the lumped model was given as the dropping of customer identities. Explain the preservation of the time advance, transition, and output functions by the mapping h in the terms of Section 8.4.

PROBLEMS

1. In Problem 1 of Chapter 6, you were asked to provide a DEVS model of the bus system of Example 5, Chapter 1. Since this model does not keep track of passenger identities, consider it to be a lumped model for a base model that does. Construct such a model and establish a homomorphism to demonstrate the validity of the lumped model in an appropriate experimental frame.

2. Modify the grocery store base model to permit it to recognize two classes of customers (regular and express), each with characteristic SHOPPING · TIME and SERVICE · TIME distributions. Show that the lumped model of Section 8.5 is no longer valid in Frame 3 but that it can be modified readily to be valid again in this Frame.

Part Two

Chapter Nine

Hierarchy of
System Specifications

In this chapter we provide formal equivalents for the descriptions and processes discussed in Part 1. This presentation is draped around a hierarchy of levels of system specification starting at the lowest behavioral level and ascending to the highest structural level. Each level can be viewed in two enlightening ways: (1) as a level of description, or (2) as a level of knowledge. The levels of the hierarchy and their interrelations are summarized in Section 9.19 (to which the reader may wish to refer from time to time).

We begin by developing the basic formal concepts of systems theory.

9.1 TIME BASE

Fundamental to the notion of "dynamic system" is the passage of time. Time is conceived as flowing along independently, and all events are ordered by this flow.

Formally, we say that a *time base* is a set T. The set T may be isomorphic to the reals R, in which case we call the time base *continuous*, or it may be isomorphic to the integers I, in which case, the time base is said to be *discrete*.

In both the discrete and continuous cases we employ the following properties of the reals and the integers:

(a) *Linear ordering.* There is a relation $<$ (less than) such that for any pair of instants t, t', exactly one of the following cases holds: (1) $t < t'$ (t occurs before t'), (2) $t' < t$ (t occurs after t'), or (3) $t = t'$.

(b) *Abelian group.* There is a binary operation $+$ on T such that $(T, +)$ is an abelian group; that is, for every pair $t, t' \in T$: there is an element $t'' \in T$ such that $t + t' = t' + t = t''$; there is an element $0 \in T$ such that $t + 0 = t$; there is a unique element $-t$ such that $t + (-t) = 0$ [we write $t + (-t')$ as $t - t'$). Finally, $+$ is associative $[t + (t' + t'') = (t + t') + t''$ for all triples $t, t', t'' \in T]$.

(c) *Unbounded extension.* There is *no* upper bound $t_u \in T$ such that for every $t \in T$, $t < t_u$; dually, there is no lower bound t_l such that for every $t \in T$, $t_l < t$. We denote by ∞ and $-\infty$ the fictitious upper and lower bounds.

(d) *Addition is order preserving.*

$$t < t' \Rightarrow t + t'' < t' + t'' \qquad \text{for} \quad \text{all } t'' \in T$$

The time base is represented in Figure 1a.

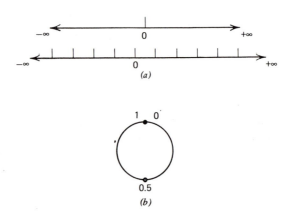

Figure 1   (a) Continuous and discrete time bases. (b) A toroidal time base.

The linear ordering property enables us to codify the notions of past and future relative to the present. For if $t \in T$ is interpreted as the *present*, then $\{t'|t' < t\}$ is the *past* and $\{t'|t' > t\}$ is the *future*. Moreover, the past and future are disjoint (as is required in a world where each moment counts and cannot be recaptured in the future once it is past).

The group property allows us to consider translation of trajectories. The unbounded extension property enables us to deal with trajectories of finite but arbitrarily large length.

The preservation of order by addition ensures that when a trajectory is translated, the chronology of the events it records is preserved.

Exercise. Look ahead to the definition of "trajectory" in Section 9.2. For each of the properties *a* through *d* answer the question: what unexpected result could occur when we apply the translation operator of Section 9.7 if this property were not present?

For example, consider the time base $T = [0, 1)$ (the real interval from 0 to 1, not including 1). Wrap the ends around to form a circle as in Figure 1*b*. To add t and t', take their normal sum $t + t'$ and subtract 1 if the sum exceeds or equals 1. This is called mod 1 addition, and it corresponds to moving around the circle in a clockwise direction.

The set T so constructed satisfies *a* and *b* but not *c* and *d*. What happens to a segment as it is translated around the circle? (This is especially relevant to the order preservation property.)

We see that is possible to consider linearly ordered Abelian groups other than $(R, +, <)$ or $(I, +, <)$ as legitimate time bases or even to relax the requirements (e.g., by requiring only a linearly ordered set).

Exercise. Describe some situations in which a relaxed set or indeed a different set of axioms for the time base might be appropriate.

9.2   TRAJECTORIES AND SEGMENTS

Having a time base T, we are in a position to describe how events occur over time.

For every pair $t_0, t_1 \in T$ such that $t_0 \leq t_1$ there are associated *observation intervals* denoted (ambiguously) by $\langle t_0, t_1 \rangle$ where $\langle t_0, t_1 \rangle \in \{(t_0, t_1), [t_0, t_1), (t_0, t_1], [t_0, t_1]\}$; as is standard, $(t_0, t_1) = \{t | t_0 < t < t_1\}$, $[t_0, t_1) = (t_0, t_1) \cup \{t_0\}$, $(t_0, t_1] = (t_0, t_1) \cup \{t_1\}$, and $[t_0, t_1] = [t_0, t_1) \cup (t_0, t_1]$.

It often does not matter which of the four possibilities $\langle t_0, t_1 \rangle$ refers to. Where the distinction is significant, so that it is more convenient, for example, to deal with a particular kind of interval, we make explicit the denotation of $\langle t_0, t_1 \rangle$.

Note that $\langle t_0, t_0 \rangle$ refers either to the singleton t_0 or the empty set $\varnothing$, according to the choice of open or closed intervals.

For the interval $\langle t_0, t_1 \rangle$, t_0 is called the *initial* or *beginning* time and t_1 is called the *final* or *ending* time.

Let Z denote a set; for example, an input, state, or output set of a model. A *segment* (or *trajectory*) over Z and T is a map[†] ω from an interval of T to Z that is, for some interval $\langle t_0, t_1 \rangle$,

$$\omega : \langle t_0, t_1 \rangle \to Z.$$

[†] We allow ω to be undefined at some points (see Section 9.6).

Sometimes we write $\omega_{\langle t_0, t_1 \rangle}$ to signify a segment with domain $\langle t_0, t_1 \rangle$. Since Z may be a finite, countable (discrete), or uncountable (continuous) set, and T may be countable or uncountable, we have six kinds of segments, each appropriate to certain classes of systems. The possibilities are described in Table 1.

Table 1   Varieties of Systems

	Range Set Z		
Time Base T	Finite	Discrete	Continuous
Discrete	Finite state automata	Infinite state computers	Difference equation specified systems
		Sequential machine specified systems	
Continuous	Asynchronous finite state systems	Queueing models	Differential equation specified systems
		Discrete event specified systems	

The trajectory $\omega : \langle t_0, t_1 \rangle \to Z$ describes a motion through the set Z which begins at t_0, ends at t_1, and at every $t \in \langle t_0, t_1 \rangle$, $\omega(t)$ describes "where the motion is" at time t. If α is a variable of a program with range Y, a segment $\omega : \langle t_0, t_1 \rangle \to Y$ would describe a sequence of values $\omega_\alpha(t_0)$, $\omega_\alpha(t_0 + 1), \ldots, \omega_\alpha(t_1)$ assumed by the variable α during a run beginning at t_0 and ending at t_1 (here $T = I$ and $\langle t_0, t_1 \rangle = [t_0, t_1]$). In fact, as we see later, this formalism provides the "good" notation for describing trajectories previously described in the "bad" notation $\alpha(t_0), \ldots, \alpha(t), \ldots, \alpha(t_1)$ of Section 5.1.

We let (Z, T) *denote the set of all segments over Z and T.* Thus $\omega \in (Z, T) \Leftrightarrow$ there is an interval $\langle t_0, t_1 \rangle$ of T and $\omega : \langle t_0, t_1 \rangle \to Z$.

9.3   I/O RELATION OBSERVATION

Having developed a means for recording the behavior of variables over time, we can specify what we mean by knowledge of a system at the most basic experimental level.

Suppose we have isolated a real system and have specified a set of input and output variables. Recall that an input variable is one we consider to influence the system but not to be directly influenced by it; an output variable is directly observable by means of some kind of measurement process. If $\alpha_1, \ldots, \alpha_n$ denote the input variables and $X_1, \ldots, X_n$ are their range sets, the cross product $X_1 \times X_2 \times \cdots \times X_n$ represents the set of all possible value assignments. Let us use values coming from some subset X of this cross product to stimulate the system. We call X an *input* set and at the basic level of knowledge, where we are starting, we consider X to be an *abstract* set, independent of any representation as a subset of a cross product of input variables. In the words of Section 9.18, X is not coordinatized or is unstructured. The implication here is that in the abstract theory we are not interested in any system properties that are tied to a particular structuring of the input set X—if X is represented as a subset of a cross product of the range sets of another set of input variables $\alpha'_1, \ldots, \alpha'_{n'}$, nothing will change in our perception of the system properties at this basic level. Likewise we consider an abstract set Y as the *output* set.

Thus, very simply, we have a set X of values that can appear at the input to the system and a set Y of values that can appear at its output.

We can now conduct an experiment: we apply to the input a segment from (X, T) and we observe at the output a segment from (Y, T). Thus we have the picture of Figure 2. A segment $\omega \in (X, T)$ is called an *input* segment; $\rho \in (Y, T)$ is an *output* segment (or trajectory). We adopt the reasonable convention that the output segment observed in response to an input segment is recorded over the same observation interval (other conventions are possible). Thus if ω and ρ are to be associated, the domain of ω equals the domain of ρ. We call such a pair (ω, ρ), an *input-output* (or I/O) pair.

Figure 2 A typical experiment.

If we continue experimenting, we will collect a set of such I/O pairs, which we call an *I/O relation*. Since we have only a finite time to do this experimentation, we can collect only a finite number of I/O pairs. Moreover, often we are interested in experimenting with only a subset of all possible input segments, denoted by Ω.

To gather together what has been said, we make the following definition: An *I/O relation observation* (*IORO*) is a structure

$$(T, X, \Omega, Y, R)$$

where T is a time base

    X is a set—the input value set

    Y is a set—the output value set

    Ω is a set—the input segment set

    R is a relation—the I/O relation[†]

with the constraints that (a) $\Omega \subseteq (X, T)$ and (b) $R \subseteq \Omega \times (Y, T)$ where $(\omega, \rho) \in R \Rightarrow \text{dom}(\omega) = \text{dom}(\rho)$. Here we use the notation $\text{dom}(\omega) = $ domain of ω.

Often we denote the structure (T, X, Ω, Y, R) by its defining relation R.

Our definition does not require that R be finite because we want to deal with models that attempt to characterize the *potential* data observable from a real system. Such data are assumed to be infinite even though we can collect only a finite portion of the full amount.

Example 1. An IORO is often the underlying form used when the behavior of a system is described by means of a differential equation such as:

$$\frac{d^3y}{dt^3} + \frac{2\,d^2y}{dt^2} + \frac{8\,dy}{dt} + 7y = x$$

This equation implies that time is continuous and that the input and output sets are also one-dimensional continuous variables. Thus in an explicit IORO $\langle T, X, \Omega, Y, R \rangle$, we have $T = X = Y = R$. Since input segment set Ω is not specified by the equation however, we are at liberty to choose it, to meet the modelling situation at hand (more about this is said in Chapter 11). One natural choice is the set of *bounded piecewise continuous (bpc) segments*, that is, the set of $\omega \in (X, T)$ such that ω is continuous except possibly at a finite number of points and the range of ω has a finite upper bound. Now it follows that

$$R = \{(\omega, \rho)|\ \text{dom}(\omega) = \text{dom}(\rho)$$

and

$$\frac{d^3\rho(t)}{dt^3} + \frac{2\,d^2\rho(t)}{dt^2} + \frac{8\,d\rho(t)}{dt} + 7\rho(t) = \omega(t) \qquad \text{for all } t \in \text{dom}(\omega)$$

This means that we would pair an output segment ρ with an input segment ω over the same observation interval, if ω and ρ satisfy the differential equation at each point in time. Of course ρ would have to have derivatives up to the third order at each point in the interval.

[†] We use R to denote both an I/O relation and the reals. The context will clarify which meaning is intended.

Exercise. $L:(R, R) \to (R, R)$ is a *differential operator of order n* if $L(\rho)$ is defined just in case ρ has derivatives up to the *n*th order and $L(\rho)(t)$ is an arithmetic combination of the *n* derivatives of ρ at *t*. In our example,

$$L(\rho)(t) = \frac{d^3}{dt^3}\rho(t) + \frac{2\, d^2\rho(t)}{dt^2} + \frac{8\, d\rho(t)}{dt} + 7\rho(t)$$

Characterize an IORO to be naturally associated with *L*. Why would you expect that many ρ's might be paired with the same ω?

An IORO, as we have shown, summarizes what can be known about the system as a black box viewed externally. Two problem areas immediately suggest themselves. First we have the problem of *going from structure to behavior*: if we know what lies inside the box, we ought to be able to describe, in one way or another, the behavior of the box as viewed externally. The second area relates to the reverse situation: *going from behavior to structure*; that is, the problem of trying to infer the internal structure of a black box from external observation.

The first problem (the structure-to-behavior direction) is a recurrent theme of this chapter. Each time we introduce a new, more structured level of system description, we show how to convert such a description into a description at a less structured level. Hence by a number of steps one may always convert a higher level structural description into one at the most basic level—that of I/O relation observation.

The problem in the behavior-to-structure direction is much more difficult, and its consideration is deferred until Chapter 14.

9.4 I/O FUNCTION OBSERVATION

We know from Chapter 3 how, given a model, we may associate a set of states with it. Now we develop the concept of state in more fundamental and, at first, more abstract form, focusing on the role of states in uniquely determining the transformation of input segments to output segments.

Suppose we undertake several simulation experiments on a model such that we reset the model to the *same initial state* every time we apply an input segment. By the initialization and run repetition properties of state variables (Section 3.2), we know that under these circumstances there will be one and only one, output segment associated with a particular input segment. Thus in this case we collect a set of I/O pairs constituting on I/O *function* [a function is a relation such that (ω, ρ) and (ω, ρ') both belong to the relation only if $\rho = \rho'$].

If we carried out this experimentation for a number of states of the model, we would collect a set of I/O functions, one function for each such state. This leads us to formulate a next higher level of system knowledge. We make the following definition.

An *I/O function observation* (IOFO) is a structure

$$(T, X, \Omega, Y, F)$$

where T, X, Ω, and Y are as before, and F is a set (the set of I/O functions) with the constraint that

$$f \in F \Rightarrow f \subseteq \Omega \times (Y, T) \text{ is a function,}$$

and if $\rho = f(\omega)$, then dom $(\rho) = $ dom (ω).

Note that f may be a partial function; that is, for some segment ω, $f(\omega)$ need not be defined, or equivalently, there is no pair of the form (ω, ρ).

Given an IOFO (T, X, Ω, Y, F), we associate with it an IORO (T, X, Ω, Y, R) where $R = \bigcup_{f \in F} f$. In other words, by collecting together all the I/O segment pairs that were formerly partitioned into functional groupings, we obtain an I/O relation. In this process, we lose the information about which individual functions were so united. This is what we would expect, since the IOFO represents a higher level of knowledge than the IORO.

Example 2. In the case of behavior described by a differential equation such as

$$\frac{d^3y}{dt^3} + \frac{2\,dy^2}{dt^2} + \frac{8\,dy}{dt} + 7y = x$$

it is well known how to characterize an appropriate set of I/O functions. In our example, we have an IOFO (T, X, Ω, Y, F), where T, X, Ω, Y are as in the IORO of Example 1, and

$$F = \{f_{a, b, c} | a, b, c \in R\}$$

where $f_{a, b, c} : \Omega \to (Y, T)$ is defined by

$$f_{a, b, c}(\omega) = \rho$$

where $\dfrac{d^3\rho(t)}{dt^2} + \dfrac{2\,d^2\rho(t)}{dt^2} + \dfrac{8\,d\rho(t)}{dt} + 7\rho(t) = \omega(t)$ for $t \in$ dom $(\omega) =$ dom $(\rho) = \langle t_1, t_2 \rangle$

and

$$\frac{d^2\rho(t_1)}{dt} = a, \qquad \frac{d\rho(t_1)}{dt} = b, \qquad \rho(t_1) = c$$

In general, given a differential operator of order n, we require n parameters to specify an I/O function, corresponding to the specification of the initial values of the derivatives

$$y, \frac{dy}{dt}, \ldots, \frac{dy^{n-1}}{dt^{n-1}}$$

Exercise.   Give an IOFO corresponding to a differential operator L.

Note that at the IOFO level we are allowed to observe the initial state of the system (before we experiment), but not its final state (after we experiment). In the next higher level of knowledge, we are allowed to observe both initial and final states, and in this way to know directly the transition and output functions. This is the level at which the general notion of input-output system is defined.

9.5   I/O SYSTEM

First let us supply some preliminaries to the definition of I/O systems. A pair of segments $\omega, \omega' \in (Z, T)$ are said to be *contiguous* if their domains are contiguous, that is for some t_0, t_1, t_2 in T, $\omega : \langle t_0, t_1 \rangle \to Z$ and $\omega' : \langle t_1, t_2 \rangle \to Z$.

We can "patch" a pair of contiguous segments together to form a new segment. Given $\omega : \langle t_0, t_1 \rangle \to Z$ and $\omega : \langle t_1, t_2 \rangle \to Z$, a *composition* of ω and ω' is a segment μ such that $\mu : \langle t_0, t_2 \rangle \to Z$ and

$$\mu(t) = \begin{array}{ll} \omega(t) & \text{for } t \in \langle t_0, t_1 \rangle - \{t_1\} \\ \omega'(t) & \text{for } t \in \langle t_1, t_2 \rangle - \{t_1\} \end{array}$$

Since $\mu(t_1)$ is not specified in the definition for a given pair ω, ω', it is possible to imagine any number of distinct compositions, each differing only in the value at the overlap point t_1. Once the type of interval $\{(\ ), [\ ), (\ ], [\ ]\}$ has been specified, however, it is desirable to have a unique value prescribed, which allows the resulting composition operation to be associative. In other words, we postulate the following.

There is a binary operation on (Z, T) which is defined only for contiguous segments: COMPOSITION(ω, ω') is a composition of ω and ω' for contiguous ω, ω'; moreover, COMPOSITION is *associative*; that is, if ω, ω' are contiguous, and ω', ω'' are contiguous, COMPOSITION(COMPOSITION$(\omega, \omega'), \omega'') = $ COMPOSITION$(\omega, $ COMPOSITION$(\omega', \omega''))$.

Often we write COMPOSITION$(\omega, \omega') = \omega \cdot \omega'$ or just $\omega\omega'$.

Exercise. Let $\langle \ \rangle$ mean $[\ )$. Show that the operation taking ω and ω' into $\omega \cdot \omega'$ is an associative composition where

$$\omega \cdot \omega'(t) = \begin{array}{ll} \omega(t) & \text{for } t \in [t_0, t_1) \\ \omega'(t) & \text{for } t \in [t_1, t_2) \end{array}$$

(note that $\omega\omega'(t_1) = \omega'(t_1)$.)

Provide choices of $\omega\omega'(t_1)$ for each of the other interval types yielding associative composition operators. Note that an equally valid choice of two natural possibilities exists in the case $\langle \ \rangle = [\ ]$. Try employing a fixed constant in the case $\langle \ \rangle = (\ )$.

The notion of composition allows us to formalize the performing of successive I/O experiments on a system. If we inject an input segment ω and immediately follow this with a second input segment ω', then $\omega \cdot \omega'$ represents the resulting compound experiment as in Figure 3. A subset Ω of (Z, T) is said to be *closed under COMPOSITION* if for every contiguous pair $\omega, \omega' \in \Omega$, we have $\omega \cdot \omega' \in \Omega$.

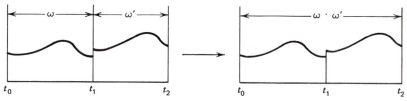

Figure 3   Composition of segments.

We employ sets of segments closed under COMPOSITION as our system input sets. Thus if we can consider the injection of contiguous segments ω, ω' separately, we can consider the COMPOSITION (ω, ω') also. We are now ready to consider our most basic concept of "system." An *input-output system* (*I/O system*, or just *system*) is a structure

$$S = \langle T, X, \Omega, Q, Y, \delta, \lambda \rangle$$

where T is a time base
  X is a set—the input value set
  Ω is a subset of (X, T)—the input segment set
  Q is a set—the state set
  Y is a set—the output value set
  δ is a function—the state transition function
  λ is a function—the output function

subject to the constraints

1. Ω *is closed under COMPOSITION.*
2.   *Deterministic response.* δ is a mapping from $Q \times \Omega$ into Q

$$\delta : Q \times \Omega \rightarrow Q;$$

λ is a mapping from Q into Y

$$\lambda : Q \rightarrow Y$$

3.   *Composition property.*   For every contiguous pair of segments $\omega, \omega' \in \Omega$

$$\delta(q, \omega \cdot \omega') = \delta(\delta(q, \omega), \omega')$$

The interpretation of the functions δ and λ is as illustrated in Figure 4.

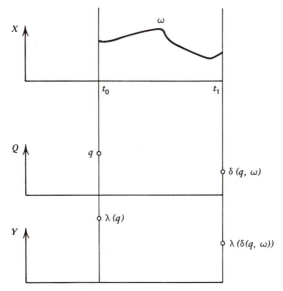

Figure 4   The basic systems functions.

Suppose that the system is in state $q \in Q$ at time $t_0 < t$; we inject an input segment $\omega : \langle t_0, t_1 \rangle \rightarrow X$; the system responds to this segment and finishes in state $\delta(q, \omega)$ at time t_1. Thus $\delta(q, \omega)$ specifies the *final* state reached starting from q with input ω. It says nothing about the intermediate states traversed to arrive there. We observe the output of the system at time t_1, which is $\lambda(\delta(q, \omega))$. Again $\lambda(\delta(q, \omega)$ tells us the final output only and nothing about the interior outputs generated within the observation interval $\langle t_0, t_1 \rangle$.

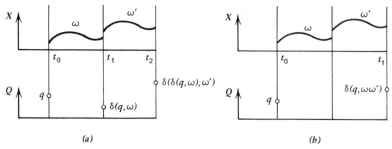

Figure 5 The composition property. (*a*) Results of a two-part experiment. (*b*) Result of a single composite experiment.

To interpret the composition property (Axiom 3) refer to Figure 5. Suppose that the system is in state $q \in Q$ at time $t_0 \in T$; we inject $\omega : \langle t_0, t_1 \rangle \to X$; this transfers the system from state q to state $\delta(q, \omega)$ at time t_1. We immediately inject $\omega' : \langle t_1, t_2 \rangle \to X$; this transfers the system from state $\delta(q, \omega)$ at time t_1 to state $\delta(\delta(q, \omega), \omega')$ at time t_2, which is the final state of the experiment. Axiom 3 asserts that this should also be the final state $\delta(q, \omega \cdot \omega')$ obtained by applying the composite segment $\omega \cdot \omega' : \langle t_0, t_2 \rangle \to X$ to the same initial state q. Thus we require that $\delta(\delta(q, \omega), \omega') = \delta(q, \omega\omega')$.

Exercise. Returning to Section 3.2, convince yourself that the present axioms correctly encode the intuitive concept of state developed there. In particular, show how Axiom 2 [determinism] relates to properties *a* and *b* [initialization and repetition of a run] of the prototype simulation program and how Axiom 3 [composition property] relates to properties *c* and *d* [interrupting and restarting a run] of that program.

Exercise. Verify the statement made earlier that if we are allowed to directly observe both initial and final states of an experiment, we can go about constructing the transition and output functions.

9.6 FROM SYSTEM STRUCTURE TO BEHAVIOR

Having an internal structure of a system, we ought to be able to generate its behavior. In terms of knowledge levels, given the I/O system structure $S = \langle T, X, \Omega, Q, \delta, \lambda \rangle$, we ought to be able to associate with S an I/O function observation and an I/O relation observation which are complete in the sense of containing all possibly observable input-output pairs.

To do this we have to be able to describe the time course of state and output values in response to an input segment along the entire observation interval. The system description, however, provides the state and output responses only at the end of an observation interval. Thus we need an operator that will chop a segment into successive parts to which the transition and output function can be applied. The operator, called segmentation, is illustrated in Figure 6.

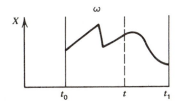 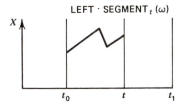

Figure 6 Left segmentation.

Let $\omega : \langle t_0, t_1 \rangle \to Z$. Then for $\tau \in \langle t_0, t_1 \rangle$, LEFT $\cdot$ SEGMENT$_\tau(\omega) = \omega'$, where $\omega' : \langle t_0, \tau \rangle \to Z$ such that $\omega'(t) = \omega(t)$ for $t \in \langle t_0, \tau \rangle$. Often we use the shorter notation $\omega_{\tau\rangle}$ for LEFT $\cdot$ SEGMENT$_\tau(\omega)$.

Exercise. Define RIGHT $\cdot$ SEGMENT$_\tau(\omega)$ (also denoted by $\omega_{\langle\tau}$).

It is only natural that having split a segment into parts, we should be able to put it back together again. Thus we require that

$$\text{COMPOSITION}(\omega_{\tau\rangle}, \omega_{\langle\tau}) = \omega$$

Exercise. Show that the COMPOSITION operators defined in Section 9.6 for $\langle \ \rangle \in \{ [\ ), (\ ], [\ ] \}$ satisfy the COMPOSITION requirement. What happens in the case $\langle \ \rangle = (\ )$?

With each state $q \in Q$ and each input segment $\omega : \langle t_0, t_1 \rangle \to X$ in Ω, we associate a *state trajectory*, STRAJ$_{q, \omega} : \langle t_0, t_1 \rangle \to Q$; for each $\tau \in \langle t_0, t_1 \rangle$,

$$\text{STRAJ}_{q, \omega}(\tau) = \delta(q, \text{LEFT} \cdot \text{SEGMENT}_\tau(\omega))$$

Note that because δ is a function, STRAJ$_{q, \omega}$ has a unique value everywhere it is defined—but it need not be defined everywhere, since for some $\tau \in \langle t_0, t_1 \rangle$, the appropriate left segment of ω may not belong to Ω. Thus δ is not defined for that segment, and STRAJ$_{q, \omega}(\tau)$ will be undefined for that point τ.

Often it is convenient to make sure that all left segments are in the input segment set. We say that S is *left input segmentable* if Ω is closed under left segmentation.

Exercise. Show that if S is left input segmentable, STRAJ$_{q, \omega}$ is fully defined for each $q \in Q$ and $\omega \in \Omega$.

A state trajectory is a time record of the states passed through by a system as it moves from initial to final state. There may be gaps in the record—points at which no state is recorded—because the set of allowable input segments may not be sufficiently extensive. The states themselves, however, are not observable; therefore we need a second trajectory, the output trajectory, to record the trace of output values observed.

With each $q \in Q$ and $\omega : \langle t_0, t_1 \rangle \to X$ in Ω, we associate an output trajectory $\text{OTRAJ}_{q, \omega} : \langle t_0, t_1 \rangle \to Y$, where for each $\tau \in \langle t_0, t_1 \rangle$

$$\text{OTRAJ}_{q, \omega}(\tau) = \lambda(\text{STRAJ}_{q, \omega}(\tau))$$

Thus $\text{OTRAJ}_{q, \omega}$ is derived from $\text{STRAJ}_{q, \omega}$ by applying the output map ω to the state traversed at each instant τ; of course $\text{OTRAJ}_{q, \omega}$ is undefined wherever $\text{STRAJ}_{q, \omega}$ is undefined. These concepts are illustrated in Figure 7. Starting in state q, an input segment $\omega \in \Omega$ is applied. At point τ_1, $\text{LEFT} \cdot \text{SEGMENT}_{\tau_1}(\omega) \in \Omega$; thus $\text{STRAJ}_{q, \omega}(\tau_1)$ is defined and equals q', the state reached by the system by applying $\text{LEFT} \cdot \text{SEGMENT}_{\tau_1}(\omega)$ to the system in state q; $\text{OTRAJ}_{q, \omega}(\tau_1)$ is also defined and equals $\lambda(q')$. In contrast, at point τ_2, $\text{LEFT} \cdot \text{SEGMENT}_{\tau_2}(\omega)$ is not in the specified set Ω, and $\text{STRAJ}_{q, \omega}(\tau_2)$ and $\text{OTRAJ}_{q, \omega}(\tau_2)$ are undefined.

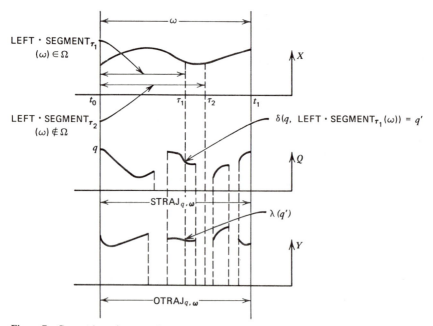

Figure 7   Generation of state and output trajectories.

Now with each state $q \in Q$ we can associate a function $\tilde{\beta}_q : \Omega \to (Y, T)$, called the *I/O function of state q*, where for each $\omega \in \Omega$,

$$\tilde{\beta}_q(\omega) = OTRAJ_{q, \omega}$$

The set of functions $\tilde{B}_S = \{\tilde{\beta}_q | q \in Q\}$ is called the *I/O behavior of S*. Thus with S we associate the I/O function observation $(T, X, \Omega, Y, \tilde{B}_S)$—call it IOFO$_S$.

Exercise.   Show that $(T, X, \Omega, Y, \tilde{B}_S)$ satisfies the prerequisites of an IOFO.

The *I/O relation R_S* is defined to be the union of all the functions $\tilde{\beta}_q$ in $\tilde{B}_S$, hence is the set of all input-output pairs possibly observable for S. .

Exercise.   Show that

$$R_S = \{(\omega, \rho) | \omega \in \Omega, \rho = OTRAJ_{q, \omega} \qquad \text{for some } q \in Q\}$$

So we associate with S the I/O relation observation (T, X, Ω, Y, R_S), which we denote by IORO$_S$.

With each state $q \in Q$, we can also associate a function $\beta_q : \Omega \to Y$, called the *last output I/O function of state q*, where for each $\omega \in \Omega$,

$$\beta_q(\omega) = \lambda(\delta(q, \omega))$$

The relationship between $\tilde{\beta}_q$ and β_q is given by

$$\tilde{\beta}_q(\omega)(t) = \beta_q(\omega_{t\rangle}) \qquad \text{for } t \in \text{dom}(\omega)$$

Exercise.   Prove this.

Knowing either one of the functions β_q, $\tilde{\beta}_q$ is tantamount to knowing the other one.

Exercise.   Show how to define β_q, having been given $\tilde{\beta}_q$.

Thus the set of function $B_S = \{\beta_q | q \in Q\}$ carries the same information as the set $\tilde{B}_S$.

To summarize, given a system description $S = \langle T, X, \Omega, Q, Y, \delta, \lambda \rangle$, we can always define the observable behavior it can produce. This behavior can be observed at two levels. If we have *no access* to the initial state of the system at the beginning of an experiment, we can collect the I/O pairs in R_S; if we *know* the initial state, we can separate the I/O pairs into functional relations, indexed by initial states, thus obtaining the set of functions $\tilde{B}_S$ or the related set B_S.

9.7 TIME INVARIANT SYSTEMS

Until now we have not automatically allowed ourselves the freedom of sliding a segment around so that if $\omega:\langle t_0, t_1 \rangle \to X$ is applicable at time t_0, for example, we can also apply "it" at some other time t_2. To formalize this idea, we consider a class of unary operators on (X, T) called "translation" operators.

For each $\tau \in T$, define a unary operator

$$\text{TRANS}_\tau : (Z, T) \to (Z, T)$$

where if $\omega:\langle t_0, t_1 \rangle \to Z$ and $\text{TRANS}_\tau(\omega) = \omega'$, then $\omega':\langle t_0 + \tau, t_1 + \tau \rangle \to Z$ and $\omega'(t + \tau) = \omega(t)$ for $t \in \langle t_0, t_1 \rangle$.

We say that $\text{TRANS}_\tau(\omega)$ is the τ-*translate of* ω, and it has the same shape as ω except that it has been translated by τ units, as in Figure 8.

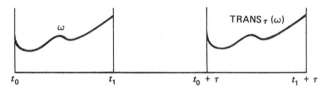

Figure 8 The translation operator.

Exercise. Show that the relation "is a translate of" on (Z, T) is an equivalence relation, where ω' *is a translate of* ω if and only if for some $\tau \in T$, ω' is a τ-translate of ω.

We say that $\Omega \subseteq (Z, T)$ is *closed under translation* if $\omega \in \Omega \Rightarrow$ for every $\tau \in T$, $\text{TRANS}_\tau(\omega) \in \Omega$.

The concept of time invariance was introduced in Section 1.4.1 and used in Section 3.3. Having before us the notion of translation, we can now formally define time invariance. System $S = \langle T, X, \Omega, Q, Y, \delta, \lambda \rangle$ is *time invariant* if

(a) Ω *is closed under translation.*

(b) δ *is time independent*: for every $\tau \in T$, $\omega \in \Omega$, and $q \in Q$

$$\delta(q, \omega) = \delta(q, \text{TRANS}_\tau(\omega))$$

For a time invariant system, if a segment can be applied somewhere in time, it can be applied anywhere in time; moreover, anywhere the same-shaped segment is applied to the same initial state, the same result will be achieved.

Exercise. Let S be a structure $\langle T, X, \Omega, Q, Y, \delta, \lambda \rangle$, where $T = X = Q = Y = R$, $\Omega = (X, T)$, and $\lambda(q) = q$, and consider four possibilities for δ:

1. $\delta_1(q, \omega_{\langle t_0, t_1 \rangle}) = qt_1$
2. $\delta_2(q, \omega_{\langle t_0, t_1 \rangle}) = q(t_1 - t_0)$
3. $\delta_3(q, \omega_{\langle t_0, t_1 \rangle}) = q \exp(t_1^2 - t_0^2)$
4. $\delta_4(q, \omega_{\langle t_0, t_1 \rangle}) = q + (t_1 - t_0)$

Let S_i be the foregoing structure with δ_i in the role of δ. Justify the following statements:

1. S_1 is not a system because δ_1 does not have the composition property and, moreover, δ_1 is not time independent.
2. S_2 is not a system because δ_2 does not have the composition property, even though it is time independent.
3. S_3 is a system because δ_3 has the composition property but S_3 is not time invariant.
4. S_4 is a time invariant system.

From here on, we restrict our treatment to time invariant systems. Most of our concepts carry through to time varying systems, perhaps with some modification, but the time invariance enables certain simplifications in notation which make exposition more straightforward.

Since for a time invariant system S, Ω is closed under translation, all segments can be represented by those beginning at some particular time—we pick $0 \in T$.

Formally, for $\omega : \langle t_0, t_1 \rangle \to Z$ let the *standard translation* of ω, $\mathrm{STR}(\omega) = \mathrm{TRANS}_{-t_0}(\omega)$. Then $\mathrm{STR}(\omega)$ is the translate of ω beginning at 0 ($\mathrm{STR}(\omega)$: $\langle 0, t_1 - t_0 \rangle \to Z$). Let $\Omega_0 = \mathrm{STR}(\Omega) = \{\mathrm{STR}(\omega) | \omega \in \Omega\}$. Then Ω_0 is the set of all segments beginning at zero.

Exercise. Show that Ω is the translation closure of Ω_0 (i.e., the least set containing Ω_0 and closed under translation).

Again since δ is time independent, it can be fully defined simply by specifying its values for all segments in Ω_0. Thus if $\delta_0 : Q \times \Omega_0 \to Q$, then $\delta : Q \times \Omega \to Q$ is defined by

$$\delta(q, \omega) = \delta_0(q, \mathrm{STR}(\omega)) \qquad \text{for} \quad \omega \in \Omega$$

Exercise. Which axiom justifies the foregoing statement?

We know that Ω is not a semigroup because the composition operation, although associative, is not defined for all pairs of segments. If we define a natural composition on Ω_0, however, Ω_0 becomes a semigroup.

First we define the length operator $l:\Omega \to T_0^+$ by $l(\omega) = t_2 - t_1$, where dom $(\omega) = \langle t_1, t_2 \rangle$. Thus $l(\omega)$ is the length of the observation interval on which ω is defined.

Now define COMPOSITION$_0 : \Omega_0 \times \Omega_0 \to \Omega_0$ by

$$\text{COMPOSITION}_0(\omega, \omega') = \omega \cdot \text{TRANS}_{l(\omega)}(\omega')$$

for all $\omega, \omega' \in \Omega_0$.

Usually we write COMPOSITION$_0(\omega, \omega') = \omega \cdot \omega'$ or just $\omega\omega'$ when the context is clear. COMPOSITION$_0$ is illustrated in Figure 9.

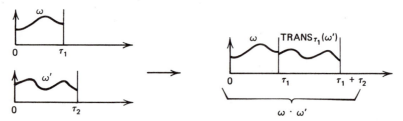

Figure 9 Composition of segments beginning at zero. To compose with ω', translate ω' until it is contiguous with ω.

Exercise. Show that COMPOSITION$_0$ is always defined and associative and that Ω_0 is a semigroup that is a homomorphic image of the groupoid Ω; that is, the map $h:\Omega \to \Omega_0$, where $h(\omega) = \text{STR}(\omega)$ is such that $h(\omega\omega') = h(\omega) \cdot h(\omega')$.

Thus we are led to a working specification for time invariant systems. A *time invariant system in short form* is a structure

$$S_0 = \langle X, T, \Omega_0, Q, Y, \delta_0, \lambda \rangle$$

where X, T, Q, Y, and λ are as before but Ω_0 is semigroup of segments beginning at 0 ($\Omega_0 \subseteq \text{STR}(X, T)$), and $\delta_0 : Q \times \Omega_0 \to Q$ satisfies the *composition property*: for all $q \in Q$, $\omega, \omega' \in \Omega_0$

$$\delta_0(q, \omega \cdot \omega') = \delta_0(\delta_0(q, \omega), \omega')$$

The expanded form of S_0 is the structure

$$S = \langle X, T, \Omega, Q, Y, \delta, \lambda \rangle$$

where Ω is the translation closure of Ω_0 and $\delta(q, \omega) = \delta_0(q, \text{STR}(\omega))$ for all $q \in Q, \omega \in \Omega$.

Exercise. Show that S is a time invariant system—be sure to check the composition property.

Example 3. Linear Systems. Let $S_{A, B, C}^{\text{con}} = \langle X, T, \Omega_0, Q, Y, \delta_0, \lambda \rangle$, where X, Q, Y are finite-dimensional vector spaces over R; $T = R$; Ω is the set of bpc segments beginning at 0; $\delta_0 : Q \times \Omega_0 \to Q$ is given by

$$\delta_0(q, \omega) = e^{Al(\omega)}q + \int_0^{l(\omega)} \exp\left(A(l(\omega) - t')\right)B\omega(t') \, dt'$$

and $\lambda : Q \to Y$ is given by

$$\lambda(q) = Cq$$

where $A : Q \to Q$
$\qquad B : X \to Q$
$\qquad C : Q \to Y$

are linear transformations. In addition,

$$e^A = \sum_{i=0}^{\infty} A^i/i!$$

where $A = I$, $A^{i+1} = A \cdot A^i$.

Let $S_{A, B, C, F}^{\text{dis}} = \langle X, T, \Omega_0, Q, Y, \delta_0, \lambda \rangle$ where X, Q, Y are finite-dimensional vector spaces over a field F; $T = I$; $\Omega_0 = (X, T)_0$; $\delta_0 : Q \times \Omega_0 \to Q$ is given by

$$\delta_0(q, \omega) = A^{l(\omega)}q + \sum_{i=0}^{l(\omega)-1} A^{l(\omega)-1-i}B\omega(i)$$

and $\lambda : Q \to Y$ is given by

$$\lambda(q) = Cq$$

Exercise. Show that $S_{A, B, C}^{\text{con}}$ and $S_{A, B, C, F}^{\text{dis}}$ are systems in short form and provide the corresponding expanded versions.

We say that $S_{A, B, C}^{\text{con}}$ is the *linear continuous time system* specified by $\{A, B, C\}$. Similarly, $S_{A, B, C, F}^{\text{dis}}$ is the *linear discrete time system* specified by $\{A, B, C, F\}$.

Since we are restricting our attention to time invariant systems, we henceforth work only with systems in short form. Moreover, we drop the subscript zeros in the description.

9.8   ITERATIVE SPECIFICATION OF SYSTEMS

In Section 3.4, we saw how the concept of sequential machine underlies the discrete time simulation of a model. The sequential machine structure is an example of a means for specifying a system in a compact way. Such specifications do *not* directly describe the salient elements of a system (e.g., its input set Ω or its transition function δ), but they do provide the essential information, which when correctly interpreted *will* uniquely specify these elements. This idea is illustrated in Figure 10.

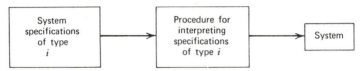

Figure 10   Interpretation of iterative system specifications.

First note that there are various types of system specifications. For example, the class of all sequential machines is one type, and the class of a differential equation system specifications is another. For each specification type, we have a procedure that will accept as input a particular system specification of that type. The procedure will produce as output, the system specified by the input specification. For example, if the procedure receives a particular sequential machine 5-tuple $M = \langle X_M, Q_M, Y_M, \delta_M, \lambda_M \rangle$ it will produce as output the system specified by M, call it $S = \langle T, X, \Omega, Q, Y, \delta, \lambda \rangle$. The elements $T, X, \Omega, Q, Y, \delta, \lambda$ are determined by the elements $X_M, Q_M, Y_M, \delta_M, \lambda_M$ *and* the fact that M is known to be a sequential machine specification—and therefore is to be interpreted in a way appropriate to specifications of this type. For example, T is set equal to I (the integers) because a sequential machine presupposes discrete time operation. Rules of interpretation such as this are sensitive only to the type of specification, not to the particular specification. We call these *background conventions*. On the other hand, the particular δ that appears as part of the system structure S is very much related to the particular δ_M appearing as part of the specification M. The rules by which δ is constructed from δ_M are sensitive to the particular given specification. We call rules of this kind *specificity* rules.

In formulating a specification for a class of systems, the goal is to represent explicitly only those elements which distinguish one member of the class from another. These elements furnish information to the specificity rules. The elements that are common to all members of the class of systems do not have to be explicitly stated and should be introduced by the background conventions.

The following general scheme for generating system specifications is sub-sequently employed to produce more specialized types of specifications.

9.8.1   Generator Segments

Consider (Z, T) the set of all segments $\{\omega : \langle 0, t_1 \rangle \to Z | t_1 \in T\}$, which is a semigroup with the composition discussed in Section 9.7.[†]

For a subset Γ of (Z, T), we designate by Γ^+ the *composition closure of* Γ (also called the *semigroup generated by* Γ). Then Γ^+ can be constructed as follows. Let $\Gamma^1 = \Gamma$ and let $\Gamma^{i+1} = \Gamma^i \cdot \Gamma = \{\omega\omega' | \omega \in \Gamma^i \text{ and } \omega' \in \Gamma\}$. Then $\Gamma^+ = \bigcup_{i \in I^+} \Gamma^i$. The proof is given in the following:

Exercise.   Show that $\Gamma^i = \{\omega_1 \omega_2 \cdots \omega_i | \omega_j \in \Gamma \text{ for } j = 1, \ldots, i\}$. Then show that as the least semigroup containing Γ, Γ^+ is included within $\bigcup_{i \in I^+} \Gamma^i$. On the other hand, since Γ^+ contains Γ, it also contains Γ^2; hence by induction $\Gamma^2, \Gamma^3, \ldots, \Gamma^i$ for each $i \in I^+$, and $\bigcup_{i \in I^+} \Gamma^i \subseteq \Gamma^+$. Conclude that $\Gamma^+ = \bigcup_{i \in I^+} \Gamma^i$.

Example 4.   Consider the following sets of segments:
1. bc = bounded continuous segments.
2. CONST = $\{a_\tau | \tau > 0, a_\tau(t) = a \text{ for } t \in \langle 0, \tau \rangle, a \in R\}$ (constant segments of variable length).
3. $\{\omega\}$ where ω is a segment.

Exercise.   Show that bc generates bpc, CONST generates P.CONST (piecewise constant segments), and $\{\omega\}$ generates PER_ω [periodic segments with period $l(\omega)$].

Now given a set of segments Ω, we are interested in finding a set Γ with the property that $\Gamma^+ = \Omega$. If Γ has this property, we say it is a *set of generators for* Ω or that Γ *generates* Ω.

We say that $\omega_1, \omega_2, \ldots, \omega_n$ is a *decomposition of* ω *by* Γ if $\omega_i \in \Gamma$ for each $i = 1, \ldots, n$ and $\omega = \omega_1 \cdot \omega_2 \cdots \omega_n$.

Exercise.   Show that Γ generates Ω if and only if each $\omega \in \Omega$ has a decomposition by Γ.

It happens in general that if Γ generates Ω, we cannot expect each $\omega \in \Omega$ to have a unique decomposition by Γ; that is, there may be distinct decompositions $\omega_1, \ldots, \omega_n$ and $\omega'_1, \ldots, \omega'_m$ such that $\omega_1 \cdot \omega_2 \cdots \omega_n = \omega'_1 \omega'_2 \cdots \omega'_m = \omega$.

Exercise.   Show that unique decompositions exist in the case of Γ equals $\{\omega\}$ but not in the cases bc and CONST. Consider what properties Γ might have to ensure that each $\omega \in \Gamma^+$ has a unique decomposition.

[†] Since all systems will be time invariant, we shall work with the short form and omit the zero subscript.

Of the many possible decompositions, we are interested in selecting a single representative, or *canonical* decomposition. We go about selecting such a decomposition by a process called *maximal length segmentation*. First we find ω_1, the longest generator in Γ which is also a left segment of ω. This process is repeated with what remains of ω after ω_1 is removed, generating ω_2, and so on. If the process stops after n repetitions, then $\omega = \omega_1 \omega_2 \cdots \omega_n$, and $\omega_1, \omega_2, \ldots, \omega_n$ is the decomposition sought.

We call a decomposition obtained by this process a *maximal length segment* (mls) decomposition.

More formally, a decomposition $\omega_1, \omega_2, \ldots, \omega_n$ is an *mls decomposition* of ω by Γ if for each $i = 1, \ldots, n$, $\omega' \in \Gamma$ is a left segment of $\omega_i \cdot \omega_{i+1} \cdots \omega_n$, $\Rightarrow \omega'$ is a left segment of ω_i. In other words, for each i, ω_i is the longest generator in Γ which is a left segment of $\omega_i \cdots \omega_n$.

It is not necessarily the case that mls decompositions exist, (i.e., that the just-mentioned processes will stop after a finite number of repetitions). Thus we are interested in checkable conditions on a set of generators which will guarantee that each segment generated has an mls decomposition.

Exercise. Let $\Gamma = \{a_{\tau_1} 0_{\tau_2} | \tau_1, \tau_2 > 0\} \cup \{a_{\tau_1} 0_{\tau_2} a_{\tau_3} | \tau_1, \tau_2, \tau_3 > 0\}$. Show that $a_{\tau_1} 0_{\tau_2} a_{\tau_3} 0_{\tau_4} \in \Gamma^+$ but has no mls decomposition.

Fortunately, a segment can have at most one mls decomposition.

Exercise. Show that ω_1 is a left segment of ω_1' and ω_1' is a left segment of ω_1 if and only if $\omega_1 = \omega_1'$. Hence show that if ω has a mls decomposition by Γ, it is unique.

Let us say that Γ is an *admissible* set of generators for Ω if Γ generates Ω and for each $\omega \in \Omega$, a unique mls decomposition of ω by Γ exists. (We also say Γ admissibly generates Ω.)

We now provide a set of conditions guaranteeing that Γ is an admissible set of generators. It should be noted that these conditions are too strong in some cases—for example, when all segments have unique decompositions. We provide a weaker set of conditions in Section 9.8.2.

Exercise. Check whether conditions a and b of the following theorem hold for bc, CONST, $\{\omega\}$.

THEOREM 1.   SUFFICIENT CONDITIONS FOR ADMISSIBILITY

If Γ satisfies the following conditions, it admissibly generates Γ^+:

(a)   *Existence of longest segments*:

$$\omega \in \Gamma^+ \Rightarrow \max \{t | \omega_t \rangle \in \Gamma\} \text{ exists}$$

(b) *Closure under right segmentation*:

$$\omega \in \Gamma \Rightarrow \omega_{\langle t} \in \Gamma \qquad \text{for all } t \in \text{dom}(\omega)$$

Proof. In our proof by induction, the parameter of the induction is the length of a decomposition—a decomposition $\omega_1, \omega_2, \ldots, \omega_n$ of ω by Γ is said to have length n, the number of generators in it. The induction statement is

$P(n) \equiv [\omega$ has a decomposition by Γ of length $n \Rightarrow \omega$ has an mls decomposition by Γ of length n or less$]$

To establish $P(1)$, the basis case, note that "ω has a decomposition by Γ of length 1" implies $\omega \in \Gamma$ (i.e., ω is itself a generator). It follows directly that ω is an mls decomposition by Γ of itself of length 1.

Exercise. Show that ω is an mls decomposition by Γ of itself, having length 1.

For the inductive step, assume $P(i)$ true for all $i < n$. We must show that $P(n)$ follows. As in Figure 11, let ω have a decomposition $\omega_1, \omega_2, \ldots, \omega_n$ by Γ of length n. We wish to resegment ω to obtain an mls decomposition $\omega'_1, \omega'_2, \omega'_3, \ldots, \omega'_m$ with $m < n$. Let us call the points $t_0, t_1, t_2, \ldots, t_n$ the break points of the decomposition $\omega_1, \omega_2, \omega_3, \ldots, \omega_n$ (i.e., $\omega_1 = \omega_{t_1\rangle}$, $\omega_2 = \omega|_{\langle t_1, t_2\rangle}$, etc.).

Let t'_1 be the greatest value of t such that $\omega_{t\rangle} \in \Gamma$; this exists by condition a of the hypothesis of Theorem 1. Then t'_1 is the first breakpoint of the mls decomposition and $\omega'_1 = \omega_{t'_1\rangle}$ (by construction, ω'_1 is the longest generator in Γ which is a left segment of ω).

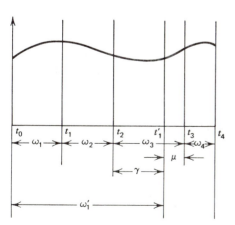

Figure 11 Initial segment of mls decomposition.

Let k be the integer such that $t_k \le t'_1 < t_{k+1}$. Note that $k \ge 1$, since ω_1 is a generator in Γ which is a left segment of ω and as the longest such segment, ω'_1 is at least as long as ω_1 ($k = 2$ in Figure 11).

Now ω_k is split by t'_1 into left and right segments, call these γ and μ, respectively. By condition b, μ is a generator in Γ. Now $\mu \in \Gamma$ and $\omega_{k+2} \cdot \omega_{k+3} \cdots \omega_n \in \Gamma^+$, which means that the right segment of ω caused by t'_1, namely $\omega_{\langle t'_1} = \mu \cdot \omega_{k+2} \cdot \omega_{k+3} \cdots \omega_n$ (by the postulated property of composition that composition of left and right subsegments of a segment yields the original). Thus $\mu, \omega_{k+2}, \ldots, \omega_n$ is a decomposition of $\omega_{\langle t'_1}$ of length $n - (k+1) + 1 = n - k$. Since $k \ge 1$, $n - k \le n - 1$, and we can employ $P(n - k)$ to obtain an mls decomposition by Γ of $\omega_{\langle t'_1}$ of length $n - k$ or less; call it $\bar{\omega}_1, \bar{\omega}_2, \ldots, \bar{\omega}_m$ (where $\bar{m} \le n - k$). We now claim that ω'_1, $\bar{\omega}_1, \ldots, \bar{\omega}_{\bar{m}}$ is the desired mls decomposition of ω of length $m < n$.

First $\omega'_1 \cdot \bar{\omega}_1 \cdots \bar{\omega}_{\bar{m}} = \omega_{t'_1\rangle} \cdot \omega_{\langle t'_1} = \omega$ (composition of left and right segments); thus $\omega'_1, \bar{\omega}_1, \ldots, \bar{\omega}_{\bar{m}}$ is a decomposition of ω by Γ.

Second, ω'_1 is an mls segment and $\bar{\omega}_1, \bar{\omega}_2, \ldots, \bar{\omega}_{\bar{m}}$ is an mls decomposition of $\omega_{\langle t'_1}$; thus $\omega'_1, \bar{\omega}_1, \ldots, \bar{\omega}_{\bar{m}}$ is an mls decomposition of ω.

Third, $\omega'_1, \bar{\omega}_1, \ldots, \bar{\omega}_{\bar{m}}$ has length $m = 1 + \bar{m} \le 1 + n - k \le n$ as required.

Having shown $P(n)$, we are entitled by the induction scheme to assert that $P(i)$ is true for all $i = 1, 2, \ldots$. But this means that every $\omega \in \Gamma^+$ has an mls decomposition, since $\omega \in \Gamma^+$ implies $\omega \in \Gamma^i$ for some $i = 1, 2, \ldots$, and then $P(i)$ applies to ω. By a previous exercise, the mls decomposition is unique and thus the theorem is established. ∎

9.8.2 Extension of Generator Transformations

Having established a terminating process for obtaining mls decompositions, we wish to use these decompositions to help us generate a transition function given only that function's action on the generators. In other words, let Ω_G be an admissible generating set for Ω and suppose we have defined a function $\delta_G : Q \times \Omega_G \to Q$, which we call a *single segment transition function*.

Let $\omega_1, \omega_2, \ldots, \omega_n$ be the mls decomposition of ω. Having δ_G defined for each segment ω_i, we wish to piece together these parts to obtain compound transition associated with ω itself. We do this by iteration: if q_0 is the initial state, $q_1 = \delta_G(q_0, \omega_1)$ is the state after injecting ω_1, $q_2 = \delta_G(q_1, \omega_2)$ is the state after injecting ω_2, and so on.

Formally, we define a function $\bar{\delta}_G : Q \times \Omega_G^+ \to Q$, called the *extension* of δ_G to Ω_G^+ by

$$\bar{\delta}_G(q, \omega) = \begin{array}{ll} \delta_G(q, \omega) & \text{for } \omega \in \Omega_G \\ \bar{\delta}_G(\delta_G(q, \omega_1), \omega_2, \ldots, \omega_n) & \text{for } \omega \in \Omega_G^+, \text{ where } \omega_1, \omega_2, \ldots, \omega_n \\ & \text{is the mls decomposition for } \omega \end{array}$$

Exercise. Show by induction that $\bar{\delta}_G$ is well defined, that is, $\bar{\delta}_G(q, \omega)$ exists and is unique for each $q \in Q$, $\omega \in \Omega_G^+$. Use (1) the uniqueness of the mls decomposition, and (2) the fact that $\omega_1, \omega_2, \ldots, \omega_n$ is the mls decomposition of ω, which implies that $\omega_i, \omega_{i+1}, \ldots, \omega_n$ is the mls decomposition of $\omega_i \cdot \omega_{i+1} \cdots \omega_n$ for each $i = 1, 2, \ldots, n$. In fact, show that $\bar{\delta}_G(q, \omega_1 \cdots \omega_n) = \delta_G(\bar{\delta}_G(\cdots \bar{\delta}_G(\bar{\delta}_G(q, \omega_1), \omega_2) \cdots), \omega_n)$.

So far so good—$\bar{\delta}_G$ satisfies the first requirement of a bona fide transition function: it is a mapping from $Q \times \Omega_G^+$ into Q. But this does not imply that it satisfies the second requirement, namely, the "composition property." The reason? Consider Figure 5 once more. On the one hand, $\bar{\delta}_G(q, \omega)$ is defined according to the mls decomposition of ω; $\bar{\delta}_G(\bar{\delta}_G(q, \omega), \omega')$ is then defined according to the mls decomposition of ω'. On the other hand $\bar{\delta}_G(q, \omega\omega')$ is defined according to the mls decomposition of $\omega\omega'$. Although both $\bar{\delta}_G(q, \omega\omega')$ and $\bar{\delta}_G(\bar{\delta}_G(q, \omega), \omega')$ exist and are unique, they need not be equal because the mls decomposition of $\omega\omega'$ is not necessarily the mls decomposition of ω followed by the mls decomposition of ω'.

Exercise. Show that if (a) $\omega_1, \ldots, \omega_n$ is the mls decomposition of ω, (b) $\omega_1', \ldots, \omega_m'$ is the mls decomposition of ω', and (c) $\omega_1, \ldots, \omega_n, \omega_1', \ldots, \omega_m'$ is the mls decomposition of $\omega\omega'$, then $\bar{\delta}_G(q, \omega\omega') = \bar{\delta}_G(\bar{\delta}_G(q, \omega), \omega')$. In general, however, when ω is joined to ω', it may be possible to extend ω_n to a longer mls. The new mls may encompass part or all of ω', thus displacing all its old breakpoints.

Thus we are led to seek conditions that will guarantee that $\bar{\delta}_G$ has the composition property. Having such conditions, we can employ Ω_G and δ_G as the basis for a system specification. Since other specification schemes are possible, and since iteration is at the basis of the present scheme, we designate it "iterative specification."

An *iterative specification* of a system is a structure

$$G = \langle T, X, \Omega_G, Q, Y, \delta_G, \lambda \rangle$$

where T is a set—the time base
$\quad X$ is a set—the input value set
$\quad \Omega_G$ is a set—the input segment generator set
$\quad Q$ is a set—the state set
$\quad Y$ is a set—the output value set
$\quad \delta_G$ is a function—the single segment transition function
$\quad \lambda$ is a function—the output function

with the restrictions that

$$\Omega_G \subseteq (X, T)$$
$$\delta_G : Q \times \Omega_G \to Q$$
$$\lambda : Q \to Y$$

and, most important, Ω_G is an *admissible set of generators* and $\delta_G : Q \times \Omega_G^+ \to Q$ *has the composition property.*

With an iterative specification $G = \langle T, X, \Omega_G, Q, Y, \delta_G, \lambda \rangle$ we may associate a system $S_G = \langle T, X, \Omega_G^+, Q, Y, \bar{\delta}_G, \lambda \rangle$.

We can provide a set of conditions guaranteeing that a structure is an iterative specification. Since these conditions are based on those for admissibility, they are not as weak as they might be. A weaker set of conditions can be found in the exercise following Theorem 2.

THEOREM 2.   SUFFICIENT CONDITIONS FOR ITERATIVE SPECIFICATION

Let $G = \langle T, X, \Omega_G, Q, Y, \delta_G, \lambda \rangle$ be a structure with T a time base set; X, Q, Y the input, state, and output sets, respectively; $\Omega_G \subseteq (X, T), \delta_G : Q \times \Omega_G \to Q$; and $\lambda : Q \to Y$. Then if the following conditions hold, G is an iterative specification and S_G is a system:

(a)   *Existence of longest segments*

$$\omega \in \Omega_G^+ \Rightarrow \max \{t \,|\, \omega_t \in \Omega_G\} \text{ exists}$$

(b)   *Closure under right segmentation*

$$\omega \in \Omega_G \Rightarrow \omega_{\langle t} \in \Omega_G \qquad \text{for } t \in \mathrm{dom}\,(\omega)$$

(c)   *Closure under left segmentation*

$$\omega \in \Omega_G \Rightarrow \omega_{t \rangle} \in \Omega_G \qquad \text{for } t \in \mathrm{dom}\,(\omega)$$

(d)   *Consistency of composition*

$$\omega_1, \omega_2, \ldots, \omega_n \in \Omega_G \qquad \text{and} \qquad \omega_1 \cdot \omega_2 \cdots \omega_n \in \Omega_G$$
$$\Rightarrow \delta_G(q, \omega_1 \cdot \omega_2 \cdots \omega_n) = \delta_G(\cdots \delta_G(q, \omega_1), \ldots), \omega_n)$$

Proof.   Requirements a and b were shown by Theorem 1 to guarantee that Ω_G is admissible, which means that mls decompositions always exist. This in turn implies that $\bar{\delta}_G : Q \times Q_G^+ \to Q$ is a well-defined function as required. Thus the theorem is established once we can show that $\bar{\delta}_G$ has the composition property. We do this as follows.

Let $\omega : \langle 0, \tau \rangle \to X$ be a segment. A *partition* of $\langle 0, \tau \rangle$ is a finite subset $\{t_1, t_2, \ldots, t_n\}$ of $\langle 0, \tau \rangle$. A partition is said to be a *breakpoint partition* if its points form the breakpoints of a decomposition of ω by Ω_G, that is, if $t_1 < t_2 < \cdots < t_n$, for each $i = 1, \ldots, n - 1, \omega_{\langle t_i, t_{i+1} \rangle} \in \Omega_G$ (where $t_1 = 0$ and $t_n = \tau$).

A partition A *refines* a partition B if $B \subseteq A$ (so the intervals $\langle t_i, t_{i+1} \rangle$ defined by B may be split up by A). The *common refinement* of partitions A and B is the partition $A \cup B$.

For a breakpoint partition $\{t_1, t_2, \ldots, t_n\}$ we define $\delta_\omega^*(q, \{t_1, t_2, \ldots, t_n\}) = \delta_G(\cdots \delta_G(q, \omega_{\langle 0, t_1 \rangle}), \ldots), \omega_{\langle t_n, \tau \rangle})$, that is, the state reached starting from q and applying the successive subsegments of ω.

LEMMA 1

If B is a breakpoint partition, any refinement of B is also a breakpoint partition.

Proof. Let A refine B. Then every interval $\langle t_i, t_{i+1} \rangle$ due to B can be segmented further into intervals $\langle t_i, \tau_1 \rangle$, $\langle \tau_1, \tau_2 \rangle$, ..., $\langle \tau_n, t_{i+1} \rangle$ due to A. Since B is a breakpoint partition, $\omega_{\langle t, t_{i+1} \rangle} \in \Omega_G$, and since by hypotheses a and b, Ω_G is left and right segmentable, the subsegments $\omega_{\langle t_i, \tau_1 \rangle}$, $\omega_{\langle \tau_1, \tau_2 \rangle}$, ..., $\omega_{\langle \tau_n, t_{i+1} \rangle}$ are all in Ω_G. Thus A is a breakpoint partition.

LEMMA 2

If A refines B and B is a breakpoint partition, $\delta_\omega^*(q, A) = \delta_\omega^*(q, B)$, for all $q \in Q$.

Proof. By Lemma 1, A is also a breakpoint partition. Moreover, from the requirement of composition consistency (part c), we have

$$\delta_G(q, \omega_{\langle t_i, t_{i+1} \rangle}) = \delta_G((\cdots \delta_G(q, \omega_{\langle t_i, \tau_1 \rangle}), \ldots) \omega_{\langle \tau_n, t_{i-1} \rangle})$$

for any interval $\langle t_i, t_{i+1} \rangle$ due to B and the finer intervals $\langle t_i, \tau_1 \rangle, \ldots, \langle \tau_n, t_{i+1} \rangle$ due to A. By induction, it follows that $\delta_\omega^*(q, A) = \delta_\omega^*(q, B)$ for all $q \in Q$.

Exercise. Show that the equation in δ_ω^* is true.

Having these lemmas, we can complete the proof of Theorem 2. Let $\bar{A}$ be the breakpoint partition defined by the mls decomposition of $\omega\omega'$. Now notice that if $\omega_1, \omega_2, \ldots, \omega_n$ and $\omega_1', \omega_2', \ldots, \omega_m'$ are mls decompositions of ω and ω', respectively, then $\omega_1, \omega_2, \ldots, \omega_n, \omega_1', \omega_2', \ldots, \omega_m'$ is a decomposition (although not necessarily an mls decomposition!) of $\omega\omega'$. Let $\bar{B} = B_\omega \cup B_{\omega'}$ be the breakpoint partition defined by this decomposition, where B_ω and $B_{\omega'}$ are points in the domains of ω and ω', respectively. Then we have

$$\bar{\delta}_G(\bar{\delta}_G(q, \omega), \omega') = \delta_\omega^*(\delta_\omega^*(q, B_\omega), B_{\omega'}) \quad \text{(by definition)}$$
$$= \delta_\omega^*(q, \bar{B}) \quad \text{(by an easy induction)}$$
$$= \delta_\omega^*(q, \bar{A} \cup \bar{B}) \quad \text{(by Lemma 2)}$$
$$= \delta_\omega^*(q, \bar{A}) \quad \text{(by Lemma 2)}$$
$$= \bar{\delta}_G(q, \omega\omega') \quad \text{(by definition)} \qquad \blacksquare$$

Exercise. Conditions b and c, requiring left and right segmentability in the definition of iterative specification, can be weakened while still enabling the theorem to be true. Replace b and c by

(d) For $\omega \in \Omega_G^+$, if $t^* = \max \{t | \omega_{t} \in \Omega_G\}$ and $t_k < t^* < t_{k+1}$, then $\omega_{\langle t_k, t^* \rangle} \in \Omega_G^+$ and $\omega_{\langle t^*, t_{k+1} \rangle} \in \Omega_G$ (see Figure 12).

Show that G is an iterative specification.

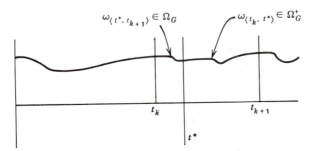

Figure 12   Relaxed conditions for Theorem 2.

To summarize, an iterative specification G specifies a time invariant system S_G. Since we have already seen in Section 9.6 how to associate an I/O behavior set and an I/O relation with a system such as S_G, we can associate these objects with the specification G.

9.9   SPECIALIZATION OF ITERATIVE SPECIFICATION

We now present two important specializations of our scheme for iterative specification—the discrete time and the discrete event system specifications. The approach is depicted in Figure 13. The procedure referred to in Figure 10 is shown to involve two phases. The first is a translation of the specification into the iterative specification format; in this phase all the background

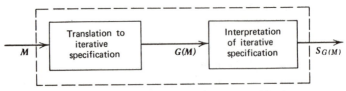

Figure 13   Translation and interpretation of iterative specifications.

conventions are operating. The second phase converts the specification into a system by employing the extension process underlying Theorem 2 (i.e., by extending Ω_G to Ω_G^+ and δ_G to $\bar{\delta}_G$). Note that this extension is done in a uniform way, but the rules involved are of the specificity type, depending as they do on the specific input Ω_G and δ_G.

It is now time to show how the discrete time models discussed in Chapter 3 fit into the iterative specification scheme. The *discrete time system specification* is often called a *sequential machine*, which is a structure

$$M = \langle X_M, Q_M, Y_M, \delta_M, \lambda_M \rangle$$

where X_M, Q_M, Y_M are sets, $\delta_M : Q_M \times X_M \to Q_M$, and $\lambda_M : Q_M \to Y$. We associate with M a structure

$$G(M) = \langle T, X, \Omega_G, Q, Y, \delta_G, \lambda \rangle$$

where $T = I$
$\quad X = X_M$
$\quad \Omega_G = \{\omega | \omega : \langle 0, 1 \rangle \to X\}$
$\quad Q = Q_M$
$\quad Y = Y_M$
$\quad \delta_G : Q \times \Omega_G \to Q$ is defined by $\delta_G(q, \omega) = \delta_M(q, \omega(0))$
$\quad \lambda = \lambda_M$

We interpret $\langle t_0, t_1 \rangle$ as $[t_0, t_1)$. Since T is a discrete time base, $[t_0, t_0 + 1)$ is another name for $[t_0]$. Why?

The generators in Ω_G are in one-to-one correspondence with the input values X. This is because $\omega : \langle 0, 1 \rangle \to X$ (equivalently $\omega : [0] \to X$) is uniquely determined by its value $\omega(0) \in X$. We can therefore describe Ω_G more conveniently as

$$\Omega_G = \{\omega_x | x \in X, \omega_x : \langle 0, 1 \rangle \to X, \omega_x(0) = x\}$$

The natural composition (Section 9.5) is appropriate and satisfies the required postulates. Thus we have

$$\Omega_G^+ = \{\omega_{x_1}\omega_{x_2} \cdots \omega_{x_n} | x_i \in X^+, \quad i = 1, 2, \ldots, n; \quad n = 1, 2, \ldots \}$$

Exercise. We define X^+ as the set of all finite sequences of elements of X; that is, $\{x_1, x_2, \ldots, x_n | x_i \in X, i = 1, 2, \ldots, n; n = 1, 2, \ldots\}$. Show that Ω_G^+ corresponds one to one with X^+.

The extension of δ_M to X^+ is defined by

$$\bar{\delta}_M : Q \times X^+ \to Q$$

where $\bar{\delta}_M(q, x_i) = \delta_M(q, x_i) \qquad$ for $x_i \in X$
$\quad \bar{\delta}_M(q, x_i x) = \bar{\delta}_M(\delta_M(q, x_i), x) \qquad$ for $x_i \in X, x \in X^+$

Exercise. Show that $\bar{\delta}_G(q, \omega) = \bar{\delta}_M(q, \omega(0)\omega(1) \cdots \omega(n))$, where the domain of ω is $\langle 0, n + 1 \rangle$.

It is well known that $\bar{\delta}_M$, hence $\bar{\delta}_G$, is well defined and has the composition property. This can be proved directly by showing that $G(M)$ satisfies the requirements of an iterative specification.

Exercise. Show that $G(M)$ is an iterative specification, hence that $S_{G(M)}$ is a time invariant system.

Example 5. Linear Sequential Machines. A sequential machine

$$M = \langle X, Q, Y, \delta, \lambda \rangle$$

is *linear* if X, Q, Y are vector spaces over a field F and

$$\delta(q, x) = Aq + Bx$$
$$\lambda(q) = Cq$$

for appropriate matrices $\{A, B, C\}$.

Exercise. Show that $S_{G(M)}$ is the linear discrete time system $S_{A, B, C, F}^{\text{dis}}$.

Exercise. We say that Ω_G has the *prefix property* if no generator is a left subsegment of another generator; that is, $\omega \in \Omega_G \Rightarrow \omega_{t\rangle} \notin \Omega_G$ for each proper left segment $\omega_{t\rangle}$. The Ω_G of the sequential machine is an example. Show that if Ω_G has the prefix property, any structure $\langle T, X, \Omega_G, Q, Y, \delta_G, \lambda \rangle$, where $\Omega_G \subseteq (T, X)$ and $\delta_G : Q \times \Omega_G \to Q$ is an iterative specification.

Exercise. A structure $M = \langle X_M, Q_M, Y_M, \delta_M, \lambda_M \rangle$ can be interpreted also as operating in discrete time jumps on a continuous time base. For example, let $G = \langle T, X, \Omega_G, Q, Y, \delta_G, \lambda \rangle$

where $T = R$
$\quad X = X_M \cup \{\phi\} \quad (\phi \notin X_M$ is a special symbol$)$
$\quad \Omega_G = \{x_h | x \in X_M, x_h : [0, h] \to X; x_h(0) = x, x_h(t) = \phi \quad$ for $0 < t \le h\}$

$$Q = Q_M$$
$$Y = Y_M$$

$\delta_G : Q \times \Omega_G \to Q$ is defined by

$$\delta_G(q, x_h) = \delta_M(q, x)$$
$$\lambda = \lambda_M$$

Figure 14 depicts the alternative translation of sequential machine specifications. Show that G is an iterative system specification and describe S_G.

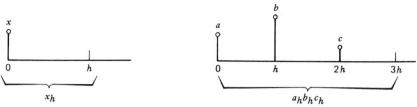

Figure 14   Alternate translation of sequential machine specifications.

9.10   DIFFERENTIAL EQUATION SYSTEM SPECIFICATION

As noted in Section 1.4, systems can be specified in many ways and at many levels of abstraction. A very common specification type employs differential equations. This form of system specification, the earliest to be developed, derives from Newton's successful attempts to account for the motion of the planets around the sun. Differential equations specify the instantaneous rates of change of state variables as functions of the state variables and the input variables. Thus in contrast to the sequential machine and discrete event specifications, next states are not prescribed directly but must be computed on the basis of information supplied about how the *changes* in state are to occur.

In this section we show how to interpret the differential equation system specification as input to an iterative specification, which in turn specifies a class of systems.

A *differential equation system specification* (DESS) is a structure

$$D = \langle X, Q, Y, f, \lambda \rangle$$

where X is a set—the input value set
$\quad Q$ is a set—the state set
$\quad Y$ is a set—the output value set
$\quad f$ is a function—the rate of change function
$\quad \lambda$ is a function—the output function

with the following restrictions:

(a) X, Q, *and* Y *are real vector spaces* (i.e., there are nonnegative integers n_x, n_y, and n_q such that $X = R^{n_x}$, $Q = R^{n_q}$, and $Y = R^{n_y}$).
(b)   *Deterministic responses*

$$f : Q \times X \to Q$$
$$\lambda : Q \to Y$$

We shall want to associate an iterative specification with the DESS. The background conventions are that the time base T is to be the real number set, and the input segment generators are the bounded continuous (bc) functions from finite intervals of T into X. With this understood, we can interpret the function f by showing how it specifies the one-segment transition function of the iterative specification.

Let $\omega : \langle 0, \tau \rangle \to X$ and $q \in Q$ be a given input segment from bc and a state respectively. We say that a segment $\Phi : \langle 0, \tau \rangle \to Q$ is a *solution associated with ω and q* if

1. $\Phi(0) = q$

2. $\dfrac{d\Phi(t)}{dt} = f(\Phi(t), \omega(t))$ for each $t \in \langle 0, \tau \rangle$

Conditions 1 and 2 provide the precise definition of the term "solution of a differential equation." They state that the solution will depend on a given initial value ($\Phi(0) = q$) and must satisfy the differential equation given in item 2 at each point in time. Thus the f function does not directly specify how state transitions are to occur but only provides a test by which to determine whether motions through the state space are solutions.

In general, for given ω and q, no solutions may exist or more than one solution may exist. The DESS will specify a system, however, when exactly one solution is associated with every pair ω and q. In this case the solution will turn out to be a state trajectory of the specified system.

Formally, a DESS has *unique solutions* if there is a unique solution $\Phi_{q, \omega}$ associated with every $q \in Q$ and bounded continuous segment of the form $\omega : \langle 0, \tau \rangle \to X$. Conditions on f that guarantee unique solutions, such as those involving the Lipschitz conditions, are known (see Problems, Chapter 16).

The transition function for the iterative specification is then obtained as the mapping that is carried out by a solution in taking an initial state (at the beginning of the observation interval) into the corresponding final state (reached at the end of the observation interval). To put this all together, we associate with a unique solution DESS $D = \langle X_D, Q_D, Y_D, f_D, \lambda_D \rangle$, the structure

$$G(D) = \langle T, X, \Omega_G, Q, Y, \delta_G, \lambda \rangle$$

where $T = R$

$X = X_D$

$\Omega_G = \{\omega | \omega : \langle 0, \tau \rangle \to X$ is a bounded continuous function and $\tau > 0\}$

$Q = Q_D$

$Y = Y_D$

$\lambda = \lambda_D$

and $\delta_G : Q \times \Omega_G \to Q$ is given by $\delta_G(q, \omega) = \Phi_{q, \omega}(\tau)$, where $\omega : \langle 0, \tau \rangle \to X$ and $\Phi_{q, \omega}$ is the unique solution associated with q and ω.

Just as in the previous cases we can show this works by demonstrating that $G(D)$ is an iterative specification. It then follows that $S_{G(D)}$ is a time invariant system. The steps, which are left to the reader to carry out, are as follows.

1. The Ω_G^+ is the set of piecewise bounded continuous segments on finite intervals of T into X. (Exercise, Section 9.8.1).
2. Maximal length segments are uniquely determined by the points of discontinuity of a segment.
3. The piecewise continuous segments are closed under both left and right segmentation.
4. For any continuous segment $\omega_{\langle 0, \tau \rangle}$ and any $t \in \langle 0, \tau \rangle$, $\delta_G(q, \omega) = \delta_G(\delta_G(q, \omega_{t \rangle}), \omega_{\langle t})$. (Show this by piecing together the solutions corresponding to each of the segments).

Example 6.   Linear differential systems.   A DESS $D = \langle X, Q, Y, f, \lambda \rangle$ is *linear* if X, Q, Y are vector spaces over the reals and

$$f(q, x) = Aq + Bx$$
$$\lambda(q) = Cq$$

Exercise.   Show that $S_{G(D)}$ is the linear continuous time system $S_{A, B, C}^{\text{cont}}$.

Exercise.   In Example 2 we saw how to associate an IOFO with a differential operator of order n. Show how to associate a DESS D with the operator such that $\text{IOFO}_{S(D)}$ is the IOFO of Example 2.

9.11   DISCRETE EVENT SYSTEM SPECIFICATION

In Chapter 6, we discussed discrete event models and the underlying time advance idea that distinguishes them from discrete time models. Now, by formalizing the discrete event models within the iterative specification scheme, the similarities and differences can be placed in sharpened perspective.

A *discrete event system specification* (DEVS) is a structure

$$M = \langle X_M, S_M, Y_M, \delta_M, \lambda_M, t \rangle$$

where X_M is a set—the external event set
   S_M is a set—the sequential states
   Y_M is a set—the output value set

δ_M is a function—the quasitransition function

λ_M is a function—the output function

t is a function—the time advance function

with the restrictions that:

(a) t is a mapping from S into the nonnegative reals with ∞:

$$t : S \rightarrow R_{0,\,\infty}^+$$

[$t(s)$ is to be interpreted as the time the system is allowed to remain in state s]

(b)   with $Q_M = \{(s, e) | s \in S_M, 0 \leq e \leq t(s)\}$, and ϕ a special symbol not in X_M, δ_M maps $Q_M \times (X \cup \{\phi\})$ into S_M:

$$\delta_M : Q_M \times (X \cup \{\phi\}) \rightarrow S_M$$

such that $\delta_M(s, e, \phi) = \delta_\phi(s)$ for all $(s, e) \in Q_M$, where $\delta_\phi : S \rightarrow S$. [$Q_M$ will become the state set of the specified system; a pair (s, e) is a sequential state s together with the time elapsed e during which the system has been in that state.]

The nonevent (no external event occurring) is denoted by ϕ. If no external events arrive, the system remains in state s a time $t(s)$ and transitions instantaneously to next state $\delta_\phi(s)$. Thus δ_ϕ is an autonomous transition function; if an event $x \in X$ arrives, and the system has been in state s for an elapsed time e, it transitions immediately to next state $\delta_M(s, e, x)$. Thus δ_M gives the next sequential state component of the total state (s, e)—the behavior of the elapsed time component e will be provided by a background convention, as will the interpretation that the state remains fixed between events.

(c) λ_M is a mapping from Q_M into Y_M,

$$\lambda_M : Q_M \rightarrow Y_M$$

9.12   DEVS MODELS FOR SOME GPSS PRIMITIVES

We give some examples of DEVS models of common queueing components. A GPSS equivalent of each component appears in Figure 15.

1.   *Passive register* (Figure 15a)

$X_M = A, S_M = A, Y_M = A; \delta_\phi(a) = a, \delta(a, b, e) = b, t(a) = \infty, \lambda(a) = a$

The register retains its last entry indefinitely without loss unless dis-

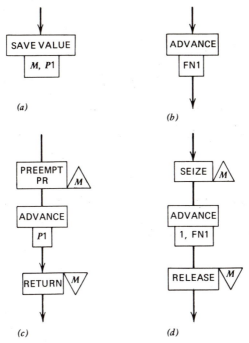

Figure 15   GPSS primitives: (a) passive register, (b) input independent delay, (c) FIFO queue with priority interrupt, (d) FIFO queue.

turbed by a new entry, in which case, it is instantaneously reset to this entry. In GPSS, SAVE VALUE cell M is set to the current contents of parameter P1 of the entering transaction.

2. *Input dependent delay* (Figure 15b)

$$X_M = A, S_M = 2^{A \times R^+}, Y_M = 2^A; \ t\left(\{(a_i, \tau_i)\}\right) = \min \{\tau_i\}$$

$$\delta_\phi(\{(a_i, \tau_i)\}) = \{(a_j, \tau_j - \min \{\tau_i\}) | \tau_j \neq \min \{\tau_i\}\}$$

$$\delta(\{(a_i, \tau_i)\}, e, a) = \{(a_i, \tau_i - e)\} \cup \{(a, \text{ADVANCE}(a))\}$$

$$\lambda(\{(a_i, \tau_i)\}, e) = \begin{cases} \{a_k | \tau_k = \min \{\tau_i\}\} & \text{if } e = 0 \\ \phi & \text{otherwise} \end{cases}$$

Entering object a is delayed an amount ADVANCE(a) before emerging. Objects scheduled to leave at the same time are not ordered sequentially in the version of Figure 15b—this could be achieved by imposing an order on the pairs $\{(a_i, \tau_i)\}$ constituting the state at any time. (See Section 6.4) In the GPSS version, a transaction is delayed by an amount determined by FNI, a function defined on the contents of parameter P1 (of the entering transaction) to correspond with the ADVANCE function of the DEVS. The GPSS simulator imposes an order on simultaneously emerging transactions according to time of arrival and priority.

3. *FIFO queue with priority interrupt* (Figure 15c)

$$X_M = A \times I \times R_0^+ ; S_M = X_M^*, Y_M = A$$

$$\delta_\phi((a, i, p)x) = x \qquad \text{for } (a, i, p) \in X_M, x \in X_M^*$$

$$\delta((a, i, p)x, e, (a', i', p')) = \begin{cases} (a', i', p')(a, i, p - e)x & \text{if } i' > i \text{ and } e < p \quad (1) \\ (a', i', p')x & \text{if } i' > i \text{ and } e = p \quad (2) \\ (a, i, p - e)\text{PLACE}((a', i', p'), x)) & \text{otherwise} \quad (3) \end{cases}$$

$$t((a, i, p)x) = p$$

$$\lambda((a, i, p), e, x) = \begin{matrix} a & \text{if } p = e \\ \phi & \text{otherwise} \end{matrix}$$

$$(\delta_\phi(\Lambda) = \Lambda; t(\Lambda) = \infty, \lambda(\Lambda) = \phi)$$

A job of the form (a', i', p') arrives at the server where a' is a name, i' an integer priority, p' a real valued processing time. In lines 1 and 2, the entering job has priority greater than that of the currently processed job, which it therefore displaces from the server's attention. (In line 2 the existing job has just finished.) In line 3 the arrival does not have high enough priority, thus is placed among the waiting jobs according to the function PLACE (e.g., at the end of the section of jobs with equal priority).

The GPSS version employs a PREEMPT, RETURN pair, which is the interrupt-permitting version of the SEIZE, RELEASE pair. The entering transactions have a distinguished parameter containing its priority level; processing time is contained in parameter 1.

Exercise.   Give a DEVS model for the GPSS diagram of Figure 15d.

9.13   TRANSLATION TO ITERATIVE SPECIFICATION

To translate the structure M into an iterative specification, we interpret $\langle t_0, t_1 \rangle$ as $[t_0, t_1)$ with the composition of Section 9.5, proceeding as follows. We consider two related kinds of input segment generators.

Ω_ϕ is the set of segments of finite length where no external event occurs:

$$\Omega_\phi = \{\phi_\tau | \tau \text{ nonnegative}, \qquad \phi_\tau : \langle 0, \tau \rangle \to \{\phi\}\}$$

Ω_X is the set of segments of finite nonzero length, where no external event occurs except at zero:

$$\Omega_X = \{x_\tau | \tau \text{ nonnegative, } x_\tau : \langle 0, \tau \rangle \to X \cup \{\phi\}$$
$$x_\tau(0) = x, \; x_\tau(t) = \phi \qquad \text{for } t \in (0, \tau)\}$$

Graphically we depict these as in Figure 16.

Thus the generator set of the iterative specification will be $\Omega_G = \Omega_\phi \cup \Omega_X$.

To fashion the single segment transition function δ_G, we must encode the background conventions implied by the interpretations given to δ_M and t. We say that

$$\delta_G : Q_M \times \Omega_G \to Q_M$$

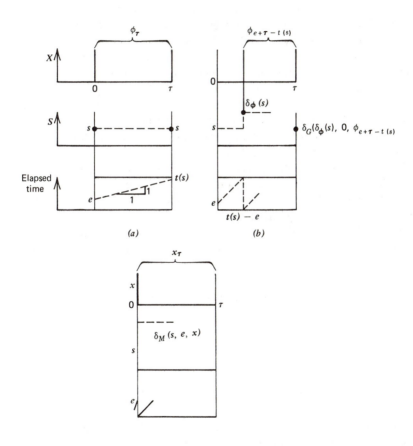

Figure 16   Definition of the generator transition function.

is defined by

$$\delta_G(s, e, \phi_\tau) = \begin{cases} (s, e + \tau) & \text{if } e + \tau \le t(s) \quad (1) \\ \delta_G(\delta_\phi(s), 0, \phi_{e+\tau-t(s)}) & \text{otherwise} \quad (2) \end{cases}$$

$$\delta_G(s, e, x_\tau) = \delta_G(\delta_M(s, e, x), 0, \phi_\tau) \qquad (3)$$

Although formidable in appearance, the definition is intuitively straight-forward and consonant with the given interpretations.

Line 1 says that if no external events occur in an interval $\langle 0, \tau \rangle$ and the total elapsed time [the sum of the elapsed time current at the beginning of the interval e and the length of the period τ] is less than that associated with the current state $t(s)$, the system remains in this state (note that the elapsed time component is updated accordingly). See Figure 16a.

Line 2 says that if no external events occur and the allowed time in the current state s is exceeded, at time $t(s) - e$, an instantaneous state transition is made to $\delta_\phi(s)$, and what happens thereafter is recursively defined in terms of the new sequential state $\delta_\phi(s)$, the new elapsed time 0, and the remaining no-event segment of length $\tau - (t(s) - e) = e + \tau - t(s)$. See Figure 16b.

Line 3 says that if an external event occurs at time 0, and none occur in the interval $(0, \tau)$, the system will instantaneously jump to state $\delta_M(s, e, x)$, the elapsed time must be set to zero, and lines 1 and 2 apply using the no-event segment ϕ_τ. See Figure 16c.

Since δ_G is defined recursively, it is not immediately apparent that it is well defined (i.e., that the recursion stops and produces a unique result). In fact, we provide a condition that is sufficient (and also necessary) for this convergence to be guaranteed.

To develop this condition, we note that in intervals in which no external event occurs, the system operates very much like an autonomous sequential machine except that state transitions occur at intervals controlled by the time advance function. Formally, we extend δ_ϕ to I_0^+ so that $\bar{\delta}_\phi(s, n)$ is the state reached from state s after n transitions; that is,

$$\bar{\delta}_\phi : S \times I_0^+ \to S$$

is defined by

$$\bar{\delta}_\phi(s, 0) = s$$
$$\bar{\delta}_\phi(s, n + 1) = \delta_\phi(\bar{\delta}_\phi(s, n))$$

(See Section 9.9.)

Then we define a function $\sum$ so that $\sum(s, n)$ is the total time used by the system to make n transitions beginning in state s. Formally, we write

$$\sum : S \times I_0^+ \to R_{0, \infty}^+$$

is defined by

$$\sum(s, 0) = 0$$

$$\sum(s, n) = \sum_{i=0}^{n-1} t(\delta_\phi(s, i))$$

Starting in state s, with elapsed time e, how many transitions will be made in an interval $\langle 0, \tau \rangle$? Let this number be $m_{s,e,\tau}$. Then if it exists, it satisfies

$$\sum(s, m_{s,e,\tau}) < e + \tau \leq \sum(s, m_{s,e,\tau} + 1)$$

Or more explicitly, we define

$$m_{s,e,\tau} = \max\ \{n | \sum(s, n) < e + \tau\}$$

It is not difficult to see that the curve of $\sum(s, n)$ versus n is nondecreasing. But if the curve flattens out and tends toward a finite limit L, then for $e + \tau > L$, $m_{s,e,\tau}$ will not exist (i.e., the system will never advance in time beyond L, no matter how many transitions are taken).

Thus we are led to

ASSERTION 1

$m_{s,e,\tau}$ exists for every

$$e + \tau > 0 \Leftrightarrow \lim_{n \to \infty} \sum(s, n) = \infty$$

(i.e. for every $t \geq 0$ there is an n_t such that $\sum(s, n_t) > t$).

Exercise.   Formally prove Assertion 1.

Finally, we can say that $\delta_G(s, e, \phi_s)$ exists just in case $m_{s,e,\tau}$ exists, and in fact we state

ASSERTION 2

If $m_{s,e,\tau}$ exists, then

$$\delta_G(s, e, \phi_\tau) = (\overline{\delta}_\phi(s, m_{s,e,\tau}), \tau + e - \sum(s, m_{s,e,\tau}))$$

Exercise.   Assertion 2 states that if a finite number $m_{s,e,\tau}$ transitions are made in the interval $\langle 0, \tau \rangle$, the final sequential state attained is $\overline{\delta}_\phi(s, m_{s,e,\tau})$, and the time elapsed in that state is $\tau + e - \sum(s, m_s, e, \tau)$. Prove Assertion 2 using the induction parameter $m_{s,e,\tau}$.

We say that a DEVS M is *legitimate* if for each $s \in S_M$, $\lim_{n \to \infty} \sum(s, n) \to \infty$.

Exercise. Show that a DEVS M is legitimate if S_M is finite and $t(s) > 0$ for each $s \in S_M$, or if S_M is infinite but $\inf \{t(s) | s \in S_M > 0\}$ (i.e., there is a lower bound $b > 0$ such that $t(s) > b$ for each $s \in S_M$).

We can now provide the translation of the legitimate DEVS M into an iterative specification.

With a legitimate DEVS $M = \langle X_M, S_M, Y_M, \delta_M, \lambda_M, t \rangle$ we associate a structure $G(M) = \langle T, X, \Omega_G, Q, Y, \delta_G, \lambda \rangle$

where $T = R$ (real time base)

$$X = X_M \cup \{\phi\} \text{ (external events and nonevent)}$$
$$\Omega_G = \Omega_\phi \cup \Omega_X = \{\phi_\tau | \tau \in R^+\} \cup \{x_\tau | \tau \in R^+\}$$
$$Q = Q_M = \{(s, e) | s \in S_M, 0 \le e \le t(s)\}$$
$$Y = Y_M$$
$$\lambda = \lambda_M$$

and

$$\delta_G : Q \times \Omega_G \to Q$$

is defined by lines 1, 2, and 3 or in explicit form (Assertion 2):

$$\delta_G(s, e, \phi_\tau) = (\bar{\delta}_\phi(s, m_{s, e, \tau}), \tau + e - \Sigma(s, m_{s, e, \tau}))$$

and

$$\delta_G(s, e, x_\tau) = \delta_G(\delta_M(s, e, x), 0, \phi_\tau)$$

Exercise. Which parts of the foregoing translation are the results of background conventions and which are due to specificity rules?

THEOREM 3

Let M be a legitimate DEVS. Then $G(M)$ is an iterative specification and $S_{G(M)}$ is a time invariant system.

Proof. The proof proceeds through the following sequence of steps, which are left to the reader to prove.

1. *Characterization of Ω_G^+.* The set Ω_G^+ is the set of finite length segments having a finite number of events arbitrarily spaced, that is, $\Omega_G^+ = \{\omega | \omega : \langle 0, \tau \rangle \to X$ such that there exists a finite subset of $\langle 0, \tau \rangle, \tau_1, \tau_2, \dots, \tau_n,$ for which $\omega(\tau_1) \in X_M$ and $\omega(t) = \phi$ for $t \notin \{\tau_1, \dots, \tau_n\}\}$.

2. *Existence of longest generators.* $\omega \in \Omega_G^+ \Rightarrow t^* = \max \{t | \omega_{t\rangle} \in \Omega_G\} = \min (\{\tau_i | \omega(\tau_i) \in X_M\} \cup \{\tau\})$ where $\text{dom } \omega = \langle 0, \tau \rangle$; ($t^*$ is τ if $\omega = \phi_\tau$, and the time of the first event otherwise)

3.   *Closure of Ω_G under nontrivial left segmentation*

$$\text{LEFT} \cdot \text{SEGMENT}_t(\phi_\tau) = \phi_t$$
$$\text{LEFT} \cdot \text{SEGMENT}_t(x_\tau) = x_t$$

From items 2 and 3 we conclude that Ω_G is admissible. In fact, we have

4.   *Characterization of mls decompositions.*   We have that $\omega_1, \omega_2, \ldots, \omega_n$ is
     the mls decomposition of $\omega \in \Omega_G^+$ if and only if $\omega_i \in \Omega_G$ for each
     $i = 1, 2, \ldots, n$, and $\omega_i \in \Omega_\phi \Rightarrow i = 1$.
         The mls decomposition of ω in Figure 17 is $\phi_{\tau_1}, a_{\tau_2 - \tau_1}, b_{\tau_3 - \tau_2}, c_{\tau_4 - \tau_3},$
     $d_{\tau - \tau_4}.$

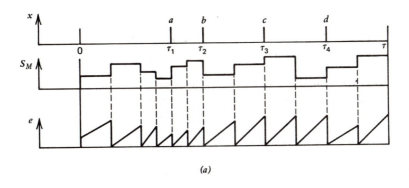

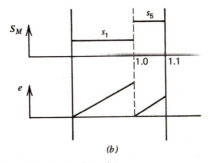

(b)

Figure 17   Input, state, and output trajectories.

5.   *Closure under nontrivial right segmentation*

$$\text{RIGHT} \cdot \text{SEGMENT}_t(\phi_\tau) = \phi_{\tau - t}$$
$$\text{RIGHT} \cdot \text{SEGMENT}_t(x_\tau) = \phi_{\tau - t}$$

6. *Relations on the generators*

$$\omega_1, \omega_2, \ldots, \omega_n \notin \Omega_G \quad \text{and} \quad \omega_1 \cdot \omega_2 \cdots \omega_n \in \Omega_G \Rightarrow n = 2 \quad \text{and} \quad \omega_2 \in \Omega_\phi$$

$$[\phi_\tau \phi_\sigma = \phi_{\tau + \sigma}, x_\tau \phi_\sigma = x_{\tau + \sigma}; \phi_\tau x_\sigma \notin \Omega_G, x_\tau x_\sigma \notin \Omega_G]$$

7. *Consistency of composition for* δ_G. We show

$$\delta_G(q, \phi_{\tau + \sigma}) = \delta_G(\delta_G(q, \phi_\tau), \phi_\sigma)$$

using the explicit characterization in Assertion 2. It then follows using line 3 that

$$\delta_G(q, x_{\tau + \sigma}) = \delta_G(\delta_G(q, x_\tau), \phi_\sigma)$$

Hint. Establish the following lemmas first:

(a) $\sum(s, n_1) + \sum(\delta_\phi(s, n_1), n_2) = \sum(s, n_1 + n_2)$

(b) $m_{s, e, \tau + \sigma} = m_{s, e, \tau} + m_{s', e', \sigma}$

where $s' = \delta_\phi(s, m_{s, e, \tau})$ and $e' = \tau + e - \sum(s, m_{s, e, \tau})$.   ∎

Exercise. The composition property is a test of whether the proper state space has been chosen for the system specification. For example, if S_M had been chosen rather than Q_M (in which case elapsed time would not be updated), $\delta_G : S_M \times \Omega_G \to S_M$, where we might define

$$\delta_G(s, \phi_\tau) = \bar{\delta}_\phi(s, m_{s, 0, \tau})$$

Show that this δ_G would not have the composition property.

Having the discrete event specified system $S_{G(M)}$, we can apply the standard definitions (Section 9.6) to describe its state and output trajectories, hence its I/O behavior $B_{S_{G(M)}}$ and I/O relation $R_{S_{G(M)}}$. Since Ω_G^+ is closed under non-trivial left segmentation, the state and output trajectories are defined everywhere on the observation interval except at zero. (See Figure 17).

Recall that associated with $\omega : \langle 0, \tau \rangle \to$ and initial state $(s, e) \in Q$ we have $\text{STRAJ}_{s, e, \omega} : \langle 0, \tau \rangle \to Q$, where $\text{STRAJ}_{s, e, \omega}(t) = \bar{\delta}_G(s, e, \omega_{t\rangle})$.

We consider the interesting phenomena involving *transitory* states. A state is *transitory* if $t(s) = 0$ (i.e. causes a zero time advance). The system may pass through a succession of these states at some instant without causing the clock to advance. Which of these states is the system "in" at such an instant? The formalism says none of them!

For example, examine the sequence of successor states s_1, s_2, s_3, s_4, s_5 $(s_{i+1} = \delta_\phi(s_i))$, where $t(s_1) = 1.0$, $t(s_2) = t(s_3) = t(s_4) = 0$, and $t(s_5) = 1.0$. We see that

$$\delta_G(s_1, 0, \phi_{0.9}) = (s_1, 0.9) \qquad \text{since } 0 + 0.9 \le 1.0$$

$$\delta_G(s_1, 0, \phi_{1.0}) = (s_1, 1.0) \qquad \text{since } 1.0 \le 1.0$$

$$\delta_G(s_1, 0, \phi_{1.1}) = \delta_G(s_2, 0, \phi_{0.1}) \qquad \text{since } 1.1 > 1.0 \text{ and } s_2 = \delta_\phi(s_1)$$
$$= \delta_G(s_3, 0, \phi_{0.1}) \qquad \text{since } 0.1 > 0 \text{ and } s_3 = \delta_\phi(s_2)$$
$$= \delta_G(s_4, 0, \phi_{0.1}) \qquad \text{since } 0\cdot1 > 0 \text{ and } s_4 = \delta_\phi(s_3)$$
$$= \delta_G(s_5, 0, \phi_{0.1}) \qquad \text{since } 0\cdot1 > 0 \text{ and } s_5 = \delta_\phi(s_4)$$
$$= (s_5, 0.1) \qquad \text{since } 0.1 \le 1.0$$

Thus the state trajectory associated with $(s_1, 0)$ and $\phi_{1.1}$ looks like that of Figure 17b. The system stays in state s_1 until and including time 1.0; at any time slightly after 1.0 it is in state s_5—none of the transitory states ever appears explicitly!

Exercise.   It is not uncommon in discrete event simulation for the programmer to allow his program to get into a repetitive loop of zero time actions; thus the computer grinds away but the simulation clock never advances. This is actually a model problem, in that the model is not well defined and has its counterpart in the DEVS, which is not legitimate. Show that a DEVS is not legitimate if there is a cycle consisting only of transitory states in the state diagram of δ_ϕ. For a finite DEVS, prove the characterizing:

THEOREM 4.

If M is a finite DEVS (i.e., S_M is a finite set), then M is legitimate if and only if every cycle in the state diagram of δ_ϕ contains a nontransitory state.

Exercise.   Given a legitimate DEVS m, construct a DEVS M' having no transitory states and generating the states and output trajectories of M associated with its nontransitory states. *Hint.* Let $S_{M'} = \{s \mid s \in S_M, t(s) > 0\}$ (the nontransitory states) and let $\delta'_\phi(s)$ be the first nontransitory state encountered in the autonomous trajectory of M beginning with s.

9.14   NETWORKS OF SYSTEM SPECIFICATIONS

In Chapter 5, we gave a general model description language in which a model is specified by a set of statements. The set of statements can be interpreted as describing a network in which memory functions are interconnected by instantaneous functions, with the external stimulation being provided by time functions. We have now provided the basis for the formalization of such network specifications, since we have available the notion of system specification by which the memory functions are to be characterized. With this we can develop the network specification as an interconnection of systems by means of instantaneous maps. Each system is specified according to an iterative specification. We are interested in describing the result of this interconnection as schematized in Figure 18—as a system specified according to

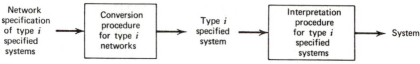

Figure 18   Network specification of systems.

an interative specification of the same type. A network specification of type-i-specified systems is to be converted by a standard procedure into a type-i-specified system representing the overall behavior of the network. Such a type-i-specified system, of course, can be further interpreted as a general system according to the procedure for type i specifications.

We shall provide such a network-to-system conversion procedure for the cases of discrete time, differential equation, and discrete event specification types. As indicated in Section 5.7, arbitrary continuous time systems present a problem because of the instantaneous nature of the interaction. At this writing, essentially only the three specification types just mentioned have known straightforward conversion procedures.

In principle, the result of a network interconnection can be obtained by dealing with the component systems at the input-output behavior level. But then the result is also known only at I/O level, and this approach does not satisfy the following requirements:

1. If every specification of type i can be readily implemented as a computer simulation program, a network of type-i-specified systems should also be readily implemented as a simulation program.
2. The result of converting a network of systems specified at a given level ought to be a system specified at a higher, more structural (more detailed) level.

We can see that the compound procedure of Figure 18 will satisfy the first (Why?) The second requirement asserts that knowing the parts and their interconnection tells us more about the whole than we know from knowing the whole alone. This requirement is also satisfied with the help of the conversion procedure of Figure 18, as demonstrated in Section 9.18.

The form of network specification we study is illustrated in Figure 19. The boxes represent memory functions that are to be considered systems of the form $\langle T, X, \Omega, \delta, Q \rangle$. These are called *transition systems* since only the state transition aspects have been specified and the output related components (Y, λ) do not appear. The circles represent instantaneous functions that map the states of boxes into inputs for the boxes they immediately influence. For example, in Figure 19 system S_δ is the only INFLUENCER of S_α. Accordingly, Z_α maps Q_δ into X_α, thus carries out the instantaneous translation of

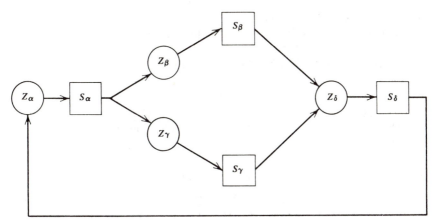

Figure 19   An example of a network.

the state of S_δ into an input value of S_α. Similarly, the INFLUENCERS of S_δ are S_β and S_γ, and this influence is specified by $Z_\delta : Q_\beta \times Q_\gamma \rightarrow X_\delta$.

Note that in effect, the Z maps provide the output maps not given in the transition system specifications for the components.

Connecting up the transition systems in this way will produce an autonomous transition system, (i.e., a system without inputs or outputs). This is a result of our not having specified input or output variables for the network. We have chosen this simplifying course for ease of exposition, and the reader who understands the approach will be easily able to extend the process to the more general case involving external input variables, and/or work with component systems that come fully dressed, with their output maps specified.

Exercise.   Given a network described in the language of Section 5.2, show how to convert it to the form of Figure 19.

9.15   DISCRETE TIME (SEQUENTIAL MACHINE) NETWORKS

A *discrete time (sequential machine) network specification* is a structure SMN = (INDEX · SET,   COMPONENTS,   INFLUENCER · SETS, Z-MAPS), where

INDEX · SET is a set (of names for the COMPONENTS)
COMPONENTS is a set (of transition sequential machines)
INFLUENCER · SETS is a family of sets (giving for each COMPONENT
   the COMPONENTS directly influencing it)
Z-MAPS is a family of maps (the connecting instantaneous maps)

with the following restrictions:

Let D denote the INDEX $\cdot$ SET. Then for each $\alpha \in D$,

1. There is a COMPONENT M_α in COMPONENTS such that

$$M_\alpha = \langle X_\alpha, Q_\alpha, \delta_\alpha \rangle$$

is a transition sequential machine (so $\delta_\alpha : Q_\alpha \times X_\alpha \to Q_\alpha$);

2. There is a member $I_\alpha \in$ INFLUENCER SETS such that

$$I_\alpha \subseteq D$$

3. There is a member Z_α in Z-MAPS such that

$$Z_\alpha : \underset{\beta \in I_\alpha}{\times} X_\beta \times Q_\alpha \to X_\alpha$$

Thus alternatively, a sequential machine network specification is a structure

$$\text{SMN} = (D, \{M_\alpha | \alpha \in D\}, \{I_\alpha | \alpha \in D\}, \{Z_\alpha | \alpha \in D\})$$

or in shorter form

$$\text{SMN} = (D, \{M_\alpha\}, \{I_\alpha\}, \{Z_\alpha\})$$

We provide a procedure for converting an SMN into an autonomous sequential machine as follows:

Given an SMN $= (D, \{M_\alpha\}, \{I_\alpha\}, \{Z_\alpha\})$, we associate with it a structure

$$M = \langle Q, \delta \rangle$$

where

$$Q = \underset{\alpha \in D}{\times} Q_\alpha$$

$$\delta : Q \to Q$$

is defined indirectly by

If $q = (q_{\alpha_1}, q_{\alpha_2}, \ldots, q_{\alpha_i}, \ldots,) \in Q$, then $\delta(q) = (q'_{\alpha_1}, q'_{\alpha_2}, \ldots, q'_{\alpha_i}, \ldots,)$, where for $\alpha_i \in D$, $q'_{\alpha_i} = \delta_{\alpha_i}(q_{\alpha_i}, x_{\alpha_i})$, where if $I_{\alpha_i} = \{\beta_1, \beta_2, \ldots, \beta_j, \ldots\}$, then $x_{\alpha_i} = Z_{\alpha_i}(q_{\beta_1}, \ldots, q_{\beta_j}, \ldots)$.

The construction of M is the formal equivalent of the simulation processes carried out in Section 5.4. The next state q'_{α_i} of each COMPONENT α_i is computed by applying its transition function δ_{α_i} to its present state q_{α_i} and the input symbol x_{α_i}, where x_{α_i} is derived from the present states of its INFLUENCERS I_{α_i} via the map Z_{α_i}.

THEOREM 5

The structure $M = \langle Q, \delta \rangle$ is an autonomous transition sequential machine.

Proof.   Show as an exercise that $\delta : Q \to Q$ is well defined.   ∎

When the components are delay elements, the definition of δ takes a particularly simple form. For if M_{α_i} is a delay element, $\delta_{\alpha_i}(q_{\alpha_i}, x_{\alpha_i}) = x_{\alpha_i}$; thus $q'_{\alpha_i} = Z_{\alpha_i}(q_{\beta_1}, \ldots, q_{\beta_j}, \ldots)$.

9.16   DIFFERENTIAL EQUATION NETWORKS

Networks of differential-equation-specified systems can be specified in a manner exactly paralleling that of the sequential machine case. The interpretation of the network as a DESS proceeds formally in the same way. For completeness, we shall sketch the development.

A *DESS network specification* is a structure

$$\text{DEN} = (\text{INDEX} \cdot \text{SET, COMPONENTS,}$$
$$\text{INFLUENCER SETS, } Z\text{-MAPS})$$

where all entities have the same meaning as in the SMN case except that now the COMPONENTS consist of DESSs of the form

$$D_\alpha = \langle X_\alpha, Q_\alpha, f_\alpha \rangle$$

Given a differential equation network (DEN), we associate with it a DESS

$$D = \langle Q, f \rangle$$

where Q is the cross product of the Q_α's and f is derived from the f_α's as it was for the SMN case.

When the components are integrators, we have a situation entirely analogous to the delay component case for sequential machine networks.

Exercise.   Show that an integrator is specified by a DESS $D = \langle X, Q, f \rangle$, where $X = Q = R$, and $f(q, x) = x$.

9.17   DISCRETE EVENT NETWORKS

In our original development of the DEVS (Chapter 6), the countdown clock variables appeared explicitly in the state variable set. We need the corresponding formal version of DEVS to discuss networks of DEVS, and we call this version the "explicit form," as in the following.

A DEVS $M = \langle X, S, Y, \delta, \lambda, t \rangle$ is in *explicit form* if

$$S = \mathscr{S} \times R_{0,\,\infty}^+$$

and for $(\measuredangle, \sigma) \in S$, $t(\measuredangle, \sigma) = \sigma$.

A *discrete event network specification* is a structure

$$\text{DEVN} = (\text{INDEX} \cdot \text{SET, COMPONENTS, INFLUENCEE} \cdot \text{SETS,}$$
$$Z\text{-MAPS, SELECT})$$

where INDEX · SET is a set (of names for the COMPONENTS)

COMPONENTS is a set (of transition DEVS)

INFLUENCEE · SETS is a family of sets (giving for each COMPO-
NENT the components it influences)

Z-MAPS is a family of maps (determining the effect of a COM-
PONENT on its INFLUENCEES)

SELECT is a function (providing the tie-breaking rule for simultaneously scheduled events)

with the restrictions that if the INDEX · SET is denoted by D, then for each $\alpha \in D$:

1. There is a COMPONENT M_α such that

$$M_\alpha = \langle X_\alpha, S_\alpha, \delta_\alpha, t_\alpha \rangle$$

is a DEVS in explicit form.

2. There is an INFLUENCEE · SET $I_\alpha \subseteq D$ where $\alpha \notin I_\alpha$.

3. For each $\beta \in I_\alpha$, there is a Z-MAP

$$Z_{\alpha, \beta} : S_\alpha \to X_\beta$$

4. And finally,

$$\text{SELECT}: 2^D \to D$$

such that for each $D' \subseteq D$

$$\text{SELECT}(D') \in D'$$

In the short form, we write

$$\text{DEVN} = (D, \{M_\alpha\}, \{I_\alpha\}, \{Z_{\alpha, \beta}\}, \text{SELECT})$$

With a DEVN, we associate a structure

$$M = \langle S, \delta_\phi, t \rangle$$

where

$$S = \underset{\alpha \in D}{\times} S_\alpha$$

Let $s = ((\mathit{4}_{\alpha_1}, \sigma_{\alpha_1}), (\mathit{4}_{\alpha_2}, \sigma_{\alpha_2}), \ldots, (\mathit{4}_{\alpha_i}, \sigma_{\alpha_i}), \ldots,)$

$$t: S \to R_{0, \infty}^+$$

is defined by

$$t(s) = \min_{\alpha \in D} \{\sigma_\alpha\}$$

Let $\text{IMM}: S \to 2^D$ be defined by

$$\text{IMM}(s) = \{\alpha | \sigma_\alpha = t(s)\}$$

[IMM(s) is the set of imminent COMPONENTS, i.e., those scheduled to become active at the next event time.]

Let $\bar{\alpha}: S \to D$ be defined by

$$\bar{\alpha}(s) = \text{SELECT}(\text{IMM}(s))$$

[$\bar{\alpha}$ is the COMPONENT from IMM(s) selected to become activated by the tie-breaking rules.]

Then

$$\delta_\phi : S \to S$$

is defined by

$$\delta_\phi(s) = s' = ((\mathbf{\mathit{4}}'_{\alpha_1}, \sigma'_{\alpha_1}), (\mathbf{\mathit{4}}'_{\alpha_2}, \sigma'_{\alpha_2}), \ldots, (\mathbf{\mathit{4}}'_{\alpha_i}, \sigma'_{\alpha_i}), \ldots,)$$

where

1. For $\beta = \bar{\alpha}(s), (\mathbf{\mathit{4}}'_\beta, \sigma'_\beta) = \delta_{\phi, \beta}(\mathbf{\mathit{4}}_\beta, \sigma_\beta).$
2. For $\beta \in I_{\bar{\alpha}(s)}, (\mathbf{\mathit{4}}'_\beta, \sigma'_\beta) = \delta_\beta((\mathbf{\mathit{4}}_\beta, \sigma_\beta), t(s), x)),$
   $$\text{where } x = Z_{\bar{\alpha}(s), \beta}(\mathbf{\mathit{4}}'_{\bar{\alpha}(s)}, \sigma'_{\bar{\alpha}(4)}).$$
3. Otherwise $(\mathbf{\mathit{4}}'_\beta, \sigma'_\beta) = (\mathbf{\mathit{4}}_\beta, \sigma_\beta - t(s)).$

In line 1, the component $\bar{\alpha}(s)$ selected from imminent set carries out its state transition. In line 2, if β is an INFLUENCEE of $\bar{\alpha}(s)$, it receives the external event x generated by the instantaneous Z-map applied to the new state of COMPONENT $\bar{\alpha}(s)$; having been in its state $(\mathbf{\mathit{4}}_\alpha, \sigma_\beta)$ for an elapsed time $e = t(s)$, it jumps to state $\delta_\beta(\mathbf{\mathit{4}}_\beta, \sigma_\beta, e, x)$. In line 3 every other component remains in its partial state $\mathbf{\mathit{4}}_\beta$, but the next scheduled state transition of each one is hastened by the $t(s)$ units that have already elapsed.]

THEOREM 6

The structure M is an autonomous transition DEVS.

Proof.   Show as an exercise that δ_ϕ and t are well defined.   ■

9.18   STRUCTURED SYSTEM SPECIFICATIONS

Section 9.14 revealed how a system can be specified by a network of component system specifications. We now show how the system specification obtained in this way represents a higher level of structural specification. Roughly, this means that we know not only the system's sets and functions as abstract entities, but the manner in which these sets and functions arise from more primitive sets and functions. This concept is the formal equivalent of the model description by components, descriptive variables, component interactions, and influence diagrams introduced in Chapter 1 and refined in the discussion of structured models in Chapters 4 and 7.

To further discuss this idea, we first examine the case of sequential machine specifications. Section 9.15 reveals how a network of machines $\{M_\alpha\}$ specifies a composite machine $M = \langle Q, \delta \rangle$, where Q is the cross product of the component states sets and δ is the cross product of component functions.

Now consider the reverse question: suppose we are given an abstract machine $M = \langle Q, \delta \rangle$ and we wish to design a network of machines that realizes it. We must choose a set D (which will turn out to be the names of the machines), for each $\alpha \in D$, a range set Q_α and a transition function δ_α such that Q is a subset of the cross product of the $\{Q_\alpha\}$ and δ is a subfunction of the cross product of the $\{\delta_\alpha\}$. To allow Q and δ to be a subset of the cross products means that the actual network we build may be much larger than the portion of interest to us. In addition, given $M = \langle Q, \delta \rangle$, there may be many, many distinct choices of D, $\{Q_\alpha\}$, and $\{\delta_\alpha\}$.

As modellers, we wish to construct a valid model of a real system by choosing components, descriptive variables, and interaction rules—the informal correlates of the set D, $\{Q_\alpha\}$, and $\{\delta_\alpha\}$. There are many alternatives to choose from, so the selection of one of them amounts to stating a hypothesis about how the real system works. Moreover, in testing our model we rarely consider all possible initial states, thus we are dealing with a subset of all possible state and transition combinations. To develop this idea further we require some of the concepts relating to embedding sets and functions into cross products.

A *structured* (or *coordinatized*) set is a structure

$$\mathscr{A} = \langle A, D, \{A_\alpha | \alpha \in D\}, i \rangle$$

where A is a set (the set to be structured)

  D is an ordered set $\alpha_1, \alpha_2, \ldots, \alpha_j, \ldots$ (the coordinates)

  A_α is a set, for each $\alpha \in D$ (the range set of α)

  i is a function (the assignment function)

with the restrictions

$$i : A \rightarrow \bigtimes_{\alpha \in D} A_\alpha$$

is one to one.

The elements of A may sometimes be called entities. The coordinates of D may be called variables, attributes, descriptors, or parameters. The elements of range set A_α may be called values, attribute values, descriptor values, or parameter values.

The map i identifies each element of A (entity) with a tuple of values (attribute values). Thus $i(a) = (a_{\alpha_1}, a_{\alpha_2}, a_{\alpha_3}, \ldots)$ means that entity a has attribute value a_{α_1}, for attribute α_1, a_{α_2} for attribute α_2, and so on. Since i is one to one, every pair of distinct entities a and b must have at least one coordinate in which they differ; that is, $a_{\alpha_j} \neq b_{\alpha_j}$ for some $\alpha_j \in D$.

Since $i(A) \subseteq \times_{\alpha \in D} A_\alpha$, we often suppress mention of i and write $A \subseteq \times_{\alpha \in D} A_\alpha$ and say that A is structured by $\{A_\alpha | \alpha \in D\}$.

Example.   Description of People.   Tom, Dick, Harry, and Jane are four people; each is to be described by sex, age, and hair color.

We have

$$\mathscr{A}_{\text{PEOPLE}} = \langle A, D, \{A_\alpha | \in D\}, i \rangle$$

where $A = \{\text{Tom, Dick, Harry, Jane}\}$
$D = \{\text{SEX, AGE, HAIR} \cdot \text{COLOR}\}$
$A_{\text{SEX}} = \{\text{MALE, FEMALE}\}$
$A_{\text{AGE}} = \{1, 2, 3, \ldots, 120\}$
$A_{\text{HAIR} \cdot \text{COLOR}} = \{\text{BLOND, BROWN, RED}\}$

and $i: A \rightarrow A_{\text{SEX}} \times A_{\text{AGE}} \times A_{\text{HAIR} \cdot \text{COLOR}}$ is given by Figure 20a.

ENTITY	SEX	AGE	HAIR · COLOR
Tom	Male	6	Blond
Dick	Male	6	Red
Harry	Male	10	Brown
Mary	Female	10	Brown
Jane	Female	33	Red

(a)

ENTITY	FAMILY · NAME	GRADE · IN · SCHOOL
Tom	SMITH	E
Dick	SMITH	VG
Harry	SMITH	G
Mary	JONES	E
Jane	JONES	VG

(b)

Figure 20   Examples of set structures.

Thus, for example,

$$i(\text{TOM}) = (\text{MALE, 6, BLOND})$$

or, in shortened form

$$\text{TOM} = (\text{MALE, 6, BLOND})$$

There may be many different ways of describing a given set (i.e., different structure assignments). In this example, consider a second structure

$$\mathscr{B}_{\text{PEOPLE}} = \langle A, E, \{\mathscr{A}_\beta | \beta \in E\}, j \rangle$$
$$E = \{\text{FAMILY} \cdot \text{NAME}, \text{GRADE} \cdot \text{IN} \cdot \text{SCHOOL}\}$$
$$A_{\text{FAMILY} \cdot \text{NAME}} = \{\text{SMITH}, \text{JONES}\}$$
$$A_{\text{GRADE} \cdot \text{IN} \cdot \text{SCHOOL}} = \{\{\text{E}, \text{VG}, \text{G}, \text{F}\}$$
$$j : A \to A_{\text{FAMILY} \cdot \text{NAME}} \times A_{\text{GRADE} \cdot \text{IN} \cdot \text{SCHOOL}}$$

is given by Figure 20*b*.

Exercise. What attributes serve to distinguish the twins, Tom and Dick; the mother, Jane, and the daughter, Mary?

We say that $\mathscr{A} = \langle A, D, \{A_\alpha | \alpha \in D\}, i \rangle$ is a *Cartesian* structure if i is an onto function, that is, $i(A) = \bigtimes_{\alpha \in D} A_\alpha$. In the short reference, we say that A is *Cartesian* structured by $\{A_\alpha | \alpha \in D\}$ if $A = \bigtimes_{\alpha \in D} A_\alpha$.

Exercise. If A is Cartesian structured by $\{A_\alpha | \alpha \in D\}$, how many elements does it have?

Having a structure for a set A, we can ask questions about its entities. For example, what attribute value does entity a have for attribute α? Such questions are captured by the formal concept of projection.

With a structure $\mathscr{A} = \langle A, D, \{A_\alpha| \in D\}, i \rangle$ we associate with each co-ordinate $\alpha_i \in D$, a map $\text{proj}_{\alpha_i} : A \to A_{\alpha_i}$ defined as follows: for each $a \in A$, let $i(a) = (a_{\alpha_1}, a_{\alpha_2}, a_{\alpha_3}, \ldots)$; then $\text{proj}_{\alpha_i}(a) = a_{\alpha_i}$.

Example. In $\mathscr{A}_{\text{PEOPLE}}$, TOM = (MALE, 6, BLOND). Thus

$$\text{proj}_{\text{SEX}}(\text{TOM}) = \text{MALE}$$
$$\text{proj}_{\text{AGE}}(\text{TOM}) = 6$$
$$\text{proj}_{\text{HAIR} \cdot \text{COLOR}}(\text{TOM}) = \text{BLOND}$$

Since $\text{proj}_\alpha(a)$ is the value of attribute α for entity a, we can use the following alternate expressions:

"The α of a is $\text{proj}_\alpha(a)$"   or   "a's α is $\text{proj}_\alpha(a)$,"

as in

"The HAIR $\cdot$ COLOR of TOM is BLOND,"

or

"TOM's HAIR $\cdot$ COLOR is BLOND."

Exercise. Display the projection $\text{proj}_{\text{HAIR} \cdot \text{COLOR}} : \{\text{TOM}, \text{DICK}, \text{HARRY}, \text{MARY}, \text{JANE}\} \to \{\text{BROWN}, \text{BLOND}, \text{RED}\}$ as a set of pairs (person, person's HAIR $\cdot$ COLOR).

For a subset SUBSET $\subseteq D$, we call $\text{proj}_{\text{SUBSET}}$, the *projection associated with SUBSET.* $\text{Proj}_{\text{SUBSET}}(a)$ is the list of values of attributes in SUB-SET that characterize a. More formally, with a structure $\mathscr{A}$ we associate with each nonempty subset $\{\beta_1, \beta_2, \dots\}$ of D, a map $\text{proj}_{\{\beta_1, \beta_2, \dots\}}(a) = (\text{proj}_{\beta_1}(a), \text{proj}_{\beta_2}(a), \dots)$. With the empty set $\varnothing$ we associate the function $\text{proj}_\phi : A \to \{\varnothing\}$.

Example.   In $\mathscr{A}_{\text{PEOPLE}}$, since MARY $= $ (FEMALE, 10, BROWN)

$$\text{proj}_{\text{SEX, AGE}}(\text{MARY}) = (\text{FEMALE, 10})$$

$$\text{proj}_{\text{SEX, HAIR} \cdot \text{COLOR}}(\text{MARY}) = (\text{FEMALE, BROWN})$$

Exercise.   Make a table giving the value $\text{proj}_{\text{SUBSET}}(\text{MARY})$ for all $2^3 = 8$ subsets SUBSET of D.

Exercise.   Construct the projection that tells for each person his or her SEX and HAIR $\cdot$ COLOR.

Just as we can embed a set into a cross product of sets, we can embed a function into a cross product of functions. The result of doing this is called a structured function.

First let us define "cross product of functions."

Let $\{f_\beta | \beta \in E\}$ be a family of functions such that for each $\beta \in E$, f_β maps a set A into a set B_β. The *cross product* is a function $f : A \to \times_{\beta \in E} B_\beta$ such that $f(a) = (f_{\beta_1}(a), f_{\beta_2}(a), \dots)$; that is, for each $\beta \in E$, $\text{proj}_\beta(f(a)) = f_\beta(a)$. We denote the cross product by $\times_{\beta \in E} f_\beta$.

A *structured function* is a structure

$$\langle f, \mathscr{A}, \mathscr{B}, \mathscr{I}, \mathscr{F} \rangle$$

where $f : A \to B$ is a function

$\mathscr{A} = \langle A, D, \{A_\alpha\}, i\rangle$	is a structure for A
$\mathscr{B} = \langle B, E, \{B_\beta\}, j\rangle$	is a structure for B
$\mathscr{I} = \{I_\beta | \beta \in E\}$	is a family of sets (INFLUENCERS)
$\mathscr{F} = \{f_\beta | \beta \in E\}$	is a family (of local functions)

with the restrictions that, for each $\beta \in E$

1. $I_\beta \subseteq D$.
2. $f_\beta : \times_{\alpha \in I_\beta} A_\alpha \to B_\beta$.
3. $\text{proj}_\beta(f(a)) = f_\beta(\text{proj}_{I_\beta}(a))$ for each $a \in A$.

Using our cross product notation, we can rewrite 3 as 3'.

3'. $f = \bigtimes_{\beta \in E} f_\beta \circ \mathrm{proj}_{I_\beta}$ restricted to A. ($f_\beta \circ \mathrm{proj}_{I_\beta}$ is the *composition* of f_β with proj_{I_β}, i.e., $f_\beta \circ \mathrm{proj}_{I_\beta}(a) = f_\beta(\mathrm{proj}_{I_\beta}(a))$).

We have assumed that i and j are the identities in writing 3 and 3'. In shortened form we say that f is structured by $(D, \{A_\alpha\}, E, \{B_\beta\}, \{I_\beta\}, \{f_\beta\})$.

Exercise. Explain 3' by providing an algorithm to compute $f(a)$ for $a \in A$.

Since an autonomous transition function takes the form $\delta : Q \to Q$, a function structure for it will take the form in which both range and domain sets are the same and have the same set structures. This leads us to the following concept.

A machine $M = \langle Q, \delta \rangle$ is a *structured machine* if we have given

D (a set of coordinates)
$\{Q_\alpha | \alpha \in D\}$ (a family of range sets)
$\{I_\alpha | \alpha \in D, I_\alpha \subseteq D\}$ (a family of INFLUENCERS)
$\{\delta_\alpha | \alpha \in D, \delta_\alpha : \bigtimes_{\beta \in I_\alpha} Q_\beta \to Q_\alpha\}$ (a family of local transition functions)

such that

$$Q \subseteq \bigtimes_{\alpha \in D} Q_\alpha$$

and

$$\delta = \bigtimes_{\alpha \in D} \delta_\alpha \circ \mathrm{proj}_{I_\alpha} \qquad \text{restricted to } Q$$

$(D, \{Q_\alpha\}, \{I_\alpha\}, \{\delta_\alpha\})$ is called the *structure* of M.

With the structured machine M, we associate *influence digraph* (directed graph) $D(M)$ as follows: the points (vertices) of $D(M)$ are in one to one correspondence with the coordinates D; for every pair of points α, β there is an arrow (edge) from α to β just in case $\alpha \in I_\beta$. Thus the points sending arrows directly to a point β are its INFLUENCERS I_β.

Exercise. The structured machine concept for nonautonomous machines $M = \langle X, Q, \delta \rangle$ was presented informally in Section 4.7. Define the corresponding formal concept in the style just given.

Example. Let $M = \langle Q, \delta \rangle$, where $Q = \{0, 1, 2\}$ and $\delta(q) = (q + 1) \bmod_3$ (a simple cycle of three states). We provide two alternative function structures for C based on the same set structure for Q.

Let Q be structured by $\{Q_\alpha | \alpha \in D\}$, where $D = \{\alpha_1, \alpha_2, \alpha_3\}$ $Q_\alpha = \{0, 1\}$ for each $\alpha \in D$, and $0 = (1, 0, 0)$, $1 = (0, 1, 0)$, $2 = (0, 0, 1)$. In the first structure assignment for δ, we choose $\{I_\alpha | \alpha \in D\}$ such that $I_{\alpha_1} = \{\alpha_3\}$, $I_{\alpha_2} = \{\alpha_1\}$, and $I_{\alpha_3} = \{\alpha_2\}$. Then the set $\{\delta_\alpha | \alpha \in D\}$ is given by $\delta_{\alpha_1} : Q_{\alpha_3} \to Q_{\alpha_1}$, $\delta_{\alpha_2} : Q_{\alpha_1} \to Q_{\alpha_2}$, and $\delta_{\alpha_3}: Q_{\alpha_2} \to Q_{\alpha_3}$, where each δ_α is the identity function, $\delta_\alpha(x) = x$; that is, we have the tables

q_{α_3}	δ_{α_1}
0	1
1	0

q_{α_2}	δ_{α_3}
0	0
1	1

q_{α_1}	δ_{α_2}
0	0
1	1

Letting $\tilde{\delta}$ denote the cross product, we find that for $q \in \{0, 1\} \times \{0, 1\} \times \{0, 1\}$

$$\tilde{\delta}(q) = \underset{\alpha \in D}{\times}\ \delta_\alpha \circ \text{proj}_{I_\alpha}(q) = (\delta_{\alpha_1} \circ \text{proj}_{I_{\alpha_1}}(q),\ \delta_{\alpha_2} \circ \text{proj}_{I_{\alpha_2}}(q),\ \delta_{\alpha_3} \circ \text{proj}_{I_{\alpha_3}}(q))$$
$$= (\delta_{\alpha_1} \circ \text{proj}_{\alpha_3}(q),\ \delta_{\alpha_2} \circ \text{proj}_{\alpha_1}(q),\ \delta_{\alpha_3} \circ \text{proj}_{\alpha_2}(q))$$
$$= (\text{proj}_{\alpha_3}(q),\ \text{proj}_{\alpha_1}(q),\ \text{proj}_{\alpha_2}(q))$$

With $Q = \{(1, 0, 0), (0, 1, 0), (0, 0, 1)\}$, we work out the table

q_{α_1}	q_{α_2}	q_{α_3}	$\tilde{\delta}$		
1	0	0	0	1	0
0	1	0	0	0	1
0	0	1	1	0	0

which has the corresponding state graph

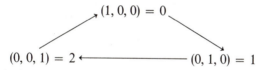

$(1, 0, 0) = 0$

$(0, 0, 1) = 2 \longleftarrow \qquad (0, 1, 0) = 1$

This shows that $\delta = \tilde{\delta}$ restricted to Q as required.

The digraph associated with this structure is

α_1

$\alpha_3 \longleftarrow \alpha_2$

We see that in this structure assignment, each state in Q is represented by a pulse in one of three positions. A cycle of length 3 is obtained as the pulse is in effect sent around the cycle in the influence graph $\alpha_1 \to \alpha_2 \to \alpha_3 \to \alpha_1$.

Exercise.   Complete the table of $\tilde{\delta}$ for all eight entries.

In our second structure assignment for δ we set $I_{\alpha_1} = \{\alpha_1, \alpha_2\}$, $I_{\alpha_2} = \{\alpha_2, \alpha_3\}$, and $I_{\alpha_3} = \{\alpha_3, \alpha_1\}$.

Then $\{\delta_\alpha | \alpha \in D\}$ is given by the tables

q_{α_1}	q_{α_2}	δ_{α_1}		q_{α_2}	q_{α_3}	δ_{α_2}		q_{α_3}	q_{α_1}	δ_{α_3}
1	0	0		1	0	0		1	0	0
0	1	0		0	1	0		0	1	0
0	0	1		0	0	1		0	0	1
1	1	—		1	1	—		1	1	—

Exercise. Show that this structure assignment is valid (the cross product restricted to Q is δ) and draw its influence digraph.

We see that even given the same state structure there may be many function structures, or choices of local transition functions and influence digraphs, which realize the same local transition function. Thus the structured machine represents a higher level of specification than the level of abstract sequential machine specification.

Exercise. The entry $\delta_\alpha(1, 1)$ is undefined in our second assignment because the $\text{proj}_{I_\alpha}(q)$ is never $(1, 1)$ for $q \in Q$, $\alpha \in D$. (This is called a "don't care" in sequential machine realization.)

Show that no matter which choice of $\{0, 1\}$ is made for this entry, the second structure will not predict the same next state for $(1, 1, 1)$ that was predicted by the first structure assignment.

Thus although many transition function structure assignments are "degenerate" on a restricted state space, they may become distinct when the state space is expanded, (e.g., when more states are traversed in subsequent experiments).

Exercise. Cast the Game of Life machine in the form of a structure machine. Provide a specification format for cellular automata which specifies only the local state set, transition function, and neighborhood of CELL(0, 0). Derive an interpretation that employs the background conventions of spatial translation invariance and homogeneity to map the specification into a structured machine.

In Chapter 5 we discussed a translation process by which the network description of a model is converted into a sequential machine format. The formal equivalent to this translation process is that of going from network to structured machine as indicated in the following exercise.

Exercise. Assuming a network specification $SMN = (D', \{M'_\alpha\}, \{I'_\alpha\}, \{Z'_\alpha\})$, where $M'_\alpha = \langle X'_\alpha, Q'_\alpha, \delta'_\alpha \rangle$, give the structure $(D, \{Q_\alpha\}, \{I_\alpha\}, \{\delta_\alpha\})$ of the machine specified by the network. (In particular, what is the relation between the function δ_α and δ'_α?)

Thus, there is a unique structured machine associated with a given network specification. However, the structured machine concept is slightly more abstract than the network specification because the translation of outputs to inputs done by the Z-maps is lost in the conversion process. As a consequence, more than one network specification may specify the same structured machine.

Exercise.   More generally, we have the concept of *structured system specification*. Show how to define this concept in the case of differential equation system specifications.

Exercise.   In Chapter 7 we discussed three forms of structured discrete event models. For each form, provide the formal structured DEVS equivalent.

Exercise.   Show how to convert a network of DEVSs, as defined in Section 9.17, into a structured DEVS. Which if any of the forms discussed previously are obtained?

9.19   GATHERING UP THE STRANDS

The hierarchy of levels at which a system may be known or specified is summarized in Table 2. As the level in the table increases, we move in the direction of increasing structural specificity (i.e., from behavior to structure). Let us briefly restate what new knowledge is introduced at each level of the hierarchy.

Table 2   Hierarchy of System Specifications

Level	Specification	Formal Object
0	I/O relation observation	$\langle T, X, \Omega, Y, R \rangle$
1	I/O function observation	$\langle T, X, \Omega, Y, F \rangle$
2	I/O system	$S = \langle T, X, \Omega, Q, Y, \delta, \lambda \rangle$
3	Iterative specification	$G = \langle T, X, \Omega_G, Y, \delta_G, \lambda \rangle$
4	Structured system specification	$(D, \{Q_\alpha\}, \{I_\alpha\}, \{\delta_\alpha\})^*$
5	Network of specifications	$SMN = (D, \{M_\alpha\}, \{I_\alpha\}, \{Z_\alpha\})^*$

* Given for sequential machine case.

At level 0 we deal with purely observational recordings of the behavior of a system. This is the set of I/O segment pairs called its I/O relation.

At level 1 we study the set of I/O functions that partitions a system's I/O relation. Each function is associated with a state of the system as it is described at level 2.

At level 2 the system is described by abstract sets and functions. The state space, transition, and output functions are introduced at this level. The transition function describes the state-to-state transitions caused by the input segments; the output function describes the state-to-observable-output mapping.

At level 3 we consider shorthand forms of specifying a system at level 2 by presenting only its input generator segments and the state-to-state transitions caused by these segments. Level 3 is superseded by a second level at which various classes of systems are specified by supplying only the information required to distinguish one member of a class from another. Classes considered were the sequential machine, discrete event, and differential equation systems.

At level 4 the abstract sets and functions of lower levels are presented as arising as cross products of more primitive sets and functions. This corresponds to the level at which models are often informally described.

At level 5 a system is specified as an interconnection of component systems specified at level 3. This level is often employed for conveniently describing a model to a simulator.

We showed how to convert a system specification at each level (except the lowest) to one at the next lower level. Thus by a multistep process we can express the observable behavior associated with a system specified or known at any of the levels. To review this process briefly, assume we are given a network at level 5. We first abstract the intermediary role played by the connecting maps and the component system specifications; thus we can describe the local state transition functions directly as required in level 4.

Given a structure at level 4, we compound the component sets and functions by the cross product operation to obtain the sets and functions required at level 3.

Given a specification at level 3, we expand it by iteration into a specification at level 2; that is, input segments are constructed by successive composition of generator segments, and multistep transitions are built up by successive application of single-step transitions.

Given a system at level 2, we associate with each state its I/O function, by pairing the output trajectory generated by the system started in the state, with the input segment that caused this trajectory.

Given a set of I/O functions at level 1, we construct the associated I/O relation by collecting together all the I/O pairs contained in the set of functions.

The process of going from a system specification at the highest level to one at the lowest is the formal equivalent of the simulation of a model by a computer. The machine computes, step-by-step, successive states and outputs; each step involves the component-by-component calculation of descriptive variable values. Sequences of states and outputs constitute trajectories, and collections of such trajectories constitute the behavior of the model.

Exercise. Review Chapters 3, 4, and 5, and correlate the translation and simulation procedures given there with the formal process discussed in this chapter.

We have now come full circle. We began in Chapter 2 with the informal description of models given in terms of components, descriptive variables, and component interaction and influence diagram. We can now see that the formal version of this description is the structured machine (in the case of discrete time systems, or the structured system specification, more generally). We remarked when introducing the informal description scheme that models can be described at other levels as well, and we traced through the various levels of system description from most behavioral to most structural. Each can be used for model description, but for simulation purposes the more structured levels—the network specification and the structured system specification—are most appropriate. However, the other levels must be brought in if we are to properly deal with the relation between structure and behavior.

9.20 SOURCES

Good expositions of mathematical systems theory are available.[1-4]. The realization of sequential machines by discrete time networks is the subject of many books on switching theory and automata.[5, 6]

1. L. Padulo and M. A. Arbib, *System Theory*. Saunders, Philadelphia, Pa., 1974.

2. A. W. Wymore, *A Mathematical Theory of Systems Engineering: The Elements*. Wiley, New York, 1967.

3. M. Harrison, *Lectures on Linear Sequential Machines*. Academic Press, New York, 1969.

4. L. A. Zadeh and C. A. Desoer, *Linear System Theory, The State Space Approach*. McGraw-Hill, New York, 1963.

5. E. F. Moore (Ed.), *Sequential Machines: Selected Papers*. Addison-Wesley, Reading, Mass., 1964.

6. G. Klir, *Introduction to the Methodology of Switching Circuits*. Van Nostrand, New York, 1972.

7. B. P. Zeigler, "Towards a Formal Theory of Modelling and Simulation: Structure Preserving Morphisms," *Journal of the Association for Computing Machinery*, **19** (4), 1972, 742–764.

PROBLEMS

1. *The lattice of all partitions and those induced by coordinatization.*   In this problem we develop a calculus for dealing with structured sets and functions. The material is taken from Reference 7,[†] to which the reader may turn for help.

Given a set A structured by $\{A_\alpha | \alpha \in D\}$, we write $P_{D'}$ as short for $\text{proj}_{D'}$, where D' is a subset of D.

(a)   Show that $P_{D'} = \bigtimes_{\alpha \in D'} P_\alpha$.

(b)   Every subset $D' \subseteq D$ induces a partition $\Pi_{D'}$ on A as follows:

$$a\pi_{D'}a' \Leftrightarrow P_{D'}(a) = P_{D'}(a')$$

(a, a' are in the same block of $\pi_{D'}$ if and only if they have the same projections on the coordinate in D'). We write π_α for $\pi_{\{\alpha\}}$.

Let $\mathcal{P}_A$ denote the set of all partitions on A. It is well known that $\mathcal{P}_A$ is a lattice with underlying partial order $\leq$ given by

$$\pi_1 \leq \pi_2 \Leftrightarrow (\forall\, a, a' \in A)(a\pi_1 a' \Rightarrow a\pi_2 a')$$

This is read: π_1 refines π_2.

The least upper bound (lub) and greatest lower bound (glb) operators are denoted $\cup$ and $\cap$, respectively. The glb $\cap$ is defined by

$$a(\pi_1 \cap \pi_2)a' \Leftrightarrow a\pi_1 a' \qquad \text{and} \qquad a\pi_2 a'$$

The lub operator is defined by

$$a(\pi_1 \cup \pi_2)a' \Leftrightarrow \text{there exist } a = a_1, a_2, a_3, \ldots, a_n$$
$$= a' \text{ such that } a_i\pi_1 a_{i+1} \text{ for all odd } i, \text{ and}$$
$$a_i\pi_2 a_{i+1} \text{ for all even } i$$

These definitions satisfy the required conditions, namely, that $\pi \leq \pi_i$ ($i = 1, 2$) implies $\pi \leq \pi_1 \cap \pi_2$ and $\pi_i \leq \pi$ ($i = 1, 2$) implies $\pi_1 \cup \pi_2 \leq \pi$; O is the finest, and I the coarsest, partitions of $\mathcal{P}_A$ are defined by

$$aOa' \quad \text{if and only if} \quad a = a' \quad \text{and} \quad aIa' \quad \text{if and only if} \quad a, a' \in A$$

The subset of $\mathcal{P}_A$ of partitions induced by coordinate subsets is denoted $\mathcal{P}_A^D$. Thus $\mathcal{P}_A^D = \{\pi_{D'} | D' \subseteq D\}$. We note that $O = \pi_D \in \mathcal{P}_A^D$, and $I = \pi_\phi \in \mathcal{P}_A^D$. It is readily established that for all $D', D'' \subseteq D$, $\pi_{D'} = \bigcap_{\alpha \in D'} \pi_\alpha$, and $D' \subseteq D''$ implies $\pi_{D''} \leq \pi_{D'}$.

The latter assertion means that $D' \mapsto \pi_{D'}$ is an order-reversing map

---

[†] Reprinted from Reference 7, pp. 747–754, Copyright © 1972, by The Association for Computing Machinery, Inc. Reprinted by permission.

between 2^D and $\mathscr{P}_A^D$. However $\mathscr{P}_A^D$ is not in general a sublattice of $\mathscr{P}_A$ anti-isomorphic to 2^D. It is easily verified that for all $D_1, D_2 \subseteq D, \pi_{D_1} \cap \pi_{D_2} = \pi_{D_1 \cup D_2}$. The $\mathscr{P}_A^D$ fails to be a sublattice of $\mathscr{P}_A$ because it may happen that $\pi_{D_1} \cup \pi_{D_2} \neq \pi_{D_1 \cap D_2}$. We can determine necessary and sufficient conditions for $\mathscr{P}_A^D$ to be a sublattice of $\mathscr{P}_A$ anti-isomorphic to 2^D as follows.

We say that $D' \subseteq D$ is a *location* for $\pi \in \mathscr{P}_A$ if $\pi_{D'} \leq \pi$ and for all $D'' \subseteq D'$ if $\pi_{D''} \leq \pi$ then $D'' = D'$. In other words, a location D_π of π is a least subset of D with the property that π_{D_π} refines π.

A coordinatization $\{A_\alpha | \alpha \in D\}$ is *irredundant* if every partition $\pi \in \mathscr{P}_A$ has a unique location.

Prove the

THEOREM

$\{A_\alpha | \alpha \in D\}$ is irredundant just in case for all $D_1, D_2 \subseteq D, \pi_{D_1} \cup \pi_{D_2} = \pi_{D_1 \cap D_2}$.

(c)   Show that a Cartesian coordinatization is irredundant.

We say that a coordinate $\alpha \in D$ is *dependent* whenever $\pi_{D-\alpha} \leq \pi_\alpha$; α is *independent* if it is not dependent. Two kinds of dependence may be distinguished: $\alpha \in D$ is called a *constant* if $\pi_\alpha = I$. The term is appropriate, since $P_\alpha(a)$ is constant over $a \in A$. Clearly $\pi_\alpha = I$ implies $\pi_{D-\alpha} \leq \pi_\alpha$.

More generally, when $\pi_{D-\alpha} \leq \pi_\alpha < I$, we say that α is *completely determined*. In this case, P_α is not a constant function, but the values it can take on are completely determined by the other coordinate values.

For example, let $|A| = n$ and consider the well-known coordinatization of $A = \{a_i | 1 \leq i \leq n\}$ by $\{A_{\alpha_i} | 1 \leq i \leq n\}$, where for each i, $a_i = (0, 0, \ldots, 1, \ldots, 0)$ (only $P_{\alpha_i}(a_i)$ is nonzero). No more than $n - 1$ coordinates of these n can be independent, thus as the reader may directly verify, any one coordinate in this coordinatization is completely determined by the rest.

We say that a coordinatization is *independent* if all its coordinates are independent.

(d)   Show that if a coordinatization is irredundant and has no constant coordinates, it is also independent. Provide a counterexample to show that independence does not imply irredundance.

(e)   Let A be a finite set of n elements. Show that an independent coordinatization of A has at most $n - 1$ elements.

(f)   Let g be a function with domain A. We say that g *depends* on a set $C \subseteq D$ if for all $a, a' \in A$

$$P_C(a) = P_C(a') \Rightarrow g(a) = g(a').$$

Then C is a *location* for g, written loc g if g depends on C, and for any $C' \subseteq C$, if g depends on C', then $C' = C$.

The *kernel partition induced by* g is a partition on A defined by $a\pi a' \Leftrightarrow g(a) = g(a')$ for all $a, a' \in A$.

Let $\{A_\alpha | \alpha \in D\}$ be a coordinatization of A. Show that this coordinatization is irredundant if and only if every function with domain A has a unique location.

(g) Show that g depends on C if and only if there is a unique function g_C with domain $P_C(A)$ such that $g_C \circ P_C = g$. Call g_C the *function of* C *defined by* g.

(h) A function g' with domain $P_C(A)$ is in *reduced form* if C is a location of g' (relative to the coordinatization $P_C(A) \subseteq \bigtimes_{\alpha \in C} A_\alpha$). Show that if C is a location of g, then g_C is in reduced form.

(i) A structured function $f : A \to B$ is in *reduced form* if every f_β, $\beta \in E$, is in reduced form.

Given an abstract machine $M = \langle Q, \delta \rangle$ and a structure $\{Q_\alpha | \alpha \in D\}$ of Q, for each $\alpha \in D$, let $I_\alpha \subseteq D$ be such that $P_\alpha \circ \delta$ depends on I_α, and let δ_α be the function of I_α defined by $P_\alpha \circ \delta$. Show that $(D, \{Q_\alpha\}, \{I_\alpha\}, \{\delta_\alpha\})$ is a structure for M. Characterize the choices $\{I_\alpha\}$, $\{\delta_\alpha\}$ which are reduced form structures for δ.

Chapter Ten

Hierarchy of
Preservation Relations

The essence of modelling lies in establishing relations between pairs of systems. These relations pertain to the validity of representation of the real system by a base model, the validity of a lumped model relative to a base model, and correctness of the simulation program with respect to the lumped model.

Corresponding to each of the various levels at which a system may be known, described, or specified, is a relation appropriate to a pair of systems specified at that level. We call such a relation a *preservation relation* or *morphism* because it establishes a correspondence between systems whereby features of the one system are preserved in the other. An example of a preservation relation is the homomorphism between discrete event systems, which we met first in Chapter 8. Such a relation preserves the time advance, transition, and output functions of one DEVS in another and is therefore a preservation relation at the iterative specification level.

We take the point of view illustrated in Figure 1, where S represents a "big" system and S' a "little" system. For example, S could be a base model and S' a lumped model, or S could represent the simulation program and S' the model being simulated. In either case, S is "bigger" than S' in that S is capable of "doing" whatever S' can do, and maybe much more. Accordingly, the basic orientation is that a part of the behavior of the big system S is mapped onto all the behavior of the little system S'; or, as we say, a "preservation morphism runs from (big) S to (little) S'." To avoid later confusion, we point out that some of the mappings we employ in such a morphism may run the other way (i.e., from S' to S). This is not inconsistent with what has been said, since these mappings can be taken to be *injective*, that is,

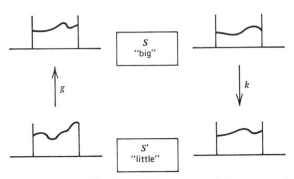

Figure 1   A morphism from a big system to a little system.

one-to-one maps that "embed" S' in S. In effect, such injective maps tell where to look in the big system S for the appropriate part relatable to little system S'. On the other hand, other mappings we employ go in the "right" direction, from S to S'; these are *surjective* or *onto* maps, which ensure that all the behavior of S' is being covered by the behavior of S.

We shall develop morphisms appropriate to each level of system specification. These morphisms are such that higher level morphisms imply lower level morphisms; that is, a morphism that preserves the structural features of one system in another at one level, also preserves the features at all lower levels. This hierarchy is summarized in Section 10.9. Chapter 15 demonstrates that this hierarchy is strict in that lower level morphisms do not imply higher level ones.

10.1   THE I/O RELATION OBSERVATION MORPHISM

Let S and S' be represented by I/O relation observations (T, X, Ω, Y, R) and $(T', X', \Omega', Y', R')$, respectively. As indicated just now, we want to represent the condition wherein the I/O behavior R' of S' can be "found in" the I/O behavior R of S. We take this to mean that if we apply an input segment ω' to S' and observe an output segment ρ', there ought to be an I/O pair $(\omega, \rho) \in R$ corresponding to $(\omega', \rho') \in R'$. This correspondence is to be established by mappings between the segment spaces as follows.

Let $g : \Omega' \to \Omega$; we call g an *encoding* map or encoder. If we apply $\omega' \in \Omega'$ to S', it tells us which $\omega \in \Omega$, namely, $g(\omega')$, to apply to S. (Note that this is an example of a "wrong-way" map, from "little" system to "big" system.)

Let $k : (Y, T) \xrightarrow{\text{onto}} (Y', T')$; we call k a decoding map, or decoder. If we observe an output segment $\rho \in (Y, T)$, it tells which $\rho' \in (Y', T')$ this represents, namely, $k(\rho)$. (This is an example of a "right way" map, from "big" to "little" system.)

The condition that every pair $(\omega', \rho') \in R'$ has a corresponding pair $(\omega, \rho) \in R$ can now be stated as follows: an *I/O relation morphism* from (T, X, Ω, Y, R) to $(T', X', \Omega', Y', R')$ is a pair (g, k) such that

1. $g : \Omega' \to \Omega$.
2. $k : (Y, T) \xrightarrow{\text{onto}} (Y', T')$.
3. For every $(\omega', \rho') \in R'$, there exists $(\omega, \rho) \in R$ such that $\omega = g(\omega')$ and $k(\rho) = \rho'$.

Exercise. Show that line 3 is equivalent to

3'. For every $\omega' \in \Omega'$, $R'(\omega') \subseteq k(R(g(\omega')))$.

(For a relation $R \subseteq A \times B$, $R(a) = \{b | (a, b) \in R\}$; for a map $h : A \to B$, and $A' \subseteq A$, $h(A') = \{h(a) | a \in A'\} \subseteq B$.) Show that line 3' is *not* equivalent to $R' \subseteq k(R(g(\Omega')))$).

Example 1. To illustrate how the I/O morphism captures the inclusion of the behavior of one system in another quite literally, let $R' = (T', X', \Omega', Y', R')$ be an IORO. We embed R' in a larger object by putting it in series with a second IORO $U = (T', Y, \Omega_U, Z, U)$. We call this larger system $R' \circ U$, and it looks like the system in Figure 2a.

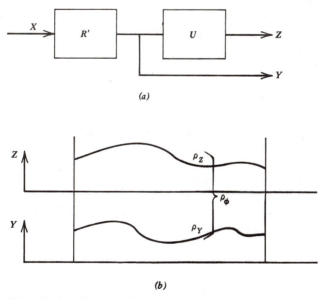

(a)

(b)

Figure 2 A series composition.

We define $R' \circ U = (T', X, \Omega', Y \times Z, R' \circ U)$, where $R' \circ U$ formalizes the notion of applying the output of R' as the input to U as follows. First note that a typical output segment $\rho: \langle t_0, t_1 \rangle \to Y \times Z$ is of the form $\rho = \begin{pmatrix} \rho_Z \\ \rho_Y \end{pmatrix}$ where $\rho(t) = \begin{pmatrix} \rho_Z(t) \\ \rho_Y(t) \end{pmatrix}$ for $t \in \langle t_0, t_1 \rangle$, as in Figure 2b. Then $\left(\omega, \begin{matrix} \rho_Z \\ \rho_Y \end{matrix} \right) \in$ $R' \circ U \Leftrightarrow (\omega, \rho_Y) \in R'$ and $(\rho_Y, \rho_Z) \in U$.

Exercise. Assume U has at least one response to every input segment derived from R', that is,

$$(\omega, \rho_Y) \in R' \Rightarrow \exists \, \rho_Z \in (Z, T') \text{ such that } (\rho_Y, \rho_Z) \in U$$

Show that (g, k) is an I/O morphism from $R' \circ U$ to R', where

$$g: \Omega' \to \Omega \text{ is the identity mapping} \quad \text{and} \quad k: (Y \times Z, T') \to (Y, T')$$

is the projection, $k \begin{pmatrix} \rho_Z \\ \rho_Y \end{pmatrix} = \rho_Y$.

Exercise. Note the importance of having the Y output available in establishing the morphism. What goes wrong if we try to establish an I/O morphism from the composition of Figure 2a, with Z as the output variable, to R'?

The decoder k can be viewed as imposing a lumping of the "big" output segment space (of S) into the "little" segment space (of S'). That is, any function imposes a partition on its domain, such that two elements are in the same block of the partition, or are equivalent, if they are mapped to the same range element. This partition is called the *kernel* partition. (See Problem 1f, Chapter 9.)

Exercise. Show that if $T = T'$, $X = X'$, $\Omega = \Omega'$, and $Y' = Y'$; then the case $R' \subseteq R$ is represented by the morphism (i, i), where i is the identity function.

10.2 THE I/O FUNCTION OBSERVATION MORPHISM

Corresponding to the level of system knowledge characterized by the I/O function observation (where the starting state of an experiment is given) is the following preservation concept.

An *I/O function morphism* from an IOFO (T, X, Ω, Y, F) to an IOFO' $(T', X', \Omega', Y', F')$ is a pair (g, k) where

1. $g: \Omega' \to \Omega$
2. $k: (Y, T) \xrightarrow{\text{onto}} (Y', T')$
3. For each $f' \in F'$ there is an $f \in F$ such that $f' = k \circ f \circ g$; that is, for all $\omega' \in \Omega'$, $f'(\omega') = k(f(g(\omega')))$

We say that f' *divides* f using (g, k) if $f' = k \circ f \circ g$. This is depicted in the commutative diagram:

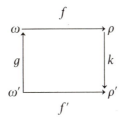

This is interpreted as follows: suppose the "little" system S' is in a state whose I/O function is f'; now an input segment ω' is injected into S' and an output segment $\rho' = f'(\omega')$ is observed—this is the bottom arrow. On the other hand, suppose the "big" system S is in a state whose I/O function is f; then we encode ω' to obtain $\omega = g(\omega')$, inject ω into S, observe the result $\rho = f(\omega)$, and decode ρ to $k(\rho)$—this is the arrow path labeled $\overset{g}{\to} \overset{f}{\to} \overset{k}{\to}$. The result is the same for both processes, namely, $f'(\omega') = k(f(g(\omega)))$.

Thus, an I/O function morphism runs from S to S', if and only if, each of the I/O functions of S' divides at least one I/O function of S using the same pair (g, k)—every "capability" of "little" S' can be found in "big" S with uniform encoding and decoding rules.

Example 2. To relate two systems that are essentially the same except that they operate at different rates, let the IOFO $F = (T, X, \Omega, Y, F)$ be derived from the differential equation

$$\frac{dy}{dt} = x$$

and the IOFO $F' = (T', X', \Omega', Y', F')$ be derived from the differential equation

$$\frac{dy}{dt} = \tau x$$

Then both systems F and F' are integrators, but F' runs at a rate τ times that of F. (Consider their responses to a constant input, for example.)
Let $g : \Omega' \to \Omega$ be given by

$$g(\omega')(t) = \omega'\left(\frac{t}{\tau}\right)$$

with $l(g(\omega')) = l(\omega') \times \tau$.
Let $k : (Y, T) \to (Y', T')$ be given by

$$k(\rho)(t') = \rho(\tau t')$$

with $l(k(\rho)) = (1/\tau)l(\rho)$.

Note that g dilates (stretches) a segment to τ times its original width, whereas k does the inverse dilation. (All segments are assumed to begin at zero.)

Exercise. Show that (g, k) is an I/O function morphism from F to F'.

Exercise. Given a differential operator L, construct a corresponding operator L' which operates at an increased rate τ. Show that (g, k) is an I/O function morphism between the corresponding IOFOs.

Exercise. Show that if $T = T'$, $X = X'$, $\Omega = \Omega'$, and $Y = Y'$, the case $F' \subseteq F$ is given by the I/O function morphism (i, i).

Exercise. Relative to the (g, k) function morphism, define a relation $\equiv$ on Ω, where $\mu \equiv v \Leftrightarrow (\forall f \in F)(k \circ f(\mu) = k \circ f(v))$. Show that $\equiv$ is an equivalence relation (μ and v are equivalent if they cause the same decoded output when applied to each I/O function in F).
Let $\bar{\Omega} = \bigcup_{\omega' \in \Omega'} [g(\omega')] \subseteq \Omega$, the union of all equivalence classes due to $\equiv$ which contain a code image of some $\omega' \in \Omega'$. Define a map $l : \bar{\Omega} \overset{\text{onto}}{\to} \Omega'$, such that $l(\omega) = \omega' \Leftrightarrow \omega \equiv g(\omega')$. Show that $\equiv_l = \equiv$. Show that for each $f' \in F'$, there is an $f \in F$ such that $f' \circ l = k \circ f$.

The map l lumps the restricted subset $\bar{\Omega}$ into equivalence classes of input segments, just as the map k lumps the output segments. Thus although it is not apparent at first sight, the morphism (g, k) does imply a lumping of both input and output spaces.

Exercise. Conversely, given a pair (l, k) and a subset $\bar{\Omega} \subseteq \Omega$ such that $l : \bar{\Omega} \overset{\text{onto}}{\to} \Omega'$ and $k : (Y, T) \overset{\text{onto}}{\to} (Y', T')$ and $(\forall f' \in F')(\exists f \in F)(f' \circ l = k \circ f)$, construct an I/O function morphism (g, k).

Thus whether we choose to think in terms of encoding by g or restricting and lumping by l, the concepts are equivalent at the I/O level.
We can now see the first example of a situation in which the existence of a stronger relation implies the existence of a weaker one.

THEOREM 1

If (g, k) is an I/O function morphism from (T, X, Ω, Y, F) to $(T', X', \Omega', Y', F')$, then (g, k) is also an I/O relation morphism from the IORO associated with (T, X, Ω, Y, F) to the IORO associated with $(T', X', \Omega', Y', F')$.

Proof. Recall that (T, X, Ω, Y, R) is the IORO associated with (T, X, Ω, Y, F) where $R = \bigcup_{f \in F} f$ and similarly, for the primed case.

Let $(\omega', \rho') \in R'$. Then $\rho' = f'(\omega')$ for some $f' \in F'$. Since (g, k) is an I/O function morphism, we have (from line 3 of the definition) that for some $f \in F$

$$\rho' = f'(\omega') = k(f(g(\omega')))$$

Call $\omega = g(\omega')$ and call $\rho = f(\omega)$ so that $(\omega, \rho) \in R$. Now by the foregoing equation, $\rho' = k(\rho)$.

Thus for each $(\omega', \rho') \in R'$, there is a pair $(\omega, \rho) \in R$ with $\omega = g(\omega')$ and $\rho' = k(\rho)$ as required by line 3 of the I/O relation morphism definition.

Since (g, k) satisfies lines 1 and 2 directly, we have proved that (g, k) is an I/O relation morphism.   ∎

Exercise.   Show directly that $F' \subseteq F$ implies $R' \subseteq R$ (as would be inferred by applying Theorem 1 to (i, i)).

10.3   THE I/O SYSTEM MORPHISM

Moving to the next level, where more about the insides of S and S' is specified, we have, appropriately, a morphism that preserves the specified structural features. As a specialization, this morphism includes the classical notion of homomorphism. Since the major element introduced at this level is the state space, we must explain an additional mapping that establishes a correspondence between the "big" and "little" state sets. We refer to the new morphism as a system morphism or a generalized homomorphism.

A *system morphism* from $S = \langle T, X, \Omega, Q, Y, \delta, \lambda \rangle$ to $S' = \langle T', X', \Omega', Q', Y', \delta', \lambda' \rangle$ is a triple (g, h, k) such that

1. $g : \Omega' \to \Omega$
2. $h : \bar{Q} \overset{\text{onto}}{\longrightarrow} Q'$, where $\bar{Q} \subseteq Q$
3. $k : Y \overset{\text{onto}}{\longrightarrow} Y'$,

and for all $q \in \bar{Q}$, $\omega' \in \Omega'$

4. $h(\delta(q, g(\omega'))) = \delta'(h(q), \omega')$ *transition function preservation.*
5. $k(\lambda(q)) = \lambda'(h(q))$ *output function preservation.*

In interpreting line 4, which pertains to preservation of the transition function, we start "big" system S in one of the states q in the restricted set $\bar{Q}$. The map h yields a corresponding state in the "little" system $q' = h(q)$. We then inject a segment ω' into S' and its encoded version $g(\omega')$ into S—sending them to states $\delta'(q', \omega')$ in S' and $\delta(q, g(\omega))$, respectively. These states also correspond under h; that is, $h(\delta(q, g(\omega'))) = \delta'(q', \omega') = \delta'(h(q), \omega')$.

Line 5, pertaining to output function preservation, is interpreted as follows. When "big" system S is in state q and "little" system S' is in corresponding state $q' = h(q)$, the output values observed in these states are $y = \lambda(q)$ and $y' = \lambda'(q')$, respectively; the value y' is also obtained by decoding y with k, that is, $y' = k(y)$ or $\lambda'(q') = k(\lambda(q))$.

Exercise. Draw commutative diagrams to represent lines 4 and 5.

Exercise. Show that for the equation in line 4 to be well defined (both sides defined and equal), $\bar{Q}$ must be *closed under* $g(\Omega')$; that is, for all $q \in \bar{Q}$, $\omega' \in \Omega'$, $\delta(q, g(\omega')) \in \bar{Q}$.

Consider systems S and S' described over the same observational base, (i.e., $T = T'$, $X = X'$, $\Omega = \Omega'$, $Y = Y'$). We call such a pair of systems a *compatible* pair.

S' is a *homomorphic image* of S if (g, h, k) is a system morphism, where g and k are identity maps and $\bar{Q} = Q$; the map h is said to be a *homomorphism* in this case.

Exercise. Show that for compatible systems S and S', $h: Q \overset{\text{onto}}{\longrightarrow} Q'$ is a homomorphism if

$$(a) \quad h(\delta(q, \omega)) = \delta'(h(q), \omega).$$
$$(b) \quad \lambda(q) = \lambda'(h(q)).$$

If, in addition, h is one-to-one (as well as onto), it is an *isomorphism*, and S' and S are said to be *isomorphic*.

When S' is a homomorphic image of S, both systems turn out to have the same I/O function behavior (see Theorem 3), but the difference is that the state space of S' may be much "smaller" than that of S—all the state space Q of S is lumped by h onto that, Q' of S'.

When S and S' are isomorphic, there is no essential difference in their structural descriptions at the I/O system level, although they may differ very significantly at higher levels of specification involving more structural detail.

Example 3. Linear System Homomorphisms. Let S and S' be compatible linear systems specified by $\{A, B, C\}$ and $\{A', B', C'\}$, respectively (in discrete time, let a common field F be assumed).

The existence of a homomorphism from S to S' can be reduced to relatively simple relation involving the specifications $\{A, B, C\}$ and $\{A', B', C'\}$ as is shown by

THEOREM 2

Let $H: Q \overset{\text{onto}}{\longrightarrow} Q'$ be a linear mapping. Then H is a homomorphism from S to S' if and only if the following conditions hold:

$$1. \quad A'H = HA$$
$$2. \quad HB = B'$$
$$3. \quad C'H = C$$

Exercise. Prove Theorem 2. Note that the cases of discrete and continuous time must be treated separately. For the discrete time case, make use of the sequential machine morphism of Section 10.5.1.

A *subsystem* of $S = \langle T, X, \Omega, Q, Y, \delta, \lambda \rangle$ is a system $\hat{S} = \langle T, X, \Omega, \hat{Q}, Y, \hat{\delta}, \hat{\lambda} \rangle$ where $\hat{Q} \subseteq Q$, $\hat{\delta} = \delta|\hat{Q}$, and $\hat{\lambda} = \lambda|\hat{Q}$.

Exercise. Since $\hat{S}$ is asserted to be a system, $\hat{\delta}$ must be well defined. Accordingly, show that $\hat{Q}$ must be closed under Ω; that is, $q \in \hat{Q}$, $\omega \in \Omega \Rightarrow \delta(q, \omega) \in \hat{Q}$.

Exercise. Show that if (i, h, i) is a system morphism from S to S' (a compatible pair), then S' is a homomorphic image of a subsystem of S (note that the premise does not assert that $\bar{Q} = Q$).

10.4   STRUCTURE PRESERVATION IMPLIES
BEHAVIOR PRESERVATION

To establish the basic foundation on which the utility of the structure preservation concepts just introduced rests, we first show that if S' is a homomorphic image of S, then S and S' have the same I/O function behavior. This result can be generalized to demonstrate that the holding of a general preservation relation between systems at the I/O system level implies the existence of preservation relations at the lower (behavioral) levels.

We say that two states (of the same or different systems) are *behaviorally equivalent* if they have the same I/O function; that is,

$$q \equiv q' \qquad \text{if} \quad \tilde{\beta}_q = \tilde{\beta}_{q'}$$

We say that systems S and S' are *behaviorally equivalent* if $B_S = B_{S'}$, that is, if for each state $q \in Q$, there is a state $q' \in Q'$ such that $\tilde{\beta}_q = \tilde{\beta}_{q'}$ (q and q' are equivalent), and conversely.

Exercise. Show that $\tilde{B}_S = \tilde{B}_{S'} \Rightarrow R_S = R_{S'}$ (S, S' are *relationally equivalent*).

We can now consider the fundamental theorem on behavioral equivalence of compatible systems.

THEOREM 3

Let $h: Q \xrightarrow{\text{onto}} Q'$ (onto) be a homomorphism from S to S'. Then $\tilde{B}_S = \tilde{B}_{S'}$ (S and S' are behaviorally equivalent).

Proof. We show first that for each $q \in Q$, $h(q)$ is equivalent to q. Consider the last output function $\beta'_{h(q)}$. For $\omega \in \Omega$,

$$
\begin{aligned}
\beta'_{h(q)}(\omega) &= \lambda'(\delta'(h(q), \omega)) \\
&= \lambda'(h(\delta(q, \omega))) \quad &\text{(line } a \text{ of definition)} \\
&= \lambda(\delta(q, \omega)) \quad &\text{(line } b \text{ of definition)} \\
&= \beta_q(\omega)
\end{aligned}
$$

Thus $\beta'_{h(q)} = \beta_q$.

Exercise. Show that $\beta'_{h(q)} = \beta'_q \Rightarrow \tilde{\beta}'_{h(q)} = \tilde{\beta}_q$.

Since h is onto Q', every state q' of S' has a representative state $q \in h^{-1}(q')$ such that $h(q) = q'$. Thus $\tilde{B}_{S'} = \{\tilde{\beta}'_{q'} | q' \in Q'\} = \{\tilde{\beta}'_{h(q)} | q \in Q\} \subseteq \tilde{B}_S$. But also, since h is defined on all of Q, for each $q \in Q$ there is a state $h(q) \in Q'$, thus $B_S \subseteq B_{S'}$. Thus $\tilde{B}_S = \tilde{B}_{S'}$. ∎

The essentials of Theorem 3 generalize to broader kinds of system morphisms. First we have

THEOREM 4.

If (i, h, i) is a system morphism from S to S', then (i, i) is an I/O function morphism from IOFO_S to $\text{IOFO}_{S'}$ (hence an I/O relation morphism from IORO_S to $\text{IORO}_{S'}$). In other words, if S' is a homomorphic image of a submachine of S, then $\tilde{B}_{S'} \subseteq \tilde{B}_S$ and $R_{S'} \subseteq R_S$.

Proof. An easy corollary of Theorem 3. ∎

We should now want to show more generally that, if (g, h, k) is a system morphism from S to S', there is also an I/O function morphism from S to S'. Unfortunately, this is not necessarily true for an arbitrary encoding g. To see why, consider the following lemma.

LEMMA

Let (g, h, k) be a system morphism from S to S'. Then for each $q \in Q$, we have

$$
\beta'_{h(q)} = k \circ \beta_q \circ g
$$

Exercise. Prove the lemma.

This tells us that the last output functions of corresponding states match up, but it does not allow us to conclude that the same is true for the I/O functions, which are obtained by applying the last output functions to successive left segments to obtain segment-to-segment mappings. The correspondence between last outputs must be maintained as this extension is being performed. More specifically, the g mapping must preserve left segmentation. Also, since the k map of the I/O function morphism cannot look at the input segment, the g map must allow such a map to be definable on the basis of k alone.

Thus let us say that $g:\Omega' \to \Omega$ is *invertable* if

1. *g preserves left segmentation*: ω' is a left segment of $\omega \Rightarrow g(\omega')$ is a left segment of $g(\omega)$.
2. *g is one-to-one on lengths*: $l(\omega) = l(\omega') \Leftrightarrow l(g(\omega)) = l(g(\omega'))$.

These properties of g are precisely the ones enabling us to match up instants in an observation interval of the little system with uniquely corresponding instants in the corresponding observation interval of the big system: This is shown by the

LEMMA

g is an invertable coding if and only if there is a one-to-one (partial) function $\text{MATCH}: T_0'^+ \to T_0^+$ such that

$$\text{MATCH}(l(\omega)) = l(g(\omega))$$

$$g(\omega_{t_\gamma}) = g(\omega)_{\text{MATCH}(t)\rangle}$$

With this matching of computation instants $l(\omega)$ and $l(g(\omega))$, we can define a decoding map $k:(Y, T) \to (Y', T')$ as follows.

For any $\rho \in (Y, T)$, $k(\rho)$ has length $l(k(\rho)) = \text{MATCH}^{-1}(l(\rho))$ and

$$k(\rho)(t') = k(\rho(\text{MATCH}(t'))) \qquad \text{for } t' \in \text{dom}(k(\rho))$$

Exercise.   Check that k is well defined in carrying any segment ρ of the big system to a unique segment $k(\rho)$ of the little system.

Now using the two previous lemmas we can obtain the strengthened

LEMMA

Let (g, h, k), where g is invertable, be a system morphism from S to S'. Then for each $q \in Q$,

$$\tilde{\beta}'_{h(q)} = k \circ \tilde{\beta}_q \circ g$$

where k is as defined before.

Exercise.   Prove the foregoing lemma.

Finally we have the desired

THEOREM 5

If (g, h, k), where g is invertable, is a system morphism from S to S', there is an I/O function morphism (g, k) from IOFO_S to $\text{IOFO}_{S'}$, hence an I/O relation morphism from IORO_S to $\text{IORO}_{S'}$.

Proof. The proof follows the lines of Theorem 4 and is left as an exercise for the reader.   ■

Exercise. If h is a homomorphism from S to S', show that for each $q' \in Q'$, the set $h^{-1}(q')$ is a set of equivalent states.

We learn in Section 10.7 that the converse of the last statement is true, also. That is, if we are given a partition of the states of S whose blocks consist of equivalent states, we can construct a homomorphic image of S.

10.5 SYSTEM MORPHISM FOR ITERATIVELY SPECIFIED SYSTEMS

We have seen that it is possible to implicitly specify a system structure by providing an iterative specification G. A major advantage of such an approach is illustrated in Figure 3: if we have a pair of specifications G and G', and are able to establish the appropriate preservation relation from G to G', we can be assured that a system morphism runs from S_G (the system specified by G) to $S_{G'}$.

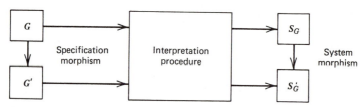

Figure 3   Motivation for specification morphism.

We define a "specification morphism" from G to G' which, when G is expanded to S_G and G' is expanded to $S_{G'}$, will imply the existence of a system morphism running from S_G to $S_{G'}$. In effect, we can consider the interpretation procedure to be augmented to permit expansion of a specification morphism into a system morphism.

To develop the concept we must first construct an input segment encoding map in such a way that a segment may be encoded by composing the encoded versions of the generators in its mls decomposition.

Thus let Ω_G and Ω'_G be admissible sets of generators. Let $g:\Omega'_G \to \Omega^+_G$ be a *generator encoding* map, so that with each generator $\omega' \in \Omega'_G$ (the "little" input generator set) there is associated a segment $g(\omega')$, its coded version (which is not necessarily a generator in the "big" input generator set). We extend g to an encoder $g:\Omega'^+_G \to \Omega^+_G$ by the definition

$$g(\omega') = g(\omega_1)g(\omega_2)\cdots g(\omega_n) \qquad \text{for } \omega' \in \Omega'^+_G,$$

where $\omega_1, \omega_2, \ldots, \omega_n$ is the mls decomposition for ω.

Now g is well defined because of the uniqueness of the mls decomposition.

For iterative specifications $G = \langle T, X, \Omega_G, Q, Y, \delta_G, \lambda \rangle$ and $G' = \langle T', X', \Omega'_G, Q', Y', \delta'_G, \lambda' \rangle$, a *specification morphism* from G to G' is a triple (g, h, k) such that

1. $g:\Omega'_G \to \Omega^+_G$
2. $h:\bar{Q} \xrightarrow{\text{onto}} Q'$ where $\bar{Q} \subseteq Q$.
3. $k:Y \xrightarrow{\text{onto}} Y'$,

and for all $q \in \bar{Q}$, $\omega' \in \Omega'_G$

4. $h(\bar{\delta}_G(q, g(\omega'))) = \delta'_G(h(q), \omega')$.
5. $k(\lambda(q)) = \lambda'(h(q))$.

Note that lines 4 and 5 are very similar to lines 4 and 5 of the system morphism definition. The major difference is that, in the present specification morphism, the transition function preservation need only be checked for the *generators* of the "little" system Ω'_G.

We say that g is *generator preserving* if $g(\Omega'_G) \subseteq \Omega_G$. Since in this case, for each generator $\omega' \in \Omega'_G$, $g(\omega')$ is also a generator, the function δ_G need not be extended, and line 4 can read:

4'. $h(\delta_G(q, g(\omega'))) = \delta'_G(h(q), \omega')$.

This means that the specification morphism can be checked directly by examining the generator transition functions δ_G and δ'_G.

The next theorem establishes the procedure for expanding a specification morphism into a system morphism. The importance of this, as we have indicated, is that to check whether a system morphism runs from a "big" to a "little" system, we need verify only that a specification morphism runs from the iterative specification of the one to that of the other—the expansion procedure, is then guaranteed by the theorem and need not be carried out.

THEOREM 6

If (g, h, k) is a specification morphism from G to G', then (g, h, k) is a system morphism from S_G to $S_{G'}$ where g is the extension of g.

Proof. We need show only that line 4 holds in the system morphism definition. This is done using induction on the proposition
$P(n) \equiv [$if $\omega' \in \Omega_G^+$ has the mls decomposition $\omega'_1, \omega'_2, \ldots, \omega'_n$, then for all $q \in \bar{Q}$,

$$h(\bar{\delta}_G(q, g(\omega'))) = \bar{\delta}'_G(h(q), (\omega')]$$

$P(1)$ is just line 4 of the specification morphism definition. Assuming that $P(n-1)$ holds, we can show that $P(n)$ holds. Let ω' have mls decomposition $\omega'_1, \omega'_2, \ldots \omega'_n$ and let $q \in \bar{Q}$, then write

$$
\begin{aligned}
h(\bar{\delta}_G(q, g(\omega'_1\omega'_2 \cdots \omega'_n)) &= h(\bar{\delta}_G(q, g(\omega_1)g(\omega'_2 \cdots \omega'_n) && \text{(definition of } g) \\
&= h(\bar{\delta}_G(\delta_G(q, g(\omega_i)), g(\omega'_2 \cdots \omega'_n))) \\
&\quad \text{(composition property of } \bar{\delta}_G) \\
&= \bar{\delta}_{G'}(h(\bar{\delta}_G(q, g(\omega'_1))), \omega'_2 \cdots \omega'_n) && (\text{P}(n-1)) \\
&\quad \text{using } \omega'_2, \ldots, \omega'_n \text{ as the mls decomposition of} \\
&\quad \omega'_2 \cdots \omega'_n) \\
&= \bar{\delta}_{G'}(\delta_{G'}(h(q), \omega'_1), \omega'_2 \cdots \omega'_n) && (\text{P}(1)) \\
&= \bar{\delta}_{G'}(h(q), \omega'_1\omega'_2 \cdots \omega'_n) \\
&\quad \text{(composition property of } \bar{\delta}_{G'})
\end{aligned}
$$

Thus $P(n)$ holds, and by the principle of induction, the theorem, which asserts $P(n)$ for all n, is established.   ∎

Exercise. Show that if (g, h, k) is a system morphism from S_G to $S_{G'}$, then (g, h, k) is specification morphism from G to G' where $g = g|\Omega'_G$. Thus there is a system morphism from S_G to $S_{G'}$ if and only if there is a specification morphism from G to G'.

Just as we can further specialize the iterative specification scheme to the discrete time, differential equation, and discrete event cases, we can provide appropriate specializations of the specification morphism. The procedure, which is parallel to that developed in Section 9.9, is depicted in Figure 4.

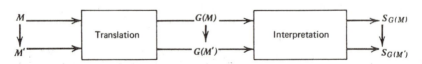

Figure 4 Specialization of specification morphisms.

10.5.1   Sequential Machine Case

Let $M = \langle X_M, Q_M, Y_M, \delta_M, \lambda_M \rangle$ and $M' = \langle X'_M, Q'_M, Y'_M, \delta'_M, \lambda'_M \rangle$ be sequential machines. The appropriate morphism is as follows: (g, h, k) is a *sequential machine morphism* from M to M' if

1. $g : X'_M \to X_M^+$
2. $h : \bar{Q}_M \xrightarrow{\text{onto}} Q'_M$, where $\bar{Q}_M \subseteq Q_M$
3. $k : Y_M \to Y'_M$,

and for all $q \in \bar{Q}_M, x' \in X'_M$

4. $h(\bar{\delta}_M(q, g(x'))) = \delta'_M(h(q), x')$
5. $k(\lambda_M(q)) = \lambda'_M(h(q))$

The translation to a specification morphism is very straightforward in this case. The translated morphism is (g, h, k) running from $S_{G(M)}$ to $S_{G(M')}$, where $g : \Omega_{G(M')} \to \Omega_{G(M)}$ is defined by $g(\omega_x) = \omega_{g(x)}$.

10.5.2   Discrete Event Case

We give as an example the construction of a homomorphism for discrete event specifications. Let $M = \langle X_M, S_M, Y_M, \delta_M, \lambda_M, t_M \rangle$ and $M' = \langle X'_M, S'_M, Y'_M, \delta'_M, \lambda'_M, t'_M \rangle$ be legitimate DEVSs, where $X_M = X'_M, Y_M = Y'_M$.

A *DEVS homomorphism* from M to M' is a map h such that

1. $h : S_M \xrightarrow{\text{onto}} S'_M$,

and for each $x \in X_M, (s, e) \in Q_M$.

2. $h(\delta_M(s, e, x)) = \delta'_M(h(s), e, x)$.
3. $\lambda'_M(h(s), e) = \lambda_M(s, e)$.
4. $h(\delta_{M, \phi}(s)) = \delta_{M', \phi}(h(s))$.
5. $t_M \cdot (h(s)) = t_M(s)$.

The translation of the morphism h, to a specification morphism is given by

THEOREM 6

Let h be a DEVS homomorphism from M to M'. Let $h : Q_M \to Q'_M$ be a map such that $h(s, e) = (h(s), e)$ for all $(s, e) \in Q_M$. Then h is a (specification) homomorphism from $G(M)$ to $G(M')$.

Proof. The proof employs the following sequence of assertions, which are left to the reader as an exercise.

(a) h is an onto map.
(b) $m_{s, e, \tau} = m_{h(s), e, \tau}$.

(c) $h(\bar{\delta}_{M,\,\phi}(s, m_{s,\,e,\,\tau})) = \bar{\delta}'_{M,\,\phi}(h(s), m_{h(s),\,e,\,\tau})$.

(d) $h(\delta_G(s, e, \phi_\tau)) = \delta_{G'}(h(s, e), \phi_\tau)$.

(e) $h(\delta_G(s, e, x_\tau)) = \delta'_G(h(s, e), x_\tau)$.

(f) $\lambda'(h(s, e)) = \lambda(s, e)$.

Assertions d, e, and f show that (i, h, i) is a specification morphism from $G(M)$ to $G(M')$, and since h has domain Q_M, h is a homomorphism from $G(M)$ to $G(M')$.   ■

Exercise. In Chapter 8 we considered a homomorphic mapping of a base, to a lumped model of a grocery store. Using the formal DEVS versions of these models developed in Chapter 9, show that there is indeed a DEVS homomorphism, as defined here, running from base to lumped system.

10.6 STRUCTURED SPECIFICATION MORPHISM

The notion of structured system specification clearly captures the informal description of a model by means of components, descriptive variables, component interaction, and influence diagram. Models specified at this level can be interrelated by means of structure preserving morphisms appropriately designed to maintain structural properties specified at this level.

Again we restrict attention to the autonomous sequential machine case, for simplicity of exposition.

Recall that a homomorphism from $M = \langle Q, \delta \rangle$ to $M' = \langle Q', \delta' \rangle$ is a map h such that

$$h : Q \xrightarrow{\text{onto}} Q'$$

$$h(\delta(q)) = \delta'(h(q)) \qquad \text{for all } q \in Q$$

Now let M and M' be structured by $(D, \{Q_\alpha\}, \{I_\alpha\}, \{\delta_\alpha\})$, and $(D', \{Q'_\alpha\}, \{I'_\alpha\}, \{\delta'_\alpha\})$, respectively.

A map $d : D \xrightarrow{\text{onto}} D'$, called a *coordinate mapping*, partitions the coordinates of D, the big machine, into blocks each of which are represented by a single coordinate of the small machine. That is, denote by (α') the set $d^{-1}(\alpha') = \{\alpha | d(\alpha) = \alpha'\}$. Then (α') is the block of coordinates of D, represented by α' of D', and the family $\{(\alpha') | \alpha' \in D'\}$ is a partition of D.

A map $h_{\alpha'}$ from $\times_{\alpha \in (\alpha')} Q_\alpha$ onto Q'_α is called the *local mapping* of α'. The $h_{\alpha'}$ maps the state assignments to the coordinates of block (α') to the range set of α'. By applying, simultaneously, local maps for each of the coordinates α' of D' we obtain a global map $h : Q \to Q'$, where $h = \times_{\alpha' \in D'} h_{\alpha'} \cdot \text{proj}_{(\alpha')}$. This map is called the *aggregation* associated with d and $\{h_{\alpha'} | \alpha' \in D'\}$.

A *weak structure morphism* from M to M' is a pair $(d, \{h_{\alpha'} | \alpha' \in D'\})$ such that the aggregation h (associated with d and $\{h'_\alpha\}$) is a homomorphism from M to M'.

Thus a weak structure morphism is a homomorphism constructed in a way that relates the state structures of two structured machines. This does not imply necessarily that the local transition function structures are related, although of course the global transition functions are. That is, the manner in which components interact in the small machine M' need not reflect the interaction in the big machine M of the components they represent. For preservation of local interaction, we need a stronger concept developed as follows: the coordinate map $d: D \to D'$ is a *digraph morphism* if for every arrow in the digraph of M' there is a corresponding arrow in the digraph of M (i.e., fór all α', $\beta' \in D'$ such that $\alpha' \in I_{\beta'}$, there exist $\alpha \in (\alpha')$ and $\beta \in (\beta')$ such that $\alpha \in I_\beta$.

A *strong structure morphism* is a weak structure morphism $(d, \{h_{\alpha'}\})$ such that d is a digraph morphism.

Because of its construction by aggregation of local maps, the structure morphism can be rephrased to emphasize that the global homomorphism condition reduces to a series of local function preserving conditions.

Let
$$h_{I'_{\beta'}} = \underset{\alpha' \in I'_{\beta'}}{\times} h_{\alpha'} \cdot \mathrm{proj}_{(\alpha')}$$

and

$$\delta_{(\beta')} = \underset{\alpha \in (\beta')}{\times} \delta_\alpha \cdot \mathrm{proj}_{I_\alpha}$$

then we have the

PROPOSITION

$(d, \{h_{\alpha'}\})$ is a weak structure morphism if and only if for all $\beta' \in D'$, we have

$$\delta'_{\beta'} \cdot h_{I'_{\beta'}} = h_{\beta'} \cdot \delta_{(\beta')}$$

Proof.   Exercise for the reader.   ∎

Structure morphisms can be further specialized for cellular spaces. In this case, since all the local transition functions are copies of a single prototype, if d is a uniform coordinate map and each local map $h_{\alpha'}$ is a copy of a single prototype, the local condition of the proposition need be checked only for a single coordinate.

More discussion of the meaning of the proposition is provided in Section 15.5.

Example 4.   Structure Morphism for Linear Systems.   For simplicity consider a linear system having no inputs and outputs. Such a system is specified by a single matrix A and *we* have either a discrete time specification $M = \langle Q, \delta \rangle$ in which Q is a vector space over a field and $\delta(q) = Aq$ or a continuous time system $S_A^{\text{cont}} = \langle T, Q, \delta \rangle$ in which $T = R$, Q is a vector space over the reals and $\delta(q, 0_t) = e^{At}q$, where we use 0_t (zero-valued input of length t) to represent the running of the system for an observation interval of length t.

For two systems specified by A and A' we know from Example 3 that a linear map $H : Q \xrightarrow{\text{onto}} Q'$ is a homomorphism just in case

$$A'H = HA$$

But now let us restrict H so that it carries out an aggregation. This permits us to derive conditions on A which allow S_A to be lumped to a system S_A'.

Let $\{e_1, e_2, \ldots, e_n\}$ be a basis for Q so that every element q of Q is represented by a list $(q_1, q_2, \ldots, q_n)$ such that $q = \sum_{i=1}^n q_i e_i$. Thus the basis vectors $\{e_i\}$ become the coordinates of a coordinatization of Q, and their range sets are the same underlying field. Note that another choice of basis set $\{f_1, f_2, \ldots, f_n\}$ would induce another coordinatization of Q, where each element q would be represented by a list $(q_1', q_2', \ldots, q_n')$. The primed q's are related to the unprimed q's because $q = \sum_{i=1}^n q_i' f_i = \sum_{i=1}^n q_i e_i$. (Linear algebra, of course, tells us that all such bases have the same number of elements.)

With respect to basis $\{e_i\}$, the linear mapping $A : Q \to Q$ is represented by a matrix $[a_{ij}]$ so that the operation $\bar{q} = Aq$ is represented by

$$\begin{bmatrix} \bar{q}_1 \\ \vdots \\ \bar{q}_n \end{bmatrix} = \begin{bmatrix} a_{11} & \cdots & a_{1n} \\ \vdots & & \vdots \\ a_{n1} & \cdots & a_{nn} \end{bmatrix} \begin{bmatrix} q_1 \\ \vdots \\ q_n \end{bmatrix}$$

or in other words,

$$\bar{q}_i = \sum_{j=1}^n a_{ij} q_j \qquad \text{for} \quad i = 1, 2, \ldots, n$$

Exercise. In the discrete time case show how the foregoing operation provides a structure for the transition function δ.

Now let us consider a partition of the coordinates $D = \{e_1, \ldots, e_n\}$. Call the partition $D' = \{e_1', \ldots, e_m'\}$ so that each e_i' is a subset of D, disjoint from the rest, and the union of all such blocks is exactly D. For example, if $D = \{e_1, e_2, \ldots, e_n\}$, then D' might be $\{e_1', e_2', e_3'\}$, where $e_1' = \{e_1, e_2, e_3\}$, $e_2' = \{e_4, e_5, e_6\}$, and $e_3' = \{e_7, e_8\}$. Now D' will serve as the coordinate set for our little system, and each coordinate will have the same range set. This will be the same field given previously. Thus the state set Q' of the little system will be a vector space of dimension m where each element q' is represented by a list $(q'_1, \ldots, q'_m)$ such that $q' = \sum_{i=1}^{m} q_i e'_i$.

Our coordinate mapping $d : D \xrightarrow{\text{onto}} D'$ is the natural one given by $d(e_i) = e'_j$, where $e_i \in e'_j$. In our example, $d(e_1) = e'_1$, $d(e_4) = e'_2$, and so on.

Exercise. Show that because D' is a partition of D, d is well defined and onto.

Now we will require that $H : Q \to Q'$ operate by summing up the coordinate values in a block, separately for each block. In other words, for each coordinate e'_i, the local mapping h_{e_i} is given by

$$h_{e_i}(q_j, q_k, \ldots, q_s) = q_j + q_k + \cdots + q_s$$

where $e'_i = \{e_j, e_k, \ldots, e_s\}$. Then H is the aggregation of the $\{h_{e_i}\}$.

Actually it is easy to show that H has a very simple specification, namely, that for each $e_j \in D$,

$$He_j = d(e_j)$$

Exercise. Show that the preceding statement is true. Also show that H is onto.

This leads to a very simple matrix representation for H, consisting entirely of columns containing exactly one 1 and the rest zeros. Also at least one 1 is found in any row. In our example, H is represented by

$$\begin{bmatrix} 1 & 1 & 1 & 0 & 0 & 0 & 0 & 0 \\ 0 & 0 & 0 & 1 & 1 & 1 & 0 & 0 \\ 0 & 0 & 0 & 0 & 0 & 0 & 1 & 1 \end{bmatrix}$$

Now we ask under what circumstances is there a linear map $A' : Q' \to Q'$ for which $A'H = HA$? This is answered in

THEOREM 8.   CONDITIONS FOR LUMPABILITY

Given A and linear aggregation H, there is a matrix A' such that $A'H = HA$ if and only if for each $e'_r \in D'$, and $e_j, e_k \in e'_p$, we have

$$\sum_{e_i \in e'_r} a_{ij} = \sum_{e_i \in e'_r} a_{ik}$$

The conditions in Theorem 8 place special requirements on matrix A, namely, that if it is blocked off according to the partition D' in both vertical and horizontal directions, *sums of elements down columns within blocks must be equal*. In our example, considering the blocks $\{4, 5, 6\}$ and $\{7, 8\}$, we must have the sums $a_{47} + a_{57} + a_{67}$ and $a_{48} + a_{58} + a_{68}$ equal, as illustrated in Figure 5a.

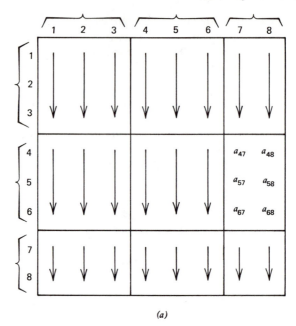

(a)

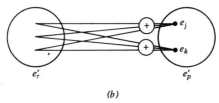

(b)

Figure 5 Illustrating the lumpability condition—sums along the arrows within the cells must be equal.

Exercise. Convince yourself that Theorem 8 is true by one or more of the following methods.

(a) Argue directly from the basic meaning of homomorphism in the sequential machine case.
(b) Examine the matrix equation $A'H = HA$ when H takes the special matrix form indicated.
(c) Give a formal abstract algebra proof, examining the equation $A'He_j = HAe_j$ for an arbitrary basis vector e_j.

The lumpability condition expresses a principle of "uniformity of influence" that we meet with again in Chapter 12. As indicated in Figure 5b, it requires that for every pair of blocks e'_r and e'_p, the total influence of block e'_r on elements of e'_p be the same for all the elements of e'_p.

This concludes our survey of the hierarchy of preservation relations. The results are summarized in Section 10.9.

10.7 THE REDUCED VERSION OF A SYSTEM

Any system S has a "reduced version" that represents the most that can be inferred about the structure of S from external observation. The reduced version S_R has a number of interesting and useful properties that become important when we consider the problem of structural inference in Chapter 14.

From here on, we restrict our attention to systems whose input segment set Ω has the null segment Λ as a member. This segment has the useful properties that $\delta(q, \Lambda) = q$ for any system state q, and $\Lambda\omega = \omega$ for any segment ω. This restriction is a matter of convenience, since essentially the same results can be obtained without it.

When the equivalence concept of Section 10.3 is applied to states of the same system S, we have a relation $\equiv$ on its state Q.

Exercise. Show that $\equiv$ is an equivalence relation (i.e., reflexive, symmetric, and transitive).

The equivalence relation induces a partition on the set Q consisting of the equivalence classes we denote by

$$Q/\equiv \ = \ \{[q]|q \in Q\}$$

Exercise. Show that $\tilde{\beta}_q(\omega\omega') = \tilde{\beta}_q(\omega)\tilde{\beta}_{\delta(q,\,\omega)}(\omega')$.

Moreover, the equivalence relation is a *congruence* with respect to both the transition and output function, that is,

LEMMA 1

(a) $q \equiv q' \Rightarrow (\forall\, \omega \in \Omega)(\delta(q, \omega) \equiv \delta(q, \omega))$.
(b) $q \equiv q' \Rightarrow \lambda(q) = \lambda(q')$.

Proof

(a) $q \equiv q' \Rightarrow \tilde{\beta}_q = \tilde{\beta}_{q'} \Rightarrow (\forall\, \omega \in \Omega)(\tilde{\beta}_q(\omega) = \tilde{\beta}_{q'}(\omega))$
$\quad\Rightarrow (\forall\, \omega \in \Omega)(\forall\, \omega' \in \Omega)(\tilde{\beta}_q(\omega\omega') = \tilde{\beta}_{q'}(\omega\omega'))$
$\quad\Rightarrow (\forall\, \omega \in \Omega)(\forall\, \omega' \in \Omega)(\tilde{\beta}_q(\omega)\tilde{\beta}_{\delta(q,\,\omega)}(\omega') = \tilde{\beta}_{q'}(\omega)\tilde{\beta}_{\delta(q',\,\omega)}(\omega'))$
$\quad\Rightarrow (\forall\, \omega \in \Omega)(\forall\, \omega' \in \Omega)(\tilde{\beta}_{\delta(q,\,\omega)}(\omega') = \tilde{\beta}_{\delta(q',\,\omega)}(\omega'))$
$\quad\Rightarrow (\forall\, \omega \in \Omega)(\delta(q, \omega) \equiv \delta(q, \omega'))$.

(b) $q \equiv q' \Rightarrow \tilde{\beta}_q(\Lambda) = \tilde{\beta}_{q'}(\Lambda) \Rightarrow \lambda(\delta(q, \Lambda)) = \lambda(\delta(q', \Lambda))$
    $\Rightarrow \lambda(q) = \lambda(q')$.   ∎

Lemma 1a asserts that all successors of equivalent states are, themselves, equivalent. Lemma 1b asserts that equivalent states yield the same output.

Both these statements can be generalized to apply to states related by the division relation (see Problem 1).

The *reduced version* S_R of S is defined as follows:

$$S_R = \langle X, T, \Omega, Q/\equiv, Y, \delta_R, \lambda_R \rangle$$

where $\delta_R : Q/\equiv \times \Omega \to Q/\equiv$

is defined by $\delta_R([q], \omega) = [\delta(q, \omega)]$

and $\lambda_R : Q/\equiv \to Y$

is defined by $\lambda_R([q]) = \lambda(q)$.

PROPOSITION

If S is a system, so is S_R.

Proof.   Use Lemma 1 to show that δ_R and λ_R are well defined. Then check that δ_R has the composition property.   ∎

We say that a system S is *reduced* if for all pairs $q, q' \in Q$, $\tilde{\beta}_q = \tilde{\beta}_{q'} \Rightarrow q = q'$. In other words, each state q has a distinct I/O function β_q associated with it.

Exercise.   Show that S is reduced if and only if for each distinct pair $q, q' \in Q$, there is a input segment $\omega_{q, q'}$ that will cause S to respond with different output segments when started in states q and q'.

Theorem 9 presents the important properties of the reduced version S_R.

THEOREM 9

(a) S_R is reduced.
(b) S_R is a homomorphic image of S.
(c) S_R is behaviorally equivalent to S.
(d)   For any system S', if S' is behaviorally equivalent to S and is reduced, S' is isomorphic to S_R.

Proof.   We show first by straightforward expansion

$$\beta_{[q]} = \beta_q \qquad \text{for each } q \in Q$$

Then a and c follow immediately from this result. For b, we consider the mapping $h:Q \to Q/\equiv$ given by $h(q) = [q]$. Then by direct verification h is a homomorphism. We defer the proof of d until Chapter 15 (see Problem 2). ∎

10.8   CHARACTERIZATION OF REALIZABLE I/O RELATIONS AND FUNCTIONS

Consider the lower three levels of system description—the IORO (I/O relation observation), the IOFO (I/O function observation), and the I/O system. Given a system S, which is at the highest of the three levels, we have seen how to associate the lower level objects $IOFO_S$ and $IORO_S$ with it. Our definitions of IORO and IOFO, however, allowed considerable freedom, and we would like to know whether every such object can be associated with some system. The problem can be phrased as follows: an IORO (IOFO) is said to be *realizable* if there is an I/O system S such that $IORO = IORO_S$ ($IOFO = IOFO_S$). In other words, an IORO is realizable if we can find a system that has exactly the same IORO associated with it.

Our problem then is to characterize the class of realizable IOROs and IOFOs by looking for necessary and sufficient conditions that will distinguish a realizable IORO (IOFO) from a non realizable IORO (IOFO). The simpler these conditions are to check, the more useful characterization we will have achieved. After all, one characterization of a realizable IORO is given by the definition of "realizable" itself. But given an IORO, this would require us to search through all possible systems to determine whether there is, or is not, a system S for which $IORO = IORO_S$.

Our characterizations are based on the characterization of realizable I/O functions.

A function f is said to be *realizable* if there is an I/O system $S = \langle T, X, \Omega, Q, Y, \delta, \lambda \rangle$ and a state $q \in Q$ such that $f = \tilde{\beta}_q$.

THEOREM 10.   CHARACTERIZATION OF REALIZABLE FUNCTIONS

A function $f:\Omega \to \Omega'$ is realizable if and only if the following conditions hold.

1. Ω *and* Ω' *are of the right form.* There are sets X, Y, and time base T such that
    $$\Omega \subseteq (X, T) \text{ and } \Omega' \subseteq (Y, T).$$

2. Ω *is closed under translation and composition.*
3. f *is length preserving and in step*: for all $\omega \in \Omega$, dom $(f(\omega)) =$ dom (ω).
4. f *is time invariant*: for all $\omega \in \Omega$, $\tau \in T$.
    $$f(\text{TRANS}_\tau(\omega)) = \text{TRANS}_\tau(f(\omega))$$

5. f *is causal*: for all ω, $\omega' \in \Omega_0 (= STR(\Omega))$, and $t \in \text{dom}(\omega) \cap \text{dom}(\omega')$.

$$\omega_{t\rangle} = \omega'_{t\rangle} \Rightarrow f(\omega)_{t\rangle} = f(\omega')_{t\rangle}$$

6. f *has last values defined*: for all $\omega \in (X, T)_0$

$$f(\omega)(l(\omega)) \in Y \Leftrightarrow \omega \in \Omega_0$$

Proof. The necessity of the six listed properties is established by considering the definition of an I/O function β_q of an arbitrary system S. The reader is given the exercise of showing that β_q has these properties.

For establishing sufficiency, we suppose that a function f has the given properties. Based on these properties, we construct a system S_f^* which realizes f, using the following lemmas.

LEMMA 2. f PRESERVES LEFT SEGMENTATION

For all $\omega \in \Omega_0$, $t \in \text{dom}(\omega)$

$$f(\omega)_{t\rangle} = f(\omega_{t\rangle})$$

Proof. It follows easily from the definition of left segmentation that

$$\begin{aligned}
\omega_{t\rangle} &= \text{LEFT} \cdot \text{SEGMENT}_t(\omega) \\
&= \text{LEFT} \cdot \text{SEGMENT}_t(\text{LEFT} \cdot \text{SEGMENT}_t(\omega)) \\
&= (\omega_{t\rangle})_{t\rangle}
\end{aligned}$$

Setting $\omega = \omega$ and $\omega' = \omega_{t\rangle}$ in the causality property 5, we have

$$f(\omega)_{t\rangle} = f(\omega_{t\rangle})_{t\rangle}$$

But by the length-preserving property 3, $\text{dom}(f(\omega_{t\rangle})) = \text{dom}(\omega_{t\rangle}) = \langle 0, t \rangle$; so $f(\omega_{t\rangle})_{t\rangle} = f(\omega_{t\rangle})$. Thus $f(\omega)_{t\rangle} = f(\omega_{t\rangle})$, as desired. ∎

LEMMA 3. f IS SPECIFIABLE BY A LAST VALUE FUNCTION f

There exists a function $f:\Omega_0 \to Y$ such that for all $\omega \in \Omega_0$, $t \in \text{dom}(\omega)$, $f(\omega)(t) = f(\omega_{t\rangle})$.

Proof. Define $f:\Omega_0 \to Y$ by $f(\omega) = f(\omega)(l(\omega))$ for $\omega \in \Omega_0$. By property 6, f is defined for every $\omega \in \Omega_0$. Moreover,

$$\begin{aligned}
f(\omega)(t) &= f(\omega)_{t\rangle}(t) && \text{(property of left segmentation)} \\
&= f(\omega_{t\rangle})(t) && \text{(Lemma 2)} \\
&= f(\omega_{t\rangle}) && \text{(definition of } f, \text{ noting } l(\omega_{t\rangle}) = t)
\end{aligned}$$
∎

With the help of Lemma 3 we construct an object $S_f^* = \langle T, X, \Omega, Q^*, Y, \delta^*, \lambda^* \rangle$, where Ω is the given domain of f and T, X, Y are the sets guaranteed to exist by property 1. In addition, $Q^* = \Omega_0$, $\delta^*:\Omega_0 \times \Omega \to \Omega_0$ is defined by

$$\delta^*(\omega, \omega') = \omega \cdot \mathrm{STR}(\omega')$$

and $\lambda^*:\Omega_0 \to Y$ is defined by $\lambda^* = f$.

We are assuming for simplicity that $\Lambda \in \Omega_0$ so that in particular $\delta^*(\Lambda, \omega) = \mathrm{STR}(\omega)$. (If $\Lambda \notin \Omega_0$, we set $Q^* = \Omega_0 \cup \{\Lambda\}$, slightly complicating the definition of λ^*.)

By Lemma 3, λ^* is well defined and it is easy to check that S_f^* is a system, which moreover is time invariant.

Finally, note that for $\omega \in \Omega_0$

$$\beta_\Lambda(\omega) = \lambda^*(\delta^*(\Lambda, \omega))$$
$$= f(\omega)$$

so that $\beta_\Lambda|\Omega_0 = f$, and it is then easy to check that $\tilde\beta_\Lambda = f$. Thus S_f^* realizes f as required.
∎

Having this characterization for realizable functions, we can develop a characterization for realizable IOFOs.

THEOREM 11.   CHARACTERIZATION OF REALIZABLE IOFOs

An IOFO (T, X, Ω, Y, F) is realizable if and only if the following conditions hold.

1.   *Each function $f \in F$ is realizable.*
2.   *The set F is closed under derivatives*

$$f \in F \Rightarrow \forall\, \omega \in \Omega, \quad \widehat{fL_\omega} \in F$$

where f is the last output function guaranteed to exist by the realizability of f, f_{L_ω} is called the ωth *derivative* of f and is defined by $fL_\omega(\omega') = f(\omega\omega')$ for all $\omega' \in \Omega$, and $\widehat{fL_\omega}$ is the segment-to-segment mapping specified by fL_ω.

Proof.   The necessity of the conditions follows by considering an arbitrary system and examining its associated IOFO. Let $S = \langle T, X, \Omega, Q, Y, \delta, \lambda \rangle$ and $\mathrm{IOFO}_S = \langle T, X, \Omega, Y, \tilde{B}_S \rangle$, where, as we recall, $\tilde{B}_S = \{\tilde\beta_q | q \in Q\}$. Clearly each $\tilde\beta_q$ is realizable. Moreover, the reader should verify that $\tilde\beta_q L_\omega = \tilde\beta_{\delta(q,\,\omega)}$; that is, the derivatives of the I/O function of state q are the I/O functions of all the states accessible from q. Thus $\tilde{B}_S$ is closed under derivatives.

To show that the conditions are sufficient, we construct a system S for which IOFO_S is the given IOFO. Since each function f is realizable, we can construct a system S_f^* that realizes it. Now each of these systems has the same state space Ω_0, but it is an easy matter to relabel each of these sets so that they are disjoint.

Naturally, the transition and output functions are likewise altered. For example, let $S_f^* = \langle T, X, \Omega, \Omega_0 \times \{f\}, \delta_f^*, \lambda_f^* \rangle$, where $\delta_f^*((\omega, f), \omega') = (\omega\omega', f)$, and $\lambda_f^*(\omega, f) = f(\omega)$. We can then "lay all the separate systems next to each other" in an operation called the disjoint union. Formally this results in an object $S_F^* = \langle T, X, \Omega, Q_F^*, \delta_F^*, \lambda_F^* \rangle$, where $Q_F^* = \bigcup_{f \in F} (\Omega_0 \times \{f\})$, $\delta_F^* | (\Omega_0 \times \{f\}) = \delta_f^*$ and $\lambda_F^* | (\Omega_0 \times \{f\}) = \lambda_f^*$. It is easy to check that S_F^* is a time invariant system. Moreover, we claim that $\text{IOFO}_{S_F^*} = \text{IOFO}$. Certainly $F \subseteq \tilde{B}_{S_F^*}$, since each f is realized by S_f^*, a part of S_F^*. On the other hand, given $q \in Q_F^*$, it belongs uniquely to some component $\Omega_0 \times \{f\}$, that is, $q = (\omega, f)$ for some $\omega \in \Omega_0$ and $f \in F$. But since (ω, f) is accessible from (Λ, f), we have that $\tilde{\beta}_{(\omega, f)}$ is a derivative of $\tilde{\beta}_{(\Lambda, f)}$. Noting that $\tilde{\beta}_{(\Lambda, f)} = f$ and that F is closed under derivatives, we have that $\tilde{\beta}_{(\omega, f)} \in F$. This allows us to conclude that $\tilde{B}_{S_F^*} \subseteq F$, hence $\tilde{B}_{S_F^*} = F$, as required. ∎

Finally, we have the

COROLLARY.   CHARACTERIZATION OF REALIZABLE IOROs

An IORO $\langle T, X, \Omega, Y, R \rangle$ is realizable if and only if there is a realizable IOFO $\langle T, X, \Omega, Y, F \rangle$ such that $R = \bigcup_{f \in F} f$.

10.9   GATHERING UP THE STRANDS

Our hierarchy of preservation relations for systems is summarized in the Table 1. The hierarchy of preservation relations runs parallel to the hierarchy of system specification levels. For each level of system specification there is a corresponding relation that preserves features introduced at this level. (We have not considered such a relation for level 5, but this could be done.)

Table 1   Hierarchy of Preservation Relations

Level	Preservation Relation	Formal Object
0	I/O relation morphism	(g, k)
1	I/O function morphism	(g, k)
2	System morphism	(g, h, k)
3	Specification morphism	(g, h, k)
4	Structure morphism (weak and strong)	$(d, \{h_\alpha\})$

As the level of the table increases, the strength of the corresponding morphism also increases, because as the level increases, more and more structure is introduced by the system specification. Accordingly, higher level morphisms preserve more structure than do lower level ones; thus higher level morphisms are stronger in the sense of preserving more structure.

It is natural then that the existence of a stronger morphism relating a pair of systems should imply the existence of a weaker morphism relating the same pair. In fact, we showed for each level (except the lowest) how to convert a morphism at that level to one at the next lowest level. Figure 6 displays the chain of implications obtained in this way and indicates where the implications were presented.

---

morphism at level i $\Rightarrow$ morphism at level $i - 1$
strong structure morphism
$\Rightarrow$ weak structure morphism (definition)
  $\Rightarrow$ specification morphism (definition)
    $\Rightarrow$ system morphism (Theorem 6)
      $\Rightarrow$ I/O function morphism (Theorem 4)
        $\Rightarrow$ I/O relation morphism (Theorem 1)

Figure 6   Downward implications property of preservation morphisms.

The utility of a high level morphism, however, lies in the guarantee that a lower level morphism exists, not necessarily in the actual construction of the latter. Indeed the higher level morphisms allow us to check by comparison of structures whether two systems are behaviorally equivalent, without having to compare their behavior directly. For this reason, higher level morphisms are important in model simplification (as we have already seen in Chapter 8) and in simulation program verification (as Chapters 4 and 7 have informally indicated).

Although stronger preservation relations imply weaker ones, the reverse is not generally true. This means that as a rule we cannot infer structure uniquely from behavior. The importance of this restriction for modelling is revealed in Chapter 15.

10.10   SOURCES

Homomorphisms of general algebras and systems are discussed by Cohn[1] and by Foo.[2] The relationship between the I/O function morphism and the system morphism is derived from Krohn and Rhodes[3] and by Hartmanis and Stearns.[4] Realization of I/O functions is discussed in a number of books.[5, 6] Category theory is invoked by some authors to characterize canonical realizations.[7] Cellular space morphisms are discussed in References 8 and 9. Aggregations are treated in References 10 and 11.

1. P. Cohn, *Algebra*, Vol. 1. Wiley, New York, 1974.

2. N. Y. Foo, *Homomorphic Simplication of Systems*. Doctoral dissertation, University of Michigan, Ann Arbor, 1974.

3. K. B. Krohn and J. L. Rhodes, "Algebraic Theory of Machines," in *Mathematical Theory of Automata*, Polytechnic Press, Brooklyn, New York, 1963, 371–391.

4. J. Hartmanis and R. E. Stearns, *Algebraic Structure Theory of Sequential Machines*. Prentice-Hall, Englewood Cliffs, N.J., 1969.

5. R. E. Kalman, P. L. Falb, and M. A. Arbib, *Topics in Mathematical Systems Theory*. McGraw-Hill, New York, 1962.

6. A. H. Zemanian, *Realizability Theory for Continuous Linear Systems*, Academic Press, New York, 1972.

7. E. G. Manes, *Category Theory Applied to Computation and Control*. Mathematics Department, University of Massachusetts, Amherst, Mass., 1974.

8. H. Yamada and S. Amoroso, "Structural and Behavioral Equivalences of Tessellation Automata," *Information and Control*, **18** (1), 1971, 1–31.

9. A. G. Barto, *Cellular Automata as Models of Natural Systems*. Doctoral dissertation, University of Michigan, Ann Arbor, 1975.

10. M. Aoki, "Control of Large-Scale Dynamic Systems by Aggregation," *Institute of Electrical and Electronic Engineers, Transactions on Automatic Control*, **13** (3), 1968, 246–253.

11. H. A. Simon and H. Ando, "Aggregation of Variables in Dynamic Systems," *Econometrica*, **29** 16, 1961, 111–138.

PROBLEMS

1. *Generalization of Lemma 2 (Section 10.7) to the division relation.* Prove the

LEMMA

Let g be invertable and let k be derived from $\tilde{k}$ as in Section 10.4. Then

$$\tilde{\beta}_{q'}|_{(g,\,k)}\tilde{\beta}_q \Leftrightarrow \beta_{q'}|_{(g,\,k)}\beta_q$$

where we write $f'|_{(g,\,k)}f'$ to denote $f' = k \circ f \circ g$ (f' divides f using (g, k)).

The lemma shows that division of I/O functions is equivalent to division of last output functions, provided g is invertable and the natural decoding map k is used.

Now consider the generalization of the equivalence relation that couples two states together if their I/O functions are in the division relation. Specifically, given g and k, define $\alpha \subseteq Q \times Q'$ by $q\alpha q' \Leftrightarrow \beta_{q'}|_{(g,\,k)}\beta_q$. We know from the preceding lemma that this equivalent to

$$q\alpha q \Leftrightarrow \tilde{\beta}_{q'}|_{(g,\,k)}\tilde{\beta}_q$$

Now to generalize Lemma 2, (Section 10.7) we must place another constraint on the encoding map g, namely, that it operate in such a way that when segments are composed together in the small system, the encoded result is the same as would be obtained by composing the coded versions of the original segments.

In other words we say that $g:\Omega' \rightarrow \Omega$ is a *semigroup homomorphism* if $g(\omega\omega') = g(\omega)g(\omega')$ for all $\omega,\ \omega' \in \Omega'$.

Furthermore, we require that g preserve the empty segment. We say that a homomorphism g is a *monoid homomorphism* if $g(\Lambda) = \Lambda$.

Now by mimicking the proof of Lemma 2 you can prove the

LEMMA

Let g be a monoid homomorphism. Then

(a) $q\alpha q' \Rightarrow (\forall\, \omega' \in \Omega')(\delta(q,\, g(\omega'))\alpha\, \delta'(q',\, \omega'))$.
(b) $q\alpha q' \Rightarrow k(\lambda(q)) = \lambda'(q')$.

2. *Construction of canonical realizations.* The realizations S_f^* and S_F^* given in Theorems 10 and 11 employ state spaces that may be much larger than necessary.

   (a) Formulate the state equivalence relation $\equiv$ for S_f^* and S_F^* and show that it is precisely the Nerode equivalence; that is, for S_f^*, $\omega \equiv \omega' \Leftrightarrow fL_\omega = fL_{\omega'}$ and for S_F^*, $(\omega, f) \equiv (\omega', f') \Leftrightarrow fL_\omega = f'L_{\omega'}$.
   (b) Apply Section 10.7 to construct the reduced versions S_f and S_F of S_f^* and S_F^* respectively.

   (Problems 8 to 10 of Chapter 15 deal with the canonicity of these systems.)

3. Consider functions of the form $f:\Omega \rightarrow \Omega'$, where $\Omega \subseteq (X,\, T)$ is closed under translation and composition and $\Omega' \subseteq (Y,\, T)$. For each of the following properties provide a function that does not have that property: length preserving and in step; time invariant; causal; has last values defined.

Part Three

Chapter Eleven

Framework for Modelling and Simulation

The basic framework introduced in Chapter 2 consists of twelve postulates, now presented formally. The postulates are to be understood as making certain claims about the nature of reality and the meaning of terms (such as "model" and "validity") commonly employed in the enterprise of modelling and simulation. An explanatory discussion follows the statement of the postulates. Then a brief exposition of a number of problems to which the framework is oriented permits the reader to see at a glance the operation of the postulates. The problems are considered in more detail in subsequent chapters.

11.1 FUNDAMENTAL POSTULATES

Postulate 1. There exists a real system $\mathcal{R}$, which is identified as a universe (set) of potentially acquirable data.

Postulate 2. There exists a model that structurally characterizes the universe of potentially acquirable data $\mathcal{R}$. We call such a model a *base model* and denote it by B.

The base model is a time invariant transition system (a system without output).

$$B = \langle T_B, X_B, (X_B, T_B), Q_B, \delta_B \rangle$$

Postulate 3. There exists a set of experimental frames restricting experimental access to the real system. We denote this set by $\mathscr{E}$ and a typical member frame by E.

Postulate 4. An experimental frame is a structure

$$E = \langle \Omega_E, Y_E, \lambda_E, V_E \rangle$$

where Ω_E is a set (the input segments applicable in E)

Y_E is a set (the output value set observable in E)

λ_E is a function (the observation function in E)

V_E is a set (the range of validity of E)

with the restrictions

1. *Closure of Ω_E.* Ω_E is a subset of (X_B, T_B) which is closed under the translation and composition of segments.
2. *Deterministic observations.* λ_E is a mapping from Q_B to Y_E (i.e., $\lambda_E : Q_B \to Y_E$).
3. *Range of validity determined in observation space.* V_E is a nonempty subset of Y_E.

Postulate 5. The real system observed within the experimental frame E is structurally characterized by a model denoted by B/E and called the *base model in E*.

Postulate 6. The base model in E is a structure

$$B/E = \langle T, X, \Omega, Q, Y, \delta, \lambda \rangle$$

where $T = T_B$ (time base of base model)

$X = \{\omega(t) | \omega \in \Omega_E, t \in \text{dom}(\omega)\}$ (union of generator ranges)

$\Omega = \Omega_E$ (input segments specified by the frame)

$Q = \lambda_E^{-1}(V_E) \cup \{\phi\}$ (the set of base model states yielding readings that lie within the valid output set together with a distinct special symbol ϕ)

$Y = V_E \cup \{\phi\}$ (the nonvalid output region is collapsed into ϕ)

$\delta : Q \times \Omega \to Q$ is defined by

$$\delta(q, \omega) = \begin{cases} \delta_B(q, \omega) & \text{if } \delta_B(q, \omega_t) \in \lambda^{-1}(V_E) \quad \text{for all } t \in \text{dom}(\omega) \\ \phi & \text{otherwise} \end{cases}$$

for $q \neq \phi$, and $\qquad\qquad \delta(\phi, \omega) = \phi$

$\lambda : Q \rightarrow Y$ is defined by

$$\lambda(q) = \begin{matrix} \lambda_E(q) & \text{if } q \neq \phi \\ \phi & \text{if } q = \phi \end{matrix}$$

PROPOSITION

The base model in E, B/E is a time invariant system.

Proof. Straightforward except for demonstrating that the composition property $\delta(q, \omega\omega') = \delta(\delta(q, \omega), \omega')$ holds for the case $\delta(q, \omega\omega') = \phi$. This is left as an exercise for the reader. ∎

Since B/E is a system, it has associated with it an input-output relation $R_{B/E}$ and an input-output relation observation $\text{IORO}_{B/E}$, defined in Section 9.3.

Postulate 7. The data potentially acquirable by observations of the real system within experimental frame E are identified with the I/O relation of the base model in E, $R_{B/E}$.

Postulate 8. The real system $\mathscr{R}$ is the set of data potentially acquirable by observations within any of the experimental frames in the set $\mathscr{E}$, that is,

$$\mathscr{R} = \bigcup_{E \in \mathscr{E}} R_{B/E}$$

Postulate 9. A lumped model is an iterative system specification M. Let $S(M)$ be the system specified by M.

Postulate 10. A lumped model M is *valid for the real system in experimental frame E* if its I/O relation $R_{S(M)} = R_{B/E}$.

Postulate 11. A computer is an iterative system specification C.

Postulate 12. A computer C is *a valid simulator of a lumped model M* if there is a specification morphism from C to M.

11.2 DISCUSSION OF POSTULATES

Postulate 1. We assert that there is an agreed-upon operational procedure for isolating out a part of reality, labeling it a real system, and collecting data by observations of it. The real system is nothing more than a source of potentially acquirable data.

At any point in time we will have collected only a finite subset of this potential universe which, by Postulate 8, will turn out to be an infinite set.

Postulate 2. We assert that there is a structure of a particular kind that characterizes the real system data in a particular way. This structure, the base model, is a time invariant transition system, and its behavior, as observed through experimental frames, will constitute the universe of potentially acquirable data. Note that we need not assert the uniqueness of such an explanatory base model, merely its existence.

The base model B is assumed to have a time base T_B, an input value set X_B, and all possible mappings from finite intervals of T_B into X_B are allowed as input segments. The set X_B delimits the possible "alphabet" of real system stimulation, but beyond this the base model is not constrained in terms of the potential input it may receive. The set of permissible input segments may well be constrained, however, by the environment of the real system, and this is explicated in Postulates 3 and 4 on experimental frames.

The essential components postulated for the base model are its state set Q_B and its transition function δ_B. Here we are asserting that there exists a hypothetical deterministically operating mechanism that constitutes the internal structure of the real system. This mechanism can be thought of as being in a definite state (an element of Q_B) at any time and as changing its states under the influence of an input segment. The law that uniquely determines the state-to-state transitions, is the transition function δ_B.

With this postulate we agree to behave as if a base model actually underlies the real system observations. However, it is an attribution to reality, which must always lie beyond the possibility of complete confirmation. See the discussion of Chapter 15.

Postulate 3. We assert that there are limitations to the possible ways of stimulating and observing the real system determined by the experimental environment or context in which it is placed. Such a context, or experimental frame E, is characterized structurally by reference to the base model B.

The limitations in experimenting with the real system may arise from one or a combination of the following factors.

(a) *Technological factors*—the state of the art of instrumentation will determine which measurements, observations, and other quantifications are possible, and to what level of resolution these can be made. Developments in physics, for example, were stimulated by advances in particle accelerators, which enabled observations in experimental domains well beyond those otherwise available.

(b) *Factors intrinsic to the scope of enquiry*—the point of view taken and the questions asked about a system determine the particular modes of observation and stimulation to which it will be subjected. For example, the psychological and neurophysiological approaches to human brain function can be distinguished as having different experimental frames relative to the same base model.

(c) *Factors due to state of understanding*—availability of appropriate observational modes may hinge on the degree to which relevant aspects of the system behavior have been isolated. For example, technology may ultimately make it possible to obtain simultaneous recordings of all the 10^{10} neurons in the human cortex, but it is doubtful that such a mode would be useful in and of itself. More likely, progress will depend on the discovery of ways in which this information can be meaningfully aggregated.

Postulate 4. Let us examine the significance of each of the components of frame $E = \langle \Omega_E, Y_E, \lambda_E, V_E \rangle$. The Ω_E specifies the kind of input stimulation that can be applied to the system in the frame E. An important aspect of this restriction has to do with the times at which the system can be observed. For example, let Ω_E consist of the single element 0_τ, where 0_τ takes on the value 0 over the interval $\langle 0, \tau \rangle$ and τ is a fixed number. The composition closure Ω_E^+ then consists of the segments $0_{n\tau}$, where $n = 1, 2, 3, \ldots$. This implies that the system will run "autonomously" (i.e., with constant input) over any period of time which is an integer multiple of τ. Since Ω_E has no subsegments of 0_τ, observations of the output of the base model will be defined only at the end of the generator segments (i.e., at integer multiples of τ: recall Section 9.6). Thus the time scale on which the real system may be observed has indivisible unit τ.

Exercise. Show that in general the minimum time between observations is min $\{l(\omega)|\omega \in \Omega_E\}$.

Of course, Ω_E also determines the "shape" of the input stimulation. Examples of this appeared in Sections 9.8.1 and 9.11.

In Section 3.4, we saw how the output set Y_E formalizes the notion of output variables. In this context, the output function λ_E determines the values the output variables will take on. When the base model is in state q we observe $\lambda_E(q)$. Thus λ_E characterizes formally the measuring instruments available in frame E—the range of possible readings (i.e., the observation space) is given by Y_E, and the mapping from the (unobservable) state space to the observation space is given by λ_E. All we can know about the system's motion through the state space is what λ_E allows us to see of it.

We have studied cases of experimental frames characterized by output maps in the grocery store example of Section 8.2. To fix some imagery in mind, we provide another example.

Exercise. Imagine the real system to be a ball moving according to Newtonian mechanics within a three-dimensional cubic box with side length L and suffering elastic collisions on hitting the walls. The state space is then given by the set $Q = \{(x, y, z, v_x, v_y, v_z)|0 \leq x, y, z, \leq L, v_x, v_y, v_z \in R\}$. Characterize the objects Y_E and λ_E for the frames

E_1: a pressure gauge placed on the top of the box responds with a unit pulse whenever the ball hits the top wall.

E_2: a scope placed at the origin allows viewing the position of the ball whenever it comes within a cubical region with side length $d \leq L$.

An experiment is often conducted under controlled conditions—certain variables must stay constant or remain within given bounds if the data collected are to be meaningful to the experimenter. We formalize this notion by means of the object V_E of the frame structure, where V_E represents the outputs that are meaningful within E. Postulate 6 formalizes the requirement that the observations taken from the real system are recorded only as long as the output remains within the bounds V_E; as soon as the output goes out of bounds, the subsequent recording is "blanked out."

Let us see how the validity set V_E may typically be specified. Suppose that $\gamma_1, \ldots, \gamma_n$ are the output variables with ranges $Y_1, \ldots, Y_n$ so that $Y_E = Y_1 \times Y_2 \times \cdots \times Y_n$. The variables may be divided into two disjoint sets, the *unconstrained* set U and the *constrained* set C. Typically, although not always, the variables in U are the ones whose response to input stimulation is of interest, and those in C are the "control" variables. The set C may be partitioned further into sets C_1, C_2, and C_3, where

1. Every variable $\gamma_i \in C_1$ must remain constant, say at value $c_i \in Y_i$.
2. Every variable $\gamma_i \in C_2$ must remain within a subset $V_i \subseteq Y_i$.
3. The values of variables $\gamma_{i_1}, \ldots, \gamma_{i_m}$ in C_3 must satisfy a relational predicate R. For example, a real valued function f with domain $Y_{i_1} \times \cdots \times Y_{i_m}$ is given, and the predicate R is specified by an equality

$$R(y_{i_1}, \ldots, y_{i_m}) \Leftrightarrow f(y_{i_1}, \ldots, y_{i_m}) = 0$$

or by an inequality

$$R(y_{i_1}, \ldots, y_{i_m}) \Leftrightarrow f(y_{i_1}, \ldots, y_{i_m}) < 0$$

More generally, the relational predicate is specified by a set of functions $f_1, \ldots, f_p$ so that, for example,

$$R(y_{i_1}, \ldots, y_{i_m}) \Leftrightarrow [\text{for each } i = 1, \ldots, p, f_i(y_{i_1}, \ldots, y_{i_m}) \le 0]$$

Note that the essential difference between sets C_3 and sets C_1 and C_2 is that the variables in C_3 are interdependent—the valid values one variable can assume cannot (in general) be stated independently of the values assumed by the other variables.

Finally, the validity set $V_e \subseteq Y_e$ is given in the preceding terms by

$$V_e = \{(y_1, \ldots, y_n) | y_i = c_i \qquad \text{for } \gamma_i \in C_1,$$

$$y_i \in V_i \qquad \text{for } \gamma_i \in C_2, \text{ and}$$

$$R(y_{i_1}, \ldots, y_{i_m}) \qquad \text{for } \gamma_{i_1}, \ldots, \gamma_{i_m} \in C_3\}$$

Exercise.   In a certain experimental study of bacteria, the growth of a colony is observed under the following conditions: the temperature must remain fixed, the air pressure may vary only within specified limits, and the density of the colony (its total mass divided by the volume it occupies) must not exceed a specified value. With temperature, pressure, mass, and volume as output variables, specify the output set Y_E and the range of validity V_E of the corresponding experimental frame E.

Postulates 5 and 6.   **These postulates show how to employ the experimental frame structure E to convert the base model transition system into a "full-fledged" system B/E, the base model in E. The system B/E inherits the time base and input value set (suitably restricted) from the base model. The input segment set is specified by the frame E. The state space Q consists of two parts: the first is the set of "valid states" (i.e., states that map under λ_E into valid outputs); the second is a distinct special symbol ϕ, which serves as a marker to indicate that a state trajectory has passed outside the region of valid states. This role is apparent in the definition of the transition function of B/E: it inherits the structure of the base model transition function for all transitions that remain within the valid states; however, any transition of B that would leave the valid state set is sent to state ϕ in B/E, which is, moreover, defined to be a fixed point or dead state. Thus as in Figure 1, state trajectories in the B and B/E are the same until the nonvalid region is entered. At this point, the B/E trajectory enters and subsequently remains in state ϕ, even though the trajectory in B may eventually return to the valid states.**

Note that the valid states may form a closed set under the action of the segsegments in Ω_E, in which case the state ϕ is never entered.

Finally, the output function of B/E is a similarly doctored version of the observation mapping specified by the frame E. The modification $\lambda(\phi) = \phi$

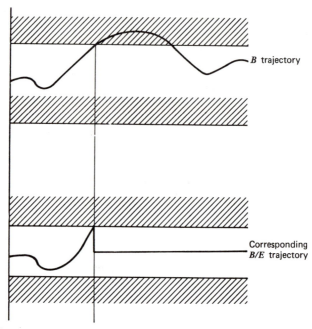

Figure 1 The correspondence between trajectories in B and B/E; cross-hatched area symbolizes invalid state set.

assumes that no attention is paid to any real system output trajectories once the range of validity has been crossed.

Postulate 7. We assert that the data collected in an experiment can be construed as a set of input-output pairs. The data potentially collectable in an experimental frame E are then identified with the infinite set of I/O pairs associated with system B/E.

Postulate 8. We assert that the set of frames $\mathscr{E}$ is complete in that if any experiment can be performed at all, it can be performed in at least one frame of $\mathscr{E}$. Thus collecting together the I/O pairs associated with all the frames of $\mathscr{E}$ yields precisely the universe of potentially acquirable data, namely, the real system $\mathscr{R}$.

Postulate 9. We assert that a lumped model is a formal object that is presented in a structural rather than a behavioral way, that is, as a set of instructions for generating state and output trajectories rather than an abstract description of the trajectories, themselves. As a consequence, the generation of trajectories must be done in a step-by-step manner by simulation or (when possible) by analysis.

Postulate 10.   At the formal level, Postulate 10, dealing with the relationship between a lumped model and the real system, may be taken to provide a definition for the relation "valid" involving a pair of systems $S(M)$ and B/E. Beyond this, however, we presume to explicate the ordinary usage of the term "valid" when applied to a model in relation to a real system. We are asserting that validity can be established, if at all, only on empirical grounds (i.e., by comparison of the data collected from the real system with those generated by the model). This is the level of relational equivalence (Section 10.4). Stronger statements concerning the degree to which the structure of the lumped model reflects that of the base model cannot be subjected to direct empirical check (see Chapter 15).

Postulate 11.   We treat the computer (program) that performs the simulation as a formal object specified by an iterative system specification. Pragmatically, this means that the actual implementation of the formal system specification is assumed to be error free—thus the real computer behaves precisely as predicted by its formal specification. (To test this assumption, we would treat the computer as a real system for purposes of the theory, the formal specification would be the model, and a second computer would be assigned to simulate the latter model, i.e., the formal computer specification.)

Postulate 12.   In the relationship between two formal objects—the lumped model M and the computer C—both are presumed to be known at the iterative specification level. Thus it is possible to demand that given an initial state q of M, we be able to specify a state in which C will generate the state and output behavior of M beginning from q.

11.3   GENERAL PROBLEMS IN MODELLING AND SIMULATION

The postulates just presented establish a framework in which a number of crucial problems in modelling and simulation may be formulated. These problems are encountered in every modelling enterprise and transcend the particular discipline in which the work is carried out. In this section we list and briefly describe the problem areas. In subsequent chapters we illustrate more specifically how the framework and the underlying systems theory can clarify these problems and suggest general methods for dealing with them. By applying the general concepts and methods in specific cases, we may discover an unlimited number of directly applicable techniques.

11.3.1   Valid Model Construction and Simplification

In earlier chapters we emphasized the utility of being able to provide a clear, informal model description. Later we illustrated the conversion of such an informal description into a completely formal one that functions as a system specification as required by Postulate 9.

Earlier chapters also gave typical ways in which modellers attempt to simplify their models by omitting interactions, aggregating variables, and so forth, and we asked, Under what conditions can such simplification techniques produce valid models?

We are now in a position to better consider this question. We suppose that the modeller has formulated a class of system specifications in which he expects to find ultimately a base model that characterizes the real system according to Postulate 2. We assume that this class is really a single model and that the values of a number of its parameters are unspecified. The grocery store of Chapter 8 is an example and should be kept in mind in the subsequent exposition. By a "candidate base model" $B*$ we mean any model of the class obtained by assigning values to the open parameters.

Next we suppose the modeller has specified an experimental frame E appropriate to the behavior of interest. This determines for every candidate base model $B*$ a system specification $B*/E$. By applying one or more simplification techniques, the modeller constructs a class of lumped models derived from the potential model class. More formally, the procedure involves mapping the states of base model $B*/E$ onto the states of the corresponding lumped model. If the mapping can be shown to be a homomorphism, then according to Section 10.4, the two models have the same behavior. Thus if a (true) base model B lies in the candidate class, the corresponding lumped model is valid in the experimental frame E according to Postulate 10.

Thus the notion of homomorphism provides a criterion by which the validity of model simplification can be assessed.

11.3.2.   Simulation Program Verification

The structure preserving concept also plays an important role in determining whether a model has been correctly implemented as a computer program. We begin considering the problem of program verification, again supposing that a model has been converted from its informal description to a formal system specification M. We also suppose that the simulation program is represented by a system specification C as in Postulate 11. The correspondences by which the model is encoded as a program then take the form of a mapping of the input segment, state, and output sets of the system C onto those of the model M. By Postulate 12, C is a valid simulator of M if the mapping can be shown to be a specification morphism.

11.3.3.   Complexity Reduction

Two tacit assumptions concerning model complexity—(1) that the limits on computational resources always force one to construct simplified lumped models, and (2) that simplification techniques always accomplish true simplification—turn out not to be self-evident when we examine the problem of complexity reduction within the context of the model-computer relationship of Postulate 12. As in the lumped–base model case, structure preserving morphisms can hold at various levels of detail. The level of a morphism represents the degree to which the static structure of the program resembles that of the model, as well as the relationship between model state transitions and their simulated program realizations. In determining the complexity of a model, both these factors must be taken into account. Accordingly, comparing the complexity of lumped and base models must be done relative to the levels of structure morphisms relating these models to the computer and to each other. We can then ask: for what kinds of complexity measures and structure morphisms is base model simplification truly necessary, and under what conditions can it be guaranteed?

11.3.4.   Goodness of Fit Criteria and Approximate Models

Implicit in Postulate 10 is a presumption that equality of I/O pairs can be determined in a strict yes-no fashion; that is, either the components of I/O pairs of real system and model are equal or they are not. Realistically however, we are rarely able to determine such equality precisely; indeed it is seldom desirable to use such a strict notion. On the real system side, accuracy of observation is limited by the finite precision of the instruments employed. In addition, often the measurements obtained are contaminated by uncontrollable extraneous influences. On the model side, since there is a finite precision with which the computer can compute model trajectories, it is usually not meaningful to require that I/O pairs agree arbitrarily closely. Moreover, often a model is considered to produce the same qualitative behavior as the real system without agreeing with it in detail.

Thus in practice one must choose criteria for evaluating the goodness of fit between real system and model I/O pairs. The judgment of model validity then becomes linked to the criterion employed. We judge I/O pairs to be "equal" if they are sufficiently close according to the chosen criterion.

The effect of error (i.e., inexact agreement) can also be examined at the structural level. Often it is fairly easy to establish that a homomorphism (or other structure preserving relation) holds approximately but not exactly between a base–lumped model pair. The lumped model may nevertheless prove to be a useful representative of the base model (i.e., valid with respect to the real system under appropriate goodness of fit criteria).

Formal theory cannot decide the choice of goodness of fit criteria, but it can clarify the concepts involved. It can also deal with the question, Under what conditions can the approximate homomorphism concept be employed to construct "valid" lumped models?

11.3.5.   State and Parameter Identification

The process of model validation is basically a process of trial and error whereby a model-testing phase is followed by a modification phase, followed by another testing phase, and so on. Often, especially at the beginning, the modeller or his mechanized equivalent is reduced to stab-in-the-dark exploration. However a more scientific approach may be possible by making use of model structure and real system data. More specifically, it may be possible to establish the range of parameter values compatible with the I/O pairs so far obtained (and even to infer uniquely what they must be).

Similarly, and this is generally less well understood by practictioners, the initial state in which the model is started for the next experiment is a choice that has to be made. Rational selection of initial state may also be based on the use of collected I/O pairs. In some cases the initial state can be inferred uniquely in this way. This strong form of state identification is intimately linked with the structural inference problem discussed below.

11.3.6   Structural Inference

According to Postulate 10, a model is valid to the degree that it reproduces the I/O behavior of a real system; that is, judgment of validity is made entirely at the observational behavioral level. Usually, however, we would like to assert a stronger degree of correspondence between model and real system. Yet as argued in Chapter 2, such a correspondence is necessarily structural, thus is meaningful only with reference to the base model hypothesized to underlie the real system. Given a lumped model that has been validated with respect to the real system in some experimental frame, then, we want to infer structural properties of the base model (which we do not know) from structural properties of the lumped model (which we *do* know, having constructed it). Although in general we cannot expect to uniquely infer what the base model must be like, we can state conditions, called "justifying conditions," which do justify some structural inferences often tacitly made by modellers. Formally, these inferences take the following form. If a structure morphism between base and lumped models holds at a (low) level of structural detail, and if a certain justifying condition holds, then a structure morphism holds also at a higher level of structural detail.

11.3.7 Model Integration

So far our framework explains how we may have several disparate models of a real system, each valid in a different experimental frame. How can these models be integrated to form a coherent whole? If the models have very little in common with each other structurally, in isolation, there may be very little guidance about to how to fit the pieces together. However, regarded as lumped models of an all-embracing base model, the models may be related both structurally and behaviorally to the base model. With the base model as maximum element, the lumped models may be placed in a latticelike structure in which models are interconnected by structure morphisms at the various levels of specification. Then we need to know how to implement such a structure as a software package and how to use it in a practical modelling and simulation environment. It is in this area that the theory of modelling and simulation may provide new and most far-reaching guiding concepts.

11.4 SOURCES

The framework discussed here, first presented in References 1 and 2, is based on a number of sources.[3-8]

1. B. P. Zeigler, "A Conceptual Basis for Modelling and Simulation," *International Journal of General Systems*, **1** (4), 1975, 213–228.
2. B. P. Zeigler, "Postulates For a Theory of Modelling and Simulation," *Proceedings of the 1975 Summer Computer Simulation Conference*, AFIPS Press, Montrale N.J., 1975, 49–54.
3. W. R. Ashby, *Introduction to Cybernetics*. Chapman & Hall, London, 1958.
4. C. W. Churchman, "An Analysis of the Concept of Simulation," in *Proceedings of the Symposium on Simulation Models*, A. C. Haggatt and F. E. Balderston (Eds.), Southwest Publishing, Cincinnati, Ohio, 1963.
5. F. Suppes, "The Meaning and Use of Models in the Empirical Sciences." Doctoral dissertation, University of Michigan, Ann Arbor, 1967.
6. G. J. Klir and M. Valach, *Cybernetics Modelling*. Iliffe Books, London, 1967.
7. A. Norris, "On Defining the Simulation Process," *Simulation*, **13** (4), 1969, 199–200.
8. R. Rosen, "On Analogous Systems," *Bulletin of Mathematical Biophysics*, **30**, 1968, 481–492.

Chapter Twelve

Valid Model Construction and Simplification

To study the use of system morphisms for model construction, we focus on two important aspects of this area; one relating to the use of structure morphisms, the other to system decomposition.

Chapter 11 placed the model simplification process within our general framework, indicating that the homomorphism formalism provides a criterion by which the validity of a lumped model may be established relative to its parent base model. As our first theme, we illustrate the use of the structure morphism to establish the validity of lumped models for a class of neural nets. An informal description of the models involved, and the context in which they were developed is given in Appendix A, to which the reader may wish to refer before proceeding. In addition, Chapter 2 sets forth some of the common simplification procedures. The central procedure employed in the neural net example is that of "grouping components and aggregation of variables." But it also illustrates the important concept of preservation of component interaction, which is formalized by the strong structure morphism.

Our second theme relates to system decomposition—the breaking down of a system into parts. We formulate the problem as one of discovering lumped models of a base model which relate to its components. Given a base and a lumped model, the issue of whether the lumped model will be valid with respect to the base model turns on the nature of the experimental frame. The role of the experimental frame is especially important in the case of system decomposition, since it determines the circumstances under which the behavior of a component can be isolated from that of the system in which it is embedded.

12.1   NEURON NET MODELLING

In Appendix A we describe informally a base–lumped model pair for neuron net simulation. We now assume that description as general background and proceed to prove the validity of the lumped model using the structure morphism concept.[†]

The base model NEURON is formalized as a sequential machine[‡]

$$M = \langle X, Q, Y, \delta, \lambda \rangle$$

where $X = R$

$\qquad Q = I_0^+ \times [0, 1]$

$\qquad Y = \{0, 1\}$

and $\delta : Q \times X \to Q \qquad$ is given by

$$\delta((i, r), x) = \begin{cases} (0, \Gamma(r)) & \text{if} \quad x + F^{-1}(r) > T(i) \quad \text{(NEURON fires)} \\ (i + 1, \Gamma(r)) & \text{otherwise} \qquad\qquad\quad \text{(it does not fire)} \end{cases}$$

for all $(i, r) \in Q$ and $x \in X$

and $\lambda : Q \to Y \qquad$ is given by

$$\lambda(i, r) = \begin{matrix} 1 & \text{if } i = 0 \\ 0 & \text{otherwise} \end{matrix}$$

The input set is the range of STRENGTH, the synapse weighted sum of excitation received by the NEURON. The state space consists of two components, $I_0^+ = \{0, 1, 2, \ldots\}$, the range of RECOVERY · STATE and $[0, 1]$ the range of a pseudorandom number generator.

The function $T : I_0^+ \to R$ is the THRESHOLD function, F is the cumulative distribution function (cdf) of the NOISE and $\Gamma : [0, 1] \to [0, 1]$ is the ideal random number generator producing numbers uniformly distributed in $[0, 1]$.

[†] The material in Sections 12.1 to 12.8, including the accompanying illustrations appeared originally in Reference 1, 382–393.

[‡] Compare this formalization with that of Section 3.6, which concerns a neuron not subject to internal noise.

The RECOVERY · STATE records the number of time steps since the NEURON last fired. The NEURON fires if its total synapse weighted input plus independently generated NOISE exceeds a threshold value determined by the THRESHOLD function applied to the RECOVERY · STATE—this is encoded in the transition function δ.

The NEURON outputs a one (pulse) when it fires, and zero (no pulse) otherwise; hence the output function λ.

12.2 SIMPLE ILLUSTRATION OF REDUCTION

We assume for convenience that the THRESHOLD becomes constant for RECOVERY · STATES beginning at some value, say i_m, that is, $T(i) = T(i_m)$ for all $i \geq i_m$. Then the NEURON state space reduces to $\{0, 1, \ldots, i_m\} \times [0, 1]$ and the new transition function is as before, except when the nonfiring case splits into

$$\begin{cases} (i + 1, \Gamma(r)) & \text{if } i < i_m \\ (i_m, \Gamma(r)) & \text{if } i \geq i_m \end{cases}$$

Exercise. Formulate the reduced NEURON as a machine M'. Show that there is a homomorphism from M to M', and conclude that the I/O behavior of the two machines is the same.

12.3 THE "NEURON" AS A STOCHASTIC AUTOMATION

If we drop the NOISE component r from the state set, the NEURON can (and must) be probabilistically described (cf. Section 6.2). RECOVERY · STATE becomes a discrete random variable (rv) R taking on values $\{0, 1, \ldots, i_m\}$. Let $p = (p(0), p(1), \ldots, p(i_m))$ denote a probability mass function (pmf) for RECOVERY · STATE, so that $p(i)$ is the probability of being in state i and

$$\sum_{i=0}^{i_m} p(i) = 1$$

If the NEURON is in state i, it can go only to state $i + 1$ (where we set $i_m + 1 = i_m$) or to state 0. The first case occurs when $x + F^{-1}(r) \leq T(i)$ (input plus noise is less than or equal to threshold), that is, when $r \leq F(T(i) - x)$. The probability of this event is thus $F(T(i) - x)$.

Thus if $p^t = (p(0), p(1), \ldots, p(i_m))$ is a pmf at some t, and $p^{t+1} = (p'(0), \ldots, p'(i_m))$ is the pmf at time $t + 1$ determined by it, then

$$p^{t+1} = p^t P(x)$$

Here $P(x)$ is a Markov conditional probability matrix

$$P(x) = \begin{bmatrix} P_x(0/0) & P_x(1/0) & 0 & \cdots & 0 \\ P_x(0/1) & 0 & P_x(2/1) & \cdots & \vdots \\ \vdots & \vdots & & \ddots & \\ P_x(0/i_m) & 0 & \cdots & & P_x(i_m/i_m) \end{bmatrix}$$

with nonzero entries

$$P_x(0/i) = 1 - F(T(i) - x) \quad \text{and} \quad P_x(i + 1/i) = F(T(i) - x)$$

12.4 A BLOCK OF IDENTICAL "NEURONS"

Now consider a block of N NEURONS $\alpha_1, \alpha_2, \ldots, \alpha_N$. The global state set of this block is $(\{0, 1, \ldots, i_m\} \times [0, 1])^N$. With a typical global state $q = ((i_{\alpha_1}, r_1), \ldots, (i_{\alpha_N}, r_N))$, we associate a distribution of RECOVERY $\cdot$ STATES $f^q = (f^q(0), f^q(1), \ldots, f^q(i_m))$, where $f^q(i)$ is the proportion of NEURONS in RECOVERY $\cdot$ STATE i, that is, $f^q(i) = N^{-1} \cdot |\{\alpha | i_\alpha = i\}|$.

Again dropping the NOISE component, at time t the N RECOVERY $\cdot$ STATE variables $R_{\alpha_1}^t, R_{\alpha_2}^t, \ldots, R_{\alpha_N}^t$ for a jointly distributed set of random variables. Let $P_{\alpha_1, \ldots, \alpha_N}^t$ denote the pmf, where $P_{\alpha_1, \ldots, \alpha_N}^t(i_1, \ldots, i_N)$ is the probability that $R_{\alpha_1}^t = i_1, \ldots, R_{\alpha_N}^t = i_N$.

We say the RECOVERY $\cdot$ STATE variables are *independent* at time t if $P_{\alpha_1, \ldots, \alpha_N}^t(i_1, \ldots, i_N) = P_{\alpha_1}^t(i_1)P_{\alpha_2}^t(i_2) \cdots P_{\alpha_N}^t(i_N)$ for suitable marginal pmfs $P_{\alpha_1}^t, \ldots, P_{\alpha_N}^t$. Furthermore, the variables are *identically distributed at time t* if all the $P_{\alpha_i}^t$ are the same function, say p^t.

Let the RECOVERY $\cdot$ STATE variables be independent and identically distributed (iid) at time t, with p^t the marginal pdf. Assume that N, the number of NEURONS, tends toward infinity so that by the strong law of larger numbers[2], the probability of the subset of global states $\{q | f^q = p^t\}$ is 1. In other words, the only global states possible at time t are those states q for which the proportion of NEURON in RECOVERY $\cdot$ STATE i, $f^q(i)$ equals the probability of any one NEURON being in i, $p^t(i)$.

Now suppose that each NEURON receives a volley of the same STRENGTH x. Since each NEURON RECOVERY $\cdot$ STATE at time t is an independent rv with pmf p^t, and the NOISE is independently generated for it, we have that $p^{t+1} = p^t P(x)$ and the RECOVERY $\cdot$ STATE variables are independent and identically distributed at time $t + 1$ with marginal pmf p^{t+1}. More formally, the successor state of a global state $q = ((i_1, r_1), \ldots, (i_N, r_N))$ is $q' = ((j_1, \Gamma(r_1), \ldots, (j_N, \Gamma(r_N))$

where $j_k = \begin{cases} 0 & \text{if } x + F^{-1}(r_k) > T(i_k) \\ j_k + 1 & \text{otherwise} \end{cases}$ for $k = 1, \ldots, N$

Thus
$$P_x\left(\frac{j_1,\ldots,j_N}{i_1,\ldots,i_N}\right) = P_x\left(\frac{j_1}{i_1}\right)P_x\left(\frac{j_2}{i_2}\right)\cdots P_x\left(\frac{j_N}{i_N}\right)$$

and
$$P^{t+1}_{\alpha_1,\ldots,\alpha_N}(j_1,\ldots,j_N) = \sum_{(i_1,\ldots,i_N)} P_x\left(\frac{j_1}{i_1}\right)\cdots P_x\left(\frac{j_N}{i_N}\right)p^t(i_1)\cdots p^t(i_N)$$
$$= p^{t+1}(j_1)\cdots p^{t+1}(j_N)$$

By the law of large numbers, the successor state q' has distribution $f^{q'} = p^{t+1} = p^t P(x) = f^q P(x)$.

To sum up this section, we have established

PROPOSITION 1

Consider a block of N NEURONS each receiving the same input volley STRENGTH x. Let q be a global state, where the RECOVERY · STATE values are chosen independently from a distribution f^q. Then for N tending to infinity, the successor state q' is such that $f^{q'} = f^q P(x)$ and in it the RECOVERY · STATE variables are independently distributed with distribution $f^{q'}$.

This completely describes the situation in which the base model consists of a single block of uncoupled NEURONS with identical input STRENGTH. The proposition suggests that we can employ a valid lumped model with the set of all probability distributions of RECOVERY · STATES as its state space and the transformation performed by $P(x)$ as its transition function (Figure 1). We defer verifying this idea until we have covered the general case of interconnected blocks of NEURONS.

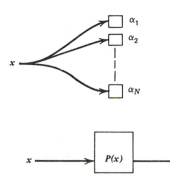

Figure 1 A block of identical NEURONS and its lumped representation.

12.5 INTERCONNECTED BLOCKS OF "NEURONS"

Consider two blocks of NEURONS (Figure 2) such that each NEURON in BLOCK 2 has n INFLUENCERS (or NEIGHBORS) in BLOCK 1, and all

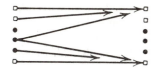

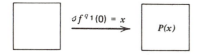

Figure 2   Two blocks of NEURONS and their lumped representation.

synaptic weights have the same value $\mathit{\Delta}/n$. For a typical NEURON β of BLOCK 2 with INFLUENCERS $\alpha_1, \alpha_2, \ldots, \alpha_n$, the input STRENGTH is

$$x_\beta = \frac{\mathit{\Delta}}{n} \sum_{\alpha=\alpha_1}^{\alpha_n} \lambda(i_\alpha, r_\alpha)$$

where (i_α, r_α) is the state of NEURON α. Dropping the NOISE component, STRENGTH at time t becomes a random variable

$$X_\beta^t = \frac{\mathit{\Delta}}{n} \sum_{\alpha=\alpha_1}^{\alpha_n} [R_\alpha^t]$$

where $[R_\alpha^t] = \begin{matrix} 1 & \text{if } R_\alpha^t = 0 \\ 0 & \text{otherwise} \end{matrix}$

Let n tend to infinity so that by the law of large numbers[2], X_β^t takes on the constant value

$$x_\beta^t = E(X_\beta^t) = \frac{\mathit{\Delta}}{n} \sum_{\alpha=\alpha_1}^{\alpha_n} E([R_\alpha^t])$$

Now if the RECOVERY · STATE variables are iid at time t with marginal distribution p^t, then $E([R_\alpha^t]) = p^t(0)$, and

$$x_\beta^t = \frac{\mathit{\Delta}}{n} \sum_{\alpha_1}^{\alpha_n} p^t(0) = \mathit{\Delta} p^t(0)$$

That is, each of the NEURONS of BLOCK 2 "samples" without error the firing activity of BLOCK 1 and receives the *same* input volley STRENGTH.

Combining this result with Proposition 1, we have

PROPOSITION 2

Consider blocks BLOCK 1 and BLOCK 2 of N NEURONS each. Let q_1, q_2 be the global states of BLOCK 1 and BLOCK 2, where the RECOVERY · STATE values are chosen independently from the distributions f^{q_1} and

f^{q_2}, respectively. Let each NEURON in BLOCK 2 have n NEIGHBORS in BLOCK 1 with synaptic weights $\measuredangle/n$. Then for N and n tending to infinity, the successor state q'_2 is such that $f^{q'_2} = f^{q_2} \cdot P(x)$, where $x = \measuredangle f^{q_1}(0)$, and in it the RECOVERY $\cdot$ STATE variables are independently distributed with distribution f^{q_2}.

12.6   CONSTRUCTION OF BASE—LUMPED MODEL PAIR

The *base model* is a structured sequential machine $B = \langle Q, \delta \rangle$ arising out of a network of NEURONS as follows. Let D be the set of NEURONS. For each NEURON $\alpha \in D$, a set $I_\alpha \subseteq D$ of INFLUENCERS (or INPUT $\cdot$ NEIGHBORS) is designated according to criteria soon to be specified; similarly we assign a connecting instantaneous map Z_α mapping $\times_{\beta \in I_\alpha} Q_\beta$ into X_α of the form

$$Z_\alpha(q_1, \ldots, q_{|I_\alpha|}) = \sum_{i=1}^{|I_\alpha|} \measuredangle_i^\alpha \lambda(q_i)$$

where the synaptic weights $\{\measuredangle_i^\alpha\}$ are chosen as indicated below.

Let $\{(\alpha')|\alpha' \in D'\}$ be a partition of D. [Then, D' will be the set of lumped components and (α') will be the BLOCK of NEURONS represented by lumped component α'.] With the number N of NEURONS in each BLOCK tending to infinity, we take as the base model state set, the set of all global states that have probability 1 of occurring according to the law of large numbers when RECOVERY $\cdot$ STATES are assigned to NEURONS in each BLOCK in iid fashion (with marginal distributions characteristic of the BLOCK). We employ Proposition 2 to show that this set is closed under the global network transition function.

Exercise.   Write out explicitly the structuring of Q by $\{Q_\alpha\}$ and δ by $\{\delta_\alpha\}$.

The *lumped model* is also a structured machine $M' = \langle Q', \delta' \rangle$ arising from a network of lumped components as follows. Let D' be the set of lumped components. Each component

$$M_{\alpha'} = \langle X_{\alpha'}, Q_{\alpha'}, \delta_{\alpha'} \rangle$$

where $X_{\alpha'} = R$

$$Q_{\alpha'} = \{p|p = (p(0), \ldots, p(i_m)), p(i) \in [0, 1] \text{ for each } i, \quad \text{and}$$
$$\sum_{i=1}^{i_m} p(i) = 1\}$$

$$\delta_\alpha : Q_{\alpha'} \times X_{\alpha'} \to Q_{\alpha'}$$

is defined by $\delta_{\alpha'}(p, x) = pP(x)$.

(The parameters specifying $P(\cdot)$ are derived from those of the base model as indicated below.)

Let $I_{\alpha'} \subseteq D'$ be the INFLUENCERS of component α' and $Z_{\alpha'}$ be a mapping $\times_{\beta' \in I_{\alpha'}} Q_{\beta'}$ to $X_{\alpha'}$ of the form

$$Z_{\alpha'}(p_1, \ldots, p_{|I_{\alpha'}|}) = \sum_{i=1}^{|I_{\alpha'}|} s_i^{\alpha'} p_i(0)$$

Exercise.   Write out explicitly the structuring of Q' by $\{Q_{\alpha'}\}$ and δ' by $\{\delta_{\alpha'}'\}$.

To establish a correspondence between base and lumped models, let $d : D \to D'$ (onto) be a coordinate mapping and for each $\alpha' \in D'$ let $h_{\alpha'}$ map

$$\times_{\alpha \in (\alpha')} Q_\alpha \xrightarrow{\text{onto}} Q_{\alpha'} \quad \text{by} \quad h_{\alpha'}(q) = f^q$$

That is, the local aggregation mapping $h_{\alpha'}$ takes a global state q of the block (α') of NEURONS and maps it into a distribution of RECOVERY · STATES in the corresponding lumped model components state set.

We wish to establish that $(d, \{h_{\alpha'}\})$ is a strong structure morphism by specifying parameters of the base model to correspond to those of the lumped model. The specifications are as follows:

1. All NEURONS α in a BLOCK(α') have the same THRESHOLD function $T_{\alpha'}$ and NOISE cdf $F_{\alpha'}$. Thus the $P(\cdot)$ matrix for lumped component α' is characterized by $T_{\alpha'}$ and $F_{\alpha'}$.
2. Consider any pair α', β' such that $\alpha' \in I_{\beta'}$ (α' is an INFLUENCER of β' in the lumped model). Then each NEURON $\beta \in (\beta')$ has the same number $n_{\alpha'}^{\beta'}$ (tending to infinity) of INFLUENCERS in BLOCK(α'); call this set $I_\beta(\alpha')$. The set I_β of all INFLUENCERS of β is the union of the INFLUENCERS $I_\beta(\alpha')$ over each of the $\alpha' \in I_{\beta'}'$.

    This guarantees that d is a digraph morphism. (In fact, a stronger relation is true: for each α', β' for which $\alpha' \in I_{\beta'}$ and for each $\beta \in (\beta')$, there are $n_{\alpha'}^{\beta'}$ points $\alpha \in (\alpha')$ such that $\alpha \in I_\beta$.)
3. The synapse weights of all the elements in $I_\beta(\alpha')$ are the same value $s_{\alpha'}^{\beta'}/n_{\alpha'}^{\beta'}$, where $s_{\alpha'}^{\beta'}$ is the weight for the influence of lumped BLOCK α' on lumped BLOCK β'.

Consider a lumped component β'. For notational convenience let $I_{\beta'} = \{\alpha_1', \ldots, \alpha_m'\}$, $s_{\alpha_i'}^{\beta'} = s_i$, and $n_{\alpha_i'}^{\beta'} = n_i$ (see Figure 3). For any NEURON β in the base model BLOCK(β') we have $|I_\beta| = \sum_{i=1}^m n_i$ and

$$Z_\beta(q_1, \ldots, q_{|I_\beta|}) = \sum_{i=1}^m s_i \left(\frac{1}{n} \sum_{\alpha \in I_\beta(\alpha_i')} \lambda(q_2) \right) \tag{1}$$

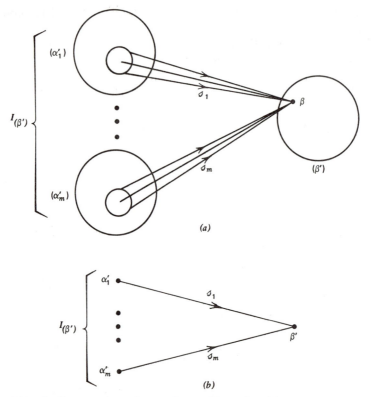

Figure 3   Correspondences between base and lumped models.

(The number of firing NEURONS among those sampled by β from BLOCK(α_i') is $\sum_{\alpha \in I_\beta(\alpha_i)} \lambda(q_2)$; each such NEURON contributes s_i/n_i to the volley received by β; the total volley STRENGTH is the sum of the contributions of the m INFLUENCER BLOCKS.)

Anticipating that the proportion $(1/n_i) \sum_{\alpha \in I_\beta(\alpha_i)} \lambda(q_2)$ turns out to correspond to a lumped model firing probability $p_i(0)$, we chose *identical* weights $\{s_i\}$ for the Z-maps of corresponding base and lumped components. That is,

$$Z_{\beta'}(p_1, \ldots, p_m) = \sum_{i=1}^{m} s_i p_i(0) \tag{2}$$

We are now ready to prove the main

THEOREM

For the base lumped model pair B, M defined earlier, the mapping $(d, \{h_{\alpha'}\})$ is a strong structure morphism.

Proof.   According to the Proposition of Section 10.6, we need only establish the commutative relation

$$h_{\beta'} \cdot \delta_{(\beta')} = \delta'_{\beta'} \cdot h_{I_{\beta'}}$$

for an arbitrary lumped component $\beta' \in D'$.

With $I_{\beta'} = \{\alpha'_1, \ldots, \alpha'_m\}$, let $q_1, \ldots, q_n$ be the global states of the base BLOCKS$(\alpha'_1), \ldots, (\alpha'_m)$. Let q be the global state of BLOCK(β') and $\bar{q}$ its successor; that is, $\delta_{(\beta')}$ applied to base model global state $(q, q_1, \ldots, q_n, \ldots)$ yields $\bar{q}$.

By the law of large numbers, we have from Equation 1,

$$Z_{\beta}(q_1, \ldots, q_m) = \sum_{i=1}^{m} \mathscr{A}_i f^{q_i}(0)$$

where f^{q_i} is, as before, the RECOVERY $\cdot$ STATE distribution associated with global state q_i of BLOCK(α'_i).

Thus each NEURON $\beta \in (\beta')$ receives the same STRENGTH

$$x = Z_{\beta}(q_1, \ldots, q_m)$$
$$= \sum_{i=1}^{m} \mathscr{A}_i f^{q_i}(0)$$

By Proposition 2 we have

$$f^{\bar{q}} = f^q \cdot P(x)$$

Proposition 2 also establishes that if $q, q_1, \ldots, q_m$ are global states arising with probability 1 from iid assignments according to $f^q, f^{q_1}, \ldots, f^{q_m}$, respectively, then $\bar{q}$ will be in the same relation to $f^{\bar{q}}$. This establishes the closure of state space Q.

Recalling that $h(q_{\alpha'}) = f^{q_{\alpha'}}$ is the aggregation mapping global state $q_{\alpha'}$ of BLOCK(α') to distribution state $f^{q_{\alpha'}}$ of lumped component α', we have

$$h_{\beta'} \cdot \delta_{(\beta')}(q, q_1, \ldots, q_m) \cdots) = h_{\beta'}(\bar{q})$$
$$= f^{\bar{q}}$$
$$= f^q \cdot P(x) \tag{3}$$

On the other hand,

$$\delta_{\beta'} \cdot h_{I_{\beta'}}(q, q_1, \ldots, q_m, \ldots) = \delta'_{\beta'}(h_{\beta'}(q), x')$$
$$= f^q \cdot P(x') \tag{4}$$

where $x' = Z_{\beta'}(h_{\alpha'_1}(q_1), \ldots, h_{\alpha'_m}(q_m))$
$$= Z_{\beta'}(f^{q_1}, \ldots, f^{q_m})$$
$$= \sum_{i=1}^{m} \mathscr{A}_i f^{q_i}(0) \quad \text{(from Equation 2)}$$
$$= x \tag{5}$$

Thus combining Equations 3, 4, and 5 we have

$$\delta'_{\beta'} \cdot h_{I_{\beta'}}(q, q_1, \ldots, q_m, \ldots) = h_{\beta'} \cdot \delta_{(\beta')}(q, q_1, \ldots, q_m, \ldots)$$

for each global state $(q, q_1, \ldots, q_m, \ldots) \in Q$, and this establishes the relation requirements for $(d, \{h_{\alpha'}\})$ to be a structure morphism from B to M. ∎

12.7   EXPERIMENTAL FRAME AND VALIDITY

We have established that a strong structure morphism runs from the structured base model $B = \langle Q, \delta \rangle$ to the structured lumped model $M' = \langle Q', \delta' \rangle$. This implies that the global aggregation h obtained from the family of local aggregations $\{h_{\alpha'}\}$ is a transition function homomorphism.

Now consider an experimental frame E in which the activity of BLOCK(α') is of interest. This means that the base model in E is a machine $B/E = \langle Q, Y_E, \delta, \lambda_E \rangle$, where $Y_E = [0, 1]$ and $\lambda_E : Q \to Y_E$ is defined by $\lambda_E(q_{\alpha'}, q_{\beta'}, \ldots) = f^{q_{\alpha'}}(0)$ ($f^{q_{\alpha'}}(0)$ is the proportion of firing NEURONS in (α')).

Expanding the lumped model to $M' = \langle Q', Y_E, \delta', \lambda' \rangle$, where $\lambda' : Q' \to Y_E$ is defined by $\lambda'(p_{\alpha'}, p_{\beta'}, \ldots) = p_{\alpha'}(0)$, we can easily establish that $\lambda' \circ h = h \circ \lambda_E$, hence

COROLLARY

(a) M' is a homomorphic image of B/E.

(b)   If B is a base model for a real system $\mathscr{R}$, M' is a valid lumped model with respect to $\mathscr{R}$ in experimental frame E.

Proof.   Exercise for the reader. (See discussion, Section 11.3.1.) ∎

12.8   THE CASE OF FINITE NEIGHBORHOOD SIZE

While retaining an effectively infinite number of NEURONS per BLOCK, we can relax without much difficulty the requirements for infinite numbers of INFLUENCERS per NEURON.

We replace specification 2 of the base model construction by

2′.   (a)   For any pair α', β' such that $\alpha' \in I_{\beta'}$, each NEURON $\beta \in (\beta')$ has the same finite number of INFLUENCERS $n_{\alpha'}^{\beta'}$ in BLOCK (α').

(b)   The set of INFLUENCERS $I_\beta(\alpha')$ is a uniform random sample from BLOCK (α').

As before, I_β is the union of the sets $I_\beta(\alpha')$ for $\alpha' \in I_{\beta'}$.

With this change, we must treat the input volley STRENGTH received by NEURON β as a nonconstant random variable, since the law of large numbers no longer applies. Thus in the preamble to Proposition 2, $(n/\varDelta)X_\beta^t$ is a random variable that is binomially distributed according to $B(n, p^t(0))$—by hypothesis, the firing variables $[R_\alpha^t]$ are iid with marginal distribution $p^t(0)$. Since X_β^t and the NOISE are independent, their sum has cdf obtained by convolution of the separate cdfs. The $P(\cdot)$ matrix of the lumped component is then characterized by this resultant cdf.

As an illustration, consider what happens when the NOISE is normally $N(0, \sigma)$ distributed. If n is sufficiently large, we may set $x_\beta^t = E(X_\beta^t + Y_\beta^t)$, where Y_β^t is $N(0, (\varDelta/n)\sqrt{p^t(0)(1 - p^t(0))})$ distributed, thus permitting Y_β^t to be regarded as the externally (to NEURON β) generated noise. The internal and external noises then combine and the total effective noise is $N(0, \sqrt{\sigma^2 + (\varDelta/n)p^t(0)(1 - p^t(0))})$ distributed. Thus the $P(\cdot)$ matrix is now parameterized by $\sqrt{\sigma^2 + (\varDelta/n)p^t(0)(1 - p^t(0))}$, where it would have been parameterized by σ in the case of $n \to \infty$.

In the derivation of the Proposition 1, the iid condition of RECOVERY $\cdot$ STATE variables $R_{\beta_1}^{t+1}, \ldots, R_{\beta_N}^{t+1}$ is predicated on the iid condition of $R_{\beta_1}^t, \ldots, R_{\beta_N}^t$ and the independence of the internal NOISE for each NEURON β_i. To maintain the truth of the proposition (hence of subsequent results), we must be assured that the externally generated noises $Y_{\beta_i}^t$ are also independent. This is guaranteed by stipulation $2'b$, which asserts that the INFLUENCERS $I_\beta(\alpha')$ are to be distributed with uniform random distribution. The intersection of any pair of sets $I_{\beta_1}(\alpha')$ and $I_{\beta_2}(\alpha')$ of size n then has expected size n/N, which vanishes as $N \to \infty$. When $I_{\beta_1}(\alpha') \cap I_{\beta_2}(\alpha') = \varnothing$, the noises $Y_{\beta_1}^t$ and $Y_{\beta_2}^t$ are independent as required.

Thus with the modifications noted, the strong structure morphism from base to lumped model is preserved.

Exercise. Show that with appropriate modifications, the strong structure morphism continues to hold (a) when synaptic weights are allowed to vary within INFLUENCER sets, and (b) when delays are allowed in the transmission of pulses.

The case of finite BLOCK population size is another story, however, and we consider it in Section 13.5.

12.9 CHARACTERISTICS OF NATURALLY OCCURRING STRUCTURE MORPHISMS

The neural net lumping of Section 12.6 suggests certain generalizations. We know that the experimental frames employable are limited to those which relate to the aggregate behavior of blocks of components. In other words, the lumped model cannot answer questions concerning the individual behaviors of components. In addition, valid lumping can be guaranteed by imposing the constraints of *homogeneity of components in a block* and *uniformity of influence among blocks.* "Homogeneity of components" indicates that all the components in a block share the same structure. In the neuron net example, uniformity of influence takes the form of the uniform influence of a block on the components of a block it influences. In general, however, it may take the form of uniform influence of components on blocks, where each component of one block influences another block in the same way. Or, it may involve both uniform influence of blocks on components and components on blocks.

Indeed the homogeneity and uniformity constraints have been shown to provide sufficient conditions for achieving lumped models valid in aggregational experimental frames in such contexts as ecological modelling[3] (see structured specification morphisms, Section 10.6) and queueing networks.[4] Also, the approach taken in the neural context has been shown to generalize to networks of arbitrary stochastic automata.[5] This suggests that homogeneity and uniformity constraints may supply sufficient conditions for establishing structure morphisms in a wide variety of naturally occurring base models. Moreover, we would like to know the extent to which these conditions are also necessary in particular contexts.

This question leads to a second problem. Suppose that homogeneity and uniformity are sufficient to guarantee lumpability, but we have some basis for believing that such constraints are not characteristic of a base model of a particular real system. To what extent can such constraints be violated while still enabling lumpability? We can approach the problem by way of the concept of approximate specification morphism introduced in the next chapter. Here one would attempt to characterize the error introduced at each time step as a function of the deviation of the base model from the homogeneity and uniformity constraints. We might hope that the reader has been inspired to look more deeply into these problems.

12.10 SYSTEM DECOMPOSITION: COMPONENT ISOLATION AND IDENTIFICATION

In this section we illustrate informally some common ways of decomposing systems (i.e., separating them into more manageable parts). The parallel formal development is sketched in problems at the end of the chapter. Our approach is the following: suppose a base model consists of an interconnection of components, $A, B, C, \ldots$; since the components may interact, we suspect that it may be rather difficult to find experimental conditions in which a given component will be observed in "isolation" (indeed, recognition of this difficulty is what systems theory is all about).

Let us formulate the problem of isolating components within the conceptual framework we have developed. Given a component A, we seek an experimental frame E_A such that the behavior of the real system observable in E_A is "essentially" due to A. If such a frame exists, the structure of A can be *identified*, in that having validated a lumped model against the real system behavior in E_A, we would be in a position to infer the structure of A from that of the model. (We treat the identification issue itself in Chapter 15.)

We consider a series of cases of increasing difficulty.

12.11   PARALLEL DECOMPOSITION

When a decomposition can be found for which the components do not interact at all, we say that there is *parallel* decomposition. This is illustrated in Figure 4, where the influence diagram of a base model consisting of components S and T appears. The concept of parallel connection is formally defined in Problem 1.

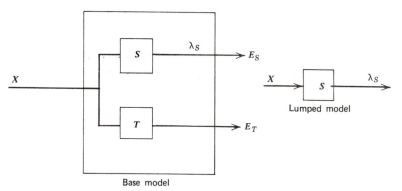

Figure 4   Base and lumped models for parallel decomposition.

To isolate S in Figure 4, we select a frame in which the base model output is affected by S only. Thus, if $Q_S \times Q_T$ is the base model state set, E_S specifies an output map λ_S, which depends only on Q_S. No other restrictions are required. We can show (Problem 1) that S is then a homomorphic image of B/E_S (the base model in E_S), hence that R_E (the observable behavior in E_S) is that of S alone. Accordingly, a valid lumped model in frame E_S is S itself.

12.12   SERIES DECOMPOSITION

In a *series* decomposition, the components may interact, but only in a nonfeedback way. Component S in Figure 5 influences component T, but is not itself influenced by T. The isolation of S may proceed exactly as in the case of parallel decomposition (Problem 2). Since S affects T, however, the same technique will not suffice for isolating T. The important special case for which some isolation can be achieved is discussed next.

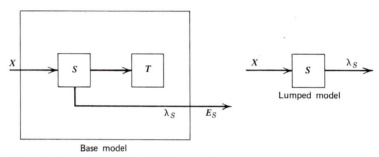

Figure 5   Base and lumped models for series decomposition.

12.13   SLOW FAST SERIES DECOMPOSITION

Suppose that the operation of S in Figure 6a is relatively fast compared to that of T. Let us call S the fast component and T the slow component. Assume that S operates so fast that its input-output function can be regarded

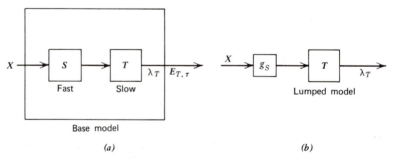

Figure 6   The case of slow-fast series decomposition.

as instantaneous, on a time scale appropriate to T's operation. Under these conditions, the dynamic response of the real system viewed at the output of T is essentially that of T, with S acting as an input encoder (see Figure 6b).

Let us take the first steps in formalizing these ideas. The basic requirements, that S "look" like an instantaneous operator on the time scale of T, can be broken down into two conditions:

1. There is a time duration τ such that the initial state of S at the beginning of an input segment has no effect on the output after τ time units have elapsed. We say that S has *definite* memory of length τ—it "forgets" what its state was, hence all previous input history prior to τ units.
2. No matter what its input segment is like, the state of T does not change appreciably during a period of length τ. For example, let $\tau = 1$ second and consider an input segment 10 seconds long. By condition 1, any effect of the initial state of S will appear in the first second; after that, the output of S will be entirely due to the input segment. By condition 2, T will be very little affected by the output of S in the first second, and its state at the end of 10 seconds will be almost entirely due to the last 9 seconds of input received from S. For example, if T has a "relaxation time" of one hour, its state changes very little during one second—in this sense, S is fast on the time scale of slower acting T.

Thus we can say that S encodes homomorphically input segments of length 10 for input to T. Observing the output of T, we see the dynamic response of T to these segments. Thus the appropriate experimental frame $E_{T,\tau}$ specifies (1) an output map λ_T which depends only on Q_T, and (2) a restriction on the admissible input segments to the real system (e.g., $\Omega_{E_{T,\tau}}$ is the subset of base model admissible segments of length 10τ). In this case the lumped model M_τ of Figure 6b is an approximate homomorphic image of $B/E_{T,\tau}$ and $R_{E_{T,\tau}}$ is approximately equal to R_{M_τ} (Problem 3b).

Thus the observable behavior of the real system in frame $E_{T,\tau}$ can be attributed to the lumped model M_τ. But since M_τ does not consist entirely of component T, we still do not know whether T itself can be isolated. The answer to this question is affirmative in the following sense.

Since S is a front component, as in Section 12.12, we can construct a valid model for S within frame E_S. This model provides us with the encoding performed by S on segments of length 10τ. Employing this encoding (called g_S in Figure 6b) and the identity decoding, it is not hard to see that there is an I/O system morphism from T to M_τ as shown in Figure 7 (see Problem 3b). Thus T and M_τ have the same structure and behavior when factored through the known pair of encoding and decoding maps.

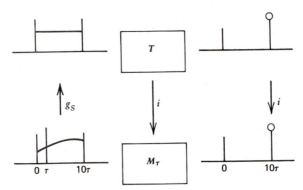

Figure 7 The relation between T and M_τ.

12.14 FEEDBACK DECOMPOSITION

Consider now the case in which components S and T interact in a symmetrical way. As in Figure 8a, there is a feedback cycle containing both components. Under the same assumptions as before, we can still isolate component S, but we must exercise greater control on the experimental conditions. In fact we must begin to use the "range of validity" component of experimental frames. By assumption, the state of T therefore its output, is approximately constant in an interval of length τ. Thus the output of S over such an interval reflects its response to an input consisting of the external input and the constant input from T arriving via the feedback path. Over such an interval, a lumped model of the form in Figure 8b would be valid with the parameter value set to that of the feedback to S in the base model. As soon as T changes its output, however, the parameter setting is no longer valid and must be reset to correspond to the new T output.

The appropriate experimental frame is then really a class of frames $\{E_{S,T,c} | c \in \lambda(Q_T)\}$. Since each frame $E_{S,T,c}$ specifies the same output map $\lambda_S \times \lambda_T$ [$\lambda_S \times \lambda_T(q_S, q_T) = (\lambda_S(q_S), \lambda_T(q_T))$], we can distinguish outputs of each of the components separately. However, the range of validity of a frame is parameterized by its "c" component, namely, $V_{E_{S,T,c}} = \{(\lambda_S(q_S), c) | q_S \in Q_S\}$. In other words, frame $E_{S,T,c}$ is valid as long as the output observed from T remains constant at value c.

In this case the sense in which component S can be isolated is less straightforward than before. It would be natural to consider as a lumped model the parameterized system S_c—which is component S with T-originating input wire held at the (parameter-specified) value c. In frame $E_{S,T,c}$, however, model S_c is valid in a weakened sense—while the real system remains within the range of validity, the two I/O behaviors agree; but when this range

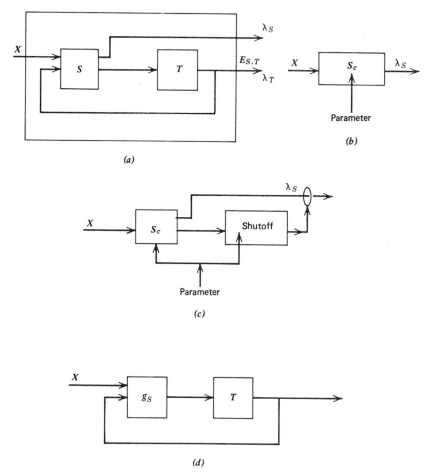

Figure 8   The case of feedback decomposition.

is violated, the behaviors disagree, since $B/E_{S, T, c}$ would be emitting the blank symbol ϕ and S_c would continue on its merry way. The complete validity required by Postulate 10 would call for the augmentation of S_c by a shutoff component (Figure 8c), which would predict the points at which the range of validity is violated. This component would be in effect a model of T needed only to predict whether a change in T's output occurs. Many unsolved problems are opened up by this observation. (See Problem 4.)

Finally, let us attempt to isolate the slow component T. It appears that the best we can hope for is the model in Figure 8d, where component S is represented as an instantaneous map. In this case, because of the feedback loop, there is no experimental frame in which the behavior of the real system can be identified with that of T. However, it may still be advantageous to employ the frame $E_{T,\,\tau}$. Having identified S in the frames $\{E_{S,\,T,\,c}\}$, the representation of S as an instantaneous operator may yet greatly decrease the amount of experimentation necessary to identify the T component.

12.15 SOURCES

Stochastic automata are discussed by Paz.[6]

1. B. P. Zeigler, "Statistical Simplification of Neural Nets," *International Journal of Man–Machine Studies*, 7, 1975. 371–393.

2. W. Feller, *An Introduction to Probability Theory and Its Applications*, Vol. I. Wiley, New York, 1957.

3. B. P. Zeigler, "The Aggregation Problem," in *Systems Analysis and Simulation in Ecology*, Vol. 4, B. C. Patten (Ed.). In preparation.

4. B. Melamed, "Analysis and Simplification of Stochastic Systems with Applications to Jackson Queueing Networks." *Doctoral Dissertation*, University of Michigan, Ann Arbor, 1976.

5. S. Aggarwal, "Ergodic Machines—Probabilistic and Approximate Homomorphic Simplification." Doctoral dissertation, University of Michigan, Ann Arbor, 1975.

6. A. Paz, *Introduction to Probabilistic Automata*. Academic Press, New York, 1971.

7. J. N. Perram, "Relaxation Times in Bacteriological Culture and the Approach to Steady State." *Journal of Theoretical Biology*, **38** (3), 571, 578 1973.

PROBLEMS

Let $S = \langle T_S, X_S, \Omega_S, Q_S, Y_S, \delta_S, \lambda_S \rangle$ and $T = \langle T_T, X_T, \Omega_T, Q_T, Y_T, \delta_T, \lambda_T \rangle$ be I/O systems.

1. A *parallel* connection of S and T is a structure

$$S \times T = \langle T, X, \Omega, Q, Y, \delta, \lambda \rangle$$

where $T = T_S = T_T$; $X = X_S = X_T$; $\Omega = \Omega_S = \Omega_T$; $Q = Q_S \times Q_T$; Y is an arbitrary set; $\lambda: Q \rightarrow Y$ an arbitrary mapping, and $\delta(q_1, q_2, \omega) = (\delta_S(q_1, \omega), \delta_T(q_2, \omega))$.

(a) Show that $S \times T$ is an I/O system.

(b) Show that S is a homomorphic image of $S \times T$, provided

$$Y = Y_S \qquad \text{and} \qquad \lambda(q_1, q_2) = \lambda_S(q_1).$$

(c) Using previous theorems, conclude that $\tilde{B}_{S \times T} = \tilde{B}_S$ and

$$R_{S \times T} = R_S \qquad \text{for the given choice of } \lambda.$$

2. A *series* connection of S and T is a structure

$$S \ominus T = \langle T, X, \Omega, Q, Y, \delta, \lambda \rangle$$

where $T = T_S = T_T; X = X_S; \Omega = \Omega_S; Q = Q_S \times Q_T; Y$ is an arbitrary set; $\lambda : Q \to Y$ is an arbitrary mapping, and

$$\delta(q_1, q_2, \omega) = (\delta_S(q_1, \omega), \delta_T(q_2, \tilde{\beta}_{q_1}(\omega)))$$

(a) Show that if $Y_S \subseteq X_T$ and $\text{proj}_1(R_S) \subseteq \Omega_T$, then $S \ominus T$ is a system.
(b) Show that S is a homomorphic image of $S \ominus T$, provided

$$Y = Y_S \qquad \text{and} \qquad \lambda(q_1, q_2) = \lambda_S(q_1).$$

(c) Give a counterexample to show that in general there is no choice of Y and λ that will make T a homomorphic image of $S \ominus T$.

3. In this problem we show how to formulate slow-fast series decomposition when conditions 1 and 2 (page 321) hold exactly. Consideration of the more realistic case, involving approximation, is delayed until after the relevant concepts have been introduced (see Problem 2, Chapter 13). Consider the series connection $S \ominus T$ as in Problem 2a.

We say that S has *definite memory of order* Δ, if $\beta_{q_1}(\omega) = \beta_{q_i'}(\omega)$ for all pairs $q_1, q_1' \in Q_s$ and $\omega \in \Omega$ such that $l(\omega) \geq \Delta$.

We say that *T is slow in* Δ if $\delta_T(q_2, \omega) = q_2$, for all $q_2 \in Q_T$ and $\omega \in \Omega_T$ such that $l(\omega) = \Delta$.

Consider a structure $M_\tau = \langle T, X, \Omega_\tau, Q, Y, \delta_\tau, \lambda \rangle$, where $T = T_S = T_T; X = X_S; \Omega_\tau = \{\omega | \omega \in \Omega_S, l(\omega) = \tau\}; Q = Q_T; Y = Y_T; \lambda = \lambda_T;$ and $\delta_\tau : Q_T \times \Omega_\tau \to Q_T$ is given by

$$\delta_\tau(q, \omega) = \delta_T(q, Z(\omega))$$

where $Z : \Omega_\tau \to (Y_S, T_S)$ is given by

$$Z(\omega) = \tilde{\beta}_{\bar{q}_1}(\omega) \qquad \text{for some fixed } \bar{q}_1 \in Q_s$$

(a) Show that M_τ is an iterative specification and characterize the system S_{M_τ}.
(b) Show that (g, h, k) given below is a system morphism from $S \ominus T$ to S_{M_τ}, provided $\tau \geq \Delta$, Ω_S is segmentable at Δ, $Y = Y_T$, and $\lambda(q_1, q_2) = \lambda_T(q_2)$. The triple (g, h, k) is defined by

$$g : \Omega_\tau^+ \to \Omega_S$$

is the identity embedding $g(\omega) = \omega$ (note $\omega \in \Omega_\tau^+$ has length an integral multiple of τ).

$$h : Q_S \times Q_T \to Q_T$$

as the projection $h(q_1, q_2) = q_2$; and $k : Y_T \to Y_T$ is the identity mapping $i(y) = y$.

(c)   Show that (g_S, i, i) is a system morphism from T to S_{M_τ} where $g_S:\Omega_\tau^+ \to \Omega_T$ is the extension of the encoding

$$g_S:\Omega_\tau \to \Omega_T$$

where $g_S(\omega) = Z(\omega)$

4.   Provide a formalization of the concepts developed for feedback decomposition in Section 12.14.

5.   In a chemical reactor the bacteria concentration s and the nutrient concentration x interaction is modelled by

$$\frac{dx}{dt} = x(f(s) - D)$$

$$\frac{ds}{dt} = D(u(t) - s) - xf(s) \tag{1}$$

where $f(s)$ governs the rate of conversion of nutrient to bacteria at nutrient level s, D is a constant representing the constant rate at which the reactor is flushed, and $u(t)$ is the input at time t which determines the total bacteria–nutrient concentration possible.[†]

(a)   Formalize the differential equations as a DESS without outputs and consider this to be the base model B.

(b)   Formalize the equation

$$\frac{dz}{dt} = D(u(t) - z)$$

as a DESS M and show that it is a homomorphic image of B. *Hint.*   Consider the aggregation mapping $(x, s) \mapsto x + s$ (i.e., set $z = x + s$ in Equation 1). For which experimental frame E is M, with a suitable output map, valid with respect to B/E?

(c)   Show that the DESS B' formalizing the equations

$$\frac{dz}{dt} = D(u(t) - z)$$

$$\frac{ds}{dt} = D(u(t) - s) - f(s)(z - s) \tag{2}$$

is isomorphic to B. *Hint.*   Consider the map $(x, s) \to (x + s, s)$.

(d)   Note that B' is a series composition of components S and T with state variables z and s, respectively. It happens that often the total concentration z equilibrates rapidly compared with that of the

---

[†] This problem is based on an analysis by J. N. Perram.[7]

(original) component concentrations. Thus in these cases S and T can be taken as the fast and slow components as in Section 12.13.

Formalize an experimental frame in which input segments are piecewise constant of length $30D$ and the output is nutrient concentration. Characterize the coding g_S and the model of Figure 6b. *Hint.* If $u(t) \equiv a$, $z(t)$ approaches a with relaxation time D; substitute $z = a$ in Equation 2; the model actually has analytic solutions in cases such as $f(s) = (k \cdot s)/(k^2 + s)$.

Chapter Thirteen

Approximation and Error Tolerance

To aspire to the strict agreement of I/O pairs demanded by Postulate 10 would be unrealistic in most modelling situations on two counts: (1) strict equality may be impossible to determine and (2) the construction of approximate but nevertheless useful models, would be inhibited. (We have already seen such situations in Chapter 12.) Thus it becomes important to augment the basic framework to allow looser notions of validity. Unfortunately the theory of approximation in modelling has not received the attention it deserves in the literature,[1, 2] and we can only sketch the main considerations.

Likewise, approximation is an ever-present participant in the simulation relation. One aspect of this problem, however, has received much attention—namely, the simulation of differential equation systems by digital computers. Because much literature is available on this subject, (see Reference 4 of Chapter 5), we simply place the problem in a systems perspective. This formulation is found in Problem 1, Chapter 16.

13.1 GOODNESS OF FIT CRITERIA

The selection of *goodness of fit* measures (for determining how well the model and real system I/O pairs agree) is a fundamentally important choice the modeller must make. Abstractly, we phrase the problem as one of selecting a metric[†] on the space of all input-output pairs. Let (X, T) and (Y, T) be the input and output segment spaces. A metric d assigns a real number as a distance between any two I/O pairs; $d((\omega, \rho), (\omega', \rho'))$, the distance determined by the metric between pairs (ω, ρ) and (ω', ρ'), can be interpreted as the magnitude of the error (deviation or disagreement) between the pairs. Examples of such metrics follow the first set of exercises.

Having chosen his goodness of fit measures, the modeller finds himself making judgments of the following kind: "The output generated by the model is in reasonable agreement with the observed data," or, "The fit between model and real system curves is acceptable for the purposes at hand."

When making these judgments, the modeller is setting a level for deciding when model and real system I/O pairs *are close enough for the purposes for which the model is intended.* What the modeller may informally refer to as "reasonable" or "acceptable" agreement may then be captured more rigorously by the notion of *tolerance,* which can be defined with reference to an *acceptance level L*—a model pair (ω', ρ') is within *tolerance* of a real system pair (ω, ρ) if $d((\omega', \rho'), (\omega, \rho)) \leq L$.

In other words, "(ω', ρ') is within tolerance of (ω, ρ)" means that (ω', ρ') is close enough to (ω, ρ) to be judged to be in "reasonable" or "acceptable" agreement with it. How close is "close enough" is determined by the acceptance level L selected by the modeller.

The concept of model validity put forth in Postulate 10 may accordingly be weakened to

Postulate 10′. **A lumped model M is valid *within tolerance* or *acceptably valid* with respect to frame E if for every pair $(\omega, \rho) \in R_{S(M)}$, there is a pair $(\omega', \rho') \in R_{B/E}$ within tolerance, and conversely.**

In short, "equality" is replaced by "within tolerance."

Exercise. Show that tolerance is a reflexive, symmetric, but not necessarily transitive, relation.

Exercise. Show that when $L = 0$, the tolerance becomes an identity relation and the "acceptable validity" of Postulate 10′ reduces to the "validity" of Postulate 10.

Often a metric on $(X, T) \times (Y, T)$ is made up of metrics separately defined on the input space (X, T) and output space (Y, T). Thus one might

---

[†] A metric on a set Z is a map $d: Z^2 \to R$ such that (1) $d(z, z) = 0$ for all $z \in Z$; (2) $d(z_1, z_2) = d(z_2, z_1)$ for all pairs $z_1, z_2 \in Z$; and (3) $d(z_1, z_3) \leq d(z_1, z_2) + d(z_2, z_3)$ for all triples $z_1, z_2, z_3 \in Z$ *(the triangle inequality).*

set $d((\omega, \rho), (\omega', \rho'))$ equal to $d_I(\omega, \omega') + d_O(\rho, \rho')$ or to max $\{d_I(\omega, \omega'),$ $d_O(\rho, \rho')\}$, where d_I and d_O are metrics chosen for (X, T) and (Y, T), respectively. Moreover, often a modeller has control over the input segments applied to both the model and the real system. In this case, he may wish to judge validity by comparing model and system output responses to the same input segment. This amounts to choosing $d_I(\omega, \omega') = \infty$ for $\omega \neq \omega'$, and $d_I(\omega, \omega) = 0$.

Exercise. Verify the foregoing statement by showing that the definitions of tolerance and acceptable validity reduce to those required.

A very commonly employed class of metrics consists of those arising from norms defined on linear spaces. The maximum, integral absolute, and integral square error criteria are familiar examples. A *norm* assigns a distance from 0 (of the linear space) to every element. Table 1 defines the examples just cited.

Table 1   Some Common Norms

Criterion	Definition of Norm
Maximum	$\|\rho\| = \max \{\rho(t) \mid t \in \text{dom}(\rho)\}$
Integral absolute	$\|\rho\| = \int_{\text{dom}(\rho)} \|\rho(t)\| \, dt$
Integral square	$\|\rho\| = \int_{\text{dom}(\rho)} \rho^2(t) \, dt$

Having a norm $\| \ \|$, the metric d_O is defined by $d_O(\rho, \rho') = \|\rho - \rho'\|$, that is, the distance between ρ and ρ' is the distance of $\rho - \rho'$ from zero. Thus, for example, for the integral square, $d_O(\rho, \rho') = \int_{[0, \tau]} [\rho(t) - \rho'(t)]^2 \, dt$, where $[0, \tau]$ is the common domain of ρ and ρ'. Since $e = \rho - \rho'$ is the error trajectory, $d_O(\rho, \rho')$ is the integral square error.

Another large class of metrics can be generated as follows. One selects a function $f : (Y, T) \to Z$, where Z has a metric d_Z; then $d_O(\rho, \rho') \underset{\text{def}}{=} d_Z(f(\rho),$ $f(\rho'))$ is a metric. (Verify this.) For example, $f(\rho)$ may be the asymptotic value of ρ, the value of ρ at a predetermined set of points, the number of events in ρ of a certain kind, the derivative of ρ at a given point, and so on. Thus f *picks out those aspects of the output segments considered to be important for determining acceptable agreement.*

As in Figure 1, different choices of f will have different consequences for deciding when real and model segments agree. The asymptotic values are of interest in the upper sketch, whereas in the lower diagram, the derivatives at time 0 are the criterion. Clearly ρ and ρ' may be judged to be close under the first choice, but far apart under the second. For the choice of acceptance

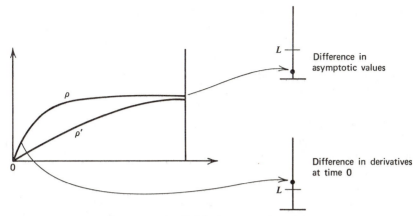

Figure 1 Two ways of measuring the distance between trajectories.

level L shown, ρ and ρ' will be accepted as within tolerance (or in reasonable agreement) in the first choice but not the second.

Exercise. Define f and Z for the case when asymptotic values are of interest and for the case when derivatives at time 0 are of interest.

Exercise. Show that the integral absolute error criterion tends to ignore large differences that occur over short periods, while the maximum error criterion ignores long periods of relatively small differences. Display two segments ρ and ρ' such that ρ is closer to zero as measured by the integral absolute error criterion but the opposite is the case when the maximum error criterion is used.

Thus we see that the choice of metric for goodness of fit criterion may be decisive in judging the validity of a model. A model may be judged to be acceptably valid with one choice of metric and rejected with another choice.

13.2 ERROR PROPAGATION

The concepts associated with relaxing the requirements used in comparing the model and real system trajectories are in the behavioral domain. We now move to the structural domain, with the aim of beginning to relate structural mismatching to behavioral consequences. Again we carry out the discussion within the sequential machine (discrete time system specification) context.

The problem is the following: suppose we have two compatible sequential machines $M = \langle X, Q, Y, \delta, \lambda \rangle$ and $M' = \langle X, Q', Y, \delta', \lambda \rangle$. Instead of an exact homomorphism (Section 10.5.1), we have a mapping $h: Q \xrightarrow{\text{onto}} Q'$ which is an approximate homomorphism in that the transition and output functions are preserved only approximately. Were h a true homomorphism, the I/O function sets, hence the I/O relations, of the two machines would be identical (i.e., we would have exact behavioral agreement). What can we say about behavioral agreement when h is only an approximate homomorphism?

This situation occurs in two contexts—in the relation between the base and the lumped models, and in the relation between the computer and the lumped model. We presented an example in Section 12.8, of an approximate homomorphism between base and lumped models. In Section 5.8, we saw how error could be generated in the computer simulation of a model. This problem has been studied extensively by numerical analysts in the context of differential equation simulation. The basic concepts, however, concern the behavioral consequences of a system morphism that holds only approximately between two system structures. These concepts can be nicely illustrated in the case of sequential machines.

13.3   OUTPUT FUNCTION MISMATCH

Sometimes the transition functions match up exactly but error is introduced in the output function. To formulate the problem, suppose we have a metric d_Y on the output set Y, and ε is a bound on the mismatch in output from corresponding states (i.e., for all $q \in Q$ we have $d_Y(\lambda'(h(q)), \lambda(q)) \le \varepsilon$.

Let us apply an arbitrary input sequence $\omega = x_1 x_2 \cdots x_n$ to both M and M'. Since we are assuming h to be an exact transition preserving homomorphism ($h(\delta(q, x)) = \delta'(h(q), x)$), we will have exactly corresponding state trajectories $q_1, q_2 \cdots q_n$ and $h(q_1) h(q_2) \cdots h(q_n)$ (where q_1 and $h(q_1)$ are the initial states). But because of the approximate output preservation, the associated output trajectories $y_1, y_2 \cdots y_n$ and $y'_1, y'_2 \cdots y'_n$ would be such that for each i, $d_Y(y_i, y'_i) \le \varepsilon$. Thus if we select the metric d_O on the output segment space Y^* such that

$$d_O(a_1 \cdots a_n, b_1 \cdots b_n) = \max_{i \le i \le n} \{d(a_i, b_i)\}$$

then

$$d_O(y_1 \cdots y_n, y'_1 \cdots y'_n) \le \varepsilon.$$

In this case there is no error buildup or "zero error propagation"—no matter how long the input segment is, the deviation between output segments remains bounded by the error introduced at each step.

Exercise. If M is B/E and M' is a lumped model, for what range of acceptance levels L would M' be acceptably valid in frame E?

13.4 TRANSITION FUNCTION MISMATCH

In the output function mismatch case just presented, there is zero error propagation because the error introduced at a step is not "fed back," thus does not influence later steps. This is not necessarily the case when transition function mismatch occurs.

For simplicity let us consider autonomous state machines $M = \langle Q, \delta \rangle$ and $M' = \langle Q', \delta' \rangle$. Let d be a metric on the state space Q'. Let ε be a bound on the mismatch in transition function preservation, so that for all $q \in Q$, we have

$$d(h(\delta(q)), \delta'(h(q))) \leq \varepsilon \tag{1}$$

Thus at every step an error may be introduced, and we must determine how this error will propagate over many time steps.

To understand the processes involved, let $q_1 q_2 \cdots q_n$ be a trajectory traced out in the state space by the big machine M. This trajectory appears in the little state space Q' as a sequence $h(q_1)h(q_2) \cdots h(q_n)$. But starting from state $h(q_1)$, M' will generate a trajectory $h(q_1)q_2' \cdots q_n'$ which, because h is only an approximate homomorphism, may differ from the true trajectory $h(q_1) \cdots h(q_n)$. There are three possibilities:

(a)   *Unbounded error propagation*—the error grows without bound.
(b)   *Ultimately bounded error propagation*—the trajectories remain finitely close together.
(c)   *Zero error propagation*—as in the output function mismatch case.

We can explain how these cases arise by seeking bounds on the maximum and minimum deviations of the trajectories $h(q_1)h(q_2) \cdots h(q_n)$ and $h(q_1)q_2' \cdots q_n'$.

In a heuristic manner and referring to Figure 2a, let us look at what happens in the first two transitions. At step 1, M is in state q_1 and M' is in state $q_1' = h(q_1)$.

At step 2, M goes to state $q_2 = \delta(q_1)$ which corresponds to state $h(q_2)$ in M_1'. At the same time, M' goes to state $q_2' = \delta'(q_1')$. Were h an exact homomorphism, $h(q_2)$ would equal q_2'. But since it is not, Equation 1 tells us that $h(q_2)$ and q_2' can differ by as many ε units. Let us suppose the worst has happened, and we have

$$d(h(q_2), q_2') = \varepsilon \tag{2}$$

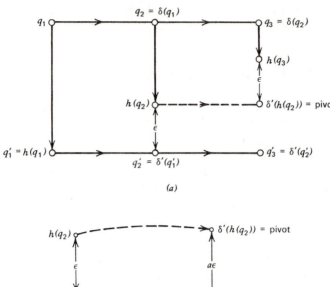

(a)

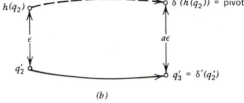

(b)

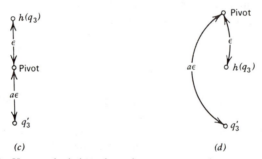

(c)   (d)

Figure 2   How to obtain bounds on the error propagation.

At step 3, M goes to state $q_3 = \delta(q_2)$, which corresponds to $h(q_3)$ in M'. At the same time M' goes to state $q'_3 = \delta'(q'_2)$. How far away apart can $h(q_3)$ and q'_3 be?

To answer this question, we examine what happens to state $h(q_2)$ of M'. At step 3, $h(q_2)$ goes to $\delta'(h(q_2))$ in M'. Let us call $\delta'(h(q_2))$ the *pivot state*, since we are going to relate the distance from $h(q_3)$ to q'_3 to the distances of the latter two states to $\delta'(h(q_2))$.

For the distance from $h(q_3)$ to the pivot state, notice that $h(q_3) = h(\delta(q_2))$, and this would equal $\delta'(h(q_2))$ for an exact homomorphism. But since h is not exact, we have from Equation 1

$$d(h(q_3), \delta'(h(q_2))) \leq \varepsilon \tag{3}$$

To find the distance from q_3' to the pivot state, we need Figure 2b, where the pivot state $\delta'(h(q_2))$ and q_3' are successor states in M' of states $h(q_2)$ and q_2'.

Now the way in which M' maps states into successors will determine how the distance between a pair of states will be transformed into the distance between their successors. We can represent the distance between the successor states $\delta'(h(q_2))$ and q_3' in terms of the distance between their predecessors $h(q_2)$ and q_2' by

$$d(\delta(h(q_2)), q_3') = d(h(q_2), q_2') \cdot a$$
$$= \varepsilon \cdot a \tag{4}$$

(using Equation 2), where a is a nonnegative number.

To put together the two distances to the pivot state, consider Figures 2c and 2d.

In Figure 2c we see that

$$d(q_3', h(q_3)) \leq a\varepsilon + \varepsilon = (a + 1)\varepsilon \tag{5}$$

Thus q_3' and $h(q_3)$ are at most $(a + 1)\varepsilon$ units apart after two steps.

Figure 2d indicates that

$$d(q_3', h(q_3)) \geq a\varepsilon - \varepsilon = (a - 1)\varepsilon \tag{6}$$

that is, q_3' and $h(q_3)$ are at least $(a - 1)\varepsilon$ units apart after two steps. (We are relying on geometrical intuition here; formally, the triangle inequality of the metric d is used as in the ensuing exercises.)

Now we can explain how the three cases of error propagation mentioned earlier can arise.

(a)   If a of Equation 4 is greater than 1, so that the distance between a pair of states is *amplified* after a single transition, we see from Equation 6 that

$$d(q_3', h(q_3)) \geq (a - 1)\varepsilon > 0 \tag{7}$$

Suppose that all succeeding transitions are characterized by the same value of a.

Then repeating the foregoing argument, at step 4 we have

$$d(q_4', h(q_3)) \geq a(a - 1)\varepsilon - \varepsilon = (a^2 - a - 1)\varepsilon \tag{8}$$

and so on to step n, where

$$d(q_n', h(q_n)) \geq (a^{n-2} - a^{n-3} - \cdots - a - 1)\varepsilon \tag{9}$$

Since $a > 1$, we see that the error

$$e_n = d(q'_n, h(q_n))$$

grows without bound as n increases (in fact, exponentially). Therefore, we have the case of *unbounded error propagation*.

(b) If a of Equation 4 is less than 1, the distance between a pair of states is *attenuated* after a single transition. Here Equation 5 proves to be the most applicable. Assuming the same value of a for successive transitions and repeating the argument, at step 4 we have

$$d(q'_4, h(q_3)) \leq a(a + 1)\varepsilon + \varepsilon = (a^2 + a + 1)\varepsilon \qquad (10)$$

and so on to step n, where

$$d(q'_n, h(q_n)) \leq (a^{n-2} + a^{n-3} + \cdots + a + 1)\varepsilon \qquad (11)$$

But now since $a < 1$, we have

$$e_n = d(q'_n, h(q_n)) \leq \left(\frac{a^{n-1} - 1}{a - 1}\right)\varepsilon \qquad (12)$$

Thus as n increases, e_n is bounded by $\varepsilon/(1 - a)$. This is the case of *ultimately bounded error propagation*, and the accumulated error is attenuated by M'. Although the error may grow at first, ultimately a balance is reached: at each step, the error introduced (ε) is offset by the attentuation of error already accumulated.

(c) Finally, for the case $a = 0$, we have from Equation 12, that for each n

$$e_n \leq \varepsilon \qquad (13)$$

This is the case of *zero error propagation*. Here, the error introduced at any step is forgotten at the next step, and no error is propagated or accumulated.

We see that how well, or how badly, the behavior of the base and lumped (or computer and lumped) models will agree over time can be predicted from two quantities:

1. The error in the homomorphism introduced at each step: ε.
2. The manner in which an error, once introduced, is amplified or attenuated by the lumped model transition function: a.

Since quantity a is a property of the lumped model alone, we can see that a lumped model has the potentiality to predict not only how a real system will behave, but how accurately one should expect its own predictions to be! More of this after we have formalized our argument.

The amplification factor referred to previously can be defined in two ways. Let

$$a_* = \inf_{\substack{q_1, q_2 \in Q' \\ q_1 \neq q_2}} \frac{d(\delta'(q_1), \delta'(q_2))}{d(q_1, q_2)}$$

$$a^* = \sup_{\substack{q_1, q_2 \in Q' \\ q_1 = q_2}} \frac{d(\delta'(q_1), \delta'(q_2))}{d(q_1, q_2)}$$

In other words, we have

$$d(\delta'(q_1), \delta'(q_2)) \geq a_* \, d(q_1, q_2) \quad \text{and} \quad d(\delta'(q_1), \delta'(q_2)) \leq a^* \, d(q_1, q_2)$$

for all distinct pairs $q_1, q_2 \in Q'$.

We say that M' is *error unstable* if $a_* > 1$ and M' is *error stable* if $a^* < 1$. Let e_n be the error at step n; that is,

$$e_n = d(h(q_n), q_n')$$

so that $e_1 = 0$.

Exercise.   Show that

(a) $e_n \leq \left(\dfrac{a^{*n-1} - 1}{a^* - 1} \right) \varepsilon.$

(b)   If M' is error stable, conclude that for all n, $e_n \leq \varepsilon/(1 - a^*)$.

(c)   If M' is error unstable, assume that $\varepsilon_1 = \varepsilon$ and show that

$$e_n \geq a^{n-2} - \left(\frac{a_*^{n-2} - 1}{a^* - 1} \right) \varepsilon$$

conclude that for large n

$$e_n \approx a_*^{n-2} \varepsilon.$$

(d)   What can be said when $a^* = 1$?

Hint.   In a use the triangle inequality

$$d(h(q_n), q_n') \leq d(h(q_n), \delta'(h(q_{n-1}))) + d(\delta'(h(q_{n-1})), q_n')$$

and in c, the triangle inequality

$$d(\delta'(h(q_{n-1})), q_n') \leq d(\delta'(h(q_{n-1}), h(q_n)) + d(h(q_n), q_n')$$

Exercise.   Let Q' be the output set of M and M' with output functions h and the identity, respectively. Using the maximum error metric, for which values of acceptance level L would M' be acceptably valid with respect to M in the case that M' is error stable? error unstable?

Exercise.   Define an approximate homomorphism between machines M and M' in which there is both transition and output function mismatch. If the output function λ' is metric preserving, what can you say about the validity of M' as a model of M? (Note that λ' is metric preserving if $d_Y(\lambda'(q_1'), \lambda'(q_2')) = d(q_1', q_2')$).

13.5 MODELLING THE ERROR AS NOISE

By characterizing the error introduced at each step only by a bound ε on its magnitude, we have been able to obtain lower and upper bounds on error propagation, but not to say what the error is likely to be. To make such probabilistic statements, we would have to be able to characterize the error introduced at each step in a probabilistic manner (i.e., to regard the error as a noise generated by some known stochastic process). We can illustrate how such an approach might work in the case of our neuron net models (Chapter 12). Consider, for simplicity, a base model consisting of a single block of N neurons and its corresponding lumped version. When $N \to \infty$, under appropriate structural conditions, the mapping h (where $h(q) = f^q$) is a homomorphism. When N is finite, however, h is only an approximate homomorphism.

Let us choose a metric d on the lumped model space Q', where

$$d(p, p') = \max_{0 \le i \le i_m} |p(i) - p'(i)|$$

(Recall that a typical state p is a probability mass function on the RECOVERY $\cdot$ STATES $\{0, 1, \ldots, i_m\}$; thus $d(p, p')$ is the largest difference in the probabilities assigned by p and p').

How shall we model the error introduced at each transition? If the lumped model is in state p, it predicts that the N RECOVERY $\cdot$ STATE variables in the base model are iid with distribution p. Thus regarding the variables as independent samples from a pot (Appendix C) with pmf p, the N samples may result in a distribution f different from p. The chi square distribution with i_m degrees of freedom is then the appropriate probabilistic characterization. To see this more formally, let $S = \{0, 1, \ldots i_m\}$ be the sample space of the pot and let p be the pmf (so that $p(i)$ is the probability of obtaining RECOVERY $\cdot$ STATE i). Each of N neurons samples from S, giving a joint sample space S^N. The random variable $X : S^N \to R$ where

$$X(s) = N \sum_{i=0}^{i_m} \frac{(f^s(i) - p(i))^2}{p(i)}$$

is approximately $\chi^2_{i_m}$ distributed (Appendix C, f^s is the distribution of RECOVERY $\cdot$ STATES obtained from sample s.) Thus

$$P(\{s | X(s) \le x_\alpha\}) = F_{\chi^2_{i_m}}(x_\alpha).$$

Let $\alpha = .01$ so that $F_{\chi^2_{i_m}}(x_{.01}) = .99$ and for a given degree of freedom i_m we can find $x_{.01}$ in the 99% column of the tabular portion of Figure 5 in Appendix C. Then

$$p\left(\left\{f\,|\,N\sum_{i=0}^{i_m}\frac{[f(i)-p(i)]^2}{p(i)}\leq x_{.01}\right\}\right)$$
$$= p(\{s\,|\,X(s)\leq x_{.01}\})$$
$$= .99$$

In other words, with probability .99, when the lumped model is in state p, by pure chance the base model may be in any state q with distribution f^q for which

$$N\sum_{i=0}^{i_m}\frac{[f^q(i)-p(i)]^2}{p(i)}\leq x_{.01}$$

The set of such distributions is bounded an ellipsoid in i_{m+1}—space centered around point p, and satisfying

$$\sum_{i=0}^{i_m}\frac{[f(i)-p(i)]^2}{p(i)}=\frac{x_{.01}}{N}$$

The extrema on the ith axis satisfy

$$\frac{[f(i)-p(i)]^2}{p(i)}=\frac{x_{.01}}{N}$$

or

$$f(i)=p(i)\pm\sqrt{p(i)\left(\frac{x_{.01}}{N}\right)}$$

Thus for any such distribution f, we have

$$d(f,p)=\max_{0\leq i\leq i_m}|f(i)-p(i)|$$
$$\leq\max_{0\leq i\leq i_m}\sqrt{p(i)\left(\frac{x_{.01}}{N}\right)}$$
$$\leq\sqrt{\frac{x_{.01}}{N}}$$

Finally, recalling that $h(q)=f^q$, we have

$$d(h(\delta(q)),\delta'(h(q)))\leq\varepsilon$$

where $\varepsilon=\sqrt{x_{.01}/N}$.

In other words, if the base model is in state q and the lumped model is in state $f^q=h(q)$, the respective next states $\bar{q}$ and $\bar{p}$ are such that $\bar{q}$ is obtained by iid sampling from $\bar{p}$ and with .99 probability $d(f^{\bar{q}},\bar{p})\leqslant\varepsilon$. Note that as $N\to\infty$, $\varepsilon\to 0$, consistent with the law of large numbers.

Now employing the given value of ε, and obtaining the quantities a^* and a_* for a given lumped model, we can determine the error propagation bounds as in the previous section. However, having developed a probabilistic description of the error introduced at each step, we can hope to achieve a better prediction of the actual error propagation. This can be done by analysis and/or simulation of the lumped model subjected at every step to error generated according to the $\chi^2_{i_m}$ distribution.

Complete analysis would require the techniques of stochastic process theory, and it is likely that analytically intractable problems would arise. However, there may well be information that can be readily obtained by mapping out the transition behavior of the lumped model. For example, suppose the state space decomposes into a number of regions as indicated in Figure 3. Each region is the set of states attracted to a particular equilibrium point. Within each region, the flow lines converge toward the attractor, thus the attenuation factor a^* may be expected to be less than one (i.e., in each region the model is error stable). At the boundaries between regions, however, the model will be error unstable because two neighboring states, one on each side of a boundary, will be attracted to different equilibria.

Consider point A in Figure 3, in the interior of the stable region 1. For given N, the ellipsoidal neighborhood centered on A might overlap into region 2. The extent of the overlap would indicate the probability that

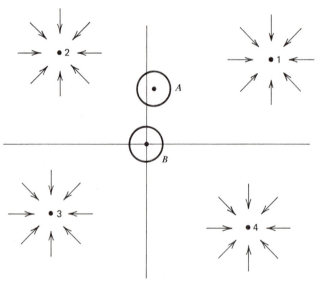

Figure 3 An illustrative case in which the lumped model state space divides into four quadrants, each having an equilibrium attractor (points 1, 2, 3, 4).

started in state A, the base model would end up at equilibrium 2, even though the lumped model would finish at equilibrium 1. As $N \to \infty$, the ellipsoidal neighborhood would contract to the point that the probability of such an ultimate error would vanish. Consider, on the other hand, point B situated on the boundary between regions. No matter how large N is, there is a nonzero probability that the base model will terminate in each of the equilibrium points.

Clearly with an analysis of this kind, much more can be ascertained about the predicted behavior of the base model than can be done by computing bounds on the error propagation alone. Again, this can be achieved with the help of a probabilistic characterization of the error introduced by the approximate homomorphism (ε) and a mapping of the amplification (or attenuation) properties (a^*, a_*) in the lumped model state space.

13.6 SOURCES

A general formulation of modelling and simulation in which approximation plays a central role has been developed by Corynen.[1] Appostal provides an excellent discussion of the various concepts of modelling and approximation.[2]

1. G. Corynen, "*A Mathematical Model of Modelling and Simulation.*" Doctoral dissertation, University of Michigan, Ann Arbor, 1974.
2. L. Appostal, "Towards the Formal Study of Models in the Non-Formal Sciences," in *The Concept and Role of the Model in Mathematics and the Natural and Social Sciences: A Colloquium*, H. Freudenthal (Ed.), D. Reidel, Dorecht, Holland, 1960, 1–37.

PROBLEMS

1. In this problem we generalize the concept of approximate homomorphism to that of approximate specification morphism. Let $G = \langle T, X, \Omega_G, Q, \delta_G \rangle$ and $G' = \langle T', X', \Omega'_G, Q', \delta_{G'} \rangle$ be iterative specifications without outputs. Let d be a metric on Q'.

    A pair (g, h) is a ε-*approximate specification morphism* (ε-morphism for short) if

    (a) $g : \Omega'_G \to \Omega^+_G$.
    (b) $h : \bar{Q} \xrightarrow{\text{onto}} Q'$, where $\bar{Q} \subseteq Q$.
    (c) $d(h(\bar{\delta}_G(q, g(\omega))), \delta_{G'}(h(q), \omega)) \leq \varepsilon$ for all $q \in Q$, $\omega' \in \Omega'_G$.

Prove that for all $q \in Q$, $\omega' \in \Omega_G^+$

$$d(h(\bar{\delta}_G(q, g(\omega'))), \bar{\delta}_{G'}(h(q), \omega'))) \leq \left(\frac{a^{*n-1} - 1}{a^* - 1} \right) \varepsilon$$

where g is the extension of g, ω has an mls decomposition of length n, and

$$a^* = \sup_{\omega' \in \Omega'} \sup_{\substack{q_1, q_2 \in Q' \\ q_1 \neq q_2}} \frac{d(\delta_G'(q_1, \omega'), \delta_G'(q_2, \omega'))}{d(q_1, q_2)}$$

2. This problem extends the results of Problem 3, Chapter 12, on slow-fast series decomposition, to the case in which approximations are made.

(a) In the series connection $S \ominus T$ we say that T is *approximately slow in* Δ if $d(\delta_T(q, \omega), q)) \leq b$ for all $\omega \in \Omega_T$ such that $l(\omega) \leq \Delta$, and $q \in Q_T$.

In other words, T moves no more than b units under a metric d for any input less than Δ long.

Let $d(\delta_T(q, \omega), \delta_T(q', \omega)) \leq a_\tau d(q, q')$ for all $q, q' \in Q_T$ and $\omega \in \Omega_T$ such that $l(\omega) = \tau$.

Show that the system morphism (g, h, k) from $S \ominus T$ to S_{M_τ} (of Problem 3b, Chapter 12) is approximate in the sense that

$$d(h(\delta(q_1, q_2, g(\omega))), \bar{\delta}_\tau(h(q_1, q_2), \omega)) \leq \varepsilon_{l(\omega)}$$

for all $(q_1, q_2) \in Q_S \times Q_T$, $\omega \in \Omega_\tau^+$, provided $\tau \geq \Delta$. *Hint*: Establish an ε-approximate *specification* morphism from $S \ominus T$ (restricted to inputs Ω_τ) to M_τ with ε determined by the quantities a_τ and b; then use the result of Problem 1.

(b) If $a_\tau < 1$, for $\tau = n\,\Delta$, what can you say about $M_{(n+1)\Delta}$ as a model of $S \ominus T$?

Chapter Fourteen

State Identification, Validation, and Prediction

As indicated in Chapter 8, the problem of state identification arises in the process of testing a model for validity. After a heuristic exposition of the problem, we clarify the issues involved with a formal treatment that also sets the stage for the consideration of structural inference, the subject of Chapter 15.

14.1 THE INITIAL STATE PROBLEM

Imagine a real system sitting on the table ready for experimentation in a given experimental frame. Imagine, too, that we also have a lumped model ready for simulation. We would like to test the model for validity. Suppose we proceed by selecting at random an input segment ω; subjecting the real system to ω, we observe an output segment ρ. We would like to subject the model to the same segment ω, but before we run the simulation, we must determine an initial state to start the model in. How do we choose such a state?

To see the problem, let us choose a state q_0 at random and run the simulation. Two things can happen: (1) the model does not produce ρ as output, or (2) it does.

In the first case we *cannot* conclude that the model is invalid, because it might produce ρ if started in some other state. Thus, we have to try another state q_1, and so on, trying q_2, q_3, . . . , until no states are left to try, whereupon the model can be rejected as invalid. Alternatively, we could happen on a state in which the model does produce ρ, which gives us Case 2.

Having arrived at Case 2, we have confirmed the model. We cannot, however, conclude that it is valid, since it has not been established that we would obtain agreement for all possible input-output pairs. There are two ways to proceed.

(a)   We could continue to try to find other states in which the model also produces ρ. (After all, what is special about the one we have found?)

(b)   We could try another experimental input segment ω'.

A lot of time could be saved if we did not have to search in a random way for appropriate starting states. Ideally we would like some assurance that a particular state was the *only* candidate. Then we need only run the model starting from this state, and

1.   If it does not produce ρ, the model is invalid (there are no other states to try).

2.   If it does produce ρ, the model is confirmed, and we go on to another experiment (again, there are no other states to try as in 1).

How could such a situation arise? Suppose that the output of the system at initial time 0 $[(\rho(0)]$ is observed to be y. If there is only one state in the lumped model with this output value, it must be the unique candidate we seek.

Exercise.   If states appear as outputs (i.e., if the output set of the model is the state set and the output function is the identity map), the foregoing hypothesis holds. But recall that this condition calls for the ability to associate each of the model state variables with directly observable variables in the real system. Referring to models in Chapters 1, 2, 3, and 7, show that this association is generally not possible.

Usually there is a set of states that produces the same output value y, that is, $\{q|\lambda(q) = y\}$. Our trials of initial states can be restricted to this set, which is better than the random selection of trials just proposed, but not a great deal better if this set is large. As we observe more and more of the output segment ρ, however, we can expect to be able to narrow down increasingly, the set of states compatible with the observation. Some I/O pairs may perform better in this regard than others. In fact, suppose there is a pair $(\bar{\omega}, \bar{\rho})$ such that when the model produces $\bar{\rho}$ in response to $\bar{\omega}$, it always finishes in a particular state q at the *end* of the experiment. (We say later that $(\bar{\omega}, \bar{\rho})$ identifies q in this case.) We can take advantage of this pair by applying the input segment $\bar{\omega}$ to the real system. *If $\bar{\rho}$ is observed, the model must be in state q at the end of the experiment. Thus q is the unique candidate state for testing with any continuation segment ω* (see Figure 1). If ρ is observed in the real system, the model must also produce output segment ρ, or be invalid—there are no other possibilities.

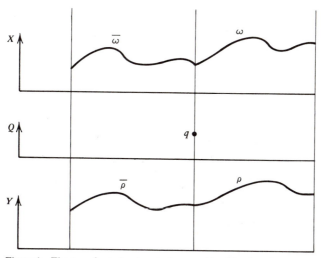

Figure 1   The use of priming inputs for state identification.

We can think of $\bar{\omega}$ as a "priming" input: if a response $\bar{\rho}$ has been observed, the real system has been primed to permit testing of the model state q.

So far, however, we are no better off than before if $\bar{\rho}$ was *not* observed, and it would be even nicer to have a segment $\bar{\bar{\omega}}$, whose every response tells us something. Then no matter which state the model starts in, its final state will be identified by some pair $(\bar{\bar{\omega}}, \bar{\bar{\rho}})$. Thus when we apply $\bar{\bar{\omega}}$ to the real system, two things may happen.

1. The observed response is not one of the $\bar{\bar{\rho}}$'s—in which case the model is invalid, since these are the only possible output segments starting from all possible starting states.
2. The observed response is one of the $\bar{\bar{\rho}}$'s—in this case a unique candidate state for continuation experiments has been identified.

Thus $\bar{\bar{\omega}}$ is a "strong priming" input: it either invalidates the model, or primes the real system, allowing testing of a unique model state (identified by the system response).

It may seem that an input with these properties (called a homing segment) is unlikely to be found in many models. Yet for finite state models such an input segment is known always to exist.[1] Also, in many models an even stronger condition applies—that of a globally attractive equilibrium; if the model is run long enough with constant input, it will forget entirely its initial state and approach a final equilibrium state. Let τ be the upper bound on time required to attain equilibrium (assuming it is finite), and let $\bar{\bar{\omega}}$ be a constant input of length τ. Then each of $\bar{\rho}$'s identifies the *same* final state and $\bar{\bar{\omega}}$ is a (very) strong priming input.

Exercise.   Think about this.

Other common model properties may be exploited to find priming input segments, such as cyclic response to periodic input and finite memory.

14.2   FORMAL TREATMENT

To formalize the concepts introduced, we work with the I/O system $S = \langle X, T, \Omega, Q, Y, \delta, \lambda \rangle$, since this is the most appropriate level at which to consider the relation of I/O behavior to state identification.

With each segment pair $(\omega, \rho) \in (X, T) \times (Y, T)$, we associate a subset of states

$$\text{INITIAL}(\omega, \rho) = \{q \in Q | \tilde{\beta}_q(\omega) = \rho\}.$$

Recall that $\tilde{\beta}_q$ is the I/O function associated with state q. Thus INITIAL (ω, ρ) is the set of states that can cause the output ρ when ω is the input. Note that INITIAL$(\omega, \rho) \neq \varnothing$ just in case $(\omega, \rho) \in R_S$. If INITIAL$(\omega, \rho) = \{q_0\}$ for some $q_0 \in Q$, we say that (ω, ρ) *distinguishes* q_0 (i.e., q_0 is the only initial state that can cause ρ to be emitted when ω is received).

Again, with any pair $(\omega, \rho) \in (X, T) \times (Y, T)$ we associate a subset of states

$$\text{FINAL}(\omega, \rho) = \delta(\text{INITIAL}(\omega, \rho), \omega).$$

FINAL(ω, ρ) is the set of possible states the system can be in at the *end* of the input segment ω (whereas INITIAL(ω, ρ) is the states it could have been at the beginning) if ρ is produced as the output.

We say that (ω, ρ) *identifies* q if FINAL$(\omega, \rho) = \{q\}$; that is, q is the only possible state the system can be in at the end of an experiment, where ω is injected and ρ is observed in response.

Clearly if (ω, ρ) distinguishes q, it also identifies $\delta(q, \omega)$. The converse is not necessarily true, since distinct states in INITIAL(ω, ρ) could be mapped into the same final state by the transition function. Thus it is generally easier to find identifying pairs than distinguishing pairs; this is fortunate because the former are the more useful to us. Recall the foregoing discussion of the use of such I/O pairs for "weak" priming inputs.

Corresponding to the "strong priming inputs," we have the following notions.

We say that ω is a *distinguishing segment* if for all $\rho \in (Y, T)$, $|\text{INITIAL}(\omega, \rho)|$ = 0 or 1.

Similarly, ω is a *homing segment* if for all $\rho \in (Y, T)$, $|\text{FINAL}(\omega, \rho)| = 0$ or 1. In other words, ω is a distinguishing (homing) segment if, whenever $(\omega, \rho) \in R_S$, (ω, ρ) distinguishes (identifies) some system state.

These concepts are borrowed from sequential machine theory, where they are usually defined in a different but equivalent, way.

Exercise. Show that ω is a distinguishing (homing) segment if and only if for all $q, q' \in Q$, $\bar{\beta}_q(\omega) = \bar{\beta}_{q'}(\omega) \Rightarrow q = q'$ ($\delta(q, \omega) = \delta(q', \omega)$).

Exercise. If ω is a distinguishing segment, there is a one-to-one correspondence $q \rightarrow \rho_q$ such that (ω, ρ_q) distinguishes q for each $q \in Q$. Thus all states are distinguished.

On the other hand, not all states need be identified; that is, if ω is a homing segment there is mapping from the set $\{\rho | (\omega, \rho) \in R_S\}$ *into* Q such that $\rho \rightarrow q_\rho$ implies that (ω, ρ) identifies q_ρ.

Exercise. If ω is a distinguishing segment, it is implied that ω is a homing segment, but not conversely.

Corresponding to the equilibrating input, we have the more general concept: ω is a *synchronizing segment* if $|\delta(Q, \omega)| = 1$, (i.e., δ maps all states into a single state under ω).

Exercise. If ω is a synchronizing segment it is implied that ω is a homing segment, but not conversely.

A system S has *definite memory of order* k if all segments of length greater or equal to k are synchronizing segments.

System S has *finite memory of order* k (or is k-definitely homable) if all segments of length greater or equal to k are homing segments.

System S is *k-definitely distinguishable* if all segments of length greater or equal to k are distinguishing sequences.

Exercise. Show that

definite memory $\Rightarrow$ finite memory   and   definitely distinguishable $\Rightarrow$ finite memory

In the finite sequential machine domain, the definite memory machines can be shown to be coextensive with (the same set as) the class of machines structured by delay nets without feedback.[2] Thus definite memory imposes a strong restriction on transition function and inner structure. This is not the case with the finite memory and the definite homability properties.

Every transition function can be the transition function of a finite memory system.

Exercise. Show that the foregoing statement is true by considering a system whose outputs are in one-to-one correspondence with its states.

See Sections 3.7.1 and 5.6.1 for examples of finite memory systems.

14.3 CONSTRUCTION OF STATE IDENTIFICATION EXPERIMENTS

In the modelling context, the last exercise indicates that the dynamics (transition function) of a model need not be tampered with to achieve desirable state identification properties. It is possible to take advantage of equilibrating inputs (synchronizing segments) when these already exist in the model, but it may not be necessary or desirable to do this in connection with the construction of homing segments. Indeed, we see that with sufficient measurement capability (the ability to measure all state variables directly in the real system), every model can be initialized with no uncertainty at the beginning of an experiment. Thus the initial state problem arises because of restricted measurement capability, and the solution is, sometimes found in expanding this capability.

The problem of constructing identifying pairs, or the more desirable homing sequences, then breaks up into two parts.

(a) Analyzing the model to see if it has the desirable properties.
(b) Augmenting the model and experimental frame to endow the model with these properties if it does not already have them.

For small finite state models it is possible to carry out the generation of all the INITIAL(. , .) and FINAL(. , .) sets in an algorithmic manner. (See Problem 1.) In the case of differential equation or Markov chain models it may be possible to obtain analytic solutions for equilibrium properties. Other than this, we have no general guidelines for analysis, and the modeller must make as much use as possible of the special properties of his model.

Suppose we have found an identifiable state, (e.g., an equilibrium state) by analysis. We next pose the following questions.

1. Is the length of the identifying pair short enough for practical application (e.g., what is the maximum time required to reach equilibrium?).
2. Are all other states accessible from the identifiable state? If not, are the "interesting states" accessible from it (see Problem 2).

If the answer to either of these questions is no, or if an identifiable state has not been found, one must then consider part b, augmentation of the model and experimental frame. As mentioned previously one can first explore the possibility of expanding the experimental frame through more precise or extensive measurement, hence expanding the output variable set of the lumped model. Output augmentation may introduce identifiable states not previously there, shorten the length of an identifying pair already known to exist, or both.

One can also investigate the idea of expanding the experimental frame by developing additional ways of stimulating the real system, thus introducing new input segments. Input augmentation may increase the set of states accessible from an identifiable state by introducing new transition possibilities. Of course this procedure requires augmentation of the transition function of the model and will be meaningful only if the resultant model validly reflects the real system behavior for the agumented inputs.

Note that in both cases of augmentation we have not destroyed the existing transition function but have added to what already existed.

We have not examined the possibility of adaptive experimentation in which we identify a state by making use of already obtained responses as guides in our choice of continuation experiments. This course of action almost certainly must be taken for complex models, but very little is presently known about its workings in the nonfinite state (hence very small model) domain.

14.4 UNIQUE PREDICTION AND RELATION OF LUMPED TO BASE MODEL

Our discussion of the state identification problem in Section 14.1 did not once include the base model. This is proper because validation is a procedure involving only the lumped model and real system. But once we introduce the base model, we can think about the problem in a perhaps more revealing way. Namely, not knowing what state to *start* the *lumped* model in, is equivalent to not knowing what state the *base* model *is* in. If we have constructed the lumped model as a simplification of the base model as in Chapters 2 and 8, we have also a mapping h from the base to the lumped state space. Given the state q of the base model, we would try only one state, $h(q)$ of the lumped model. If h were in fact a homomorphism, (and so the lumped model was valid), q and $h(q)$ would be equivalent states (recall from Section 10.4, this means that they have the same I/O functions). But since we do not know the state of the base model, we can say only that we would like to be able to drive the base and lumped models into a pair of states which, if the lumped model is to be valid, must be equivalent. We now show, formally, that this can be done when the lumped model state involved is identifiable.

Consider compatible systems $S = \langle X, T, \Omega, Q, Y, \delta, \lambda \rangle$ and $S' = \langle X, T, \Omega, Q', Y, \delta', \lambda' \rangle$. In the interpretation of interest, S is the base model B/E, in an experimental frame E, and S' is lumped model $S_{G(M)}$. Theorem 1 states that if the lumped model is valid in frame E and one of its states q is identifiable, there is an equivalent state (having the same I/O function) in the base model.

THEOREM 1

For systems S, S', let $R_{S'} = R_S$. If $q \in Q'$, is identifiable, then $\tilde{\beta}_q = \tilde{\beta}_r$ for some $r \in Q$.

Proof. Let (ω, ρ) identify q. Then for all $\omega' \in \Omega'$, we have

$$(\omega\omega', \rho\rho') \in R_{S'} \Rightarrow \rho' = \tilde{\beta}_q(\omega') \tag{1}$$

$$\begin{aligned}
[(\omega\omega', \rho\rho') \in R_{S'} &\Rightarrow \text{for some } q' \in Q', \tilde{\beta}_{q'}(\omega\omega') = \rho\rho' \\
&\Rightarrow \tilde{\beta}_{q'}(\omega)\tilde{\beta}_{\delta'(q', \omega')}(\omega') = \rho\rho' \\
&\Rightarrow \tilde{\beta}_{q'}(\omega) = \rho \quad \text{and} \quad \tilde{\beta}_{\delta'(q', \omega)}(\omega') = \rho' \\
&\qquad\qquad\qquad\qquad\qquad (\text{dom } (\omega) = \text{dom } (\rho)) \\
&\Rightarrow \delta'(q', \omega) = q \quad \text{and} \quad \tilde{\beta}_q(\omega') = \rho'
\end{aligned}$$

The last line follows because $\text{FINAL}(\omega, \rho) = \{q\}$.]

Since (ω, ρ) identifies q, $(\omega, \rho) \in R_{S'}$, and since $R_{S'} \subseteq R_S$, $(\omega, \rho) \in R_S$. Let $\bar{q} \in \text{INITIAL}(\omega, \rho)$ (for system S) so that

$$\tilde{\beta}_{\bar{q}}(\omega) = \rho$$

We can show that q is equivalent to $\delta(\bar{q}, \omega)$. For arbitrary $\omega' \in \Omega$, we have

$$\begin{aligned}
\tilde{\beta}_{\bar{q}}(\omega\omega') &= \tilde{\beta}_{\bar{q}}(\omega)\tilde{\beta}_{\delta(\bar{q}, \omega)}(\omega') \\
&= \rho\tilde{\beta}_{\delta(\bar{q}, \omega)}(\omega')
\end{aligned}$$

Thus $(\omega\omega', \rho\tilde{\beta}_{\delta(\bar{q}, \omega)}(\omega')) \in R_S$, and since $R_S \subseteq R_{S'}$, $(\omega\omega', \rho\tilde{\beta}_{\delta(\bar{q}, \omega)}(\omega')) \in R_{S'}$. But then by Equation 1, $\tilde{\beta}_{\delta(\bar{q}, \omega)}(\omega') = \tilde{\beta}_{\bar{q}}(\omega')$. Since this holds for arbitrary $\omega' \in \Omega$, we have $\tilde{\beta}_{\delta(\bar{q}, \omega)} = \tilde{\beta}_q$. ∎

The theorem has the following interpretation. Assume that the lumped model is valid and that (ω, ρ) identifies q, one of its states. Suppose that ω is applied to both base and lumped models. If ρ is observed as the output segment of both models, they have been sent to equivalent states—namely, q and $\delta(\bar{q}, \omega)$ where $\bar{q}$ is any state of the base model that can cause the response ρ to input ω.

Thus we have confirmed the second interpretation given to state identification: knowing what state the lumped model should be in is the same as knowing what state the base model is actually in (up to equivalence).

We can also study the result from the view point of using the model to make predictions about future real system behavior. If we knew the state of the base model, we could employ the lumped model initialized at the corresponding state to make a unique prediction of future real system behavior. Since we normally do not know the base model state, we cannot make such unique predictions. However, with the help of an identifying pair (ω, ρ), we can make such predictions in the appropriate circumstances.

Suppose ω is applied and ρ is observed in the real system. We then set the lumped model to state q. We can now make a very strong prediction: if we apply any segment ω', and the lumped model responds with ρ', then ρ' must be observed also from the real system. Thus if ρ' is not in fact observed, we will (regretfully) have to conclude that the lumped model is not valid.

14.5 SOURCES

The basic book on state identification for finite sequential machines is that of Gill.[1] Fishman discusses the approach to equilibrium in stochastic models.[2]

1. A Gill, *Introduction to the Theory of Finite State Machines.* McGraw-Hill, New York, 1965.

2. G. S. Fishman; *Concepts and Methods in Discrete Event Digital Simulation.* Wiley, New York, 1973.

PROBLEMS

1. (a) Show that FINAL$(\omega\omega', \rho\rho') = \delta($FINAL$(\omega, \rho) \cap$ INITIAL(ω', ρ'), $\omega')$. Conclude that if the sets INITIAL$(\omega, \cdot)$ and FINAL$(\omega, \cdot)$ are known for all generator segments $\omega \in \Omega_G$, by iteration one can generate FINAL$(\omega, \cdot)$ for any segment $\omega \in \Omega_G^+$. (Then using INITIAL$(\omega, \rho) = \delta^{-1}($FINAL$(\omega, \rho), \omega)$, one can generate INITIAL$(\omega, \cdot)$ for any $\omega \in \Omega_G^+$ if so desired.)

   (b) Complete the table for the machine given in Figure 2b.

ω	ρ	INITIAL	FINAL
1	0	a	b
0	1	a, b	a
1	1	b	b
0	0	ϕ	ϕ
10	01	?	a
10	11	?	?

(a)

	δ		λ	
	0	1	0	1
a	a	b	1	0
b	a	b	1	1

(b)

Figure 2   Tables for Problem 1b.

2. The set $\delta(q, \Omega)$ is the set of *accessible* states from q; that is, q' is accessible (or reachable) from a if there is an $\omega \in \Omega$ for which $\delta(q, \omega) = q'$. Show that if q is identifiable, so is every state accessible from it.

3. Show that every finite state reduced machine has a homing sequence (see Gill[1]). Give an upper bound on the length of the sequence.

Chapter Fifteen

Structural Inference

We demonstrated in Chapter 9 that knowledge of a real system may reside at different levels of a system specification hierarchy. Moreover, Chapter 10 revealed that corresponding to each level of knowledge there is a morphism relating systems described at this level. The morphisms at the various levels form a hierarchy in the sense that stronger (i.e., higher level) morphisms imply weaker (i.e., lower level) morphisms. In this chapter we learn that this hierarchy is a strict one; that is, higher level morphisms cannot be inferred from lower level ones, except under certain conditions, called justifying conditions. As indicated in Chapter 11, this restriction has direct implications for any attempt to infer unknown base model structure from known lumped model structure. The justifying conditions are summarized in Section 15.6.

15.1 JUSTIFYING THE INFERENCE OF I/O FUNCTIONS FROM I/O RELATIONS

The identifiability properties of a model may be exploited to facilitate initial state identification. This leads naturally to the conditions justifying the inference of morphisms at the I/O function level from morphisms at the I/O relation level—that is, for climbing up the first rung of the morphism hierarchy. Recall that initial state knowledge is at the crux of the distinction between the two levels.

Let S and S' be compatible systems as in Chapter 14, where under interpretation S is a base model and S' a lumped model.

If *all* states of a system S' are identifiable, we say that S' is *identifiable*. We have immediately, as a corollary to Theorem 1, of Chapter 14, the following.

THEOREM 1

If $R_{S'} = R_S$ and S' is identifiable, $\tilde{B}_{S'} \subseteq \tilde{B}_S$.

Exercise. We say that S' is strongly connected if for each $q' \in Q'$, $\delta(q', \Omega) = Q'$. Equivalently, every state can access all other states, or for any pair q_1, q_2 there are segments ω_1, ω_2 such that $\delta(q_1, \omega_1) = q_2$ and $\delta(q_2, \omega_2) = q_1$ (ω_1 drives q_1 to q_2 and ω_2 drives q_2 back to q_1).

Show that if S' is strongly connected and there is at least one identifiable state, S' is identifiable.

Conclude that the theorem holds, that is, $R_S = R_{S'} \Rightarrow B_{S'} \subseteq B_S$ if S' is strongly connected and has any of the following properties: definite memory, finite memory, a distinguishing segment, or a homing segment.

This theorem is important because it tells us under what conditions we can infer that the structure of a valid lumped model does reflect that of the base model. In other words, according to Postulate 11 (Chapter 11), the only way to validate a (lumped) model is to compare its I/O relation with the observable behavior of the real system. We *cannot* directly check that the structure of the lumped model reflects that of the base model, since the latter is unknown to us.[†] If the lumped model is identifiable, however, we can be sure that when it has been validated, every state of the lumped model represents an equivalent state in the base model. This equivalence, together with another condition, that the lumped model be reduced, will enable us to conclude that the lumped model is a homomorphic image of the base model. This is a very strong reflection of the inner structure, indeed, given that all we can do is compare at the observational level.

15.2 JUSTIFYING CONDITIONS

We call a condition like "S' is identifiable" a *justifying condition* because it allows us to make a stronger statement about the relation between lumped and base models (e.g., $\tilde{B}_{S'} \subseteq \tilde{B}_S$) when *a priori* only a weaker one has been established (e.g., $R_{S'} = R_S$).

When we propose a justifying condition, we would like to be assured that it is really needed—that is, dropping the condition (and not replacing it by another), we can show that the inference is not justified.

[†] Although, of course, we can check that a lumped model is structurally related to a specific *postulated* base model, as in Chapters 8 and 12.

In the case under discussion, suppose we drop the condition "S' is identifiable." We must display two systems S and S' for which S' is not identiable, $R_S = R_{S'}$, and yet $B_{S'} \nsubseteq B_S$. In sequential machine theory it is well known that there are pairs M', M which are relationally but not behaviorally equivalent. We must select such a pair in which M' is not identifiable. The machines in Figure 1 constitute such a pair. Clearly M' differs from M only in the addition of a state c. The following assertions are true:

1. The I/O function of c is included (as a set of I/O pairs) in the union of those of states a and b.

$$[\tilde{\beta}_c(0) = \tilde{\beta}_b(0) \quad \text{and} \quad \tilde{\beta}_c(0x) = \tilde{\beta}_c(0)\tilde{\beta}_a(x) = \tilde{\beta}_b(0)\tilde{\beta}_a(x) = \tilde{\beta}_b(0x)$$
$$\tilde{\beta}_c(1) = \tilde{\beta}_a(1) \quad \text{and} \quad \tilde{\beta}_c(1x) = \tilde{\beta}_c(1)\tilde{\beta}_b(x) = \tilde{\beta}_a(1)\tilde{\beta}_b(x) = \tilde{\beta}_a(1x)$$
$$\tilde{\beta}_c(\Lambda) = \tilde{\beta}_a(\Lambda) = \tilde{\beta}_b(\Lambda)$$
$$\tilde{\beta}_c \subseteq \tilde{\beta}_a \cup \tilde{\beta}_b]$$

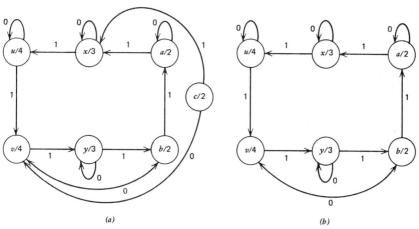

(a) (b)

Figure 1 Sequential machines (a) M' and (b) M for which M' is not identifiable, $R_{M'} = R_M$, and $\tilde{B}_{M'} \nsubseteq \tilde{B}_M$. The notation x/y means that x is a state and $y = \lambda(x)$.

2. State c cannot be accessed from any other state.
3. State c is not identifiable [since c cannot be accessed from any state, there can be no pair (ω, ρ) where $\omega \neq \Lambda$, for which FINAL$(\omega, \rho) = \{c\}$, and FINAL$(\Lambda, 2) = \{a, b, c\}$].

As a consequence of 1, $R_{M'} = \tilde{\beta}_a \cup \tilde{\beta}_b \cup \tilde{\beta}_c = \tilde{\beta}_a \cup \tilde{\beta}_b = R_M$. As a consequence of 3, M' is not identifiable.

But we also have

4. State c is not equivalent to either of states a or b $[\tilde{\beta}_c(0) \neq \tilde{\beta}_a(0), \tilde{\beta}_c(1) \neq \tilde{\beta}_b(1)]$.

As a consequence of 4, $\tilde{\beta}_c \in B_{M'}$ but $\tilde{\beta}_c \notin B_M$ so $B_{M'} \nsubseteq B_M$.

This then establishes that if we do not stipulate that "S' is identifiable", we cannot infer from $R_{S'} = R_S$ that necessarily, $B_{S'} \subseteq B_S$.

In general, a justifying condition may be a conjunction of a number of clauses. For example, from the exercise following Theorem 1 we have a justifying condition with two clauses: "S' has an identifiable state" and "S' is strongly connected." Even stronger than testing the condition as a whole, would be a test of each clause to see whether it can be dropped without destroying the inference. If we produce for each clause a counter-example that destroys the inference, we call the set a *minimal* justifying set. This means that considered as a whole, each of the clauses is a necessary component. But it does not mean that there cannot be another, perhaps smaller, set of clauses constituting a justifying condition.

For example, from Problem 1d, we have an alternate justifying condition for the inference $R_S = R_{S'}$ implies $\tilde{B}_{S'} \subseteq \tilde{B}_S$, namely: S' is finite state and strongly connected.

Note that it is meaningless to try to show that a justifying condition is necessary in that it is logically implied by the simultaneous holding of both antecedent and consequent. For example, we cannot show that $R_{S'} = R_S$ and $\tilde{B}_{S'} \subseteq \tilde{B}_S$ implies S' is identifiable, since if we put $S = S'$, we would be trying to show that every system is identifiable! (Figure 1a is a counterexample.)

Finally, note that in the present case the justifying condition refers only to the lumped model S'. This is desirable because it is the lumped model whose structure may in principle be checked to see whether the justifying condition holds.[†]

15.3 JUSTIFYING THE INFERENCE OF STRUCTURE AT THE SYSTEM LEVEL

To complement the justifying conditions for inferring knowledge at the level of I/O function behavior from knowledge at the I/O relation level, we now provide a justifying condition for inferring knowledge at the I/O system level from knowledge at the I/O function level.

[†] There is still the question of whether the justifying predicate is effectively decidable and, if so, the decision procedure practically implementable. See Zeigler[3] for a discussion of this issue.

THEOREM 2

For compatible systems S and S', if $\tilde{B}_{S'} \subseteq \tilde{B}_S$ and S' is reduced, S' is a homomorphic image of a subsystem of S.

Proof. Let S and S' be compatible with $\tilde{B}_{S'} \subseteq \tilde{B}_S$. For each $q' \in Q'$, let

$$E(q') = \{q \mid q \in Q, \tilde{\beta}_q = \tilde{\beta}_{q'}\}$$

That is, $E(q')$ is the set of states in S equivalent to q' in S'. By assumption $E(q')$ is not empty. Let

$$\bar{Q} = \bigcup_{q' \in Q'} E(q')$$

that is, $\bar{Q}$ is the set of states of S which are equivalent to states of S'.

Define the relation $h : \bar{Q} \to Q'$ where $h(q) = q'$ for which $\tilde{\beta}_{q'} = \tilde{\beta}_q$.

Since S' is reduced, h is single valued [suppose both q' and q'' are candidates for $h(q)$; then $\tilde{\beta}_{q'} = \tilde{\beta}_q$ and $\tilde{\beta}_{q''} = \tilde{\beta}_q$; thus $\tilde{\beta}_{q'} = \tilde{\beta}_{q''}$, and since S' is reduced, $q' = q''$]. Moreover, h is defined everywhere on $\bar{Q}$ and is onto Q (why?). So h is a total function from $\bar{Q}$ onto Q'.

Now the assertion that for all $q \in Q$, $\omega \in \Omega$,

$$h(\delta(q, \omega)) = \delta'(h(q), \omega) \tag{1}$$

is a restatement of a previous result (Lemma 1a, Chapter 10) that the successors of equivalent states are themselves equivalent, as we now see:

$$\tilde{\beta}_q = \tilde{\beta}_{h(q)} \qquad \text{(from the definition of } h\text{)}$$
$$\Rightarrow \tilde{\beta}_{\delta(q,\,\omega)} = \tilde{\beta}_{\delta'(h(q),\,\omega)} \qquad \text{for all } \omega \in \Omega \qquad \text{(Lemma 1a)}$$
$$\Rightarrow h(\delta(q, \omega)) = \delta'(h(q), \omega) \qquad \text{(definition of } h\text{)}$$

Similarly,

$$\lambda(q) = \lambda'(h(q)) \tag{2}$$

follows from the equivalence of q and $h(q)$ (employing $\Lambda \in \Omega$, as in Lemma 1b of Chapter 10).

Thus from Equations 1 and 2 we conclude that (i, h, i) is a system morphism from S to S' (Section 10.3) or, equivalently, that S' is a homomorphic image of a subsystem of S. ∎

Theorem 2 tells us that "S' is reduced" is a justifying condition for the implication

$$\tilde{B}_{S'} \subseteq \tilde{B}_S \Rightarrow S' \text{ is a homomorphic image of a subsystem of } S$$

We can, again, test the minimality of the condition by dropping it. We must show that there are systems S' and S for which $\tilde{B}_{S'} \subseteq \tilde{B}_S$ but S' is not homomorphically related to S (Problems 4a and 4d).

Now let us combine Theorems 1 and 2 to get:

COROLLARY

For compatible systems S and S', if $R_S = R_{S'}$ and S' is identifiable and reduced, S' is a homomorphic image of a subsystem of S.

Note that the justifying condition is obtained by combining the justifying condition for inference of I/O function knowledge from I/O relation knowledge with the justifying condition for the inference of structure at the system level from I/O function knowledge. In the interpretation, where S is the base model in frame E and S' is a lumped model, we have the following: if a lumped model has been shown to be identifiable and reduced, and if it has been validated with respect to the real system in frame E, its internal structure represents the structure of the base model in the sense that the lumped model is a homomorphic image of a subsystem of the base model.

Theorem 2 can be readily generalized to apply to the inference of a system morphism from knowledge of an I/O function morphism, as follows. Let (g, k) be an I/O function morphism from IOFO_S to $\text{IOFO}_{S'}$. To make progress we must reduce k, which is a mapping of output segments to output segments, to a map $\hat{k}$, which maps output values to output values. We can do this by finding out when the process of constructing k from $\hat{k}$ can be reversed:

Let g be invertable. We then have the function MATCH (see Section 10.4). We say that k is $\hat{k}$-*derivable* if

$$\rho_1(\text{MATCH}(t')) = \rho_2(\text{MATCH}(t')) \Rightarrow k(\rho_1)(t') = k(\rho_2)(t')$$

for all $\rho_1, \rho_2 \in (Y, T)$ and $t' \in \text{dom}(\rho_1) \cap \text{dom}(\rho_2)$. This is just what we need, as can be seen in the

LEMMA

Let g be invertable and let $k : (Y, T) \xrightarrow{\text{onto}} (Y', T')$ be $\hat{k}$ derivable. Then there is a function $\hat{k} : Y \xrightarrow{\text{onto}} Y'$ defined as follows.

Let $\omega' \in \Omega'$ be any segment. Let $t' = l(\omega')$ and so $\text{MATCH}(t') = l(g(\omega'))$. Given $y \in Y$, let ρ_y be any segment in (Y, T) passing through y at time $\text{MATCH}(t')$; that is, $\rho_y(\text{MATCH}(t')) = y$. Then by definition

$$\hat{k}(y) = k(\rho_y)(t').$$

Moreover, k and $\hat{k}$ are in the relation

$$k(\rho)(t') = \hat{k}(\rho(\text{MATCH}(t')))$$

for all $\rho \in (Y, T)$ and $t' \in \text{dom } k(\rho)$.

Exercise.   Prove the lemma.

We can now state the generalization of Theorem 2 which provides justifying conditions for inferring the existence of a system morphism, given the existence of an I/O morphism.

THEOREM 3   INFERENCE OF SYSTEM MORPHISM FROM I/O FUNCTION MORPHISM

Let (g, k) be an I/O function morphism from IOFO_S to $\text{IOFO}_{S'}$ such that g is an invertable monoid homomorphism and k is $\hat{k}$-derivable. Then if S' is reduced, there is a system morphism from S to S'.

Proof.   Consider the object $(g, \alpha, \hat{k})$ where α is the relation defined in Problem 1 of Chapter 10, and $\hat{k}$ is the function of the preceding lemma. With $Q = \text{dom}(\alpha)$, it is readily shown that α is a total function mapping Q onto Q'. That $(g, \alpha, \hat{k})$ satisfies all the conditions required of a system morphism is a restatement of the results of Problem 1, Chapter 10.   ∎

15.4   HOMOMORPHISM AND WEAK STRUCTURE MORPHISM

The next level above the system level we investigate is that of the structured specification. For simplicity we restrict our discussion to the autonomous sequential machine $M = \langle Q, \delta \rangle$. If we have two machines that are related by a homomorphism, we know that the global transition functions are related, but we do not necessarily have the assurance that the local transition functions are also related, as required by a strong structure morphism.

Let us first note that it is impossible to provide meaningful conditions that will justify the inference of even a weak structure morphism, given a homomorphism. Consider any abstract machine $M = \langle Q, \delta \rangle$ having at least three states. Then choosing a structure $\{A_\alpha | \alpha \in D\}$ for Q and any compatible structure for δ, we would have a first structure for M, call it M_A; choosing another structure $\{B_\beta | \beta \in E\}$ for Q and a compatible δ structure, we have a second structure M_B for M. Now M_A and M_B are isomorphic at the abstract level (being both isomorphic with M), but there need be little relation between the coordinatizations $\{A_\alpha\}$ and $\{B_\beta\}$, which are arbitrarily chosen. More generally, there are pairs of structured machines M and M' for which there is a homomorphism, but no weak structure morphism, from M to M'. Even stronger, there are structured machines that have nontrivial homomorphic images but no nontrivial structure morphic images (see Problem 6 for these results). This establishes that the weak structure morphism is a higher level morphism than is the homomorphism. We cannot in general infer the existence of a weak structure morphism given a homomorphism, nor are there meaningful justifying conditions that enable us to make this inference.

15.5 JUSTIFYING THE INFERENCE OF STRONG STRUCTURE MORPHISMS

We now come to the highest level of morphism to be considered. Let $M = \langle Q, \delta \rangle$ and $M' = \langle Q', \delta' \rangle$ be structured by $\{Q_\alpha | \alpha \in D\}$ and $\{Q_{\alpha'} | \alpha' \in D'\}$, respectively. Let $(d, \{h_{\alpha'}\})$ be a weak structure morphism from M to M'. Recall that this means that the state structures $\{Q_\alpha\}$ and $\{Q_{\alpha'}\}$ are related by an aggregation

$$h = \underset{\alpha' \in D'}{\times} h_{\alpha'} \circ \mathrm{proj}_{(\alpha')}$$

which is also a homomorphism of the global transition functions δ and δ'. Section 10.6 indicates that this is equivalent to the holding of a set of relations involving the local transition functions, namely

$$\delta'_{\beta'} \circ h_{I'_{\beta'}} = h_{\beta'} \circ \delta_{(\beta')} \tag{3}$$

for each $\beta' \in D'$.

We may visualize this relation for a particular α' as in Figure 2. Recall that $I_{\beta'}$ are the INFLUENCERS of β'; $(I'_{\beta'}) = d^{-1}(I_{\beta'})$ are the coordinates in D mapping onto these INFLUENCERS, call them the *pseudoinfluencers*. Also recall $\delta'_{\beta'}$ is the local transition function of β' and

$$\delta_{(\beta')} = \underset{\beta \in (\beta')}{\times} \delta_\beta \circ \mathrm{proj}_{I_\beta}$$

is the transition function for the block $(\beta') = d^{-1}(\beta')$. Accordingly,

$$I_{(\beta')} = \underset{\beta \in (\beta')}{\bigcup} I_\beta$$

is the actual set of INFLUENCERS of (β').

Equation 3 tells us that when we apply $h_{I'_{\beta'}}$ to the pseudoinfluencers to find the state of the INFLUENCERS and then apply $\delta'_{\beta'}$, we obtain the same result as first applying the block function $\delta_{(\beta')}$ to its INFLUENCERS $I_{(\beta')}$, then applying the local function $h_{\beta'}$. But it does not tell us that there is necessarily any relation between the pseudoinfluencers $(I'_{\beta'})$ and the INFLUENCERS $I_{(\beta')}$.

Such a relation would hold, however, if $(d, \{h_{\alpha'}\})$ were to be a strong structure morphism. Recall that this required that the digraphs of M and M' also match up in that if $\alpha' \in I_{\beta'}$, there are $\alpha \in (\alpha')$ and $\beta \in (\beta')$ for which $\alpha \in I_\beta$. In other words, for every INFLUENCER α' of β', there is a pseudo-

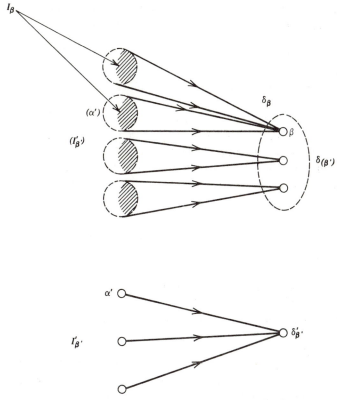

Figure 2   The relation between the INFLUENCERS $I'_{\beta'}$, the pseudoinfluencers $(I'_{\beta'})$ of β', and the INFLUENCERS $I_{(\beta')}$ of block (β'). (From Reference 4, Fig. 3, p. 759.)

influencer $\alpha \in (\alpha')$ which is actually also an INFLUENCER of some $\beta \in (\beta')$ (hence also an INFLUENCER of the block (β')). Therefore the digraph of M' does not deceptively represent the information flow of M—if there is a communication link in M', it represents a true communication link in M.

Exercise.   Show that the strong morphism does not require that the pseudoinfluencers $(I'_{\beta'})$ and the INFLUENCERS $I_{(\beta')}$ be identical sets or even that one be contained in the other.

To develop justifying conditions for the inference of strong from weak structure morphisms, we need some fairly abstract concepts of the calculus of partitions. These were developed in Problem 1 of Chapter 9, to which the reader should turn for definitions.

Given the mapping $h:Q \xrightarrow{\text{onto}} Q'$ and a partition π' of Q', we have a unique partition on Q induced by h, called $h^{-1}\pi'$, defined by

$$q_1 h^{-1}\pi' q_2 \qquad \text{if and only if} \qquad h(q_1)\pi' h(q_2)$$

for all $q_1, q_2 \in Q'$.

Thus $h^{-1}\pi'$ is the partition of Q whose blocks are inverse images of the blocks of π'.

We say that h is *location preserving* if for any pair of partitions π of Q and π' of Q' such that π is finer than $h^{-1}\pi'$ ($\pi \le h^{-1}\pi'$), given a location L of π, there is a location L' of π' such that $d(L) \supseteq L'$.

We employ location preservation as a justifying condition for inferring a strong from a weak structure morphism in the following.

THEOREM 4

Let $(d, \{h_{\alpha'}\})$ be a weak structure morphism from M to M'. Then $(d, \{h_{\alpha'}\})$ is also a strong structure morphism if

(a)   The structure of δ' is in reduced form.
(b) Q' is irredundantly coordinatized.
(c)   The aggregation h of $\{h_{\alpha'}\}$ is location preserving.

Proof. We provide a sketch and leave the details to the reader. Condition a says that each $\delta'_{\beta'}$ must actually depend on all its INFLUENCERS, that is, $I'_{\beta'}$ is a location for $\delta'_{\beta'}$, hence a location for $\pi_{\delta'_{\beta'}}$. Moreover, by condition b $I'_{\beta'}$ is the unique location for $\pi_{\delta'_{\beta'}}$.

From Equation 1, we can show by straightforward unpacking of definitions that $h^{-1}\pi_{\delta'_{\beta'}} \le \pi_{\delta_{\beta'}}$. By condition c, any location of $\pi_{\delta_{\beta'}}$ when mapped by d includes a location for $\pi_{\delta'_{\beta'}}$. But $I_{(\beta')}$ is a location for $\pi_{\delta_{\beta'}}$ and $I'_{\beta'}$ is the unique location of $\pi_{\delta'_{\beta'}}$. Thus $d(I_{(\beta')}) \supseteq I'_{\beta'}$, which is equivalent to the requirement for strong structure morphism. ∎

We investigate the minimality of the justifying conditions in Problem 7.

Exercise.   As a corollary of Theorem 4, or by direct argument, show that if $Q' = \bigtimes_{\alpha \in D} Q_{\alpha'}$ any weak morphism from M to M' is also a strong morphism from M to M'.

15.6   GATHERING UP THE STRANDS

We have now completed our study of the hierarchy of system specifications and morphisms introduced in Chapters 9 and 10. In Chapter 10 we demonstrated the truth of implications of the form

$$\text{morphism at level } i \Rightarrow \text{morphism at level } i - 1$$

In this chapter we have shown that the converse implication

$$\text{morphism at level } i - 1 \Rightarrow \text{morphism at level } i$$

is *false*.

This means that knowledge at one level of the specification hierarchy does not enable us to infer knowledge at the next level or higher. Therefore independent knowledge resides at each level. For example, the validation of a lumped model at the level of input-output observation does not imply that the model's internal structure is in any way related to the internal structure of a base model. With the help of justifying conditions, however, such structural inferences can be justified. The justifying conditions enter into the implication of strong from weak morphisms in the form

$$\begin{array}{l}\text{morphism at level } i - 1 \\ \text{and} \\ \text{justifying condition}\end{array} \Rightarrow \text{morphism at level } i$$

Table 1 summarizes the primary justifying conditions given in this chapter. It is not possible to give meaningful justifying conditions for the transition from level 2 to level 3 because of the arbitrariness of the coordinatization of sets. This imparts a fundamental limitation to our ability to infer base model structure from lumped model structure.

To see this, note that at the lower levels, the justifying conditions apply only to the lumped model. Thus we can assert that the internal structure of a model satisfying such conditions represents that of any other model whatever, as long as the second model has the same I/O behavior as the first. Thus any model that is replicatively valid and satisfies the justifying conditions, is also predictively valid and structurally valid at the level of global transition structure (to use the terms of Section 1.1). However, we cannot climb further up the morphism hierarchy in such an arbitrary way. To proceed further we must restrict our study to the base models whose state structures are preserved in the lumped model by the homomorphism inferred at the level transition $1 \rightarrow 2$. Thus the jump $2 \rightarrow 3$ severely restricts the class of base models about which we can make any strong assertions of internal structure. Note that for the transition $3 \rightarrow 4$, conditions a and b are again properties of the lumped model. But condition c further restricts the base model class by placing limitations on the relation between the state structures of base and lumped models. For base models in the class, however, we are justified in inferring that the local transition structure of a valid lumped model truly reflects that of the base model. In other words, a replicatively valid model is structurally valid with respect to any base model in the class, consistent with the justifying conditions.

This difficulty in justifying higher level inferences ought to be remembered when we are tempted to feel so confident in our models that we equate them with the actually working of reality.

Table 1   Summary of Justifying Conditions

Level Transition	Justifying Conditions	Inference
$0 \to 1$	S' is identifiable.	$R_{S'} = R_S \Rightarrow B_{S'} \subseteq B_S.$
$1 \to 2$	S' is reduced.	$B_{S'} \subseteq B_S \Rightarrow$ homomorphism from S to S'.
$2 \to 3$	None given.	Homomorphism from M to $M' \Rightarrow$ weak structure morphism from M to M'.
$3 \to 4$	(a) δ' is in reduced form (b) Q' is irredundantly structured. (c) h is location preserving.	Weak structure morphism from M to $M' \Rightarrow$ strong structure morphism from M to M'.

15.7   SOURCES

1. J. N. Gray and M. Harrison, "The Theory of Sequential Relations," *Information and Control,* **9** (5), 1966, 435–468.
2. B. P. Zeigler, "Automation Structure Preserving Morphisms with Applications to Decomposition and Simulation," in *Theory of Machines and Computations*, A. Paz and Z. Kohavi (Eds.,) Academic Press, New York, 1971, 295–312.
3. B. P. Zeigler, "A Conceptual Basis for Modelling and Simulation," *International Journal of General Systems*, **1** (4), 1974, 213–228.
4. B. P. Zeigler, "Towards a Formal Theory of Modelling and Simulation: Structure Preserving Morphisms," *Journal of the Association for Computing Machinery*, **19** (4), 1972, 742–764.

PROBLEMS

1. The identifiability concepts have been presented in a form that was stronger than necessary. Consider the following relaxation: S' is *identifiable* if its reduced version S'_R is identifiable.
    (a)   Show that Theorem 1 holds with the new definition.
    (b)   Extend the definitions of definite memory, finite memory, and the

other terms, in the same manner, and show that they amount to replacing equality by behavioral equivalence as the operative relation on the states.

(c) Show that every finite state machine has a homing sequence (in the relaxed sense). (See Problem 3, Chapter 14.)

(d) From c, conclude that in the finite state case, "S' is strongly connected" implies "S' is identifiable."

2. Show that the clauses $\{S'$ strongly connected, S' has an identifiable state$\}$ form a minimal justifying set for the inference $R_{S'} = R_S \Rightarrow \tilde{B}_{S'} \subseteq \tilde{B}_S$.

3. Provide a minimal justifying condition for the inference $R_{S'} = R_S \Rightarrow \tilde{B}_{S'} = \tilde{B}_S$. Why must S also be mentioned in the justifying condition?

4. (a) Consider the case of a system S and its reduced version S_R. If S_R has strictly fewer states than S, show that the pair S, S_R is a counterexample to the following implication: $\tilde{B}_S \subseteq \tilde{B}_{S'} \Rightarrow S$ is a homomorphic image of a subsystem of S'.

(b) Consider the class of sequential machines which count modulo some integer n. An n-counter M_n has states $\{0, 1, 2, \ldots, n - 1\}$; a 1 input symbol causes the state to incre⌒se by 1 (mod n); a 0 input causes no change in state.

By assigning outputs $\lambda(j) = j$, $j \in \{0, 1, \ldots, n - 1\}$ the M_n counter will count the number of ones in an input string mod n. Show that if m divides n, then by assigning outputs $\lambda'(j) = j \pmod{m}$, the M_n counter counts mod m. *Hint.* Show that M_m is a homomorphic image of M_n in the experimental frame λ'.

(c) Conversely, show that M_m is a homomorphic image of M_n only if m divides n.

(d) Use the foregoing results to show that there are pairs of systems S, S' such that $\tilde{B}_S = \tilde{B}_{S'}$, but neither is S a homomorphic image of S' nor is S' a homomorphic image of S. *Hint.* Consider, for example, M_4 and M_6 with mod 2 output.

5. Prove part d of Theorem 9, Chapter 10, on the uniqueness within isomorphism of the reduced version of a system.

6. (a) Two ways of describing the slate of a chess board are as follows:
(i) For each square of the board, tell the piece, if any, occupying it;
(ii) Tell where on the board, if anywhere, each piece is located.

The two representations are different structure assignments for the same set. They are equivalent in the sense that there is a one-to-one correspondence between them, but we may not be able to express this as an aggregation of local maps. For simplicity, consider the possible states that two bishops traveling on squares of different colors can be in. Specify the structure (i) of this set, which has 64 coordinates and the structure (*ii*), which has two coordinates. Do the same for the case of two queens. Show that the one-to-one correspondence between the two structures can be expressed as an aggregation in the first case but not in the second.

(b) Let $\{A_\alpha | \alpha \in D\}$ be a structure for A having at least two independent coordinates (see definitions given in Problem 3, Chapter 9). Show that there is another coordinatization of A which is not related to $\{A_\alpha\}$ by an aggregation mapping.

Hint. Let α_1 and α_2 be the independent. Then the coordinatization takes the form of the left side of the table:

α_1	α_2	α_3	$\cdots$	α_n	α'_1	α'_2	α'_3	$\cdots$	α'_n
a	a_2	a_3	$\cdots$	a_n	a	$\bar{a}_2$	a_3	$\cdots$	a_n
a'	a_2	a_3	$\cdots$	a_n	a'	a_2	a_3	$\cdots$	a_n
b_1	b	b_3	$\cdots$	b_n	b_1	b	b_3	$\cdots$	b_n
b_1	b'	b_3	$\cdots$	b_n	b_1	b'	b_3	$\cdots$	b_n

The table represents a one-to-one mapping to a second structure that is an identity except for the first n-tuple, for which a special image is created. Show that column two of the right-hand side must be computed by looking at both columns 1 and 2 of the left-hand side.)

(c) Show that every set has at least one independent coordinatization.

(d) Let $M = \langle Q, \delta \rangle$ and $M' = \langle Q', \delta' \rangle$ be structured by $\{Q_\alpha | \alpha \in D\}$ and $\{Q'_\alpha | \alpha' \in D\}$, respectively, and $h: Q \overset{\text{onto}}{\to} Q'$ be a homomorphism. Show that h induces a weak structure morphism from M to M' if and only if there are locations for the family of functions $\{P_{\alpha'} \circ h | \alpha' \in D\}$ which are pairwise disjoint.

(e) Show that there are no nontrivial weak structure morphic images of the structured machine given in Figure 3.

Hint. Note that the 6 cycle has only a 2 cycle and a 3 cycle as homomorphic images (Problem 4c). Show that neither homomorphism can be expressed as an aggregation of local maps involving at least two coordinates.[†]

7. (a) Show that the conditions *a* and *b* cannot be dropped from the justifying conditions of Theorem 4 by considering two structures for δ based on the same nonirredundant structure of Q (the examples of Section 9.18, for example).

(b) Show that the condition *c* cannot be dropped from the justifying conditions of Theorem 4.

[†] See Reference 3.

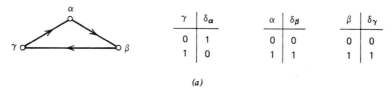

γ	δ_α
0	1
1	0

α	δ_β
0	0
1	1

β	δ_γ
0	0
1	1

(a)

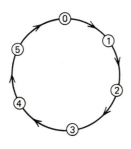

	α	β	γ
0	0	0	0
1	1	0	0
2	1	1	0
3	1	1	1
4	0	1	1
5	0	0	1

(b)

Figure 3 (a) A structured machine. (b) Global transition of machine in (a). (From Reference 2, Fig. 1, p. 312.)

Hint. Consider Figure 4 in which[‡] $A_\alpha = \{a, b, c, d\}$, $A_\beta = \{e, f, g, h\}$, and $A = \{ae, af, bg, cf, dg\}$. (Thus a line between a and e indicates $ae \in A$.)

$$A'_\alpha = \{\overline{ab}, \overline{cd}\}, \ A'_\beta = \{\overline{ef}, \overline{gh}\}, \text{ and } A' = A'_\alpha \times A'_\beta.$$

Clearly A' is irredundantly structured. Let $h_\alpha : A_\alpha \to A_{\alpha'}$ and $h_\beta : A_\beta \to A_{\beta'}$ be such that elements are mapped onto the corresponding blocks, for example,

$$h_\alpha(a) = \overline{ab}, \text{ etc.}$$

Then the aggregation h of h_α and h_β maps A onto A', for example

$$h(ae) = \overline{ab} \ \overline{ef}, \text{ etc}$$

$$\pi_h = \{\overline{ae}, \overline{af}; \overline{bg}; \overline{cf}; \overline{dg}\} = h^{-1}\pi_{\alpha,\beta}.$$

α is the location for $h^{-1}\pi_{\alpha,\beta}$ but α, β is the location for $\pi_{\alpha,\beta}$ and h is not location preserving.

Based on this idea, construct a pair of structured machines $M = \langle Q, \delta \rangle$ and $M' = \langle Q', \delta' \rangle$ such that δ' is in reduced form, Q' is irredundantly structured, and there is a weak morphism from M to M' whose aggregation map

---

[‡] The material (from problem 7b) is reprinted from Reference 4, Example 3, p. 761. Copyright © 1972, by The Association For Computing Machinery, Inc. Reprinted by permission.

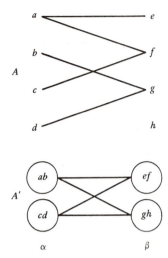

Figure 4 Structured sets A and A', which are related by an aggregation mapping that is not location preserving. (From Reference 7, Example 3, p. 761.)

is not location preserving. Moreover, the morphism is not a strong structure morphism.

8. *Canonical realization of I/O functions.* Given a realizable I/O function f and a realizable IOFO $\langle T, X, \Omega, Y, F \rangle$ we can now construct reduced systems S_f and S_F which realize f and F, respectively. Prove that $S_f(S_F)$ is canonical in the following sense: $S_f(S_F)$ realizes $f(F)$, and if any system S also realizes $f(F)$, then $S_f(S_F)$ is a homomorphic image of a subsystem of S; moreover, if S is reduced, S is isomorphic to $S_f(S_F)$.

9. (*a*) Provide a pair of systems S and S' such that $R_S = R_{S'}$ but neither $\tilde{B}_S \subseteq \tilde{B}_{S'}$ nor $\tilde{B}_S \subseteq \tilde{B}_{S'}$.
    (*b*) Provide a pair of systems S and S' such that $R_{S'} \subseteq R_S$ and S' is identifiable but $\tilde{B}_{S'} \not\subseteq \tilde{B}_S$. (This shows that the equality $R_{S'} = R_S$ is necessary in making the inference $B_{S'} \subseteq B_S$).

10. *Canonical realization of I/O relations.* In contrast to previous cases, IORO's do not in general have canonical realizations. We say that an IORO has a canonical realization S_R if $IORO_{S_R} = IORO$ and, moreover, if any system S also realizes IORO, then S_R is a homomorphic image of a subsystem of S.
    (*a*) Using the results of Problem 9, provide an IORO that does not have a canonical realization.
    (*b*) Show that if an IORO has a realization (is realized by a system) that is strongly connected, and has another realization having a finite number of states, it has a realization that is both strongly connected and finite state.

(c) Show that *b* is true with "finite memory" substituted for "finite state" throughout.

(d) Prove the following:

THEOREM

An IORO has a canonical realization if either (1) it has an identifiable realization, or (2) it has a finite state (or memory) realization and a strongly connected realization.

(e) Given a realizable IOFO $\langle T, X, \Omega, Y, F \rangle$ characterize the following properties of its canonical realization S_F as properties of $F: S_F$ is finite state, strongly connected, finite memory, identifiable (e.g., S_F is finite state $\Leftrightarrow$ F has finite cardinality).

Chapter Sixteen

Simulation Program Verification and Complexity

Back in Chapter 2 we raised the distinction between a model and its program implementation. We also indicated that the complexity of a model would be measured by the magnitude of the computational resources required by its simulation realizations. In this chapter we discuss these issues, with help of the postulates of Chapter 11, and the systems concepts of Part 2.

According to Postulates 9 and 11, both models and programs can be formalized as iterative systems specifications. The link between a model and its program realization thus should be expressable as a relation at the iterative specification level. When such a relation can be shown to be a iterative specification morphism, we are assured by Theorem 5 (Chapter 10) that an I/O function morphism runs from the program specification to the model specification. This means that for every initial model state, there is at least one initialization of the program that will cause the latter to generate the behavior of the former. According to Postulate 12, we then say that the *program correctly simulates the model*. Thus one may prove that a program correctly simulates a model by formally establishing the existence of an iterative specification morphism from the program to the model specification.

In the next section we study an example of this idea. We formalize the discrete time models and the prototypical simulation strategy of Chapter 4 as structured sequential machines. We then prove that a homomorphism runs from the program to the model at the abstract sequential machine level.

Thus although the structural features of the model specification are directly represented in the program structure, the relationship preserved is not expressable as a structure morphism.

To avoid unenlightening complications, we present a relatively simple special instance below. However, the reader may readily extend the ideas involved to the more general case.

16.1   PROGRAM VERIFICATION FOR ONE–DIMENSIONAL CELLULAR SPACE

Our model is a one-dimensional cellular space having n identical CELLS ($n \geq 2$). (For review see Chapter 4.) To preserve uniformity when computing neighborhoods, the space is wrapped into a circle. Formally we identify CELL(n) with CELL(0), as in Figure 1. Once the INTERNAL · NEIGH-BORS of CELL(0) are specified, say $N_0 \subseteq \{0, 1, \ldots, n - 1\}$, the INTER-NAL · NEIGHBORS of any CELL(i) are $N_i = (N_0 + i) \bmod n$.

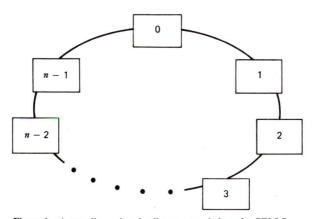

Figure 1   A one-dimensional cell space consisting of n CELLS.

The model is thus specified by a structure (n, S, N_0, τ), where n is the number of CELLS, S is the state set of each CELL, N_0 is the neighborhood of 0, and $\tau : S^{|N_0|} \to S$ is the local transition function.

This structure in turn specifies a structured autonomous sequential machine $M' = \langle Q', \delta' \rangle$, where $Q' = S^n$ and $\delta' = \bigtimes_{i=0}^{n-1} \tau \circ \text{proj}_{N_i}$. (See Section 9.18.)

Having formalized the model, we turn to formalizing the simulation program, which will be an adaptation of the procedure of Section 4.6 to one-dimensional cell spaces.

The one-dimensional arrays FLIP and FLOP, which hold the present and next states, will be placed contiguously in a one-dimensional array called GLOBAL · STATE, that is, for $i = 0, 1, \ldots, n - 1$, GLOBAL · STATE(i) = FLIP(i), and for $i = n, n + 1, \ldots, 2n - 1$, GLOBAL · STATE$(i)$ = FLOP$(n - i)$. NEIGHBOR · STATES is a one-dimensional array of size $|N_0|$, NEXT · STATE is an ordinary variable. FLIP · FLOP has the range $\{0, 1\}$. To keep track of the place in the scanning sequence, we use a variable I with range $\{0, 1, \ldots, n\}$. To compute neighborhoods we use an array INFLUENCERS of size $|N_0|$. We omit the variable CLOCK and the halt register INDICATOR, since they are extraneous to our concerns here.) The flow chart we use appears in Figure 2.

After shortening the mnemonic names, we obtain the list of MEMORY variables, with range (wr) sets indicated:

GS (GLOBAL · STATE),   wr $S^n \times S^n$
INF (INFLUENCERS),   wr $\{0, 1, \ldots, n - 1\}^{|N_0|}$
NE (NEIGHBOR · STATES),   wr $S^{|N_0|}$
NS (NEXT · STATE),   wr S
I,   wr $\{0, 1, \ldots, n\}$
FF (FLIP · FLOP),   wr $\{0, 1\}$

Marking the points shown in the flow chart as our control states, we have as the CONTROL variable.
C (CURRENT · INSTRUCTION · #),   wr $\{1, 2, \ldots, 7\}$

The formal program model is then an autonomous sequential machine $M = \langle Q, \delta \rangle$, where Q is the cross product of the ranges of GS, INF, NE, NS, I, FF, and C. To define δ we use the projection functions introduced in Section 9.18.

The definition is a series of statements of the form

$$\text{for } q \in Q, \qquad \text{proj}_A(q) = x \Rightarrow \text{proj}_B(\delta(q)) = y$$

This means, "if q is a program state in which the coordinates of A have value x, the next state $\delta(q)$ is such that the coordinates of B have value y, and no other coordinates change value" ($\text{proj}_{\bar{B}}(\delta(q)) = \text{proj}_{\bar{B}}(q)$ is understood).

The definition of δ is

$$\text{proj}_C(q) = 1 \Rightarrow \text{proj}_I(\delta(q)) = 0 \qquad \text{and} \qquad \text{proj}_C(\delta(q)) = 2$$

$$\text{proj}_C(q) = 2 \qquad \text{and} \qquad \text{proj}_I(q) = n$$
$$\Rightarrow \text{proj}_{FF}(\delta(q)) = \text{proj}_{FF}(q) \qquad \text{and} \qquad \text{proj}_C(\delta(q)) = 1$$

$$\text{proj}_C(q) = 2 \qquad \text{and} \qquad \text{proj}_I(q) \neq n$$
$$\Rightarrow \text{proj}_C(\delta(q)) = 3$$

$$\text{proj}_C(q) = 3 \Rightarrow \text{proj}_{INF}(\delta(q)) = (\text{proj}_{INF}(q) + 1) \bmod n$$
$$\text{and} \qquad \text{proj}_C(\delta(q)) = 4$$

$$\text{proj}_C(q) = 4 \Rightarrow \text{proj}_{NE}(\delta(q)) = \text{proj}_{\text{proj}_{INF}(q) + n \cdot \text{proj}_{FF}(q)} \text{proj}_{GS}(q)$$
$$\text{and} \qquad \text{proj}_C(\delta(q)) = 5$$

$$\text{proj}_C(q) = 5 \Rightarrow \text{proj}_{NS}(\delta(q)) = \tau(\text{proj}_{NE}(q))$$
$$\text{and} \qquad \text{proj}_C(\delta(q)) = 6$$

$$\text{proj}_C(q) = 6 \Rightarrow \text{proj}_{\text{proj}_I(q) + n \cdot \overline{\text{proj}_{FF}(q)}} \text{proj}_{GS}(\delta(q)) = \text{proj}_{NS}(q)$$
$$\text{and} \qquad \text{proj}_C(\delta(q)) = 7$$

$$\text{proj}_C(q) = 7 \Rightarrow \text{proj}_I(\delta(q)) = \text{proj}_I(q) + 1 \qquad \text{and} \qquad \text{proj}_C(\delta(q)) = 2$$

Now we wish to prove that the program simulates the model correctly. Formally, this can be done by showing that a homomorphism exists from the program system specification M to the model specification M' and takes the form $h: Q \xrightarrow{\text{onto}} Q'$, where $\bar{Q} \subseteq Q$ (Section 10.5).

Here $\bar{Q}$ represents the set of program states we expect to correspond to states of the model—the *correspondence states*. We set

$$\bar{Q} = \{q | q \in Q, \text{proj}_{INF}(q) = N_0, \text{proj}_I(q) = 0, \text{proj}_C(q) = 2\}$$

Thus $q \in \bar{Q}$ is a state in which the program is about to begin scanning (for the first time, or subsequently) through the CELLS to compute their next states.

We define h by

$$h(q) = \text{proj}_{\{0, 1, \dots, n-1\} + n \cdot \text{proj}_{FF}(q)} \circ \text{proj}_{GS}(q)$$

for $q \in \bar{Q}$. Thus if $\text{proj}_{FF}(q) = 0$ (the FLIP $\cdot$ FLOP indicates 0), h projects out the first half of the GLOBAL $\cdot$ STATE array, whereas if $\text{proj}_{FF}(q) = 1$, it projects out the second half.

Exercise.   Show that h is onto but not one to one.

To go from a state in $\bar{Q}$ to another state in $\bar{Q}$ we must traverse the loop (of control states) $2, 3, \dots, 7$ a total of n times (in which the CELLS are scanned), then the loop $2, 1$ (in which the FLIP $\cdot$ FLOP is complemented) before returning to control state 2. Thus we have a total of $6n + 2$ states, which we call *work states*, lying along any trajectory between successive correspondence states.

To prove correctness, we should therefore consider a single step in the model to be encoded as $6n + 2$ steps of the program; that is, we must prove that

$$h(\bar{\delta}(q, 6n + 2)) = \delta'(h(q)) \qquad \text{for all } q \in \bar{Q} \tag{1}$$

To prove Equation 1, we establish a lemma to the effect that the scanning of successive CELLS is correctly implemented, namely, let $q \in \bar{Q}$, and for $i = 0, 1, \dots, n$, let $q_i = \bar{\delta}(q, 6i)$.

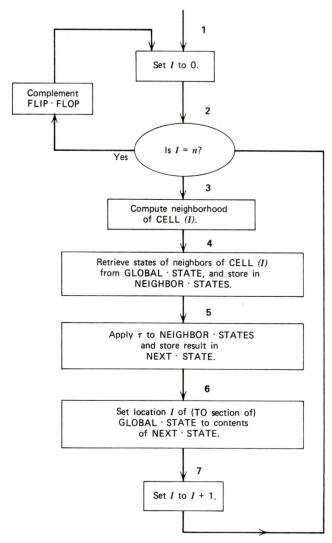

Figure 2 Flow chart for cell space simulator.

Then

$$\text{proj}_C(q_i) = 2, \text{proj}_I(q_i) = i,$$

$$\text{proj}_{FF}(q_i) = \text{proj}_{FF}(q),$$

$$\text{proj}_{INF}(q_i) = N_{i(\text{mod } n)}$$

$$\text{proj}_{\{0, 1, \ldots, n-1\} + n \cdot \text{proj}_{FF}(q_i)} \circ \text{proj}_{GS}(q_i) = \text{proj}_{\{0, 1, \ldots, n-1\} + n \cdot \text{proj}_{FF}(q_i)} \circ \text{proj}_{GS}(q)$$

and

$$\text{proj}_{\{0, 1, \ldots, i-1\} + n \cdot \overline{\text{proj}_{FF(q_i)}}} \text{proj}_{GS}(q_i)$$

$$= \underset{j \in \{0, 1, \ldots, i-1\}}{\times} \tau \circ \text{proj}_{N_{j + n\, \text{proj}_{FF(q_n)}}} \circ \text{proj}_{GS}(q_i) \qquad (2)$$

Equation 2 states nothing more than that as the program sequences through the CELLS, it returns, after examining CELL(i), to control state 2, leaves i in the I register, does not alter the flip-flop, computes the correct neighborhood N_i, leaves the FROM part of the GLOBAL $\cdot$ STATE array unaltered, and places the next state of CELL(i) in the ith location of the TO part of the GLOBAL $\cdot$ STATE array.

The proof of Equation 2, which proceeds by induction on i and amounts to tracing through the definition of δ around the loop 2, 3, $\ldots$, 7, is left as an exercise for the reader. In carrying the proof out, the reader should note the importance of the composition property of δ in formalizing the advance from state to state.

Now for $i = n$, Equation 2 gives us $\text{proj}_I(q_n) = n$, $\text{proj}_C(q_n) = 2$, and $\text{proj}_{INF}(q_n) = N_0$.

Tracing through two more states, we find $\text{proj}_I(\bar{\delta}(q_n, 2)) = 0$; $\text{proj}_C(\bar{\delta}(q_n, 2)) = 2$, and $\text{proj}_{INF}(\bar{\delta}(q_n, 2)) = N_0$. Thus, $\bar{\delta}(q, 6n + 2) = \bar{\delta}(q_n, 2)$ belongs to $\bar{Q}$ as required. Also we have

$$\text{proj}_{\{0, 1, \ldots, n-1\} + n \cdot \text{proj}_{FF(q)}} \circ \text{proj}_{GS}(\delta(q, 6n + 2))$$

$$= \underset{j \in \{0, 1, \ldots, n-1\}}{\times} \tau \circ \text{proj}_{N_{j + n \cdot \text{proj}_{FF(q)}}} \circ \text{proj}_{GS}(q)$$

Thus $$h(\delta(q, 6n + 2)) = \underset{j \in \{0, 1, \ldots, n-1\}}{\times} \tau \circ \text{proj}_{N_j} \circ h(q) = \delta' \circ h(q)$$

This proves Equation 1, thus establishes that the program charted in Figure 2 correctly simulates the cellular space model.

16.2   THE EXTENDED HOMOMORPHISM

In the next section we define complexity measures based on the simulation strategies introduced in Chapter 4. These strategies may be shown to be correct in the same manner we have employed, with the following qualification. In the case of the discrete event approach, the sequence of CELLS scanned need not remain the same nor of the same size. This means that a variable number of transitions may mediate between successive correspondence states. Accordingly, we must extend as follows our notion of homomorphism to include this possibility.

A mapping $h : \bar{Q} \xrightarrow{\text{onto}} Q'$, where $\bar{Q} \subseteq Q$, is an *extended homomorphism*, if for each $q \in Q$, there is a positive integer n_q such that

$$h(\bar{\delta}(q, n_q)) = \delta'(h(q))$$

Exercise. Define an appropriate notion of behavior and show that if an extended homomorphism runs from M to M', the behavior of M correctly matches the behavior of M' (analogous to Theorem 4, Chapter 10.)

In our construction of the simulation program we employed the local transition function τ directly. The correctness of this part of the program was thus taken for granted. For a model of some complexity, the program realization of τ would also be at issue. However, we have now reduced the problem to that of verifying the correctness of a program realization of a function. The latter problem is a general one that has begun to receive much attention.[1, 2]

To summarize, we have illustrated an approach to simulation program verification based on the Postulates of Chapter 11. In like manner, we can formulate the relationships involved in the digital simulation of continuous time systems. The approximate morphisms developed in Chapter 12 can then be applied to study the error inherent in such simulation. These concepts are elaborated in Problems 1 and 2.

16.3 THE SIMULATION COMPLEXITY OF MODELS[†]

The complexity of a model can be investigated from several points of view. In Section 2.5 we viewed the structure of a model as a compact description of its behavior, thus relating the complexity of a model to the difficulty experienced by a modeller in unraveling its structure to reveal its behavior. Recall that in Chapter 9 we set forth a hierarchy of levels at which systems may be specified, ranging from weakly structured input-output descriptions at the low end to highly structured network descriptions at the high end. At each level, measures can be defined based on the features of model structures at that level. The criterion for accepting any such measure as a measure of complexity is that it relates to the difficulty with which the behavior of a model may be inferred from its structure. This difficulty, of course, depends on the nature of the inferential process.

Were we to consider the human brain in the role of the inferential process, we would be able to characterize the intrinsic difficulty encountered by

[†] The material in Sections 16.3 to 16.6, including the accompanying illustrations, appeared originally in Reference 3.

humans in analyzing and understanding model descriptions. But this would
require an understanding of the human analysis process which we now do
not have. Instead, we turn to computer simulation of models for characterizing the inferential process. In other words, the complexity of a model
structure is related to the resources required by a computer in generating
the model behavior, employing instructions based on the model structure.

It is commonly supposed when one transforms a model structure via one
or other of the procedures of Section 2.8 that the resultant model must be
simpler than the original. Formulating this situation as involving a morphism
of an appropriate type from base model to lumped model, we can show
that this is not necessarily the case. Actually, the complexity as determined
by simulation based measures may increase, decrease, or stay the same in
such circumstances. This leads us to seek morphisms and measures for which
true simplification can be guaranteed, and more generally, to the study of
the behavior of complexity measures under morphisms.

To illustrate this idea, let us examine model structures at the level of the
structured machine (Sections 4.7, 9.18). This is the level at which one specifies
the coordinatization of the state space of a discrete time model and the
local transition function for each coordinate. One can think informally of a
directed graph as in Figure 1, in which the points represent black boxes.
The next state of a box is determined as a function of the present states of
the boxes that send lines directly to it.

The points that send directed edges to a point α are called the
INFLUENCERS of α; the points to which α sends directed edges are its
INFLUENCEES. A DIGRAPH (directed graph) is then a set of points

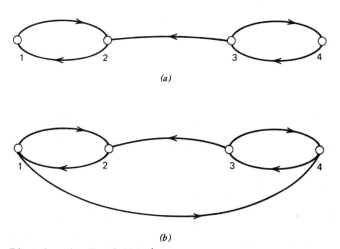

(a)

(b)

Figure 3   Directed graphs: digraph (a) is an ultrastrong morphic image of that digraph (b).

(nodes) and a relation on this set called INFLUENCES, where α IN-FLUENCES β just in case α is an INFLUENCER of β or, equivalently, β is an INFLUENCEE of α.

It is possible to define certain meaningful complexity measures directly by reference to the DIGRAPH of a model, thereby neglecting the other co-relevant elements of its structure. We consider such measures next and define a number of morphisms that interrelate digraphs. Finally, we study the behavior of the complexity measures under the morphisms.

16.4 SIMULATION COMPLEXITY MEASURES

A number of measures have been defined for arbitrary directed graphs. We provide an explanation of how each measure listed below serves as an index of complexity when a particular strategy for computer simulation is considered. We restrict our attention to discrete time simulation by a sequential digital computer.

Let DIGRAPH be an arbitrary directed graph. We consider the following measures (writing MEASURE for MEASURE (DIGRAPH)).

1. $\#\cdot$ POINTS, the number of points of the digraph, represents the number of elements in the coordinate set of the structured machine specification of a model, or less formally, the number of state variables. In a straightforward simulation strategy, a copy is saved of the present global state of the model while each of the coordinates is updated to produce the next global state. Thus this strategy utillizes a number of storage locations equal to $\#\cdot$ POINTS for next states in addition to the $\#\cdot$ POINTS locations required by every strategy for present states.[†]

2. $\#\cdot$ LINES is the number of lines of the digraph. In a sequential simulation, the coordinates must be arranged in some sequence, and the next state of each is updated in turn so that at the end of the sequence the global transition has been computed. The time required to compute the transition is thus related to the total of the times required to compute each coordinate transition. Assuming that the time required for a coordinate is directly proportional to the number of its INFLUENCERS, we find that the total time is proportional to the sum of all the INFLUENCERS, hence to the $\#\cdot$ LINES.

3.   MAX $\cdot$ STRONG $\cdot$ COMPONENT is the size of the largest strong component in the digraph. A strong component is a maximal set such

---

[†] Only $\#\cdot$ POINTS $-$ 1 additional locations are actually required, since the last local state updated can be placed directly into its present state location.

that for every pair of points α, β in the set, there is a directed path from α to β and from β to α (a point is considered to be accessible from itself by a path of length 0). For example, the digraph of Figure 3a has two strong components $\{1, 2\}$ and $\{3, 4\}$, whereas that of Figure 3b, has only $\{1, 2, 3, 4\}$. The strong components thus represent sets of coordinates that are involved in two-way interaction or feedback. For any distinct pair of strong components, the components are either disconnected from each other or are connected in a one-way interaction—components of one influence the other, but not conversely. Thus the strong components can be ordered in a sequence $S_1, S_2, \ldots S_n$ in which each S_i does not influence any S_j ahead of it ($j > i$). For example, $\{1, 2\}$ $\{3, 4\}$ is such a sequence in Figure 3a. A simulation strategy can take advantage of this ordering by first updating the local states of the coordinates in S_1, then those of S_2, and so on. After completing S_1, the old local states of these coordinates need not be saved, since S_1 does not influence any component S_j ahead of it. The same holds true for S_2, and indeed every S_i, $i = 1, \ldots, n$. Thus the computation breaks down into a series of stages such that at each stage i, at most the previous states of coordinates in S_i need be saved to compute the next states of coordinates of S_i. MAX · STRONG · COMPONENT thus represents the additional storage required by this strategy to compute a global state transition.

4. ＃ · STRONG · COMPONENTS, the number of nontrivial strong components, represents the number of times in our strategy that the additional storage area must be cleared and loaded.

5. MIN · CYCLE · BREAK · SET is the size of a smallest cycle-break set. A cycle-break set is a set of points through which all nontrivial cycles pass—removing the points in such a set from the digraph will render it acyclic (without nontrivial cycles). It is clear that a minimal cycle-break set must be the disjoint union of minimal sets, each of which breaks the cycles of a particular strong component.

Since a cycle-break set interrupts all cycles, only the past local states of its elements need to be saved to compute the next global state. To see this, consider without loss of generality a strongly connected graph, and duplicate each of the cycle-break points such that one copy has all the lines coming in to it, and nothing else, and one copy has all lines going out, exclusively (call them the NEXT and the PRESENT nodes, respectively). The resulting digraph is acyclic (Figure 4). Using the idea presented in 3, the nodes can be sequenced in such a way that each point does not influence any points ahead of it. The NEXT nodes are at the beginning of such a sequence and the PRESENT nodes can be placed at the end. Of course the next states of PRESENT nodes need not be computed (this has been done for the corresponding NEXT nodes), and

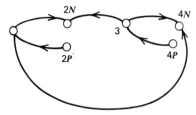
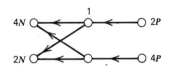

Figure 4   Splitting of the nodes of the digraph of Figure 3b.

they serve only as storage locations of present local states. Note that every cycle requires saving the present state of at least one point on it. Thus MIN · CYCLE · BREAK · SET represents the smallest number of coordinates whose present states must be saved by *any* sequential strategy in computing a global state change.

6.   MIN · MAX · INFLUENCEES is defined as follows. Let $\alpha_1, \alpha_2, \ldots, \alpha_n$ be a particular ordering of the points of DIGRAPH. For each $i = 2, 3, \ldots, n$, let INFLUENCEES$_i$ be the set of points α such that $\alpha \in \{\alpha_1, \ldots, \alpha_{i-1}\}$ and α INFLUENCES at least one $\beta \in \{\alpha_i, \ldots, \alpha_{i-1}\}$ i.e., INFLUENCEES$_i$ = $\{\alpha_1, \ldots, \alpha_{i-1}\} \cap$ INFLUENCEES · OF · $\{\alpha_1, \ldots, \alpha_n\}$. Note that INFLUENCEES$_i$ is precisely the set of coordinates whose present states must occupy the storage at stage i—any such coordinate has already had its next state computed (it comes before α_i in the sequence), but its present state is necessary to the correct computation of the next state of some coordinate further along the sequence. To visualize INFLUÉNCEES$_i$, we can imagine the DIGRAPH drawn in such a way that $\alpha_1, \alpha_2, \ldots, \alpha_n$ appear on a horizontal axis in the order stated and a vertical line is drawn to cross the horizontal axis at α_i. Then INFLUENCEES$_i$ is the set of all points to the left of the line that send out arrows that touch or cross the vertical line, as illustrated in Figure 5. Clearly INFLUENCEES$_2$ = $\{\alpha_1\}$ just in case α_1 INFLUENCES any other element, and INFLUENCEES$_n$ = INFLUENCEES · OF · α_n.

$$\max_{2 \leq i \leq n} |\text{INFLUENCES}_i|$$

represents the largest number of coordinates whose present states must be saved at any one time employing the sequence $\alpha_1, \ldots, \alpha_n$. Thus it represents the number of additional storage locations needed for a strategy based on this sequence.

MIN · MAX · INFLUENCES is the minimum overall permutations of $\alpha_1, \ldots, \alpha_n$ of $\max_{2 \leq i \leq n} |\text{INFLUENCEES}_i|$. It represents the minimum number of additional storage locations required by any sequential strategy.

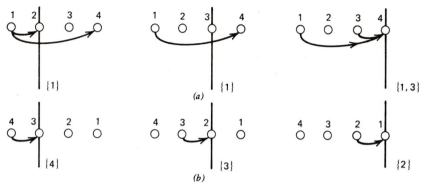

Figure 5 The temporary storage required by computation sequences 1, 2, 3, 4 and 4, 3, 2, 1 for the digraph of Figure 3b.

Since MIN · CYCLE · BREAK · SET is the least number of coordinates whose present states must be saved during the global state transition computation, we have MIN · CYCLE · BREAK · SET $\leq |\bigcup_{i=2}^{n}$ INFLU-ENCEES$_i|$ for any permutation of $\alpha_1, \ldots, \alpha_n$. The equality clearly holds for sequences employed by the strategy of 5. However, a sequence that realizes MIN · MAX · INFLUENCEES may require more than MIN · CYCLE · BREAK · SET as the total number of local states saved (see Figure 5b).

The same reasoning leads to the inequality

$$\text{MIN} \cdot \text{CYCLE} \cdot \text{BREAK} \cdot \text{SET} \leq \sum |S_i|$$

all nontrivial strong components

16.4.1 Digraph Morphisms

To define a series of digraph morphisms of increasing strength, let DIGRAPH and DIGRAPH′ have node sets D and D', respectively. Let $d : D \xrightarrow{\text{onto}} D'$ with $(\alpha') = d^{-1}(\alpha')$ denoting the block in D represented by point $\alpha' \in D'$; we also say that (α') is the block *corresponding* to α'.

The map d is a type x morphism from DIGRAPH to DIGRAPH′ if whenever α' INFLUENCES β' in DIGRAPH′, then "y," where x and y are as follows (see Figure 6):

	x	y	
1.	Weak	$\exists\, \alpha \in (\alpha'), \exists\, \beta \in (\beta')$	such that α INFLUENCES β
2a.	Strong-right	$\forall\, \beta \in (\beta'), \exists\, \alpha \in (\alpha')$	such that α INFLUENCES β
2b.	Strong-left	$\forall\, \alpha \in (\alpha'), \exists\, \beta \in (\beta')$	such that α INFLUENCES β
3.	Very strong	d is both strong-left and strong-right	
4.	Ultrastrong	$\forall\, \alpha \in (\alpha'), \forall\, \beta \in (\beta'), \alpha$ INFLUENCES β	

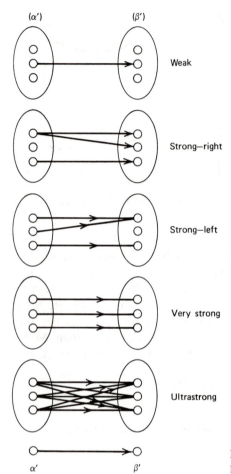

Figure 6 The hierarchy of digraph morphisms.

The morphism types form a hierarchy, ordered partially from weak to strong:

Exercise. Show that in the hierarchy, every level i morphism is also a level $i - 1$ morphism, but there are level $i - 1$ morphisms that are not level i morphisms.

We now turn to our main concern—the behavior of complexity measures with morphisms.

We say that a complexity MEASURE *tends to decrease* with morphisms of type m if whenever d is a type m morphism from DIGRAPH to DIGRAPH' (arbitrary digraphs), then MEASURE(DIGRAPH') $\leq$ MEASURE(DIGRAPH).

We say that a MEASURE is *ambivalent* with type m morphisms if it tends neither to decrease nor to increase with type m morphisms; that is, there are pairs (DIGRAPH$_1$, DIGRAPH$_1'$) and (DIGRAPH$_2$, DIGRAPH$_2'$) with respective connecting morphisms d and d' of type m, for which MEASURE (DIGRAPH$_1'$) > MEASURE(DIGRAPH$_1$) and MEASURE(DIGRAPH$_2'$) < MEASURE(DIGRAPH$_2$).

16.5   BEHAVIOR OF COMPLEXITY MEASURES WITH MORPHISMS

By testing the six complexity measures against the five morphism types, we obtain the results displayed in Table 1. The marked cells of the table represent results that can be proven directly (as we shall show). The blank cell entries can be inferred from the following easily justified assentions:

(*a*)   If a MEASURE tends to decrease with morphisms at level i, it tends to decrease with morphisms at all higher levels j, $j \geq i$.

(*b*)   If a MEASURE is ambivalent at level i, it is also ambivalent at all lower levels j, $j \leq i$.

In other words, ambivalence can be resolved only by strengthening the morphism relation, and there is a minimum level at which the nondecreasing behavior is achieved (although this may be at the highest level in which all morphisms are digraph isomorphisms).

That $\#\cdot$ POINTS and $\#\cdot$ LINES tend to decrease with weak morphisms is almost immediate. The ambivalence of $\#\cdot$ STRONG $\cdot$ COMPONENTS can be seen by noting that the morphic image digraph may have fewer lines than the preimage digraph, hence may be more disconnected (this is the case for Figures 3*b* and 3*a*, between which there is a type 4 morphism); on the other hand a nontrivial, strongly connected digraph may be mapped onto a single point (i.e., a trivial strong component). In the first case $\#\cdot$ STRONG $\cdot$ COMPONENTS increases, whereas in the second it decreases in going from preimage to image.

Table 1 Behavior of Complexity Measures

Measure	Morphism			
	1 Weak	2 Strong-Right	Strong-Left	3 Very Strong	4 Ultrastrong
# · POINTS	Tends to decrease				
# · LINES	Tends to decrease				
MAX · STRONG · COMPONENT	Ambivalent	Tends to decrease	Tends to decrease		
# · STRONG · COMPONENTS					Ambivalent
MIN · CYCLE · BREAK · SET	Ambivalent	Tends to decrease	Tends to decrease		
MIN · MAX · INFLUENCEES	Ambivalent	Tends to decrease	Tends to decrease		

The remaining results employ the following general principle: let $a_1, \ldots, a_n$ and $b_1, \ldots, b_n$ be sequences such that for each $i = 1, \ldots, m$, $a_i \leq b_i$. Then for any set A that includes $\{a_1, \ldots, a_n\}$, $\min \{a | a \in A\} \leq \min \{b, \ldots, b_n\}$; for any set B that includes $\{b_1, \ldots, b_n\}$, $\max \{b | b \in B\} \geq \max \{a_1, \ldots, a_n\}$.

In addition we require the following

LEMMA

Let d be a strong (right or left) digraph morphism from DIGRAPH to DIGRAPH'. Then for any circuit (cycle) in DIGRAPH' there is a circuit (cycle) in DIGRAPH tranversing at least as many distinct points.

Proof.   Let $\alpha_1', \alpha_2', \ldots, \alpha_p'$ be a *circuit* of DIGRAPH'; that is, $\alpha_1' = \alpha_p'$ and for each $i = 1, 2, \ldots, p - 1$, there is a line from α_i to α_{i+1}. A circuit is thus a walk beginning at some point in the graph which returns home. A *cycle* is a circuit in which all but initial and end points are distinct. Let $\alpha_{i_1}', \alpha_{i_2}', \ldots, \alpha_{i_q}'$ be the distinct points of circuit $\alpha_1', \ldots, \alpha_p'$ of which there are $q \leq p$. The corresponding blocks in DIGRAPH $(\alpha_{i_1}'), \ldots, (\alpha_{i_q}')$ are also distinct, and we claim that there is a circuit traversing each of these q blocks and therefore at least q points.

Consider the case when d is strong-left. Choose any point α_1 in (α_1'). Since d is strong-left, there is a line from α_1 to some point α_2 in (α_2') and from α_2 to some point $\alpha_3' \in (\alpha_3')$. Continuing in this way we generate a walk $\alpha_1, \alpha_2, \ldots, \alpha_{p-1}$ which traverses the q distinct blocks. Although we are guaranteed that there is a line from α_{p-1} to some point α_p in (α_1'), it is not necessarily the case that $\alpha_p = \alpha_1$. But since d is strong-left, our walk may be extended to pass again and again through the blocks $(\alpha_1), \ldots, (\alpha_{p-1})$, and since (α_1) has a finite number of points, eventually we must repeat a point. The walk starting from this point and returning to it is a circuit passing through q distinct blocks.

In the case of a strong-right morphism we follow the walk generation procedure just given in reverse. When the reverse walk closes in on itself, we will have generated a circuit of the desired kind.

When a circuit in DIGRAPH' is a cycle of size p, it can be shown that the corresponding circuit in DIGRAPH can be reduced to a cycle of size an integer multiple of p.   ∎

THEOREM

MAX · STRONG · COMPONENT and MIN · CYCLE · BREAK · SET tend to decrease with strong (right or left) morphisms and are ambivalent with weak morphisms.

Proof. Let *d* be a strong morphism from DIGRAPH to DIGRAPH′. A strong component in DIGRAPH′ is a set of points *S* which are connected by a circuit. By the lemma, there is a set of points at least as large as *S* which are connected by a circuit in DIGRAPH. Thus for every strong component of DIGRAPH′, there is a strong component of DIGRAPH that is at least as large. Applying the general principle, we have MAX · STRONG · COMPONENT (DIGRAPH′) ≤ MAX · STRONG · COMPONENT (DIGRAPH). This shows that MAX · STRONG · COMPONENT tends to decrease with strong morphisms.

Referring again to Figure 3, we see a case of the MAX · STRONG · COMPONENT strictly decreasing in going from preimage to image. On the other hand, Figure 7 shows a pair of digraphs related by a weak morphism in which the MAX · STRONG · COMPONENT strictly increases in going from preimage to image, demonstrating the desired ambivalence with weak morphisms.

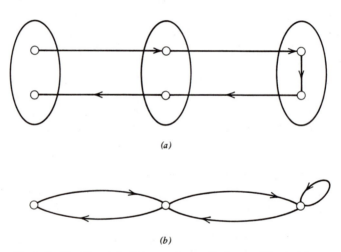

(a)

(b)

Figure 7   The digraph in (b) is a weak morphic image of that in (a).

Now again returning to any strong morphism *d* from DIGRAPH to DIGRAPH′. Let *C* be a cycle-break set in DIGRAPH. By the lemma, any cycle in DIGRAPH′ that avoids all *d(C)* has a corresponding cycle in DIGRAPH that avoids all *C*. This is a contradiction unless all the cycles of DIGRAPH′ pass through *d(C)*. Thus if *C* is a cycle-break set in DIGRAPH, *d(C)* is a cycle-break set at least as small. Thus by the general principle MIN · CYCLE · BREAK · SET (DIGRAPH′) ≤ MIN · CYCLE · BREAK · SET (DIGRAPH).

The ambivalence of MIN · CYCLE · BREAK · SET with weak morphisms is represented in Figures 7 and 8.   ∎

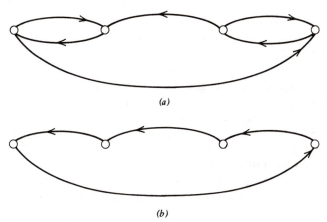

(a)

(b)

Figure 8   The digraph in (b) is a weak morphic image of that in (a).

THEOREM

MIN · MAX · INFLUENCEES tends to decrease with strong (left or right) morphisms but is ambivalent with weak morphisms.

Proof.   We consider first the case in which d is a strong-left morphism from DIGRAPH to DIGRAPH'. Let $\alpha_1, \ldots, \alpha_n$ be a sequence listing the points of DIGRAPH. Then $d(\alpha_1), \ldots, d(\alpha_n)$ is a sequence listing all points of DIGRAPH', which however may have repetitions. Mark the first appearance of every point of DIGRAPH' in this sequence. We claim that the marked sequence is a computation sequence for which max $|\text{INFLUENCEES}_i|$ in DIGRAPH' is less than or equal to max $|\text{INFLUENCEES}_i|$ for the sequence $\alpha_1, \ldots, \alpha_n$ in DIGRAPH.

Referring to Figure 9 for visualization, we say that α *corresponds* to α' if α is the element in $\alpha_1, \ldots, \alpha_n$ in the same position as the first appearance of α' in $d(\alpha_1), \ldots, d(\alpha_n)$, that is, $\alpha = \alpha_i$, where $i = \min \{j|\alpha_j \in (\alpha')\}$. Thus α maps onto α' and all elements that also map onto α' appear ahead of α in the sequence $\alpha_1, \ldots, \alpha_n$. Clearly α' appears before β' in the marked sequence if and only if the first appearance of α' comes before the first appearance of β' in $d(\alpha_1), \ldots, d(\alpha_n)$.

Let the marked sequence be $\alpha'_1, \ldots, \alpha'_m$ and consider stage i; $\alpha' \in \text{INFLUENCEES}_i$ for $\alpha'_1, \ldots, \alpha'_m$ if and only if α' appears before α'_i in the marked sequence and α' INFLUENCES' β' for some β' equal to or ahead of α_i'. Let α correspond to α' in $\alpha_1, \ldots, \alpha_n$. Then since d is a strong-left morphism, α INFLUENCES some $\bar{\beta}$ in (β'). But since β' is ahead of α_i' in the marked sequence, its corresponding β lies ahead of α_i (corresponding to α_i') in $\alpha_1, \ldots, \alpha_n$. Thus $\bar{\beta}$ must lie ahead of α_i in $\alpha_1, \ldots, \alpha_n$. Thus $\alpha \in$ INFLUENCEES$_i$ for $\alpha_1, \ldots, \alpha_n$.

Thus for each $\alpha' \in$ INFLUENCEES$_i$ of $\alpha_1', \ldots, \alpha_m'$, there is a distinct $\alpha \in$ INFLUENCEES$_i$ of $\alpha_1, \ldots, \alpha_n$. And so for each $i = 1, \ldots, m$, $|$INFLUENCEES$_i|$ for $\alpha_1', \ldots, \alpha_m'$ is less than or equal to $|$INFLUENCEES$_i|$ for $\alpha_1, \ldots, \alpha_m$. Using the general principle, we have that max $|$INFLUENCEES$_i|$ for $\alpha_1', \ldots, \alpha_m'$ is less than or equal to max $|$INFLUENCEES$_i|$ for $\alpha_1, \ldots, \alpha_n$. Applying the principle to all possible permutations of $\alpha_1, \ldots, \alpha_n$ (which cover all possible permutations of $\alpha_1', \ldots, \alpha_m'$), we have the desired result that MIN $\cdot$ MAX $\cdot$ INFLUENCEES (DIGRAPH') $\leq$ MIN $\cdot$ MAX $\cdot$ INFLUENCEES (DIGRAPH).

The proof for strong-right morphisms is similar, except that the marked sequence is obtained by marking all *last* appearances of elements in $d(\alpha_1), \ldots, d(\alpha_n)$.

The ambivalence of MIN $\cdot$ MAX $\cdot$ INFLUENCEES with weak morphisms is demonstrated by the digraph pairs in Figures 7 and 8.

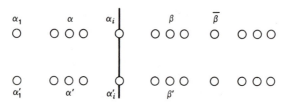

Figure 9   The relations between the original and marked sequences.

16.6 SUMMARY

We have outlined an approach to structural complexity based on (1) a hierarchy of levels of system specifications and morphisms, and (2) complexity measures related to inference of model behavior given model structure.

We restricted our application of these ideas to the case of discrete time models specified at the structure machine level and to measures and morphisms defined on their coordinate influence digraphs. The measures chosen were related to sequential simulation strategies. Our results reinforce the conclusion previously derived that complexity does not automatically decrease under common procedures designed to enable simplification. Some measures such as # $\cdot$ POINTS and # $\cdot$ LINES *do* tend to decrease under even the weakest of the morphisms considered. This agrees with the common perception that simplification involves reducing the number of variables and the numbers of interactions of a model. However, the generalization of this well-behavedness to other measures relevant to simulation does not go through, as commonly supposed. In fact some measures (MAX · STRONG · COMPONENT, MIN · BREAK · CYCLE · SET, MIN · MAX · INFLU-ENCEES) are ambivalent with the lowest level morphisms but become well behaved with higher level morphisms in which the structures of the preimage and image models are more strongly related. Finally, one measure considered (# · STRONG · COMPONENTS) is ambivalent with even the highest level morphism considered.

Clearly, the approach illustrated here may be applied at various levels of the specification hierarchy, employing various complexity measures and strategies of simulation. The result might be a better understanding of what makes models complex and of the ways in which they can be meaningfully simplified.

16.7 SOURCES

A survey of program verification work is given in Reference 1. Various preservation relations for programs are systematized in Reference 2. Simulation in automata theory is discussed in Reference 4.

1. B. Elspas, K. N. Levitt, R. J. Walinger, A. Waksman, "An Assessment of Techniques for Proving Program Correctness" *Computer Surveys*, **4** (2), 1972, 97–146.
2. J. L. Bosworth, "Software Reliability by Redundancy." Doctoral dissentation, University of Michigan, Ann Arbor, 1975.
3. B. P. Zeigler, "Simulation Based Complexity of Models," *International Journal of General Systems*, **2** (2), in press.
4. J. E. Hopcroft and J. D. Ullman, *Formal Languages and Their Relation to Automata.* Addison-Wesley, Reading, Mass., 1969.

PROBLEMS

1. In this problem we study digital simulation of continuous time and especially differential equation systems.

    Let $S = \langle T, X, \Omega, Q, \delta \rangle$ be a continuous time I/O system (without outputs). For any $h > 0$, define $S_h = \langle T, X, \Omega_h^+, Q, \overline{\delta}_h \rangle$, where $\Omega_h = \Omega|_{\langle 0, h \rangle}$ and $\delta_h = \delta | Q \times \Omega_h$. S_h represents system S as it appears when restricted to input segments of lengths that are integer multiples of h.

    (a) Show that S_h is specified by the iterative specification $G_h = \langle T, X, \Omega_h, Q, \delta_h \rangle$.

(b)   Consider the sequential machine $M_h = \langle \Omega_h, Q, \delta_h \rangle$ and show that there is a specification morphism from $G(M_h)$ to G_h. Conclude that there is a system morphism from $S_{G(M_h)}$ to S_h.

It follows from b, that every continuous time system can be simulated *exactly* by a discrete time system (hence by an ideal digital computer), provided its state trajectories are to be reproduced only at sampled intervals that are multiples of h. Note, however, that (1) the system must be known at the I/O system level (i.e., its global transition function must be known), and (2) the input set cardinality of M_h is one cardinal order above that of S_h (e.g., if X has the cardinality of the reals, Ω_h has the cardinality of the set of all real functions).

Considerations 1 and 2 mitigate against the practicality of exact simulation of continuous time models. But although the exact may not be attainable, it does provide an ideal against which to judge approximate simulation methods, and a basis for considering them.

As illustration, we consider the case of differential equation models. Let $D = \langle X, Q, f \rangle$ be a differential equation system specification (DESS) (without outputs) such that f satisfies the *Lipschitz condition*:

$$\text{for all } q, q' \in Q, x \in X, \qquad \|f(q, x) - f(q', x)\| < k \cdot \|q - q'\|$$

$\| \ \|$ is a norm on Q, and k is constant.

From Section 9.10 we know that D specifies an iterative specification $G(D)$, which in turn specifies an I/O system $S_{G(D)}$. From Problem 1b we also know that $S_{G(D)}^h$ can be exactly simulated by some sequential machine $M_h = \langle \Omega_h, Q, \delta_h \rangle$, where Ω_h is the set of bpc segments over $\langle 0, h \rangle$ mapping into X, and $\delta_h : Q \times \Omega_h \to Q$ is given by

$$\delta_h(q, \omega) = \Phi_{q, \omega}(h)$$

where Φ is the state trajectory associated with q and ω.

It is clear that to obtain such exact simulation we must have already available the global state trajectory solutions. But note that only the solutions over the interval $\langle 0, h \rangle$ need be known. This makes it possible to generate trajectories by obtaining solutions for the interval $\langle 0, h \rangle$ by one or another integration method and iterating to obtain trajectories over intervals of longer lengths. Classical numerical analysis has concentrated on the generation of complete trajectories by integration alone, and little is known about the relative merits of the combined integration-iteration approach.

2.   We illustrate the study of error propagation by considering the most basic integration method, the Euler or rectangular method, whose application is modelled by the sequential machine $M_h^a = \langle X, Q, \delta_h^a \rangle$, where $\delta_h^a : Q \times X \to Q$ is given by $\delta_h^a(q, x) = q + hf(q, x)$.

(a) Let (g, i) be a pair such that $g:\Omega_h \to X$ is given by $g(\omega) = \omega(0)$ and $i:Q \to Q$ is the identity mapping. Consider (g, i) as an approximate specification morphism from M_h^a to M_h. Using the Lipschitz condition and assuming that $\|f(q, x)\| \le M$, for all $q \in Q$, $x \in X$ show that

$$d(\delta_h(q, \omega), \delta_h^a(q, \omega(0))) = \|\delta_h(q, \omega) - \delta_h^a(q, \omega(0))\|$$
$$\le Mkh^2$$

so that (g, i) is an ε-morphism where $\varepsilon = Mkh^2$.

Hint. $\Phi_{q, \omega}(t) = q + \int_0^t f(\Phi_{q, \omega}(t'), \omega(t'))\, dt'$.

(b) Show that the error amplification factor of M_h^a, namely, the a of the relation

$$\|\delta_h^a(q, x) - \delta_h^a(q', x)\| \le a\|q - q'\|$$

is given by $a = 1 + kh$.

(c) Using the results of part a with M_h playing the role of big system and M_h^a the little system (this is acceptable because the state spaces are isomorphic), show that the error accumulated in n steps

$$e_n^h = \|\delta_h(q, \omega_1, \ldots, \omega_n) - \delta_h^a(q, \omega_1(0) \cdots \omega_n(0))\|$$

is bounded by

$$e_n^h \le Mh((1 + kh)^n - 1)$$

Now consider a fixed time t, and let n be determined as the number of steps of length h required to reach t (i.e., $n = t/h$). Show that the error between the true and approximate solutions at t, with step size h, is bounded above by $Mh(1 + hk)^{t/h}$, which approaches zero as h goes to zero.

(d) We have till now assumed that the DESS had unique solutions; hence the previous result shows that an approximate trajectory comes arbitrarily close to the corresponding true trajectory. But we can also use the technique to show that the Lipschitz condition guarantees unique solutions.

Consider the following sequence of approximation sequential machines: $M_h^a, M_{h/2}^a, M_{h/4}^a, \ldots, M_{h/2^n}^a, \ldots$. By considering $M_{h/2^{n+1}}^a$ to be a big machine and $M_{h/2^n}^a$ to be a small machine, show that the sequence generates trajectories $\{\Phi_{q, \omega}^h\}$, which converge to a fixed trajectory $\Phi_{q, \omega}$ as $n \to \infty$. Then show that $\Phi_{q, \omega}$ is a solution of the differential equation. Use the results of c to demonstrate that this solution is unique.

3. Formalize each strategy of Section 16.4 as a program specification M to simulate a one-dimensional cell space model M' and prove that a homomorphism runs from M to M'.

4. Study the behavior of MAX · INDEGREE with digraph morphisms, where MAX · INDEGREE (DIGRAPH) is the size of the largest set of INFLUENCERS of the points of DIGRAPH.

5. Formalize the next-event–last-event strategy for simulating structured machines (Section 4.8).

   (*a*) Define measures of complexity appropriate to the sizes of the NEXT · EVENTS and LAST · EVENTS lists as related to an arbitrary state transition of the machine. Study the behavior of these measures under strong structure morphisms, including the digraph morphism refinements introduced in this chapter.

   (*b*) For the case of the one-dimensional cell space, establish the correctness of the strategy using the extended homomorphism concept.

6. Using the DEVS formalism, formalize the discrete event strategies of Chapter 7, and prove that they correctly simulate the discrete event models (also DEVS formalized) of the same chapter.

Appendix A

Brain Modelling

This appendix presents in some detail a fully worked out example of the approach to modelling and simulation just introduced. Although the subject area—neuron-based models of the brain—may be of particular interest to some, the presentation is intended for the general modeller whose primary interest lies elsewhere. We want to concretize and illustrate the general principles introduced in Chapters 1 and 2 for a particular special case, and it is these principles that the reader should keep uppermost in his mind to avoid getting bogged down in details.

The presentation[†] follows the format suggested in Chapter 2. The formal descriptions of the base and lumped models are given in Chapter 12.

INFORMAL DESCRIPTION OF BASE AND LUMPED MODELS AND THEIR CORRESPONDENCE

The human brain is estimated to consist of about 10^{10} nerve cells, called *neurons*. Certain properties of these neurons and their interconnection are known or can be inferred from general knowledge of cell behavior. What is almost completely lacking is an understanding of how the higher level behavior associated with the mind—thinking, planning, deciding, creating, and so on—can arise from such a vast network of relatively primitive parts. The psychologist D. O. Hebb[2] put forth a "theory" (better put, an extensive hypothesis) on how the brain is organized, and this stimulated the development of a continuing series of simulation models.

[†] The description of base and lumped models is taken from Reference 1, pp. 371–379.

We employ a fairly simple model of the neuron. We assume that the cell body is capable of emitting or *firing*, an electrical pulse that travels down its *axon* (output fiber). The input fibers, or *dendrites*, of the neuron make contact with the axons of other neurons and are capable of relaying their pulses to the cell body. (In our base model, the pulse travel time is, in effect, ignored). The pulses arriving from various points at the cell body can combine to stimulate it to discharge a pulse. It is thought that each axon may have a different influence on the firing of the neuron—some may inhibit, some may facilitate, and to varying degrees. This differential influence is thought to arise from the chemical properties of the separating space, or *synapse* between axon and dendrite. When a neuron fires, it becomes refractory, or harder to fire, for some time, or in terms of our model, its threshold for firing increases instantly and then decays back to its original level.

Base Model   (*Figure 1a*)

Components

NEURONS—elements modelling basic behavior assumed to be characteristic of real brain cells.

INPUT · WIRES—sources of external act excitation.

Descriptive Variables

For each NEURON:

RECOVERY · STATE—with range the nonnegative integers; RECOVERY · STATE = i indicates that i time units have elapsed since the NEURON last fired; thus $i = 0$ means the NEURON is now firing.

NOISE—with range the real numbers; (when NOISE = r the actual threshold for firing of the NEURON is THRESHOLD $(i) + r$, where THRESHOLD (i) is the threshold value characteristic of RECOVERY · STATE i. NOISE is a random variable generated for each NEURON.

STRENGTH—with range the real numbers; STRENGTH = x, indicates that the sum total of all NEURON inputs is x.

FIRING · STATE—with range $\{0, 1\}$; 1 means the NEURON is firing (emitting a pulse), 0, that it is not firing.

For each INPUT · WIRE:

INPUT · LEVEL—with range the real numbers; INPUT · LEVEL = x indicates that the excitation level on the INPUT · WIRE is x (measured in the same units as STRENGTH).

The NEURONS are partitioned into disjoint groups or BLOCKS.

For each BLOCK and for each RECOVERY · STATE i

% · IN · STATE · i—with range the rationals in $[0, 100]$; the percentage of NEURONS in the BLOCK in RECOVERY STATE i.

PARAMETERS

For each BLOCK:

NOISE · DISTRIBUTION—the probability distribution for the random variable NOISE.

THRESHOLD—a real valued function with RECOVERY · STATE as argument, giving the minimum strength needed to fire a NEURON in the absence of NOISE.

For each NEURON

NEURON · NEIGHBORS—with range the subsets of NEURONS; indicates the NEURONS whose outputs impinge on the NEURON.

EXTERNAL · NEIGHBORS—with range the subsets of INPUT · WIRES indicates the external inputs impinging on the NEURON.

For each NEIGHBOR (NEURON or EXTERNAL) of the NEURON:

SYNAPS—with range the reals; determines the influence that a NEIGHBOR has on the NEURON: positive indicates facilitative negative indicates inhibiting.

Component Interaction

1. Each NEURON receives inputs from other NEURONS called NEURON · NEIGHBORS as well as from external sources called EXTERNAL · NEIGHBORS (Figure 1*a*). We just refer to NEIGHBORS when the context is clear.

2. The NEURONS are grouped into disjoint sets called BLOCKS. This partitioning of the NEURONS places the following restrictions on the possible NEURON · NEIGHBORS of a NEURON. Suppose that a NEURON α belongs to BLOCK i.

   (*a*) If α has some NEIGHBORS in BLOCK j (which may equal i) then every NEURON in BLOCK i must have at least one NEIGHBOR in BLOCK j.

   (*b*) The SYNAPS weight is the same for the outputs of all NEIGHBORS of α from the same BLOCK. The NEIGHBORS of α coming from BLOCK j all have the same "influence" on it, but this may be different from that of the neighbors of α coming from BLOCK k ($k \neq j$).

   (*c*) BLOCK j exerts the same "influence" on each NEURON in BLOCK i. We measure the "influence" of BLOCK j on α by the product of the number of α's NEIGHBORS from BLOCK j and their common SYNAPS value. This product is to take the same value for all NEURONS in BLOCK i, so that the "influence" of BLOCK j on each NEURON in BLOCK i is the same.

   (*d*) The characteristics of all NEURONS in a BLOCK, namely, the

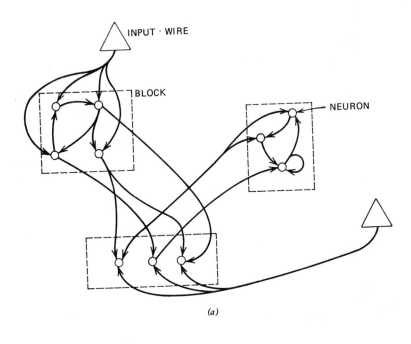

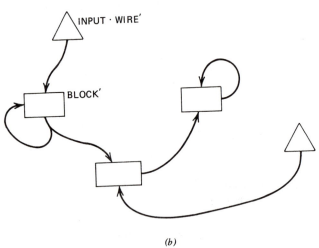

Figure 1 (a) Base model. (b) Lumped model.

THRESHOLD function and NOISE probability distribution, are the same.

(e) The EXTERNAL · NEIGHBORS and their SYNAPS weights are the same for all NEURONS in a BLOCK.

3. Each NEURON operates at each time step as follows:

(a) the STRENGTH of the input volley is computed by adding together the outputs (which may be 0 or 1) for all the EXTERNAL NEIGHBORS and NEURON · NEIGHBORS of α weighted by their respective SYNAPS values.

(b) If this STRENGTH is great enough, the NEURON will fire, (i.e., will put out a one for the next time step); otherwise it will put out a zero. The 1/0 output can be thought of as a pulse/no pulse sent out by the NEURON, with only the pulse being able to influence the activities of another NEURON.

(c) The minimum STRENGTH required to fire is dependent on the RECOVERY · STATE of the NEURON and NOISE. Generally the longer it has been since the NEURON last fired, the easier it is to fire. Indeed if it has just fired it may be impossible for it to fire for some time (this period is called the absolute refractory period). This fact is formalized in the shape of the THRESHOLD function. This function determines for each RECOVERY · STATE value i (time since last fired) a value THRESHOLD(i), which can be thought of as the minimum strength required, if there were no noise, to fire the NEURON.

It is also assumed that the NEURON is perturbed by additive noise independently generated at each step for each NEURON from the NOISE probability distribution.

Thus if the NEURON is now in RECOVERY · STATE i, the minimum STRENGTH required to fire it is THRESHOLD(i) plus the sampled value of NOISE.

(d) If NEURON fires, its RECOVERY · STATE is set to 0, otherwise it is incremented by 1. Thus, as implied, it records the time elapsed since the last firing of this NEURON occurred.

Lumped Model (Figure 1b)

Components

BLOCKS'

Each BLOCK' represents in lumped form the behavior of a corresponding BLOCK of base model NEURONS (' indicates the correspondence).

INPUT · WIRES'

Each INPUT · WIRE' of the lumped model represents a corresponding INPUT · WIRE of the base model.

Descriptive Variables

For each BLOCK', for each $i = 0, 1, 2, \ldots$

$\% \cdot$ IN $\cdot$ STATE $\cdot$ i'—with range $[0, 100]$; $\% \cdot$ IN $\cdot$ STATE $\cdot$ $i' = q$ predicts that $q/100$ of the base model NEURONS in BLOCK are in
RECOVERY $\cdot$ STATE $\cdot$ i. Thus $\% \cdot$ IN $\cdot$ STATE $\cdot$ i' of BLOCK' corresponds to $\% \cdot$ IN $\cdot$ STATE $\cdot$ i of BLOCK.

STRENGTH'—with range the real numbers; STRENGTH' $= x'$ indicates that the sum total of inputs to BLOCK' is x'.

For each INPUT $\cdot$ WIRE'

INPUT $\cdot$ LEVEL'—with range the real numbers.

PARAMETERS

For each BLOCK'

BLOCK' $\cdot$ NEIGHBORS—with range the subsets of BLOCKS'; specifies the BLOCKS' that send input to the BLOCK'.

EXTERNAL' $\cdot$ NEIGHBORS—with range the subsets of INPUT $\cdot$ WIRES'.

For each NEIGHBOR (BLOCK' or EXTERNAL')

WEIGHT'—with range the real numbers; determines the influence of the NEIGHBOR on the BLOCK'.

NOISE $\cdot$ DISTRIBUTION'—a cumulative density function (cdf) (will be the cdf of NOISE).

THRESHOLD'—a function from the nonnegative integers to the reals (to be identical with THRESHOLD).

Component Interaction

1. Each BLOCK' receives input from other BLOCKS' (called BLOCK' $\cdot$ NEIGHBORS) and external sources (called EXTERNAL $\cdot$ NEIGHBORS').

2. Each BLOCK' at each time step operates as follows:

   (*a*) The STRENGTH' of the input to the BLOCK' is computed as the WEIGHTED sum of all NEIGHBOR (BLOCK' and EXTERNAL') outputs.

   (*b*) Using this STRENGTH' and the current values of the $\% \cdot$ IN $\cdot$ STATE $\cdot$ i (one for each RECOVERY $\cdot$ STATE i) the next values of the $\% \cdot$ IN $\cdot$ STATE $\cdot$ i variables are computed: for each i, the current value of $\% \cdot$ IN $\cdot$ STATE $\cdot$ i is multiplied by a fraction—determined by THRESHOLD', STRENGTH', and NOISE $\cdot$ DISTRIBUTION' to obtain the new value of $\% \cdot$ IN $\cdot$ STATE $\cdot$ $i + 1$. If the lumped model is valid, this accounts for the fraction of base model NEURONS in RECOVERY $\cdot$ STATE i that have not fired (hence go to $i + 1$); the remainder are those that do fire (hence go to RECOVERY · STATE 0), and the lumped model reflects this as a sum of all such contributions to obtain the new $\% \cdot$ IN $\cdot$ STATE $\cdot$ 0′.

(c)   The output of BLOCK′ is just $\% \cdot$ IN $\cdot$ STATE $\cdot$ 0′, which, if the lumped model is valid, is the percentage of NEURONS in the BLOCK which are firing, that is, outputting a pulse (1). (The rest are in the various RECOVERY · STATES, and since they output a 0, will not influence any activity at the next time step.)

Correspondences Between Base and Lumped Structures

If the following correspondences hold, the lumped model is valid with respect to the base model.

Components

Each BLOCK′ (lumped model component) corresponds to a BLOCK (partition class) of NEURONS (base model components).

Descriptive Variables

For each BLOCK′
   For each $i = 0, 1, 2, \ldots$.
   $\% \cdot$ IN $\cdot$ STATE $\cdot i′ = \% \cdot$ IN $\cdot$ STATE $\cdot i$.
STRENGTH′ = STRENGTH of any NEURON in the corresponding BLOCK.

PARAMETERS
   INPUT′ · WIRES = INPUT · WIRES
      For each BLOCK′
         BLOCK′ · NEIGHBORS = the set of BLOCKS′ whose corresponding BLOCKS influence NEURONS in the BLOCK (corresponding to BLOCK′).
         EXTERNAL′ · NEIGHBORS = EXTERNAL · NEIGHBORS of any NEURON in the BLOCK (a BLOCK constant according to Postulate 2e).
         THRESHOLD′ = THRESHOLD.
         NOISE · DISTRIBUTION′ = NOISE · DISTRIBUTION for any NEURON in the BLOCK (Postulate 2d).

   For each NEIGHBOR (BLOCK′ or EXTERNAL): WEIGHT′ = the product of the number of corresponding NEIGHBORS′ and their common SYNAPS values (Postulate 2c) of any NEURON in BLOCK′.

   For each INPUT · WIRE: INPUT · LEVEL′ = INPUT · LEVEL.

PRESERVATION OF COMPONENT INTERACTION

We have just given the correspondences we expect to hold at any time step between the base and lumped models. These correspondences are significant because they enable us to correlate the behaviors of the two models through time. More specifically, if these correspondences hold, we can assert that the behavior of the lumped model validly reflects that of the base model.

But to show that these correspondences do in fact hold, and under what circumstances, requires a rigorous mathematical proof. Such a proof is given in Chapter 12.

AN ILLUSTRATIVE QUASISIMULATION

We have described a base model–lumped model pair for use in brain modelling. In actual practice, only the lumped model could be simulated on the computer and its behavior compared with the real brain system it is supposed to model. But the components of the lumped model are unlike the entities thought by neuroscientists to constitute the real brain, and even if the lumped model were to faithfully represent real brain behavior, people would be reluctant to accept it until its connection with the more familiar entities was understood. The base model has been introduced for this purpose. But precisely because it is potentially more faithful to the actual brain structure and there are thought to be about 10^{10} neurons in the real cortex, it is also infeasible to try to simulate it on a computer and test it directly for validity.

To illustrate the differences between the base and lumped models and their relationship to the real system and the computer, we are going to undertake a "quasisimulation" involving actual simulation of both lumped *and* base models. We construct a base model net consisting of a relatively small number of NEURONS, which *is* possible to simulate. We also construct a corresponding lumped model consisting of a small number of BLOCKS'. Then we program each model, simulate, and compare behaviors. Thus the base model plays the role in this instance of the "real system" itself. Note that this is a special "real system," since it is for us a very white box, rather than the blackish box that a true "real system" is.

Note that the proposed model is possible because the correspondence we have established really holds between a wide class of base–lumped model pairs, not just between a pair that would prove to faithfully represent a real brain. This is because in the description of the base and lumped models we allowed *parameters* whose many different settings may correspond to many different models, *and* we took these into account in setting up the correspondence.

A simulation package was written in FORTRAN to experiment with a wide variety of base–lumped model pairs. The essential portions of the subroutines implementing the base and lumped models appear in Figures 2 and 3.

THE EXPERIMENTAL FRAME

In Section 2.2, we state the credo that the ultimate criterion of validity of a model is the extent to which its input-output behavior agrees with the observable real system behavior. Certainly there may hold stronger structural correspondences, but their validity can only be confirmed indirectly through this basic input-output agreement. On the other hand, since stronger correspondences imply weaker ones, most modelling is a conscious attempt to reflect structural features thought to characterize the real system.

In our example, we think of the base model as being the "real system," and we suppose that there are quite severe limitations on the amount of simultaneous measurement that can be done on the "real" neural net. That is, we suppose that "electrode probes" implanted in the "brain" can obtain data on the FIRING · STATES of NEURONS in a local region but not on their RECOVERY · STATES or their NOISE generator states. Moreover the number of probes is relatively small, certainly much smaller than the number of NEURONS. These limitations are realistic in relation to the real system (without quotations marks), since what can be observed on the neurophysical level in a functioning brain is the response of an electrode to the depolorization currents in its region due to traveling of fired pulses down neuronal axons. (The concept of RECOVERY · STATE is associated with the ionic concentrations, which can be measured only for isolated nerve cells in special environmental frames.) Also with 10^{10} neurons in the real brain, it would stagger the imagination to be able to observe the simultaneous firing of them all.

Exercise. Assuming it takes a human or computer a millisecond to attend to the present FIRING · STATE of a NEURON, how many months it will take to have scanned all 10^{10} NEURONS? If 100 time steps are required for an adequate behavioral comparison, would this job be feasible even if it could be done?

Recall that the choice of output variables embodies the measurement possibilities of the real system, hence the experimental frame. Thus one choice consistent with what we said is the following:

Output Variables

Base model

For each BLOCK: % · IN · STATE · 0.

```
C MAIN PROGRAM FOR THE BASE PROGRAM
C
      EXTERNAL KBDE, A7E
      INTEGER OLDST(5,1000),SSWCH,DSWCH,FILOK
      REAL INEXT, NOISE, NOIS
C DECLARATION FOR EXTRA COMMON BLOCK VARIABLES
      INTEGER STATE(5,1000)
C BASIC COMMON BLOCK
      INTEGER T,OUTF,U,V.P.
      REAL NOIST(5,3),INPU(5)
      COMMON NBLKS,NUMBR(5),NSTAT,T,U,THPR(5,5),NOIST,INPR1(5),
     1 INPR2(5),EXINP(5,30),INPU,BKGND(5),WEIGT(5,5),OUTF,V,P
C EXTRA COMMON BLOCK FOR BASE MODEL
      COMMON STATE,NFILE,KOUNT(5)

C COMPLETE NFXT STATE (LOOP OVER ALL BLOCKS)
      CALL FOPI(NFILE)
      CALL FGETR(DUMY)
      DO 1000 I=1,NBLKS
         INPU(I) = INEXT(I)
         JFINL = NUMBR(I)
         LIMIT = KOUNT(I)
C LOOP OVER NEURONS WITHIN A BLOCK
      DO 1000 J=1,JFINL
         NOIS = NOISE(I)
         VOLLY = 0.
C SUM INPUTS TO NEURON (I.J) FROM ITS NEIGHBORS
      DO 50 K = 1, LIMIT
C NEURON (X,Y) IS ENCODED IN NBRS AS 1001 * X + Y
         CALL FGETI(NBR)
         KK1 = NBR/1001
         KK2 = NBR - KK1*1001
         IF(OLDST(KK1,KK2)) 50,40,50
   40    VOLLY = VOLLY + WEIGT(I,KK1)
   50    CONTINUE
C ADD THE EXTERNAL INPUT AND COMPUTE THRESHOLD
         VOLLY = VOLLY + INPU(I) + BKGND(I)
         THOL = NOIS + THOLD(I,OLDST(I,J))
C DOES THE NEURON FIRE?
         IF(VOLLY - THOL) 60,70,70
   60    STATE(I,J) = OLDST(I,J) + 1
         IF (STATE(I,J) - NSTAT) 1000,65,65
   65    STATE(I,J) = NSTAT - 1
         GO TO 1000
   70    STATE(I,J) = 0
 1000    CONTINUE

C UPDATE STATE VECTOR - OLDSTATE = STATE
      DO 10 I=1,NBLKS
         JFINL = NUMBER(I)
         DO 10 J=1,JFINL
   10    OLDST(I,J) = STATE(I,J)
```

Figure 2   FORTRAN implementation of the base model.

```
C EXTRA COMMON BLOCK FOR LUMPED MODEL
      COMMON FIRST, LAST(5), NBRS(25), STATE(5,20),SUMSQ(5,5),SOFLG

C COMPUTE NEXT STATE
      DO 1000 I=1,NBLKS
         0FACT = 0.0
         INPU(I) = INEXT(I)
         VOLLY = INPU(I) + BKGND(I)
         FIRS = FIRST(I)
         LAS = LAST(I)
C SUM INPUTS FROM NEIGHBORS BLOCKS
      DO 50 J= FIRS,LAS
         K = NBRS(J)
         IF(SOFLG) 50,50,40
40       0FACT = 0FACT + OLDST(K,1)*(1.0−OLDST(K,1))*SUMSQ(I,K)
50       VOLLY = VOLLY + WEIGT(I,K)*OLDST(K,1)
C COMPUTE NEW PERCENT IN STATES FOR THIS BLOCK
      SUM=0.0
      DO 100 K=2,NSTAT
         PROB = DIST(I,THOLD(I,K−2)−VOLLY,0FACT)
         STATE(I,K) = PROB*OLDST(I,K−1)
100      SUM = SUM + STATE(I,K)

C UPDATE THE STATE VECTOR
      DO 10 I=1,NBLKS
      DO 10 J=1,NSTAT
10       OLDST(I,J)= STATE(I,J)
```

Figure 3   FORTRAN implementation of the lumped model.

Lumped model
   For each BLOCK': $\% \cdot IN \cdot STATE \cdot 0'$.

This means that if the base model were truly the real system, comparison of base and lumped model behavior would involve only the comparison of the percentage of NEURONS firing in a BLOCK' with the percentage predicted for the corresponding BLOCK' by the lumped model.

   On the other hand, tests comparing all $\% \cdot IN \cdot STATE$ components of a base BLOCK with their correspondents in a lumped BLOCK' would not be allowable and would not correspond to a realistic experimental frame. Were the base model the real system, the $\% \cdot IN \cdot STATE \cdot i$ components, other than the one for $i = 0$, could not be measured directly.

Exercise.   Give the justification for the foregoing statement based on the suppositions stated earlier.

   Note however that these correspondences are the basic ones used to construct the lumped model, knowing the base model structure (i.e., to construct the homomorphism of Chapter 12). We see then the general principle operating in this particular case: the stronger correspondences motivated our construction of the lumped model, but realistically these cannot be validated directly.

If our experimental frame allowed observation of individual NEURONS, could the lumped model be employed to predict the FIRING · STATE sequence of an individual base model NEURON? The answer is no, if we intend to do deterministic point-by-point matching. As is generally the case, the lumped model is too coarse to be able to validly represent the base model's entire spectrum of behavior. Nowhere in a lumped model BLOCK' can an individual NEURON be distinguished. Since probabilistic hypotheses underlie the lumped model construction in this particular case, however, it is possible to consider a lumped model trajectory as a sequence of probabilities of individual NEURON FIRING · STATES.

A SIMULATION EXPERIMENT

A variety of tests of lumped model validity were made and have been reported,[3, 4] and the basic base–lumped model pair employed in one of these tests is illustrated in Figure 4. The lumped model consists of two BLOCKS'

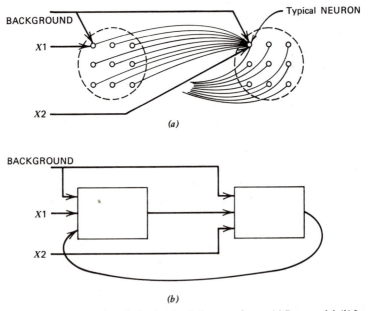

(a)

(b)

Figure 4   Base–lumped model pair for the simulation experiment. (a) Base model. (b) Lumped model.

interconnected as shown so that the one and only BLOCK′ · NEIGHBOR of BLOCK′1 is BLOCK′2, and symmetrically, the BLOCK′ · NEIGHBOR of BLOCK′2 is BLOCK′1. There are three INPUT · WIRES with INPUT · LEVELS, which we call $X1$, $X2$, and BACKGROUND, respectively. INPUT · WIRE 3 appears as an EXTERNAL · NEIGHBOR to both BLOCK′S, and INPUT · WIRE1(2) is the other EXTERNAL · NEIGHBOR of BLOCK′1(2).

The base model consists of N NEURONS divided into two BLOCKS of $N/2$ NEURONS each. The connection pattern of the base model agrees with that of the lumped model, which means that the NEURON · NEIGHBORS of any NEURON in BLOCK 1 come from BLOCK 2, and conversely for a NEURON in BLOCK 2. There were n actual NEURON NEIGHBORS for each NEURON, chosen using a uniform random distribution from the appropriate BLOCK. The NOISE · DISTRIBUTION was chosen to be Gaussian with mean zero and standard deviation SIGMA. The THRESHOLD function was chosen to be an exponential decay THRESHOLD$(i) = $ MU e^{-i}. Because THRESHOLD$(i) \cong 0$ for $i \geq 6$, the number of RECOVERY · STATES was reduced to seven (See Section 12.2). The quantities N, n, SIGMA, MU, and BACKGROUND were treated as parameters.

For parameter settings SIGMA $= 20$, MU $= 27$, and BACKGROUND $= 50$, we obtained the *flip-flop* behavior for the lumped model shown in Figure 5*a*. Notice that there are two phases:

1. The set phase: when the input level of $X1$ is suddenly raised to a high value and maintained there, the % · IN · STATE · 0 in BLOCK′ 1 should reach a high constant level and that in BLOCK′ 2, a low constant level.

2. The stay set phase: once such levels are achieved, and the level of $X1$ is again dropped to 0, the flip-flop should remain set (i.e., the disparity in levels achieved in the set phase should be maintained, even in the absence of external support).

The flip-flop thus should remember the occurrence of a sufficiently long pulse arriving on INPUT · WIRE 1. By symmetry, a similar but opposite effect should hold for INPUT · WIRE 2.

In a corresponding base model behavior in (Figure 5*b*), we see that the set phase is achieved but the stay set period is very short, indicating a serious divergence in base–lumped model behaviors. In a real situation we would have to reject the lumped model as a valid model of the "real system." But in this quasisimulation we are really testing the validity of the lumped model for the case of finite numbers of NEURONS and NEURON · NEIGHBORS. Thus before taking any radical action, we ought to try to explain the divergence on this basis.

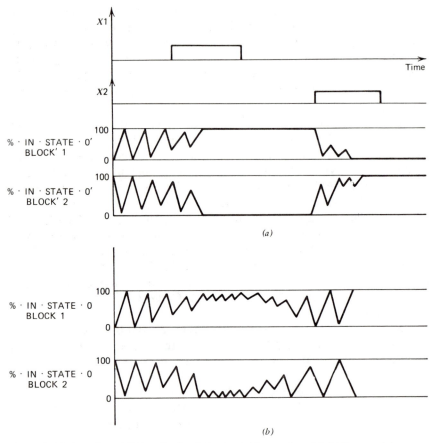

Figure 5   Trajectories exhibiting flip-flop behavior. (*a*) Lumped model. (*b*) Base model.

A series of base nets were simulated with N (number of NEURONS) ranging from 100 to 1000, and n (number of NEIGHBORS) ranging from 20 to 50. We found that n was the critical parameter. For $n = 20$, the base model did not remain set even for $N = 1000$. But with $n = 50$, the base model remained set for long periods for $N = 200$ and was in complete agreement with the lumped model for $N = 1000$.

COMPLEXITY OF BASE AND LUMPED MODELS

As we have seen, the base model is supposedly capable of more faithfully representing the behavior of the real system than its lumped counterparts, but often at the expense of very much increased usage of computer and human resources. Although such usage can be measured along a number of dimensions, we ultimately cite the dollar cost charged by the computing center for its resources and the wages paid to the project participants.

In our quasisimulation we have a sample comparison of the relative costs associated with base and lumped model. For example, the lumped model required 2 seconds of CPU time and cost $1.00 for a 100 time steps run. A base model ($N = 100$, $n = 40$) required 5.5 seconds of CPU time and cost $1.25 for a run of the same length. Since both programs fit within the minimum $32K$ allotted by the operating system, there was no cost differential in this respect.

The base model running time T can be estimated from the formula

$$T = K + N(an + b)$$

This is derived by noting that the next state computation takes the form

Loop over all neurons (N).
  Computer threshold and external input.
Loop over neighbors of this neuron (n).
  Sum up inputs.
Compare input and threshold.

In a series of runs we found that the running time in seconds was well approximated by the formula for T, with $K = 3.2$, $a = 0.001$, $b = 0.015$.

Thus as the number of NEURONS increases, while the number of BLOCKS is kept fixed, the gaps in running time, memory required, and total cost, grow rapidly until running the base model is no longer feasible. The cost of lumped model, however, would not increase at all under the same conditions.

SOURCES

1. B. P. Zeigler, "Statistical Simplification of Neural Nets," *International Journal of Man–Machine Studies*, **7**, 1975, 371–393.
2. D. O. Hebb, *Organization of Behavior*. Wiley, New York, 1949.
3. S. Aggarwal, "Ergodic Machines—Probabilistic and Approximate Homomorphic Simplification." Doctoral dissertation, University of Michigan, Ann Arbor, 1975.
4. R. Wong and E. Harth, "Stationary States and Transients in Neural Populations," *Journal of Theoretical Biology*, **36** (1), 1972, 77–92.

Appendix B

Term Project Report Form

The report should include:

1. An informal description of the lumped model (components, descriptive variables, component interaction, component-influence diagram).
2. If a base model was simulated, an informal description of it. If real data were used, a sketch of a hypothetical base model.
3. A description of the experimental frame(s) employed with reference to the base model of 2. In the case of real data, it should be made clear how the data are obtained by observations within the experimental frame(s).
4. Description of experiments run (at least four or five), giving for each experiment:
   parameter settings
   initial state
   input segment
   resultant output segment
   of lumped and base (if simulated).
5. Validation procedure employed—criteria of goodness of fit, statistics gathered, and statistical tests used, if relevant.
6. Judgment of model rejection or confirmation. Is agreement close enough for an intended application? (State such application.)
7. The relation between base and lumped models—if possible, a description of the intended homomorphic mapping.

8. If real data were used, how was lumped model initial state chosen? If the base model was simulated, how would lumped model initial state be chosen if base model initial state was unknown?

9. Comparison of base-lumped model complexities—running time, storage space, other relevant measures.

A Short Primer on Random Variables, Their Computer Realization, and Statistical Validation of Models

We begin by reviewing the random variable concept in the axiomatic spirit of present-day probability theory (as most current presentations do)[1] *and* retain this spirit as we proceed (as most presentations do not). The reader willing to invest some initial effort in assimilating the initial concepts will find the mysteries of statistical theory largely dissolved.

A *random variable* (rv) is a map $Y : S \rightarrow R$, where S is a set, called its *sample space*, and R is the set of real numbers, with which is associated a map $F_Y : R \rightarrow [0, 1]$ called its *cumulative distribution function* (cdf), where F_Y:

(a) *begins at 0*

$$\lim_{y \to -\infty} F_Y(y) = 0$$

(b) *ends at 1*

$$\lim_{y \to \infty} F_Y(y) = 1$$

(c)   *is nondecreasing*

$$y \leq y' \Rightarrow F_Y(y) \leq F_Y(y') \qquad \text{for all } y, y' \in R$$

(d)   *is continuous from the right*

$$\lim_{n \to \infty} F(y_n) = F(y) \text{ for all } y \in R \text{ and sequences } y_1 > y_2 > \cdots > y_n > \cdots$$

converging to y

Thus if we are to deal intelligently with a random variable Y, we must specify

(a)   its sample space S
(b)   its description, by a table or other means, as a set of ordered pairs $\{(s, Y(s)) | s \in S, Y(s) \in R\}$
(c)   its cdf $F_Y : R \to [0, 1]$

To interpret the typical descriptions given in Figure 1, imagine sampling an element s from the space S without being allowed to look at s but only its value $Y(s)$, a real number. The probability that this real number is less than or equal to value y is given by $F_Y(y)$. The constraints placed on the cdf F_Y are consistent with this interpretation:

(a)   The probability of getting values less than $-\infty$ is zero, since there are none to get.
(b)   The probability of getting values less than $+\infty$ is 1, since any possible value must lie in this range.
(c)   The probability of getting a value less than or equal to y cannot decrease as y increases, since more and more potential values of y are included as the increase occurs.
(d)   If F_Y takes on a value a, say, to the left of a point x, and a distinct value b, say, to the right of x, at x itself it takes on the value b.

To further explicate the term "probability" employed just now, the following definitions and axioms have become standard.

Given a set S, a *σ-algebra over S* is a family of subsets $\mathscr{F} \in 2^S$ such that

1. $\mathscr{F}$ *contains S itself.*

$$S \in \mathscr{F}$$

2. $\mathscr{F}$ *is closed under complementation.*

$$E \in \mathscr{F} \Rightarrow S - E \in \mathscr{F}$$

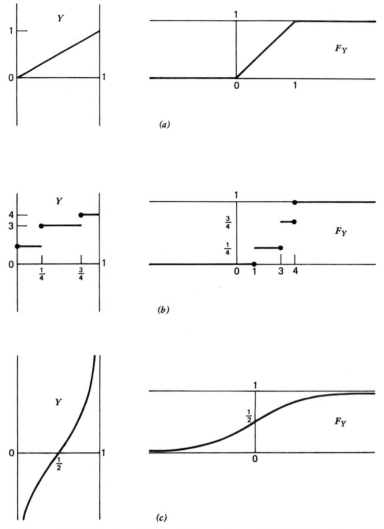

Figure 1 Some standard random variables with sample space $[0, 1]$. (a) The uniform distribution in $[0, 1]$. (b) A discrete *rv* that takes on values 1, 3, and 4 with probabilities 1/4, 1/2, and 1/4, respectively, (c) A normally distributed *rv*.

3. $\mathscr{F}$ *is closed under countable unions.*

$$E_1, E_2, \ldots, \in \mathscr{F} \Rightarrow \bigcup_{n=1}^{\infty} E_n \in \mathscr{F}$$

The sets in $\mathscr{F}$ are called *events*. The probability of an event E occurring is given by a function $P(E)$.

Formally, a function $P:\mathscr{F} \to [0, 1]$ is a *probability function* if

I. *The probability of event S is 1.*

$$P(S) = 1$$

II. *The probability of a union of mutually exclusive events is the sum of their probabilities.*

If $\qquad\qquad E_1, E_2, \ldots, \in \mathscr{F}$

and $\qquad\qquad E_i \cap E_j = \varnothing \qquad$ for all $i \neq j$

then $\qquad\qquad P\left(\bigcup_{n=1}^{\infty} E_n\right) = \sum_{n=1}^{\infty} P(E_n)$

Given an rv $Y:S \to R$ and its cdf $F_Y:R \to [0, 1]$ we can associate with it a σ-algebra $\mathscr{F}$ and a probability function $P:\mathscr{F} \to [0, 1]$ as follows:
For each $y \in R$, let

$$E_{(-\infty, y)} = \{s | Y(s) < y\}$$

where $E_{(-\infty, y)}$ is the set of sample points with Y values less than y. We can think of S as $E_{(-\infty, \infty)}$. Then $\mathscr{F}$ is the least family of sets containing the sets $\{E_{(-\infty, y)} | y \in R_\infty\}$, which is closed under complementation, and countable unions.

Thus $\qquad E_{(y, \infty)} = \bar{E}_{(-\infty, y)} = \{s | Y(s) > y\} \qquad$ is in $\mathscr{F}$

$\qquad\qquad E_{(y', y)} = E_y \cap \bar{E}_y = \{s | y' < Y(s) \leq y\} \qquad$ is in $\mathscr{F}$

and all countable unions of the sets $E_{(-\infty, y)}$, $E_{(y, \infty)}$, and $E_{(y', y)}$ are in $\mathscr{F}$. In fact this fully describes $\mathscr{F}$.[†] We say that $\mathscr{F}$ is the σ-algebra generated by $\{E_{(-\infty, y)} | y \in R_\infty\}$.
Now $P:\mathscr{F} \to [0, 1]$ is defined by

(a) $\quad P(S) = 1$
(b) $\quad P(E_{(-\infty, y)}) = F_Y(y) \qquad$ for all $y \in Y$
(c) $\quad P(E_{(y, \infty)}) = 1 - F_Y(y) \qquad$ for all $y \in R$
(d) $\quad P(E_{(y', y)}) = F_Y(y) - F_Y(y') \qquad$ for all $y, y' \in R$

and for any sequence of mutually exclusive events $E_1, E_2, \ldots$, chosen from the sets $\{E_{(-\infty, y)}\} \cup \{E_{(y, \infty)}\} \cup \{E_{(y', y)}\}$, we define

$$P\left(\bigcup_{n=1}^{\infty} E_n\right) = \sum_{n=1}^{\infty} P(E_n) = \lim_{N \to \infty} \sum_{n=1}^{N} P(E_n)$$

[†] As usual, it must be shown first that a least set exists (this is left as an exercise to those familiar with such mathematical tactics).

Exercise. Show that P is well defined and satisfies the axioms required of it. Interpret the statements a through d of its definition informally.

Conversely, given a σ-algebra $\mathscr{F}$, a probability function P, and a map $Y:S \rightarrow R$ for which the sets $E_{(-\infty, y)}$ are all in $\mathscr{F}$, we can turn Y into a random variable by giving it a cdf $F_Y:R \rightarrow [0, 1]$, where

$$F_Y(y) = P(E_{(-\infty, y)}) = P(\{s|Y(s) < y\})$$

Exercise. Show that F_Y statisfies the conditions required of it.

In sum, given an rv Y and its cdf F_Y, we can associate with it a σ-algebra of events in its sample space and a probability function, formalizing our intuitive notion that $F_Y(y)$ is the probability that Y takes on values less than or equal to y. On the other hand, if we are given a map Y, a consistent σ-algebra, and a probability function over its domain, we can compute the cdf associated with Y.

Although random variables can arise in many different ways, there is a class of rvs that represents all the others, and its members lend themselves to computer generation. We shall call these standard rvs, their sample space is the interval $[0, 1]$, and their generation reduces to application of the functional rule specifying the rv to the output of a random number generator approximating a uniform distribution on $[0, 1]$.

To see this, we let $S = [0, 1]$ and take $\mathscr{F}$ as the σ-algebra generated by the intervals $\{(0, y)|y \in (0, 1)\}$.[†] Then $P:S \rightarrow [0, 1]$ is the unique probability function satisfying

$$P(y, y') = y' - y \qquad \text{for all } y' \geq y,$$

where $y, y' \in [0, 1]$. (This uniqueness must be shown, of course.) In other words, the probability of an interval is just its length, and the probability of a mutually disjoint set of intervals is the sum of their lengths. From now on, we refer to this $S, \mathscr{F}, P$ combination as "$[0, 1]$ with uniform distribution."

A map $Y:S \rightarrow R$ is a *standard rv* if $S = [0, 1]$ with uniform distribution and Y is a nondecreasing and *left* continuous. (See Figure 1.)

The cdf associated with Y is easy to obtain. Since Y is nondecreasing and left continuous, the set $\{s|Y(s) \leq y\} = [0, s_y)$, where $s_y = \max \{s|Y(s) \leq y\}$ (exercise for the "real analysts").

Thus Y is consistent with the σ-algebra. Now

$$\begin{aligned} F_Y(y) &= P(\{s|Y(s) \leq y\}) \\ &= P(0, s_y) \\ &= s_y \end{aligned}$$

[†] These are called Borel sets.

Two rvs Y and Y' are *identically distributed* if $F_Y = F_{Y'}$. This is an equivalence relation that partitions rvs into classes having the same cdf. We now show each such class contains a standard rv.

THEOREM

Given any rv Y' with cdf $F_{Y'}$, define a map $Y:[0, 1] \rightarrow R$ such that

$$Y(s) = \min \{y | F_{Y'}(y) \geq s\}$$

Then Y is a standard rv on $[0, 1]$ with uniform distribution and $F_{Y'} = F_Y$.

Proof sketch. Since $F_{Y'}$ is nondecreasing and right continuous, $Y(s)$ is well defined at each point s in $[0, 1]$, the range of $F_{Y'}$; also Y is left continuous. In fact for any pair (s, y) such that $F_{Y'}(y) = s$, only three things can happen:

1. Y is strictly increasing around s and $F_{Y'}$ is strictly increasing around y (Figure 2a).
2. Y jumps at s and $F_{Y'}$ is constant around y (Figure 2b).
3. Y is constant around s and $F_{Y'}$ jumps at y (Figure 2c).

We give the reader the exercise of showing that in each case, $F_Y(y) = F_{Y'}(y)$. ∎

Note that when $F_{Y'}$ is strictly increasing everywhere, the definition of the equivalent standard rv reduces to

$$Y(s) = F_{Y'}^{-1}(s)$$

where $F_{Y'}^{-1}(s)$ is the unique y such that $F_{Y'}(y) = s$.

Often we have a cdf and we want to construct a standard rv that has the cdf. Theorem 1 tells us one way of doing this—note that the definition of Y in the theorem does not refer explicitly to Y' but only to its cdf $F_{Y'}$.

A pseudorandom number generator is a system that outputs sequences of numbers in the interval $[0, 1]$ which approximate a uniform distribution (See Section 3.7). Having constructed the map Y, we can use it as the output map for the random generator and can expect to have sequences of random numbers generated with the cdf originally desired.

The most common cdfs are the discrete and the continuous. A cdf F_Y is *discrete* if it has a countable number of jumps and is constant between the jumps. If $\{y_i\}$ represents the points at which jumps occur, for each i and y, y' such that (y, y') lies within (y_i, y_{i+1}), we have

$$P(E_{(y', y)}) = F_Y(y) - F_Y(y') = 0$$

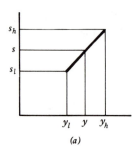

(a)

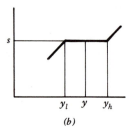

(b)

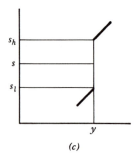

y

(c)

Figure 2   The local behavior of $F_{y'}$ (a) Cases 1. (b) Case 2. (c) Case 3.

whereas for (y, y') containing only y_i

$$P(E_{(y', y)}) = F_Y(y) - F_Y(y')$$
$$= F_Y(y_i^+) - F_Y(y_i)$$
$$= \text{the value of the jump at } y_i$$

Thus there is a function $P_Y : \{y_i\} \to [0, 1]$, call it the *probability mass function* (pmf), such that $p_Y(y_i) = F_Y(y_i^+) - F_Y(y_i)$ for jump point y_i, and for $y \in R$,

$$F_Y(y) = \sum_{y_i \le y} p_Y(y_i)$$

A cdf F_Y is *continuous* if there is a piecewise continuous function $f_Y : R \to R_0^+$ such that

$$F_Y(y) = \int_{y'}^{y} f_Y(y') \, dy \qquad \text{for} \quad y \in R$$

and then $f_Y(y) = (d/dy)F_Y(y)$ for all but a finite set of points. We call f_Y a *probability density function* (pdf). Then

$$f_Y(y)\,dy = F_Y(y + dy) - F_Y(y) = P(E_{(y,\,y+dy)})$$

To sum up, a discrete rv can take on only discrete set of values $\{y_i\}$. The probability of its assuming a value y_i is given by $p_Y(y_i)$ (which is, more precisely, the probability associated with any set $E_{(y',\,y)}$ for which $(y',\,y)$ contains y_i and no other y_j). A continuous rv can take on a continuum of values—the density function $f_Y(y)$ specifies the probability associated with the interval $(y,\, y + dy)$. It can be shown that any cdf consists of a weighted sum of a continuous cdf and a discrete cdf.

The *expectation* or *mean* of a rv Y, denoted by $E[Y]$ or $\bar{Y}$ is defined (when it exists) by

$$E(Y) = \begin{cases} \displaystyle\int_{-\infty}^{\infty} y f_Y(y)\,dy & \text{for the continuous case} \\[2mm] \displaystyle\sum_{\text{all } y_i} y_i P_Y(y_i) & \text{for the discrete case} \end{cases}$$

The *variance* of Y is defined by

$$\mathrm{var}\,(Y) = E[(Y - E(Y))^2],$$

which can be shown to be equivalent to

$$\mathrm{var}\,(Y) = E(Y^2) - (E(Y))^2$$

A very useful discrete cdf is specified by the pmf

$$p(x) = \begin{cases} \dbinom{n}{x} p^x q^{n-x} & \text{for } x = 0, 1, \ldots, n \\[2mm] 0 & \text{otherwise} \end{cases}$$

where $0 \le p \le 1$ and $q = 1 - p$. This is called the *binomial distribution*, denoted $B(n, p)$, and any rv having this cdf is said to be *binomially distributed*.

A very useful continuous cdf is specified by the pdf

$$f(x) = \frac{1}{\sigma\sqrt{2\pi}} \exp\left[-\frac{1}{2}\frac{(x - m)^2}{\sigma^2} \right] \qquad \text{for } -\infty < x < \infty$$

where $\sigma > 0$. This is called the *normal* or *Gaussian* distribution, with mean m and standard deviation σ, denoted $N(m, \sigma)$; of course any rv having this cdf is said to be *normally distributed* (Figure 3).

A second important cdf is specified by the pdf

$$f(x) = \begin{cases} \lambda \exp\,(-\lambda x) & \text{for } x \ge 0 \\[2mm] 0 & \text{otherwise} \end{cases}$$

This is called the *exponential* distribution with mean λ.

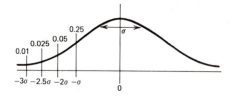

$|x|$	$f(x)$
1.0σ	0.25
2.0σ	0.05
2.5σ	0.025
3.0σ	0.01

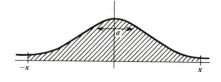

x	$F(x) - F(-x)$
	(% enclosed between $[-x, x]$)
2.0σ	95%
2.5σ	99%
4.0σ	99.8%

Figure 3   The normal distribution $N(0, \sigma)$.

A set of rvs $Y_1, Y_2, \ldots, Y_n$ are *jointly distributed* if they are defined on the same sample space (i.e., for each i, $Y_i : S \to R$ for a common sample space S). The complete specification of the probabilistic interrelation of the rvs is given by the *joint cumulative distribution function* (jcdf)

$$F_{Y_1, \ldots, Y_n}(y_1, \ldots, y_n) : R^n \to [0, 1]$$

The interpretation of this function is that

$$F_{Y_1, \ldots, Y_n}(y_1, \ldots, y_n) = P(\{s \,|\, Y_1(s) \le y_1, Y_2(s) \le y_2, \ldots, Y_n(s) \le y_n\})$$

$$= P\left(\bigcap_{i=1}^{n} \{s \,|\, Y_1(s) \le y_i\}\right)$$

$$= P\left(\bigcap_{i=1}^{n} E_{(-\infty, y_i)}\right)$$

(Since the σ-algebra on S is closed under union and complementation, it is also closed under intersection, and our definition makes sense.)

Exercise.   Show that

(a) $F_{Y_i}(y_i) = F_{Y_1, \ldots, Y_n}(\infty, \ldots, y_i, \ldots, \infty)$
(b) $F_{Y_1, \ldots, Y_n}(-\infty, \ldots, -\infty) = 0$
(c) $F_{Y_1, \ldots, Y_n}(\infty, \ldots, \infty) = 1$

Ordinarily, we can infer the so-called marginal cdf for rv Y_i (i.e., F_{Y_i}) from the jcdf $F_{Y_1, \ldots, Y_n}$, but the reverse is *not* true: knowing the individual cdfs does not allow us to derive the jcdf, which after all must contain information about the total interrelation of the rvs. However, if the rvs do not interact in a probabilistic sense, their joint behavior is a "sum" (really, a product) of their individual behavior. The rvs $Y_1, \ldots, Y_n$ are said to be *independent* if

$$F_Y(y_1, \ldots, y_n) = F_{Y_1}(y_1) \cdot F_{Y_2}(y_2) \cdots F_{Y_n}(y_n) \qquad \text{for all } (y_1, \ldots, y_n) \in R^n$$

Exercise. Show that $Y_1, \ldots, Y_n$ are independent if

$$P\left(\bigcap_{i=1}^n E_{(-\infty, y_i)} \right) = P(E_{(-\infty, y_1)}) \cdot P(E_{(-\infty, y_2)}) \cdots P(E_{(-\infty, y_n)})$$

Statistical data reduction consists in compounding individual records, usually by the elementary arithmetic operations of addition (and its inverse, subtraction) and multiplication (and its inverse, division). These operations are modelled within probability theory as follows.

Let $Y_1, \ldots, Y_n$ be jointly distributed rvs on a sample space S. Then their *sum* Y is an rv on S defined by

$$Y_\Sigma(s) = \sum_{i=1}^n Y_i(s)$$

Usually we write $\sum_{i=1}^n Y_i$ instead of Y_Σ.
Similarly the product $\prod_{i=1}^n Y_i$ is an rv on S defined by

$$\prod_{i=1}^n Y_i(s) = Y_1(s) \cdot Y_2(s) \cdots Y_n(s)$$

In particular, for example, if Y is an rv on S, then Y^2 is an rv on S where

$$Y^2(s) = Y(s) \cdot Y(s)$$

Exercise. Since a constant may be regarded as an rv that can assume only one value, show that

(a) $E(a) = a$; var $(a) = 0$
(b) $E(aY) = aE(Y)$; var $(aY) = a^2$ var (Y)
    In particular, for $a = -1$ we have
(c) $E(-Y) = -E(Y)$; var $(-Y) = $ var (Y)

Exercise. If $Y_1, \ldots, Y_n$ are jointly distributed rvs, show that

(a) $E\left(\sum_{i=1}^n Y_i \right) = \sum_{i=1}^n E(Y_i)$

(b) If $Y_1, \ldots, Y_n$ are independent, then

$$E\left(\prod_{i=1}^n Y_i \right) = \prod_{i=1}^n E(Y_i)$$

The exercise states two important principles concerning the compounding of information. The mean of the sum of any finite set of rvs defined on the same sample space is the sum of the component means. A similar statement hold for the product *if* the rvs are independent, but not in general. For example, an rv Y is not independent of itself; thus in general $E(Y^2) \neq E(Y)^2$, in fact, the difference $E(Y^2) - E(Y)^2 = \text{var}(Y)$ gives information about the shape of the cdf F_Y.

However, the mean of the product can equal the product of the means even when the rvs $\{Y_i\}$ are not independent. If this happens, the rvs are said to be *uncorrelated*.

Exercise. Show that $Y_1, \ldots, Y_n$ are uncorrelated if

$$\text{var}\left(\sum_{i=1}^{n} Y_i\right) = \sum_{i=1}^{n} \text{var}(Y_i)$$

(when the variances exist).

Thus for uncorrelated rvs, the variance of the sum is the sum of the variances.

Exercise. Show that if Y is $N(m, \sigma)$ distributed, then $(Y - m)/\sigma$ is $N(0, 1)$ distributed. Hence

$$F_{N(m, \sigma)}(y) = F_{N(0, 1)}\left(\frac{y - m}{\sigma}\right)$$

Often we assume that we can make a number of independent samples of an rv. We can imagine the sample space S as contained in a pot and the sampling of a point $s \in S$ as a blindfolded selection of an element in the pot. We are allowed to observe the value $Y(s)$ (Figure 4a). The selection of n samples is modelled by n copies of the original pot (Figure 4b). Then if $s_1, s_2, \ldots, s_n$ are n samples drawn successively from the original pot with replacement, it is the same as drawing a sample $(s_1, s_2, \ldots, s_n)$ from a "compound pot." The sample space of the "compound pot" is thus S^n. The result of the sampling is an n-tuple of values $(Y(s_1), Y(s_2), \ldots, Y(s_n))$, which is the same result obtained from n identically distributed rvs $Y_1, Y_2, \ldots, Y_n$ such that each Y_i maps $S^n \to R$ in such a way that $Y_i(s_1, \ldots, s_i, \ldots, s_n) = Y(s_i)$.

If, moreover, the sampling is to be independent, there can be no connections between the pots forming the "compound pot." In other words, the selection of a sample s_i from pot i should not affect the result of selection of a sample s_j from pot j. Thus the rvs $Y_1, \ldots, Y_n$ should be independent.

In sum, the taking of n independent samples of an rv Y is modelled by a set of n independent and identically distributed (iid) random variables $Y_1, \ldots, Y_n$ such that

$$F_{Y_1, \ldots, Y_n}(y_1, \ldots, y_n) = F_Y(y_1) \cdots F_Y(y_n)$$

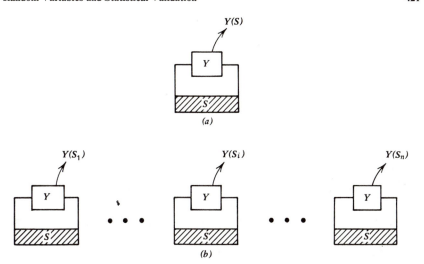

Figure 4 Sampling a random variable Y.

Given a set $Y_1, \ldots, Y_n$ representing samples of an rv Y, we can apply the arithmetic operations defined earlier. In particular, the *sample average or mean* is an rv on S^n defined by

$$U_n = \frac{1}{n} \sum_{i=1}^{n} Y_i$$

The *sample variance estimate* is an rv on S^n defined by

$$V_n = \frac{1}{n-1} \sum_{i=1}^{n} (Y_i - U_n)^2$$

$$= \frac{1}{n-1} \sum_{i=1}^{n} Y_i^2 - \frac{n}{n-1} U_n^2$$

$$\simeq \frac{1}{n} \left(\sum_{i=1}^{n} Y_i^2 - \left(\sum_{i=1}^{n} Y_i \right)^2 \right) \qquad \text{for } n \text{ large}$$

Exercise. By employing previous definitions, describe the rvs U_n and V_n; that is, define $U_n(s_1, \ldots, s_n)$ and $V_n(s_1, \ldots, s_n)$ for each point $(s_1, \ldots, s_n) \in S^n$.
  Justify the last two statements in the definition of V_n.

Since by assumption the $Y_1, \ldots, Y_n$ are iid, we know their joint distribution if we know the cdf for Y. Moreover, to compute the mean and variance of

U_n and the mean of V_n we need know only the mean and variance of Y:

	U_n	V_n
Mean	$E(U_n) = E(Y)$	$E(V_n) = \text{var}(Y)$
Variance	$\text{var}(U_n) = \dfrac{\text{var}(Y)}{n}$	

Exercise. Using the previous results on means of sums and products derive the results of the table.

Conversely, suppose we have sampled a distribution, obtaining values $Y(s_1)$, $Y(s_2)$, ..., $Y(s_n)$ and so calculating values for U_n and V_n. The table tells us that these values are good estimates of the true mean and variance of the distribution—provided the independence of sampling holds. We do not know just how good these estimates are, but we do have an indication that the larger the number of samples, the better the estimate of the mean—this is revealed by an inverse dependence of var (U_n) on n.

To estimate the amount of confidence one can have in an estimate, statisticians have devised certain tests, (e.g., Student's t-test). A test involves computing from the data a number indicating the confidence permissible in an estimate of a parameter, assuming some kind of model from which the data are generated. (The confidence given is always relative to some presumption about the underlying model—we have already seen indications of this in the sampling independence assumption.) Before discussing some of the tests, let us introduce a few new rvs on which the tests are based.

Let $Y_1, \ldots, Y_n$ be a sequence of independent normally $N(0, 1)$ distributed rvs (each has zero mean and unit variance). The rv *chi-square with n degrees of freedom* is defined by

$$\chi_n^2 = \sum_{i=1}^{n} Y_i^2$$

or to use a memory-aiding abbreviation

$$\chi_n^2 = \sum_{i=1}^{n} N^2(0, 1)$$

Exercise. (*a*) Let S^n be the common sample space of the Y_i's. Define χ_n^2 explicitly as a map from S^n to R.
(*b*) Show that $E(\chi_n^2) = n$.

Now let X and Y be independent with X distributed as χ_n^2 and Y distributed by $N(0, 1)$. Then the Student *t-statistic with n degrees of freedom* is an rv defined by

$$T_n = \frac{Y}{(X/n)^{1/2}}$$

or, in abbreviation,

$$T_n = \frac{N(0, 1)}{(\chi_n^2/n)^{1/2}}$$

Exercise. (a) If S_X and S_Y are the sample spaces of X and Y, defined T_n explicitly as a map from $S_X \times S_Y$ to R.
(b) Show that $E(T_n) = 0$.

The shapes of cdfs $F_{\chi_n^2}$ and F_{T_n} and several significant values are presented in Figures 5 and 6.

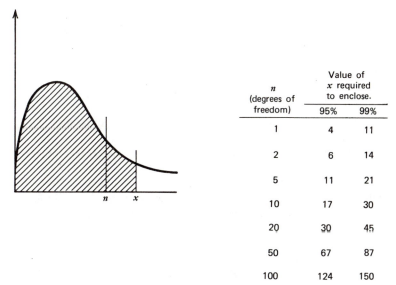

n (degrees of freedom)	Value of x required to enclose.	
	95%	99%
1	4	11
2	6	14
5	11	21
10	17	30
20	30	45
50	67	87
100	124	150

Figure 5   The chi-square distribution.

The significance tests we now consider are special cases of a more general paradigm called hypothesis testing. The procedure followed in hypothesis testing is the following.

1. Obtain data measurements M.
2. Make hypothesis H asserting that M is the outcome of sampling an rv (or set of jointly distributed rvs) with known distribution F.

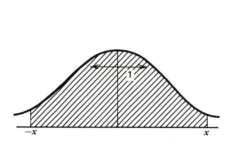

n (degrees of freedom)	Value of x required to enclose.	
	95%	99%
1	13	64
2	4	10
5	2.6	4
10	2.2	3.2
20	2.1	2.9
50	2.0	2.7
100	2.0	2.6
1000	1.96	2.58

Same as $N(0, 1)$

Figure 6   The Student t-distribution.

3.   Compute, using F, the probability of obtaining outcomes "like" M, given that H is true.
4.   If the probability is "too small," reject H; otherwise H is confirmed.

Several terms are left fuzzy in this procedure. What does "like" mean? What does "too small" mean? No a priori answers can be given. The following examples, however, illustrate certain standard interpretations.

Example 1.   Testing Whether Two Pots Are the Same Or Different.   Imagine taking n samples from a pot A and n samples from a pot B, computing the average of each sample set, and trying to decide on the basis of these two averages whether the pots are alike or different. This abstract experimental setup underlies many real situations. For example, a certain drug may be given to one group of patients and not given to another, similar, control group. These groups constitute the pots, the patients in each groups are the sample points, the relative recovery rates of the patients are the sample values, and we are trying to decide whether the drug makes any difference, on the average, in the recovery rate of a patient (i.e., whether the pots are really different).

In modelling and simulation, this situation arises in the process of validation. The real system constitutes pot A, the model the other pot, B. We make n observations of some system numerical output variable—samples from pot A; we make n simulation runs of our model and obtain values for the corresponding model output variable—samples from pot B. We compute the averages of the two sets and are trying to decide whether the averages are close enough to allow us to say that the model data could have come from the real system (i.e., are the pots the "same" or "different"?).

Step 1   Take n samples from pot A, and n samples from pot B. Compute sample averages U_A and U_B. Let $x_1, \ldots, x_n$ be the real number results from A and $y_1, \ldots, y_n$ be the real number results from B:

$$U_A = \frac{1}{n}\sum x_i \quad \text{and} \quad U_B = \frac{1}{n}\sum y_i$$

Step 2   Make hypothesis H: pots A and B are modelled by sample spaces S_A and S_B and rvs Y_A and Y_B such that Y_A, Y_B are independent and identically distributed Gaussian rvs with mean m and variance σ^2: each is $N(m\ \sigma)$.

Step 3   Consider the difference $d = U_A - U_B$. Decide that results "like the one obtained" are to be those whose magnitude of difference would be at least as great as that actually obtained. More precisely, let

$$D_d = \{(s_1^A, \ldots, s_n^A, s_1^B, \ldots, s_n^B) | (s_1^A, \ldots, s_n^A) \in S_A^n, (s_1^B, \ldots, s_n^B) \in S_B^n,$$
$$\text{and} \quad |U_n^A(s_1^A, \ldots, s_n^A) - U_n^B(s_1^B, \ldots, s_n^A)| \geq |d|\}$$

where D_d is the set of possible samples (n from A, n from B), whose sample averages computed for A and B, are at least as far apart as $|d|$.

Compute $P(D_d|H)$, the probability of getting results like the ones obtained if H is true. This is the probability of obtaining sample averages least as far apart as the actual averages computed. We show how to compute $P(D_d|H)$ in a moment. Assume for now that it has been computed.

Step 4   Decide on the meaning of "too small": choose a value $\alpha \in [0, 1]$ (e.g., $\alpha = .05$ or $\alpha = .01$), and reject hypothesis H if $P(D_d|H) < \alpha$. This means that if the probability of getting results "like the ones obtained" is smaller than α, we will reject the hypothesis that the pots A and B are "alike" (more precisely, are modelled by the same independent Gaussian distributions). In other words, there is only a small chance, less than $100\alpha\%$ (e.g., less than 5% or 1%), that results like the ones obtained would be obtained if A and B were "alike." This does not mean that the pots are really different: it is still possible that we obtained fluky results, but we are willing to take the chance that we are wrong, since the chance that the results are fluky is less than $100\alpha\%$.

Computation of $P(D_d|H)$

Suppose $(a_1, \ldots, a_n, b_1, \ldots, b_n)$ are the sample points actually obtained. Then by hypothesis, the real valued outcomes are $Y_A(a_1), \ldots, Y_A(a_n)$, $Y_B(b_1), \ldots, Y_B(b_n)$. We compute the sample means

$$U_A = U_n^A(a_1, \ldots, a_n) = \frac{1}{n} \sum_{i=1}^{n} Y_A(a_i) = \left(\frac{1}{n} \sum_{i=1}^{n} x_i\right)$$

$$U_B = U_n^B(b_1, \ldots, b_n) = \frac{1}{n} \sum_{i=1}^{n} Y_B(b_i) = \left(\frac{1}{n} \sum_{i=1}^{n} y_i\right)$$

We can also compute the sample variance estimates .

$$\sigma_A^2 = V_n^A(a_1, \ldots, a_n) = \frac{1}{n-1} \sum_{i=1}^{n} (Y_A(a_i) - U_A)^2$$

$$\sigma_B^2 = V_n^B(b_1, \ldots, b_n) = \frac{1}{n-1} \sum_{i=1}^{n} (Y_B(b_i) - U_B)^2$$

If n is large, say more than 20, we can adopt the following simplified procedure. Take σ_A^2, σ_B^2 to be good estimates of the true variance σ^2 and in fact set $\sigma^2 = (\sigma_A^2 + \sigma_B^2)/2$. Thus we proceed as if knowing the variance of the distribution $N(m, \sigma)$ common to pots A and B. From a previous exercise, $E(U_n^A) = E(U_n^B) = m$, and var (U_n^A) − var $(U_n^B) = (1/n)/\sigma^2$. Moreover it can be shown that the sum of normally distributed rvs is also normally distributed; thus U_n^A and U_n^B are $N(m, (\sigma/\sqrt{n}))$ distributed.

Since the sampling is presumed to be independent, it can be demonstrated that U_n^A and U_n^B are independent rvs. Their difference, the rv $Z = U_n^A - U_n^B$ is $N(0, (\sqrt{2}\sigma/\sqrt{n}))$ distributed.

Exercise. If Y_A and Y_B are independent rvs, show that $E(Y_A - Y_B) = E(Y_A) - E(Y_B)$ and var $(Y_A - Y_B) = $ var $(Y_A) + $ var (Y_B).

Hint. Consider $Y_A + (-1 Y_B)$ and use previous results.

Thus

$$P(D_d|H) = P(\{(s_1^A, \ldots, s_n^A, s_1^B, \ldots, s_n^B) \| U_n^A(s_1^A, \ldots, s_n^A) - U_n^B(s_1^B, \ldots, s_n^B)| \geq |d|\})$$
$$= P(\{s\|Z(s)| \geq |d|\})$$
$$= 1 - P(\{s\|Z(s)| \leq |d|\})$$
$$= 1 - P(\{s|-d \leq Z(s) \leq d\})$$
$$= 1 - (F_Z(d) - F_Z(-d))$$

Since Z is distributed by $N(0, (\sqrt{2}\sigma/\sqrt{n})$, we can merely look up $F_Z(d)$ and $F_Z(-d)$ the table of the standard normal distribution. This form arises often, however, and values of d (as a function of α) have been tabled such that $F_Z(d_\alpha) - F_Z(-d_\alpha) = 1 - \alpha$; d_α is called the confidence limit for α. If the difference obtained $d \geq d_\alpha$, we say that we reject H at level α.

Graphically (Figure 3) $F_Z(d) - F_Z(-d)$ is the area enclosed between $-d$ and d, and $1 - (F_Z(d) - F(-d))$ is the area in the tails. When $d = d_\alpha$, the area enclosed in the tails is α and the area enclosed between $-d_\alpha$ and $-d_\alpha$ is $1 - \alpha$. Only the values d_α for the case $N(0, 1)$ need be tabled, since if Z is $N(0, (\sqrt{2}\sigma/\sqrt{n}))$, then $d_\alpha = d_\alpha^{N(0, 1)}\sigma(\sqrt{2}/\sqrt{n})$ (recall from an exercise that $Z/(\sqrt{2}\sigma/\sqrt{n})$ is $N(0, 1)$ distributed).

Previously we suggested that the effect of taking more samples ought to be to increase our confidence in our estimates. In the present case, let us fix α, say at .05. Then as n increases, d_α decreases as $1/\sqrt{n}$. For example, with $n = 100$,

$$d_{.05} = d_{.05}^{N(0, 1)} \cdot \sigma \frac{\sqrt{2}}{\sqrt{100}} = 2\frac{\sigma\sqrt{2}}{10} \simeq .28\sigma$$

and with $n = 10,000$, $d_{.05} \simeq .028\sigma$. Now suppose we obtain an actual difference $d = .1\sigma$ after 100 samples and the same d after 10,000 samples. Since $d < .28\sigma$ we would not reject the hypothesis H that the pots are alike after 100 samples, but since $d > .028\sigma$ we would reject H after 1000 samples. We interpret this as follows: as more information accumulates, the less chancy our estimates U^A and U^B become, thus the more we expect that a minor difference $U^A - U^B$ will be indicative of an actual difference in pots A and B. As n increases, therefore, our test becomes more stringent; and if the hypothesis has not been rejected at level α for $n = 10,000$, we can be more confident about its ultimate validity than we can if it has not been rejected at the same level α for $n = 100$. On the other hand, if we reject the hypothesis as improbable having obtained 100 samples, it will also be rejected when 10,000 samples have been obtained (provided the same difference is observed). (Thus the life of a hypothesis is a hard one—when it asserts the similarity of two pots, at any rate.)

Since we grow more confident in our estimates as the number of samples increases, we ought to take as many samples as possible. What limits this number? First, taking a sample in real life may be very costly, and the total resources available are often limited. Second, a law of diminishing returns is operating. Since the sampling variance goes down on as $1/n$ and even worse, the confidence limits get tighter as $1/\sqrt{n}$—to gain successive decimal places .0, .00, .000, .0000, . . . , we have to take 10, 10^2, 10^4, 10^8, . . . , samples. Thus we usually have to settle for a reasonably small number of samples and employ statistical models to get the most out of the data.

When n is small (say, $n < 20$), we can no longer assume that σ is accurately estimated by $\sigma_A^2 + \sigma_B^2/2$. Since σ can no longer be assumed known, we lack the relevant parameter in $N(0, (\sqrt{2}\sigma/\sqrt{n}))$, the distribution of $U_n^A - U_n^B$. We have to arrive at an rv whose distribution is not dependent on σ. Recalling that if Y is $N(0, \sigma)$ distributed, Y/σ is $N(0, 1)$ distributed, we try

$$U_{2n} = \frac{1}{2n}\left(\sum_{i=1}^n Y_i^A + \sum_{i=1}^n Y_i^B\right) = \frac{U_n^A + U_n^B}{2}$$

$$V_{2n} = \frac{1}{2n-1}\left(\sum_{i=1}^n (Y_i^A - U_{2n})^2 + \sum_{i=1}^n (Y_i^B - U_{2n})^2\right)$$

$$W = \frac{U_n^A - U_n^B}{\sqrt{V_{2n}(2/n)}}$$

We find that W is closely related to the Student t-statistic, and in fact W is distributed as T_{2n-1}.

Exercise. Show that

$$Y = \frac{U_n^A - U_n^B}{\sigma\sqrt{\dfrac{2}{n}}}$$

is $N(0, 1)$ distributed and

$$X - \frac{(2n-1)V_{2n}}{\sigma^2}$$

is χ_{2n-1}^2 distributed (allowing loss of one degree of freedom because U_{2n} is computed from the same data). Then, assuming that $U_n^A - U_n^B$ and V_{2n} can be shown to be independent, show that $Y/(X/2n - 1)^{1/2}$ gives T_{2n-1}.

As before, having samples $a_1, \ldots, a_n, b_1, \ldots, b_n$ with outcomes $Y^A(a_1), \ldots, Y^A(a_n), Y^B(b_1), \ldots, Y^B(b_n)$, we compute

$$t = \frac{U^A - U^B}{\sigma_{A,B}}\sqrt{\frac{n}{2}} = \frac{d}{\sigma_{A,B}}\sqrt{\frac{n}{2}}$$

where $U^A = U_n^A(a_1, \ldots, a_n)$
$\quad\quad U^B = U_n^B(b_1, \ldots, b_n)$
$\quad\quad \sigma_{A,B} = \sqrt{V_{2n}(a_1, \ldots, a_n, b_1, \ldots, b_n)}$

Note that whereas d is the absolute difference in sample means, t is the difference in means *relative* to the estimate of total sample variance. Substituting t for d in the previous discussion, we arrive at the same concept of confidence limits. That is, let

$$D_t = \{(s_1^A, \ldots, s_n^A, s_1^B, \ldots, s_n^B) \mid |T_{2n-1}(s_1^A, \ldots, s_n^A, s_1^B, \ldots, s_n^B)| > t\}$$

Then

$$P(D_t|H) = 1 - (F_{T_{2n-1}}(t) - F_{T_{2n-1}}(-t))$$

and for $\alpha \in [0, 1]$, t_α is such that $F_{2n-1}(t_\alpha) - F_{T_{2n-1}}(-t_\alpha) = 1 - \alpha$. Then we reject H at level α if $|t| > t_\alpha$.

Example 2. *Testing Whether a Pot Is Modelled by an rv With Given cdf.* If we draw n samples from a pot and wish to check whether the sample outcomes could have been those of rv Y with cdf F_Y, we follow our hypothesis testing paradigm.

.1. Let $a_1, \ldots, a_n$ be the sample points taken.
2. The hypothesis H: the a_i's are independent samples of an rv $Y:S \to R$ with cdf F_Y.
3. Choose a concept of "like" results as follows. Divide the real line into m classes; that is, choose a set of points $y_1 < y_2 \cdots < y_{m-1}$ so the classes are the m intervals $(-\infty, y_1], (y_1, y_2], \ldots, (y_{m-2}, y_{m-1}], (y_{m-1}, \infty]$. With any point $s = (s_1, \ldots, s_n) \in S^n$ associate an m-tuple $(n_1^s, \ldots, n_m^s)$, where for each i, n_i is the number of sample points whose outcomes fall with interval i; that is,

$$n_i = |\{s_j|Y(s_j) \in \text{interval } i\}|$$

and $(n_1^s, \ldots, n_m^s)$ is called the *histogram* of s. Clearly $\sum_{i=1}^m n_i = n$. Since by assumption $a = (a_1, \ldots, a_n) \in S^n$ and $Y(a_1), \ldots, Y(a_n)$ are the corresponding outcomes, we can compute $(n_1^a, \ldots, n_m^a)$.

Let P_i be the probability of obtaining an outcome in interval i; that is, $p_1 = F_Y(y_1)$, $p_2 = F_Y(y_2) - F_Y(y_1), \ldots, p_m = 1 - F(y_m)$. Clearly $\sum_{i=1}^m p_i = 1$. Then consider the rv $X:S^n \to R$ defined by

$$X(s) = \sum_{i=1}^m \frac{(n_i^s - p_i n)^2}{np_i}$$

The $X(s)$ can be interpreted as a weighted square error measuring the deviation of the histogram of s, $(n_1^s, \ldots, n_m^s)$, from the "true" histogram $(p_1 n, \ldots, p_m n)$. Then the set of "results like those obtained" is the set

$$L_a = \{s \in S^n|X(s) \geq X(a)\}$$

(i.e., the set of sample n-tuples whose deviations are greater or equal to the deviation actually obtained).

To compute $P(L_a|H)$, it can be shown that the rv X has approximately the same distribution as χ_{m-1}^2, provided for each i, $p_i n > 5$. Thus

$$P(L_a|H) = 1 - F_{\chi_{m-1}^2}(X(a))$$

Again, we can set compute confidence limits beforehand such that for $\alpha \in [0, 1]$, x_α is such that $F_{\chi^2_{m-1}}(x_\alpha) = 1 - \alpha$. Then H is rejected at level α if

$$\sum_{i=1}^{m} \frac{(n_i^a - p_i n)^2}{np_i} > x_\alpha$$

That is, the histograms like the one actually obtained (having error deviations at least as great as observed) have probability of occurring less than α.

SOURCES

1. J. Neveu, *Mathematical Foundations of the Calculus of Probability*. Holden Day, San Francisco, 1965.
2. A. G. Mihram, *Simulation: Statistical Foundations and Methodology*. Academic Press, New York, 1971.

Index